THE NAMES OF
JESUS

*Discovering the Person of Jesus Christ
through Scripture*

THOMAS HOPKO

ANCIENT FAITH PUBLISHING ✠ CHESTERTON, INDIANA

Published by:
 Ancient Faith Publishing
 A Division of Ancient Faith Ministries
 P.O. Box 748
 Chesterton, IN 46304

ISBN: 978-1-936270-41-5

Printed in the United States of America

CONTENTS

FOREWORD   7

CHAPTER 1: *The Name of Jesus*   11

CHAPTER 2: *Jesus the Savior*   14

CHAPTER 3: *Jesus the Christ*   21

CHAPTER 4: *Jesus the Son of God*   28

CHAPTER 5: *Jesus as Lord*   34

CHAPTER 6: *Jesus the I AM*   39

CHAPTER 7: *Jesus as God*   43

CHAPTER 8: *Jesus the Word of God*   50

CHAPTER 9: *Jesus the Wisdom of God*   58

CHAPTER 10: *Jesus the Icon of God*   66

CHAPTER 11: *Jesus the Power of God*   73

CHAPTER 12: *Jesus the Son of Man*   79

CHAPTER 13: *Jesus the Man*   85

CHAPTER 14: *Jesus the Last Adam*   92

CHAPTER 15: *Jesus the Teacher*   100

CHAPTER 16: *Jesus the Prophet*   108

CHAPTER 17: *Jesus the Great High Priest*   116

CHAPTER 18: *Jesus the King*   *124*

CHAPTER 19: *Jesus the Good Shepherd*   *133*

CHAPTER 20: *Jesus the Lamb of God*   *141*

CHAPTER 21: *Jesus the Servant of the Lord*   *150*

CHAPTER 22: *Jesus the Suffering Servant*   *157*

CHAPTER 23: *Jesus the Righteous One*   *165*

CHAPTER 24: *Jesus the Judge*   *173*

CHAPTER 25: *Jesus the Light of the World*   *181*

CHAPTER 26: *Jesus, the Sun of Righteousness*   *189*

CHAPTER 27: *Jesus the Way*   *198*

CHAPTER 28: *Jesus the Truth*   *206*

CHAPTER 29: *Jesus the Life*   *214*

CHAPTER 30: *Jesus the Bread of Life*   *221*

CHAPTER 31: *Jesus the Resurrection*   *229*

CHAPTER 32: *Jesus the Door*   *237*

CHAPTER 33: *Jesus the True Vine*   *243*

CHAPTER 34: *Jesus Our Peace*   *251*

CHAPTER 35: *Jesus the Paraclete*   *259*

CHAPTER 36: *Jesus Our Redeemer*   *265*

CHAPTER 37: *Jesus the Firstborn*   *273*

CHAPTER 38: *Jesus the Chosen and Beloved*   *281*

CHAPTER 39: *Jesus the Bridegroom*   288

CHAPTER 40: *Jesus the Firstfruit*   298

CHAPTER 41: *Jesus the Heir*   305

CHAPTER 42: *Jesus the Holy One of God*   312

CHAPTER 43: *Jesus, Sin and Curse*   319

CHAPTER 44: *Jesus, Friend and Brother*   326

CHAPTER 45: *Jesus, Angel and Apostle*   332

CHAPTER 46: *Jesus, Pastor and Bishop*   338

CHAPTER 47: *Jesus, True & Faithful Witness*   343

CHAPTER 48: *Jesus the Physician*   349

CHAPTER 49: *Jesus the Cornerstone, Shrine, and Temple*   356

CHAPTER 50: *Jesus the Head*   363

CHAPTER 51: *Jesus, Mediator & Intercessor*   370

CHAPTER 52: *Jesus, Pioneer & Perfecter*   377

CHAPTER 53: *Jesus, Name above Every Name*   383

FOREWORD

In the month of February in the year 2008, something significant happened in the Church, though few realized it at the time. Fr. Thomas Hopko—a man aflame with the love of God and Church, deeply erudite as a professor of theology and experienced as a priest, and indisputably one of the great public speakers of our time—discovered podcasting. In the ensuing seven years, Fr. Tom committed over three hundred hours of his wisdom and learning to the hard drives of Ancient Faith Radio. From his study in Ellwood City, Pennsylvania, Fr. Tom would approach AFR's Marantz 660 recorder, press the one button he learned to press ("Record"), and speak. Beautifully.

His gifts—for oratory, for synthesizing his knowledge and wisdom, and for inspiring people—didn't mean that his podcasts came easily. Fr. Tom put a great deal of time and effort into organizing and compiling his episodes, considering carefully their theological and pastoral content. He was deeply committed to this ministry and saw it as a missionary vocation. He spoke on a wide range of topics, often making lengthy and thoughtfully conceived series out of specific themes. One of the most memorable and enduring of these was an informed and prayerful investigation into the person of Jesus Christ that went one-by-one through the names given him in the Scriptures.

Some time before his death on March 18, 2015, Fr. Tom began collaborating with Ancient Faith Publishing to adapt that series, *The Names of Jesus,* into a book. He died before its completion, but he had given the project his blessing. The volume before you is a careful adaptation from oral to written form. It captures the inimitable qualities of Fr. Tom's spoken work, yet reads like a book. For example, the editors wisely trimmed away tangents that were easy to follow from a speaker, but not so much from a writer.

The resulting book is a rare combination of genuine scholarly learning and accessible, inspiring writing. Some passages and terminology will be a challenge to some readers; their patience will be repaid. Fr. Tom was convinced that everyone without exception ought to be offered the gift of genuine theology, which can sometimes force us to think hard, and maybe to look some words up in a dictionary or lexicon. But wherever he may go in his theologically dense moments, he always leaves his readers with a pastoral word and a deeper understanding of Jesus Christ, God's love for us, and our way to salvation.

Using the names of Jesus as his thematic guide was Fr. Tom's ingenious way into understanding the person of Christ. It also takes us deeply into the Bible, with this book's every episode centering on lengthy quotations from Scripture. He walks us through verse after verse, helping us see with new eyes passages we thought we already knew. This is the same Bible read by Christians of widely different denominations and diverse beliefs about Jesus Christ, and reading Fr. Tom's commentary shows just how important it is to have a trusted guide (see Acts 8:30–31).

The book's fifty-three chapters have a number of themes that come up repeatedly, each of which evidently meant a great deal to Fr. Tom, and they should to us as well. Here are five:

1. *Jesus is truly divine*, the Son of the Father. Everything that God the Father is, Jesus is: uncreated, all-knowing, all-wise. Just as an earthly son perfectly shares human nature with his father, so Jesus perfectly shares the divine nature of His Father. Explaining Jesus' use of the Greek *ego eimi* (I Am), Fr. Tom writes:

   > Why would the guards draw back and fall on the ground when Jesus says 'I am [he]' (John 18:6)? They fall down because when they hear *ego eimi*, they hear the divine Name. He is saying the divine Name, which the Jew never said. It was the name that was written but never spoken except as "the Lord." But Jesus actually says the Name. He said to them (as an equivalent in English), "*I am God.*" (Chapter 6)

2. *This same Jesus is truly human*, the Son of Mary. Fr. Tom takes special care to emphasize that, while Jesus is not "merely" human, He is a fully human being nonetheless, with all that this implies. (Curiously enough, many people have a harder time believing that He is really human than that He is God.) Jesus, the Divine Word incarnate, was as a man subject to every human vulnerability and need, though without sin:

> Saying Jesus is a human being also means He is a particular human being in a particular time and place, with a particular culture, a particular language, particular physical features, and so on. If one is a real human being, one is limited. One learns things as a human being, with a human brain. As a man, Jesus was not omniscient. He was not omnipresent. . . . He did not know the theory of relativity. . . . He did not know the *Baghavad Gita*. Maybe He even thought the earth was flat; who knows? He was a first-century, real human being. (Chapter 13)

3. *We are called to be by grace everything Jesus is by nature.* Jesus Christ is, in His very existence, the Holy One of God, the Physician, the Mediator and Intercessor, the Truth, the Life, truly God, and truly human. It is amazing that we are called to be all of these things too—not innately, by virtue of our existence, but by grace, by the sheer gift of God. What an enormously high calling, and what immeasurable divine love this represents. Yet there is an eminently practical side to this, according to Fr. Tom. Here he writes about Jesus as "the Door" and what this means for us.

> Each one of us is to be a gate for other people to enter into communion with God. This means we should not be obstacles. We should be open doors to God's Kingdom, inviting people to enter and showing them how. (Chapter 32)

4. *Theology is reality.* Pursuit of the knowledge of God, His Son Jesus Christ and His Holy Spirit, our study of human nature, creation, and its salvation in Christ is not a philosophy, a system, a thing of mere study. It is not a game. It describes absolute reality. That means that in all its detail and complexity, in all its miraculousness and transcendence, it is real and grounded. While we can never know everything about God, theology must be reasonable; it must somehow make sense.

In meditating on "righteousness," a word that is easily misunderstood, Fr. Tom says:

> I think the term *dikaiosynē* (righteousness) is more a metaphysical term than a juridical one. *Dikaiosynē* means living according to the reality of the way things actually are, as they have been ordered and established and created by God. The laws of God are prescriptions that people should live according to reality. Therefore, when something is *made righteous* or *put right* or *justified*, it means that it is aligned up rightly. One could even say it is "according to truth." Jesus, the Righteous One, is the one who lives according to the way things really are, as coming from God. When He justifies or makes righteous, He restores to reality. Human beings, when they are made righteous, are made to be what they really are. It has to do with a person's very being, not just a person's activity. Righteousness is the reality of things being the way they really are and as they ought to be from God. (Chapter 23)

5. Finally, *be real*. Be a human being. That will ultimately entail thinking theologically and being in the Church. But these mean absolutely nothing if you are not, first and foremost, giving thanks to God, giving glory to God, and contemplating and living according to God's beauty, mercy, and love. He writes:

> It's not about figuring out the minimum you have to do to be saved. . . . What *should* we be interested in? God. Beautiful, marvelous, magnificent, splendid, glorious God Almighty. (Chapter 2)

Take your time with this book. I suggest you read no more than one chapter a day. Consider reading a chapter after prayer. It will bring you closer to Jesus Christ, and there is nothing more important, more precious and desirable than that.

Peter C. Bouteneff
Feast of the Elevation of the Cross
September 2015

CHAPTER 1

The Name of

JESUS

In the Bible, a name is a very important, sacred thing. Names are given to demonstrate being. For example, in the Book of Genesis, Adam is commanded by God to name the animals to reveal their being: "So out of the ground the Lord God formed every beast of the field and every bird of the air, and brought them to the man to see what he would call them; and whatever the man called every living creature, that was its name" (Gen. 2:19).

A name is a holy thing, and one is supposed to keep a name as holy; it should not be ridiculed or desecrated. This is true for the name of every creature, but it is especially true for the Name of God Himself. In the Bible until Moses, God is called simply "God" or *Elohim*. He is also called *El Shaddai*, or "the Most High God." However, when Moses encounters God in the burning bush, for the first time God speaks His Name: YHWH, which was pronounced "Yahweh" and meant "I am who I am," "I will be what I will be," or simply, "I am."

In ancient times, the ordinary Jew would never say that Name. We say it casually now, but it was not always that way. When the Name of God was written, instead of saying "Yahweh," the reader would substitute the word *Adonai*, which means simply "Lord." And so *Adonai* became the proper Name for God which He gave to Moses on Mount Sinai.

Why was naming so important in the ancient world? Because to know the name meant to know the person or thing the name referred to. To have a person's name was, in a sense, to have *him*. When one knew a person's name, one came to have power in relation to him. When God gives us His Name, then, He gives Himself to us as well, and yet it is a Name so holy that we dare not say it and take possession of Him.

Within this context, what does it mean to say that Jesus has a name? According to the Gospels of Matthew and Luke, the archangel tells both Mary and Joseph that "you shall call His name Jesus" (Matt. 1:21; Luke 1:31). Jesus' first name, then, is *Yeshua* or *Joshua* in Hebrew, or *Iesous* in Greek, meaning "Savior," "Victor," or "God saves."

The name of Jesus—Joshua—has immediate significance in that it reminds us of the most famous Joshua in the Old Testament: Joshua the Son of Nun. In the typology of the Old Testament Scriptures, Jesus—whom we confess as both the son of Mary and the Son of God—is given this name, not only because it means "God saves," but because it hearkens back to the Joshua of Numbers, Deuteronomy, and, of course, the Book of Joshua.

The importance of Joshua in these scriptures lies in the fact that he was Moses' successor. Having led the people of Israel out of Egypt, having wandered for forty years in the wilderness, both Moses and Aaron died in the desert. They did not cross the Jordan. They did not inherit or live in the land that God promised to Abraham from the beginning, the land flowing with milk and honey, simply because they were not faithful and because they were sinful (see Num. 20:24; 27:14). Of the generation that entered the wilderness, only Joshua and Caleb remained to cross the Jordan River and take possession of the Promised Land.

This crossing is similar in many respects to the crossing of the Red Sea. The waters are parted and the people walk as if on dry land, carrying the ark of the covenant with the tablets of the Law inside it (see Josh. 3). If Moses brought the people of Israel out of Egypt through the Red Sea, now through Joshua "God saves" the people by bringing them through the Jordan to destroy the enemies of God and take possession of the land.

This Old Testament account finds fulfillment in the New Testament. As Joshua son of Nun entered with the people of Israel into the Jordan River and placed twelve stones in the water to signify the twelve tribes, so too Jesus son of Mary is baptized in the Jordan and takes on twelve apostles to signify the twelve tribes of the new Israel of God—the Church. Joshua searched out the land with the help of the prostitute Rahab, whose life was saved as a result by the sign of a scarlet cord tied in her window (Josh. 2:18), which some of the Holy Fathers read as an allegory of sinful humanity saved by the blood of Christ. Joshua conquered Jericho and the sun stood still (Josh. 10:13), which the Orthodox liturgical tradition contrasts with the earth standing still at the birth of Christ. In short, the name and life of Joshua is evoked and fulfilled in the name and life of Jesus of Nazareth, who is God's own salvation—not just for Israel, but for the entire human race.

God gives Mary's child the name of Jesus, therefore, to teach us to contemplate Him first and foremost in the light of the foundational Old Testament narratives of Moses, Joshua, the crossing of the Jordan, and the entrance into the Promised Land. The Joshua of old was a prefiguration, a "type" (*typos*) of Him who was to come, the One who was the real embodiment of God's salvation.

Moses and the Law could not save us. Moses himself, great as he was— the man who spoke to God face-to-face, stood at the mercy seat, received the commandments, led the people—did not cross the Jordan. He did not enter the Promised Land, the land of the living. He died and was buried in Goshen. This point is literally flaunted in the Old Testament to remind us that nobody can keep the Law, not even Moses and Aaron. If they could have kept God's commandments, the Scriptures state clearly that they would never have died. However, neither Moses nor Aaron could be perfectly obedient, and so they fell before God and died.

Only Jesus of Nazareth, the new Joshua, cannot die, because he keeps the Law perfectly and totally. Therefore, He enters into the real Promised Land, the real land of the living, which is the Kingdom of heaven, the Kingdom that will fill heaven and earth when Jesus comes in glory and every knee on earth will bow before Him and glorify His Name.

There is no other name in heaven and on earth by which men can be saved except the Name of Jesus (see Acts 4:12). The Orthodox Christian tradition of the Jesus Prayer has this as its central teaching. Orthodox Christians pray the Name of Jesus for salvation. They say, "Lord Jesus Christ, the Son of God, have mercy on me, a sinner." To pronounce this holy Name has a power in and of itself, when it is connected with faith, to save us, because Jesus, Joshua, the Son of God is the only One through whom God truly saves us.

CHAPTER 2

Jesus the

SAVIOR

We know that Jesus was named "Jesus" because that word means "Savior," or "God saves." In Luke's account of the birth of Christ, the angel says to the shepherds, "Be not afraid; for behold, I bring you good news [or glad tidings, or a good message] of a great joy which will come to all the people; for to you is born this day in the city of David a Savior [*soter* in Greek], who is Christ the Lord" (Luke 2:10–11).

The words *savior, save, salvation* are used countless times in the Bible. However, the important point is that the term *the Savior* is a title for Jesus. He is *the* unique Savior, the only One who saves; salvation comes through Him. He is the great God and Savior Jesus Christ. The title *Savior* in the Holy Scripture is, first of all, a title for God Himself. The Lord God is the One who brings salvation. Mary's famous song, the *Magnificat* in Luke 1:46–55, begins with, "My soul magnifies the Lord, and my spirit rejoices in God my Savior."

In Luke 1:68–79, after John the Baptist is born, Zacharias sings his canticle, usually called the *Benedictus*, which begins:

> "Blessed be the Lord God of Israel,
> for he has visited and redeemed his people,
> and has raised up a horn of salvation for us
> in the house of his servant David,
> as he spoke by the mouth of his holy prophets from of old,
> that we should be saved from our enemies,
> and from the hand of all who hate us."

Zacharias says of John:

> "And you, child, will be called the prophet of the Most High;
> for you will go before the Lord to prepare his ways,
> to give knowledge of salvation to his people
> in the forgiveness of their sins."

God is the Savior. He saves His people from their enemies, and He gives knowledge of salvation to His people in the forgiveness of their sins. We have this teaching about salvation all through the Gospels. The famous John 3:16–21 says:

> For God so loved the world that he gave his only Son, that whoever believes in him should not perish but have eternal life. For God sent the Son into the world, not to condemn the world, but that the world might be saved through him.
> He who believes in him is not condemned; he who does not believe is condemned already, because he has not believed in the name of the only Son of God. And this is the judgment, that the light has come into the world, and men loved darkness rather than light, because their deeds were evil. For every one who does evil hates the light, and does not come to the light, lest his deeds should be exposed. But he who does what is true comes to the light, that it may be clearly seen that his deeds have been wrought in God.

The judgment is the coming of salvation. The very judgment is the light of God, the light from light, the great epiphany of God. God sends His Son as the light of the world to be the salvation of the world, that people who are in darkness would be in darkness no more, people who are caught by death would be caught by death no more, people who are captivated and enslaved by anything at all would be liberated.

The instrument of this great salvation—the *only* instrument, according to Christian faith, for anyone on earth, whether they know it or not—is the work of Jesus. If Christ had not come, if He had not died on the Cross, if He had not been raised from the dead by the power of God, and if He were not glorified at the right hand of the Father, having destroyed death and forgiven all sins and fulfilled all righteousness and revealed all truth, then human beings would not be saved. Everyone would be in darkness, ignorance, caught by disease, enslaved by their own passions, and, ultimately, they would be dead.

When we look at *salvation* and *savior* in biblical terms, we see that throughout the Old Testament, *the* Savior is God Almighty. God is the only One who can save, and salvation is of the Lord. There is no other salvation except that which is worked by God.

The term *salvation* (Greek *soteria*) is used in many ways in the Scripture, for every possible kind of salvation: salvation from disease, salvation from enemies, and ultimately salvation from sin and from death itself. "To save" means "to heal," "to destroy enemies," "to deliver from terror, torture, or death," "to liberate," "to be victorious." The term *soter*, "savior," also means "victor, conqueror."

In the Bible, we see also that only God is God, but Jesus is also called God. Only God is the Lord, the *Kyrios*, but Jesus is the *Kyrios*. This is the conviction of ancient Orthodox Christianity: that Jesus is everything God His Father is, except He is not the Father, He is the Son. He is the Son of the Father who receives everything from the Father. All of the qualities that belong essentially to God also belong to Him. He is everything God is. He has everything God has, and He has and is all these things in His humanity. The man Jesus does all the things only God can do, and all the prerogatives that belong to God alone are His.

God is the Savior, and Jesus is the Savior. God does everything that He does through and by and in and even for His Son, His eternal Son and Word who becomes the man Jesus. God creates, redeems, and saves through Jesus. Jesus is the *demiurgos*, the agent of all divine actions.

When God, who alone can save, saves the world, He does it the only way God does everything—by way of His Son: His image, His *logos*, His word, His *davar*. *Davar*, Hebrew for *word*, doesn't only mean a spoken word, a conceptual word; it means an act. The agent of all divine activities is the second Person of the Trinity, the Son of God. It is Jesus of Nazareth, who is God's Son. There is no other Savior besides Christ. And there is no other salvation that God effects except by, in, and through His Son, who is begotten of the Father before all ages and born on earth from Mary, the virgin: Jesus of Nazareth, named Jesus because He is the Savior.

What does it mean that Jesus is named the Savior? What does it mean that He *saves* us? What is this salvation?

I would like to try to convey my understanding of this by something that happened when I was a seminarian. I was sitting in a class of dogmatic theology with my beloved professor, Professor Serge S. Verhovskoy, and he said, "My dears, we must avoid this abominable preoccupation with salvation."

Well, that stunned me. I raised my hand and said, "Professor, how can you say such a thing? Isn't it *all* about salvation? Isn't Jesus our Savior? Doesn't He save the world?"

And he smiled and said, "Of course. But there are many Christians who are hardly interested in God at all. They're really not interested in Christ, in life, in the beauty of creation. They're not interested in their fellow man and their neighbor. They're not really interested in much of anything except salvation. Translated, meaning: how to get to go to heaven when you die."

A lot of Christians think of salvation as getting to go to heaven. They have radically different ideas of what it takes to go to heaven, but what many Christians have in common is that they believe one can know for sure that one is saved, and that being saved means being assured of going to heaven. They focus their whole Christian life on figuring out the minimum they have to do to be saved—and that includes Orthodox Christians as well as others.

What my professor wanted to tell us was that the faith is not about salvation in that sense. It's not about figuring out the minimum you have to do to be saved. In fact, in that sense, it is an abomination, almost a blasphemy, even to be interested, much less obsessed, with the issue of salvation and to start trying to figure out who is saved and who is not. Real, authentic Christians should never get involved in that kind of thing. It's not according to Christ. It's not according to Scripture.

What should we be interested in? God. Beautiful, marvelous, magnificent, splendid, glorious God Almighty. And His only begotten Son Jesus Christ, born of a virgin on earth; and the all-holy, life-creating Spirit who proceeds from God, dwells in the Son, and is breathed upon us. In God is life, reality, truth, peace, and joy. We need to be interested in the God who saves us, not in salvation as such. We need to be interested in loving God. Life is about God. The Bible is about God. Church is about God. Sacraments are about God.

Our faith is about the grace of God coming into us and being manifested for our salvation. God desires all to be saved and to come to a knowledge of the truth. God is the Savior of all human beings, especially those who believe (1 Tim. 4:10). Our confession has to be that God, in Christ, has already, on the Cross, saved everyone and everything. That is the gospel, the glad tidings: that He has come for Jews and Gentiles, men and women, slave and free, and even the whole earth, the galaxies and the stars and the sun and the moon. God, who created all of that, is saving all of it, and He is saving it all in Jesus Christ. That's what we have to be thrilled about. That's what we have to confess. That's what we have to live by.

If we do, then we will glorify God, and we will try to keep His commandments because we will love Him. And we will try to love Him with all our mind, all our soul, all our heart, all our strength. We will try to love our neighbor, even our worst enemy, as ourselves. We will not judge anyone for anything. Who are we to judge? God who is the Savior is the judge, and He judges us by saving us. He came to save the world, not to condemn it.

We are saved, first of all, *from* something. We are saved from ignorance, from darkness, from our sins, our madness, our diseases, our transgressions. We are saved from our own selves, from the vain imaginations of our own heart and mind. We are saved from everything that destroys, and ultimately the last enemy to be destroyed is the destroyer itself, which is death. We are saved from death. We are saved from everything that is not good, true, and beautiful; everything that is ugly, diseased, corrupted, morbid, dead, and demonic. We are saved from the power of the devil.

We are also saved *for* something. We are saved for life. What makes life, life? According to the Holy Scripture, it is the glorification of God. Human beings who are created in the image and likeness of God should strive to be in communion with God all the time, to love all the time, to give everything, to share everything, to enjoy everything. That is what it's all about.

I would suggest we strike once and for all from our life this question: "What do I need to do to be saved?" The answer is: everything and nothing, because there is nothing I can do to be saved if God doesn't save me. But once God saves me, then I have to do the works that He does, and that means I can never rest assured of my salvation. Of course, the gospel of God in Jesus Christ is that we are all saved. But the question is, do we accept that salvation? Do we live by it?

Here the teaching of Scripture and the saints would be that nobody could claim to do it. Nobody is righteous, even after baptism. We are always sinners, saying, "God be merciful to me, a sinner." I am not worthy of salvation. It is a gift. But once I realize this gift exists, then I have to take it. I have to repent every time I neglect it, forget it, or worse, refuse it and live by my own standards—because that is hell.

Once I know I am saved by Jesus, then I pray without ceasing. I give thanks in all circumstances. I rejoice in all things. I try to share everything I have. I try to do everything as well as I can, and I know that even if I do that, I am not deserving of salvation. I know there's nothing I can do externally to deserve it. I could go to a hundred Divine Liturgies and give my body to be burned, as St. Paul says in 1 Corinthians 13, but if I have not the love of God in me, if I am doing it out of arrogance and pride or trying to get to go to heaven when I die, then I'm still in the hands of the devil. My life is still an abomination. I have not yet understood salvation. Why? Because I have not yet understood God.

To understand and receive salvation, you have to understand and receive and love *God*. We love God, not salvation. And therefore, we are saved *for* loving God, glorifying God, praising God with every breath. We are saved for work, for activity, for rejoicing in one another, for serving each other. We are saved for repenting, in fact. We can only repent because we're saved, because that salvation is always available to us.

The Holy Fathers would even say, we are saved for tears. We are saved for weeping over our sins and the sins of the world. We are saved for weeping over how we have ruined our world and corrupted our planet, destroyed our universe and killed our economy, and how our greed and our competition and our racism have created a hell on the planet Earth. God has saved us in Christ from that hell, but He has not only saved us *from* hell; He has saved us *for* paradise. We are saved to be by grace everything that God in Christ is by nature.

A person who knows that is no longer obsessed with salvation as such. He is totally devoted to God as the Savior, to Christ who is the Savior. A saved person is just praying to be illumined by God to testify to the fact that we are saved, that salvation is here, eternal life is here. Everything has been redeemed, saved, delivered, protected, purified. All the enemies have been destroyed. To be saved is to be in that reality, and even more modestly, to struggle to be in that reality, to confess with tears that we are not in that reality, that we have no claim on salvation.

We certainly cannot dare to claim that we have a place reserved in heaven because we accept Jesus as our Savior. We come before the face of God always as penitents and sinners until He comes again in glory, and we say, "Save me, O Lord." The content of salvation is the outpouring of the divine *chesed* (the Hebrew word for the divine mercy, the divine love upon us), and we bask in that as our salvation. To the measure that we are in that grace, to that measure we are saved.

But it isn't over until it's over. We presume nothing, while at the same time we confess that everyone and everything in all of creation has been saved by God in the blood of Jesus. It is our task to receive that salvation every moment of every day, with every breath to be loving God, loving our neighbor, and trying to keep the commandments.

If we do that, then God will save us if He wishes, and He will know how. But we won't be interested in salvation anymore. We will be interested solely in pleasing, glorifying, worshipping, and loving God, who is love, who has loved us so much that He sent His beloved Son into the world to save us and to pour His saving power and love of the Holy Spirit into us, even now while we live in this fallen and corrupted world.

CHAPTER 3

Jesus the

CHRIST

In this chapter we will consider the term *Christ*—in Greek *Christos*, in Hebrew *mashiyach (messiah)*. This word literally means "the anointed one," one who has been anointed with oil. In the practice described in the Old Testament, the anointing of a person with oil was a sign of consecration, of sanctification, of being set apart for the service of God.

We think of it particularly in terms of the anointing of a king. But in the Torah, the Law of Moses, the priests were anointed also, as were the temple vessels and so on. Anointing things was a sign of their being made holy. Holy (in Hebrew, *kadoshet*) means being set apart, being different, belonging only to the Holy One, who is God Himself.

It is important for us to remember that in the Scripture, God was the king of the people. "God is our king before the ages" (Psalm 73:12 LXX). One of the things that distinguished the kingdom of God from all the other peoples is that for the early Israelites, the king was God. They had no human king. They had prophets; they had leaders like Moses; they had judges; but they had no king.

In the Book of 1 Samuel (1 Kingdoms LXX), the people come to God and say, "We want a king. We want to be like everybody else."

God discourages them. He says, "What do you want a king for? The whole point is that you are *not* like everybody else. I have made *you* a kingdom of priests, a holy nation. I have set you apart. I have made you a called and particular people, and what makes you called and particular is that you have no human king. God is your king."

But the people wanted a king, and God relented. Samuel the prophet is raised up to anoint Saul as the king, and Saul works out terribly. Then David is anointed and eventually becomes the king. In the Bible, quintessentially, David is virtually always considered as "the Christ," the anointed one, the one who has the oil of God placed upon him.

The kingship after David was a disaster, but still, in the Hebrew mind, and certainly in the Bible, the king was to be the anointed of God. The king was to be prophetic, royal, and pastoral, a shepherd. He was to care for the people and bring the power, truth, and wisdom of God to them, and he was to destroy their enemies.

In the Scriptures, and especially in the Psalms, wherever the expression "the anointed one" is used, that is literally "the christ." Many of the Psalms refer to "God's anointed." For example, in the second Psalm, the people rise up against the Lord and against His christ, His anointed, and the Lord protects His anointed. He gives His saving strength to His anointed. He looks upon the face of His anointed, but He also is angry with His anointed when His anointed betrays the unction.

Sometimes in the Scripture, even those who are called upon to destroy Israel—Nebuchadnezzar, Cyrus, and so on—are referred to as "God's anointed," the ones set apart by God in order to do His will.

We see in Scripture also that this anointing and oil of unction is connected to the Holy Spirit, to the power of God. The unction of God came to be connected with the Holy Spirit Himself—God pours out His Spirit upon His prophets. He pours His Spirit upon His priests.

God will put His Spirit upon him, and the one that God chooses, His anointed one, is the one upon whom and in whom His Spirit dwells, and through whom His Spirit acts. If the Spirit is there, then the Word is also there. As St. John of Damascus said, in the Bible you never have God's Spirit without God's Word, and you never have God's Word without God's Spirit, and you never have God without His Word and Spirit. This is the prefiguration in the Old Covenant of the doctrine of the Holy Trinity. You have the one true and living God, the Spirit of God, and the Word of God: the *Davar Yahweh* and the *Ruach Yahweh*.

In the New Covenant, the Word becomes flesh as Jesus, who is proclaimed immediately as *the* Christ, *the* anointed one, *the* Messiah. He is so because the Spirit of God is upon Him, because He has been anointed by the very Spirit of God, who ascends and dwells upon Him.

In the New Testament, God the Father, the Son—the Word Incarnate, and the Holy Spirit are the three divine hypostases of the Godhead, the Son being the anointed one.

In the Old Covenant, the kings who were anointed of God, christs of God, were also called "sons of God." David, the anointed, the quintessential paradigmatic christ of the Old Covenant, is called God's son, His firstborn. Why firstborn? Because the firstborn inherits everything from the father. He is the very presence of the father to others. The Old Covenant foreshadows what became central in the New Testament—that one of the sons of David would sit upon the throne, and of His kingdom there would be no end. He would be the anointed one, the Messiah, the everlasting king, *the* Son of God, the very presence of God on earth, who reigns in God's kingdom and over the whole of God's creation. This was all connected in Scripture with David.

Biblical scholarship shows us there was no consistent and clear teaching at the time of Jesus about what the messiah was, who the messiah would be, how he would act and what he would do. There was no dogmatic view in Judaism of "the messiah." Zealots had one idea and one hope, Pharisees had another, Sadducees had another, Essenes had another. It was very confused. In fact, this is true about virtually every name and title of Jesus in the Holy Scripture—Messiah, Son of God, Son of Man, the Lord. You might even say it's true about the word *Theos*, God.

Two things must be said about the first Christians, the apostles and those with them who witnessed the risen Christ. Firstly, they were themselves confused about all these things. Half the time, they didn't know what they were talking about while Jesus was still alive. That may be what led Judas to betray Him—Judas had one idea about the messiah, and Jesus didn't fit into it.

Secondly, however, we have to see that by the end of the first century, not only were certain names and titles given to Jesus in order to help people understand who He is and what He did, but also those various terms were defined in themselves and in relation to each other. The confusion about what these various names and titles meant and how they were to be fulfilled was ultimately overcome. An Orthodox Christian interpretation of these words was formulated. This interpretation was further debated, explained, codified, and defined by the ecumenical councils and the Church Fathers throughout history.

So what do we say about the term *ho Christos* (the Christ)? In the earliest Christian writings we have, Jesus is already called Lord and Christ. The first letter of Paul to the Thessalonians (which was written before the Gospels) begins, "Paul, Silvanus, and Timothy, to the church of the Thessalonians in God the Father and the Lord (*Kyrios*) Jesus (*Iesous*) Christ (*Christos*)." Jesus is Christ the Lord, *Iesous Christos Kyrios*. That is the foundational Christian creed.

The expression *Jesus Christ* is in the four Gospels right from the beginning. The most primitive Gospel, Mark, begins, "The beginning of the gospel of Jesus Christ." Some ancient manuscripts add "the Son of God." Matthew begins with "The book of the genealogy of Jesus Christ, the son of David, the son of Abraham." After the genealogy, it says, "Now the birth of Jesus Christ took place in this way."

In the Gospel of Luke, we do not see the term *Christ* in the introduction or the entire first chapter. The word appears for the first time in the second chapter, when the baby Jesus is brought to the temple on the fortieth day to be presented to the Lord. Then it says the prophet Simeon had been told by the Holy Spirit that he would not die before he had seen the Lord's Christ. This Jesus who was brought to the temple is the Lord's Christ.

John's Gospel begins with the Trinity itself. At the end of the prologue, the expression *Jesus Christ* is used. "For the law was given through Moses; grace and truth came through Jesus Christ" (John 1:17). The Gospel continues with John the Baptist, and the first thing John does is to say that he is not the Christ. *Jesus* is the Christ. At the end of John 1, Andrew says this explicitly. When he goes to call his brother Simon Peter, he says, "We have found the Messiah," and then St. John adds in parentheses, "which means Christ" (v. 41).

The term *Christ* was a title, and it had a definite article. Jesus was *the* Christ, *ho Christos*. That is the way it is used in the confessions about Jesus found in all four Gospels. When He asks, "Who do you say that I am?" in Mark, Peter says, "You are the Christ" (*Su ei ho Christos,* 8:29). In Luke, Peter answers, "The Christ of God" (9:20). In Matthew, his response is "You are the Christ, the son of the living God" (16:15–16).

You are the Christ, the Son of the Living God, the Anointed, the Spirit-filled, the Son of David, and so on. This is what we find in the Scripture. But almost immediately, the definite article "the" is dropped. Jesus is referred to not as Jesus *the* Messiah, Jesus *the* Christ, but simply as Jesus Christ, *Iesous Christos,* or Christ Jesus, *Christos Iesous.* Or Jesus *ho legomenos Christos,* the one who is called Christ.

Very early and even very publicly, Jesus Christ was the appellation for our Lord. He wasn't just Jesus; He was Jesus Christ. And the disciples were first called Christians. They were not called Jesus-ites, Yeshuites, but Christians, Messiah-ites. What characterized them was their conviction that Jesus is the Christ, the Messiah foretold in the Scriptures. The first Christians who identified Jesus as the Christ and called Him Jesus Christ and Christ Jesus had a very particular understanding of what that meant.

What it means is that Jesus is the Christ, the Son of Man (a title we will explore in chapter 12), the Lord, the Son of God. He brings the kingship of God to the world; He does the work of God in the world; He is God in the world.

That is what the Gospels are showing when they depict and narrate the actions and words of Jesus. He proclaimed the gospel to the poor. He brought the good news of the Kingdom of heaven. He performed all the signs, as St. John's Gospel calls them, that the Son of God, the Messiah, the Lord, was supposed to do, by which God would ultimately be revealed. He is the very presence and power of God in His own person as a human being on the planet Earth.

But there is one more thing that is absolutely essential and unique to ancient Orthodox Christianity: The Christ has to be crucified. Put in scriptural terms, the Christ is not only the son of David, the seat of Abraham, the messianic king, high priest, prophet, teacher, and so forth; He is the suffering servant. He is the *ebed yawheh,* the slave of Yahweh, the child of Yahweh: He is the one who is put to death. He is the one who bears the sins of the world. He is the one who is humiliated, degraded, rejected, spat upon, beaten, mocked. And this *proves* that He is the Christ.

We preach the *crucified* Christ, not anything else. And so, for Orthodox Christians, Christ is the one who is put to death by that vile, degrading, shameful death, and thereby enters into the glory of His Kingdom and brings and establishes and rules over the Kingdom of God. He sits enthroned and is revealed to the world as Christ and Lord. He is manifested, declared Christ and Lord, by what He suffers. He is put to death.

He is also raised, He is glorified, and He sits at the right hand of the Father. The Christian Orthodox conviction to this day is that all that happens because He is crucified. That is our faith, and that is the great surprise. That, we might even say, is the great messianic secret of the Holy Scripture, the secret Jesus commands people to keep until He is raised and glorified.

This is the Christian view, and until He comes again in glory, we worship God through His broken body and His shed blood. We put the sign of the Cross upon ourselves, and we are baptized into His death. But being baptized into His death, we are anointed with the same Holy Spirit with which He is anointed. As the Holy Fathers said, the Son of God is the dwelling place of the Holy Spirit from all eternity within the Godhead. And when He becomes man, the Holy Spirit descends upon Him and dwells in Him, and He does all His acts and speaks all His words by the power of the Holy Spirit. Why? Because He is the Christ.

We become christs, anointed ones of God, sons of God, and even gods also, gods by grace in and with Him, providing that we are crucified with Him, suffer and die with Him. Because there is no other way to reign with Him. There is no other way, according to ancient Orthodox Christianity, to be messiah. This is what *messiah* means.

So our understanding of *ho Christos,* the Christ, is that the *Yeshua,* the Savior, who is also the anointed, is the crucified and glorified. That is the mind-blowing teaching of ancient Christianity. That is not only why we confess Jesus as the Christ and believe in the Lord Jesus Christ, but this is what we understand it to mean. This is what we preach, this is what we glory in, this is what we live by, and hopefully this is what we are even ready to die for, because this is our confession.

"Who do you say that I am?" we are asked every day of our lives. We have to respond with the apostles and the martyrs: "You are the Christ, the Son of the living God. You are Christ crucified, raised, and glorified." That is our understanding of why Jesus is called the Christ and why we call him Christ Jesus.

CHAPTER 4

Jesus the

SON OF GOD

In Matthew 16, Jesus asks His disciples the central question, "Who do you say that I am?" (Matt. 16:15). In the Gospels of Mark and Luke, Simon Peter replies simply, "You are the Christ." In Matthew's Gospel, he continues to say, "You are the Christ, *the Son of the living God.*" What does it mean to call Jesus "the Son of God"?

In Greek, "the Son of God" is *ho huios tou theou*, of which the word for "son" is *huios*. This is important, because in the Greek there are two other words that can sometimes be translated "son": *païs*, which comes primarily from the prophet Isaiah and refers to a boy or a servant; and *tekna* or *teknon*, which is simply a child. *Huios*, however, is a very specific, technical term for the male child of a father, whether adopted or biological.

This brings us to the issue of referring to Jesus as *the* Son of God, rather than simply *a* son of God. Providentially, the Greek language contains definite and indefinite articles, much like English, and it is essential for us to pay attention in the New Testament Scriptures as to when the definite article is used and when it is not used.

To call Jesus simply *a* son of God would presuppose that many sons of God exist, of whom He is just one. Referring to Jesus as *the* Son of God implies that He is the one and only Son, and there is no other. The central point, of course, is that in the New Testament as it came to be interpreted in the early Church, Jesus is in fact *the* Son of God, the unique Son of God, outside of whom there is no son of God, and within whom and through whom and by whom we are all sons of God by faith.

Beginning in the pages of the New Testament and continuing in the development of Christian doctrine, then, we see this radical confession of Jesus as *the* Son of God in a unique way that cannot be applied to anyone else. He is not an avatar, nor is He like the kings of the Old Testament, who were often called God's sons because all their power and possessions came from God. Rather, according to Christian tradition until recently and certainly according to Orthodox Christian tradition to this day, Jesus is uniquely the only-begotten Son of God who shares the same divine nature with God the Father, and who is also born as the one and only son of Mary.

What then does it mean to call Jesus *the* Son of God? In the first place, referring to Jesus using this definite article would indicate that Jesus has no human father. God is His literal Father, which means that whatever God is, Jesus is also. This, in fact, is the teaching of the Holy Fathers of the Church, especially those Fathers of the fourth century who fought against Arianism—which said that Jesus may be *called* the Son of God, but that title is merely honorific and metaphorical, not literal. According to ancient, orthodox, catholic Christianity, Jesus is really *the* Son of God, begotten of God, and thus He really is exactly what God is.

The argument is a simple one. The Fathers taught that if I am begotten of a particular being, then I am what that being is, with no difference whatsoever, except that I am not identical to that other being. If you are a human being and a father, then your son will be a human being also. You cannot be a human being and have a son that is a dog or a horse. This is true both of fathers and mothers. If you reproduce, beget, or give birth to someone, what is born of you has to be what you are. If Jesus is begotten of God the Father and born of Mary, then the confession of faith follows that He is both what His Father is—fully divine—and what His mother is—fully human.

These dual qualities make Jesus different from the rest of humanity. Where ordinary human beings are *merely* human, Jesus is the one and only *divine* human being, with two natures—the divine from His Father and the human from His mother. In this way, Jesus is absolutely unique, since He is the only *theanthropos*: the only God-man.

As I suggested above, Jesus shares the exact divinity of God the Father, but He is not identical to the Father, any more than a human child is identical to his or her parent. Being the unique Son of God, Jesus is exactly *what* the Father is, but He is not *who* the Father is. In the theological jargon, He is a distinct Person or *hypostasis*, which means a distinct existential reality. To use the expression of St. Basil the Great, Jesus has a *tropos hyparxeos*—a mode of existence that is exactly what the Father is but not who the Father is.

When one of our daughters was in kindergarten, she said to me one morning over breakfast, "Daddy, is Jesus God?"

Wanting to end the conversation quickly and get her off to school, I said, "Yep, He's God."

She looked at me with her big, wide eyes and said, "I thought God was His Father. I thought Jesus' Father was God."

So I had to sit down and have a talk with her, and we cleared it up in about three minutes. I said, "Allie, you're Hopko and I'm Hopko, right? Mom and I, we're your parents. We gave you birth, so you are what we are. We are human beings. We're not dogs like our dog Cleo. We're not animals. We're not fish. So if I'm your father and I'm human, and you're my daughter, you've got to be human too. So if Jesus is really God's Son, and God is really His Father, then He's got to be divine too, because if the Father has a Son, the Son can't be different from what the Father is, just like you have to be a human and you have to be a Hopko."

And she said, "Okay." And from that moment she became a Nicene Orthodox Christian, following the Holy Fathers, because that is really how simple the teaching is.

If Jesus is the real, literal Son of God, then He has all the qualities that God the Father has, except that He is not the Father. It is important to note that "fatherhood" is not a quality or attribute of God. If it were, the Son of God could not be divine with the same divinity as the Father, and neither could the Holy Spirit, because they would not be everything the Father is. However, God is ever-existing, good, light, merciful, gracious, slow to anger, abounding in steadfast love and mercy. These are His attributes, all of which are the qualities of Jesus and the Holy Spirit. Indeed, when we confess that Jesus is the Son of God, we mean that He has all the qualities that belong to the divine nature of God. And, since He is also Mary's son, Jesus has the properties and characteristics that belong to human beings as well.

Calling Jesus the literal Son of God has another implication, namely, that Jesus' divinity is first and foremost the divinity of God His Father. Jesus says clearly that everything He has was given to Him by His Father (see John 17). All of His power, wisdom, glory, splendor, beauty, truth is given to Him by His Father from eternity. When the Son becomes a man, all those qualities belong to Him as a man—but it is important to note that He *receives* them, rather than counting equality with God "a thing to be grasped" (Phil. 2:6).

Therefore, while the Father and Son are "one" (John 10:30) in the same divinity, we would say that there is a priority to the Father in the Holy Trinity. This priority is called the *monarchia* of the Father. In the Orthodox Liturgy, we refer to the Father as "unoriginate" or *agenitos*, and to the Son as *genitos*, "begotten" of the Father. While the Father and the Son are the same in *what* they are, we also have to remember that the Son derives from the Father because He is not identical with the Father, and therefore has a different relationship with Him.

According to the Gospel of John, Jesus says, "The Father is greater than I" (John 14:28). In saying this, He is not saying that God is "higher" metaphysically than He is, as a human being would be "higher" than a dog. Rather, Jesus relates to the Father *as a Son,* and as a Son, He *obeys* His Father. He prays to His Father, does His Father's will, does His works, speaks His words. As such, He is subordinate to His Father, not in His divinity, but in the way He relates to Him. To put it technically, there is a kind of hypostatic subordinationism in the Holy Trinity, but there is no ontological or essential subordinationism. And while God is the *arche*, the source of the divine being of the Son and the Spirit, He expresses Himself absolutely perfectly in the Person of His Spirit and His Son, who is, as the Epistle to the Hebrews says, *charakter tes hypostasis avtou*—the exact image of His Person, His very being. As St. Paul puts it in Colossians, "In Him the *pleroma tes theotetos somatikos*—the whole fullness of deity dwells bodily" (Col. 2:9).

If Jesus is everything God the Father is, then everything He *does* is also divine. All His actions are actions only God can do, but because He is also human, He does those divine works as a human being. This indeed is the only way God can reveal Himself to creatures, by doing divine things in creaturely form. If we are really going to come to know God as human beings, then He can only reveal Himself in a way that we understand. God's instrument of revelation has to have fully created forms and qualities. If we are to know God as human beings, God has to be human.

The divine works that Jesus does—such as revealing the truth, healing, raising the dead, and so on—are also a testimonial that He is indeed *the* Son of God. In fact, Jesus Himself makes this argument in John: "If I am not doing the works of my Father, then do not believe me; but if I do them, even though you do not believe me, believe the works, that you may know and understand that the Father is in me and I am in the Father" (John 10:37–38). If the works Jesus performs are those things that only God can do, then who else can He be but *the* Son of God, who has and is everything His Father is and has?

St. John teaches that you cannot have God the Father without having God the Son. As the Son, Jesus is in the Father and the Father is in Him. Anyone who claims to confess God and does not confess Jesus as His Son is not really confessing God at all: "Any one who goes ahead and does not abide in the doctrine of Christ does not have God; he who abides in the doctrine has both the Father and the Son" (2 John 1:9). If we do not follow the teaching of the Son, we do not follow the teaching of the Father either, because Jesus as *the* Son of God is the sole agent of all God's activities and the only human being who does the divine work of God.

This leads us to a final point: If, other than the testimony of the Scriptures, Jesus' *works* are the most important argument for His identity as the Son of God, then our responsibility is to witness these works and choose to confess Him. In the New Testament, Jesus never calls himself "Son of God." When they ask Him, "Are you the Son of God?" He replies, "I am" or "You have said so," but He never actually says, "I am the Son of God." That confession is our calling. As creatures, we are called to see Him as a man, to hear Him as a man, as Israel's Messiah, as the One whom the Law, the Prophets, and the Psalms foretold. And having seen Him and heard about His works, we then must decide to confess Him as the Son of God, the very self-revelation of God.

This is why, I believe, Jesus says, "Who do you say that I am?" rather than "Come here and I am going to tell you something: I am the Christ, the Son of God." First He does the works of God that prove that He is of God, and then He asks, "Who do you say that I am?" And each and every one of us must answer that question for him or her self. Authentically, ourselves, we must make Simon Peter's confession—"You are the Christ, the Son of the living God"—based on evidence of Jesus' works, and not just on the basis of His words.

Only then can we realize that everything Jesus did, the very reason He, the eternally begotten Son of God, was born as Mary's child, was to make all of us sons of God. We are all called to become by grace what Jesus is by nature. As St. John says, "But to all who received him, who believed in his name, he gave power to become children of God" (John 1:12).

We can only truly become what Jesus is if we embrace who He is humanly, that is, through our own experience. By opening our hearts and minds and meditating on the words of God, by the power of the Holy Spirit, we can understand them and live by them, and so become ourselves sons of God and witnesses who testify in our own lives to the fact that Jesus truly is the Christ, the Son of the living God.

CHAPTER 5

Jesus as

LORD

The climactic center—literally and literarily—of the Gospels of Matthew, Mark, and Luke is the question Jesus asks the disciples, "Who do you say that I am?" This is the question of all questions as far as ancient Christianity is concerned. Jesus does not ask, "How do you relate to My teaching? Are you comfortable with My spiritual path? What do you think of My doctrine, My philosophy of life, My worldview?" but rather, "Who do you say that I am?"

If this is Jesus' first great question in the Synoptic Gospels, His second great question is what interests us now. In Matthew 22:41–46, we read:

> Now while the Pharisees were gathered together, Jesus asked them a question, saying, "What do you think of the Christ? Whose son is he?" They said to him, "The son of David." He said to them, "How is it then that David, inspired by the Spirit, calls him Lord, saying,
>> 'The Lord said to my Lord,
>> Sit at my right hand,
>> till I put thy enemies under thy feet'?
> If David thus calls him Lord, how is he his son?" And no one was able to answer him a word, nor from that day did any one dare to ask him any more questions.

The very same encounter, with some variations, is recorded in the Gospels of Mark and Luke.

The psalm verse Jesus quotes here—Psalm 110(109):1—is the most quoted Old Testament verse in the New Testament. In the Book of Acts, on the

Day of Pentecost, when the Holy Spirit is poured out on the disciples of the risen Lord, the Apostle Peter refers to this verse when he preaches the first sermon in Christian history. Having told the crowd that everything that has happened is a fulfillment of Joel's prophecy that God's Spirit will be poured out on all flesh, Peter continues:

> "Men of Israel, hear these words: Jesus of Nazareth, a man attested to you by God with mighty works and wonders and signs which God did through him in your midst, as you yourselves know—this Jesus, delivered up according to the definite plan and foreknowledge of God, you crucified and killed by the hands of lawless men. But God raised him up, having loosed the pangs of death, because it was not possible for him to be held by it. For David says concerning him,
>> 'I saw the Lord always before me,
>> for he is at my right hand that I may not be shaken;
>> therefore my heart was glad, and my tongue rejoiced;
>> moreover my flesh will dwell in hope.
>> For thou wilt not abandon my soul to Hades,
>> nor let thy Holy One see corruption.
>> Thou hast made known to me the ways of life;
>> thou wilt make me full of gladness with thy presence.'
> "Brethren, I may say to you confidently of the patriarch David that he both died and was buried, and his tomb is with us to this day. Being therefore a prophet, and knowing that God had sworn with an oath to him that he would set one of his descendants upon his throne, he foresaw and spoke of the resurrection of the Christ, that he was not abandoned to Hades, nor did his flesh see corruption. This Jesus God raised up, and of that we all are witnesses. Being therefore exalted at the right hand of God, and having received from the Father the promise of the Holy Spirit, he has poured out this which you see and hear. For David did not ascend into the heavens; but he himself says,
>> 'The Lord said to my Lord, Sit at my right hand,
>> till I make thy enemies a stool for thy feet.'
> "Let all the house of Israel therefore know assuredly that God has made him both Lord and Christ, this Jesus whom you crucified." (Acts 2:22–36)

Here then is Psalm 110(109):1, quoted again in the first Christian sermon, as it is in all the Synoptic Gospels. Most immediately, the verse shows us that there are two Lords. Just as there are two Kings, there are two Saviors (so to speak): God is the Savior, and Christ is the Savior. God is the powerful Conqueror, and Christ is the Conqueror. God is the King who makes salvation in the midst of the earth, and Jesus is that very same King. Similarly, the term "Lord" applies both to God and to Jesus. What, however, does it mean, to call Jesus "Lord"?

The juxtaposition of "Jesus," "Christ," and "Lord" is found throughout the New Testament. We might even say that *Iesous Christos Kyrios* is the foundational Christian creed, with the addition of *huios tou theou*—Son of God. Leaving behind the Gospels and Acts, throughout the Epistles we hear Jesus referred to as "Lord Christ," "Lord Jesus Christ," "Jesus Christ the Lord," "Christ Jesus the Lord," and simply "Lord." In fact, in the earliest Christian writing that exists, 1 Thessalonians, the expression "Lord Jesus Christ" is used five times and the term "Lord" many more times. The use of "Lord," therefore, is a commonplace in the Christian Scriptures.

In the Hellenic Greek language of the time, the term *kyrios* could be just an everyday term for someone who has *exousia*—authority and power. If you are a lord—a *kyrios*—you have power. You can dispose of your subjects. You can order them around. They have to obey you. Additionally, *kyrios* implies ownership. Its counterpart is *doulos*, which means a slave, a servant or bonded servant. A *kyrios*, then, is one who has *douloi*—servants or slaves. *Kyrios* could also be a title, equivalent to *Herr* in German, or the term "Lord" as it refers to an aristocrat in English. Finally, the term *kyrios* can be used in a general sense, as in "*a* lord," just as the term "son of God" could simply mean "*a* son of God" and "Christ" could mean "*an* anointed one."

We should note, however, that there is another word in the Greek New Testament that is sometimes translated in English as "lord"—*despotis*. In our Church, we sing to our bishops (since they were given civil power under the Turks) *eis polla eti despota*—"Many years to you, master (despot)." *Despota* is also used for Jesus in Scripture. For example, in the Song of Simeon in Luke 2:29, "Lord, now lettest thou thy servant depart in peace," the Greek word for "Lord" is not *kyrios*, but *despotis*, which technically means a "master of slaves." This is why Jesus uses that term in His parables when He speaks about the servants waiting for the master to come.

In the Scriptures, however, Jesus is not simply being called "lord" in the sense of being a master over slaves. Nor is He is called "lord" in some general and everyday sense. He is not just *a* lord. Rather, Jesus is confessed as *ho kyrios*, *the* Lord. And He is not just *a* king, *a* ruler with authority, but *the* ultimate ruler, *the* ultimate king.

In the Old Testament, the first name of God was *El Shaddai*, the Most High God. Later, speaking to Moses, God calls Himself another name.

> Then Moses said to God, "If I come to the people of Israel and say to them, 'The God of your fathers has sent me to you,' and they ask me, 'What is his name?' what shall I say to them?"
>
> God said to Moses, "I am who I am." And he said, "Say this to the people of Israel, 'I am has sent me to you.'" (Ex. 3:13–14)

For the first time, God gives the famous tetragrammaton, the four consonants (YHWH) between which one inserts two vowels to get the word that is usually pronounced "Yahweh" in English. From this point onward, the tetragrammaton was the name given to God, but it was a name that was pronounced only once a year, by the high priest. It was the holiest name, the name of all names, though we say it rather casually now. It means literally, "I Am Who I Am," or simply, "I Am"—*ego eimi* in the Greek translation. Some scholars, however, say that *Yahweh* should not be understood as a statement of being at all, but rather as a statement of action: "I will do what I will do," or "I cause to be what I want to be," or "I will act as I will act."

Whatever the tetragrammaton was intended to mean, when it was used in the texts of the Law and the Psalms and the Prophets and when it was chanted in the synagogue, the word itself was not pronounced in Hebrew. Rather, another term was substituted: *Adonai*, which means "the Lord." And when the Jews later translated the Holy Scriptures into Greek, they did not write *ego eimi* for *Yahweh*. They simply translated *Adonai* into the Greek word *ho kyrios*. The word that we read *ho kyrios* in Greek, then, is simply a substitution for the name of God Himself.

We see this in the Shema Yisrael of Deuteronomy 6:4–5, the very center of the Mosaic Law, which says, "Hear, O Israel: The LORD our God is one Lord; and you shall love the Lord your God with all your heart, and with all your soul, and with all your might." Reading the original Hebrew in a literal sense, we would actually hear, "Hear, O Israel, *Yahweh* is God, and you will worship *Yahweh* God, who is one, with all your mind, soul, heart, and strength."

The phrase *ho kyrios*, then, as it is attributed to Jesus in the New Testament, is an indicator that He is divine. Calling Jesus *ho kyrios* gives Him the name that belongs only to God. When Jesus is called *ho kyrios*, all His activities, even the ones He does in His humanity, are attributed to Yahweh, the Lord God. This is why, in the Gospel of John, Jesus is condemned and executed for blasphemy, for making Himself God's equal.

The term *kyrios*, then, as applied to Jesus, is the Christian confession that He is Yahweh, Adonai, the Lord God. As ancient Christians who follow the Scriptures, we confess that God is the Lord, and that this Lord God is the Father of Jesus of Nazareth, who, being the Christ, the Son of God, crucified and glorified, is also forever the Lord over all creation, the Lord over all people, the Lord of the universe, the Lord of the living and the dead. Jesus is the Lord together with God His Father.

As we say in the Creed, "I believe in one Lord Jesus Christ, the only begotten Son of God, Light from Light, true God from true God." Given what we have said above, we could equally confess Jesus Christ as "true Lord from true Lord," because *Lord* and *God* mean the same thing, according to the Scriptures. When we pray *Kyrie eleison* in the Church, then, we are addressing God the Father, the Son, and the Holy Spirit, who is also called "Lord" in the Epistle to the Corinthians and in the Creed: "I believe in the Holy Spirit, the Lord, the Giver of Life." Thus the one Lordship of God the Father is also the Lordship of the Son and the Lordship of the Holy Spirit.

Ultimately, we confess three Persons as Lord, a fact that is already prophesied in the words of Psalm 110(109):

> The Lord says to my lord:
> "Sit at my right hand,
> till I make your enemies your footstool."

CHAPTER 6

Jesus the

I AM

St. John's Gospel teaches clearly that Jesus is the I Am, the Lord, the One who spoke to Moses from the burning bush. In Greek, "I am" is *ego eimi*. Jesus uses that phrase to refer to Himself throughout the Gospels, but especially in John. Before we get to John, let's look at one use of that expression in Mark, at the time of Jesus' trial and passion:

> And the high priest stood up in the midst, and asked Jesus, "Have you no answer to make? What is it that these men testify against you?" But he was silent and made no answer. Again the high priest asked him, "Are you the Christ, the Son of the Blessed?" And Jesus said, "I am; and you will see the Son of man seated at the right hand of Power, and coming with the clouds of heaven." And the high priest tore his garments, and said, "Why do we still need witnesses? You have heard his blasphemy. What is your decision?" And they all condemned him as deserving death. (Mark 14:60–64)

Every Jew knew that "I Am" was God's name. When the high priest heard Jesus' words ("I am—*ego eimi*"), he knew Jesus was claiming to be God, which the priest saw as blasphemy.

The use of "I Am" to refer to Jesus' divinity is even more explicit in John. English translations often render the Greek *ego eimi* as "I am He," but it's important to realize the "He" is not actually there in the Greek.

Likewise, in John 4:4–42, Jesus has an encounter with a Samaritan woman. The Samaritan woman says the Christ is coming, and then Jesus says, "I who speak to you am he" (v. 26). But the Greek says, "*Legei aute, ho*

Iesous (Jesus said to her) *ego eimi* (I am) *ho lalon soi* (the one who speaks to you)." So translated literally from Greek, the verse reads, "Jesus said to her, 'I am (*ego eimi*) the one that's speaking to you." There is no "he."

In John 8 we find an astonishing conversation between Jesus and the leaders of the people about who their father is. Jesus tells them their father is the devil, and they say Jesus has a devil because he's calling God His father. It's a huge conflict. But in this chapter are three very important sentences.

First of all, verse 24 reads, "I told you that you would die in your sins, for you will die in your sins unless you believe that I am he." Jesus says unless they believe that He is the I Am, they're going to die in their sins. We can see this clearly in Greek: *Ean gar me pistevsete hoti ego eimi* (unless you believe that *I am*) *apothaneisthe en tais harmartiais humon* (you will die in your sins). (Again, there is no "he" after the "I am.")

Then, in John 8:28, Jesus says, "When you have lifted up the Son of man, then you will know that I am he." Once again, in the Greek, there is no "he." It simply says that when you have lifted up the son of man, which means when he is crucified, "*tote gnosesthe hoti ego eimi* (you will know that *I am*)." In other words, "You will know that I am *the I Am*."

However, the most striking passage in John 8 is when they start discussing Abraham in verses 48–59. Jesus says God is His father, while the Jews say they have Abraham as their father. Jesus tells them Abraham is not their father. If they really were children of Abraham, then they would know who Jesus is. But they are actually in the power of the devil, Jesus tells them. When they again make reference to Abraham, Jesus says these words: "Your father Abraham rejoiced that he was to see my day; he saw it and was glad." Then the Jews say to Him, "You are not yet fifty years old, and have You seen Abraham?"

Jesus responds, "*Amen, amen lego humin*." (This expression, "Amen, amen," is a rabbinic expression that means He is speaking with total authority, not to be contradicted, no negotiation.) He goes on, "*prin Avra'am genesthai ego eimi*." Literally, "Amen amen, I say to you, before Abraham came to be, *I am*." Then it says, "So they took up stones to throw at him; but Jesus hid himself, and went out of the temple." In other words, they are going to stone him to death for blasphemy because Jesus is saying that before Abraham existed, *He is God*.

Twice more in John we see *ego eimi* used by Jesus in the same way. When Jesus is speaking about being betrayed by Judas (13:18–19), He says the Scripture has to be fulfilled that he who eats bread with Him has lifted up his heel against Him; and then Jesus says this: "I tell you this now, before it takes place, that when it does take place you may believe *hoti ego eimi* (that *I am*)." In the English translations it says "that I am He"; but again, in Greek there is no "He."

Finally, we see this significant expression in an unexpected place. Some people don't understand this passage at all. When Jesus is in the Garden of Gethsemane (18:4–9), the temple guard comes out to arrest Him, and Jesus says to them, "Whom do you seek?" They answer him, "Jesus of Nazareth." And then Jesus says to them, "*Ego eimi.*" I am. Yet again the English translations say "I am He," but there's no "He" in Greek. Jesus says to them, "*I am.*"

When Jesus says to them, "I am," they draw back and fall to the ground. Again He asks them, "Whom do you seek?" And again they say, "Jesus of Nazareth." So Jesus says to them, "I told you that I am (*ego eimi*). So, if you seek me, let these men go." Then the disciples run away, and the guards arrest Jesus. But you could ask the question, "Why would the guards draw back and fall on the ground when Jesus says 'I am'?" They fall down because when they hear *ego eimi*, they hear the divine Name. He is saying the divine Name, which the Jew never said. It was the name that was written but never spoken except as "the Lord." But Jesus actually says the Name. He said to them (as an equivalent in English), "I am God."

In addition to the passages in John where Jesus says "I am" with no predicate, He also uses the "I am" with nine different predicate nominatives (three in #6 of this list). He says not simply "I am," but "I am (something)."

1. "I am the bread of life (*ego eimi ho artos tes zoes*)." (6:48)

2. "I am the light of the world (*ego eimi ho phos tou kosmou*)." (8:12; 9:5)

3. "I am the door of the sheep (*ego eimi he thyra ton probaton*)." (10:7)

4. "I am the good shepherd (*ego eimi ho poimen ho kalos*)." (10:11)

5. "I am the resurrection and the life (*ego eimi he anastasis kai he zoe*)." (11:25)

6. "I am the way, and the truth, and the life (*ego eimi he hodos, kai he aletheia, kai he zoe*)." (14:6)

7. "I am the true vine (*ego eimi he ampelos he alethine*)." (15:1)

He calls himself nine things, each time beginning with the expression *ego eimi*. "I Am" is the divine Name, the equivalent of the name *Yahweh*. It is what the people meant when they said "the Lord." When they read the Scripture and said "the Lord," they meant "the I Am." And we Christians, every time we hear the expression, "the Lord," have ringing in our heart and our mind the "I Am."

In our Eastern Orthodox churches, the participial form of "I Am" (which in English is "Being," or "The One Who Is") is written on icons of Jesus. In every icon of Jesus in the Orthodox Church, there is a nimbus around His head containing four Greek letters: *Ho On*, "The Existing One." The final dismissal at Vespers and Matins in the Orthodox Church contains the words "Christ our God, the existing one," or sometimes "He who is"—all translating *Ho On*, the divine Name. This is the way Jesus Christ revealed Himself to us.

CHAPTER 7

Jesus as

GOD

In the last chapter we discussed the Name of God—*Yahweh, ego eimi*, I Am. In a sense that name is a kind of mystery. The I Am, the Existing One, the Acting One: that expression shows that God is a personal God—a God who speaks, a God who acts.

In the Bible, this was the great proof of the existence of God. The Hebrews did not have much of a metaphysical mentality. They didn't think in terms of nouns, but in terms of action and power. The God of Abraham, Isaac, and Jacob, the God who reveals His name as I Am, is the only one who is living, acting, and speaking. In the ancient world, a being was identified by its action. In Genesis, when Adam is told to name the animals, he watches how they behave, and then he names them. You know what something is by seeing how it acts.

The Christian Church and the Holy Fathers likewise came to their conclusion—that Jesus Christ is divine, that He is God—because of the way He acts: He acts like God. He does things only God can do. He says things only God can say. He claims prerogatives that only belong to God. In other words, He goes around talking and acting like God, so much so that in the Gospels the question is often asked, "What manner of man is this? What kind of a man is this who does these things?" (see Matt. 8:27; Mark 4:41).

In the synoptic Gospels—Matthew, Mark, Luke—the people will say, "How can this man say your sins are forgiven? How does this man walk on the water? What manner of man is this that the winds are subject to Him?" He claims to be greater than Jonah, greater than Solomon, greater than the prophets. What is that "greater one"? The Christians would claim that Jesus is God. He is divine. He is *theos*.

He is God, and He is also man. He is divine, and He is human. He is what the one God, who is His Father, is. And from His mother, Mary, He becomes what we all are. He is really God, and He is really man. That is Eastern Orthodox Christianity. That's the way catholic, orthodox, ancient Christians interpret the Bible. This is the claim that will be explicated, explained, defended throughout Christian history.

God is one God—*deus* in Latin, *theos* in Greek. But the Divinity—*divinitas* in Latin, *theotēs* in Greek—consists of three Persons: Father, Son, and Holy Spirit. In the Eastern Orthodox Liturgy, significantly, we actually do not use the expression "triune *theos*" or "triune God." We have a triune or tri-hypostatic *theotēs*, "Divinity" or "Godhead" in English. But there is only one God.

So what about Jesus? Is He called *ho theos* ever, anywhere? Can we say, "Jesus is God," and have a scriptural reference to that particular sentence? Certainly, the New Testament teaches that Jesus of Nazareth is divine with the same divinity as God the Father. But does the phrase *ho theos* ever refer to Him?

Before we answer that, we should say one more thing: It seems pretty clear that in the New Testament, "the God" (*ho theos*)—taken by itself—refers to God the Father. That, I believe, is the way the Bible speaks. Ninety-nine percent of the time, the word "God" means the God who is the Father of Jesus, the God whose Word is Jesus Christ, the God whose personal power is Jesus Christ, the God whose wisdom is Jesus Christ, the God who has generated His Son from all eternity. This Son of God is divine. But it's the Father of Jesus who is almost always simply called "God" (*ho theos*). The same applies to the Nicene Creed and the whole Divine Liturgy.

However, there are three passages in the Gospel of John where the term *theos* is applied to Jesus. The Prologue of John contains one definite use of *theos* for Jesus and a second that is debatable.

The Gospel of John begins, "*En arche en ho logos* (In the beginning is the Word) *kai ho logos en pros ton theon* (and the Word was with [or toward or about] God), *kai theos en ho logos* (and God was the Word)." The Word is with God and is God—God without the definite article. You can turn that around and say, "*en ho logos en theos*—the Word was God." The point here is, of course, that the word God is used.

The Prologue continues, "*Houtos* (this same one) *en arche pros ton theon* (was in the beginning)." This Logos who is *theos* in the beginning was *pros ton theon*—with God, or toward God, or around God.

The next use of *theos* is in verse 18—and here we need to take some time to analyze the different readings of this passage. Most versions read, "*monogenes huios ho on eis ton kolpon tou patros* (the only-begotten son who is in the bosom [or the womb, or the interiors] of the Father)." But in some ancient versions of the Greek Scripture, it doesn't say "*monogenes huios* (the only-begotten Son)." Instead it says, "*monogenes theos* (the only-begotten God), *ho on* (who is—I Am) *eis ton kolpon tu para patros* (in the bosom of the Father)." Some of the Church Fathers probably had a version of the New Testament that did not say "the only-begotten Son" but "the only-begotten God."

Some texts say *huios*; some texts say *theos*. Which one is the variant? Which one is the original? Some argue it seems more likely from a literary criticism of the Prologue that *theos* is the proper reading, because the Prologue begins with, "In the beginning was the Word, and the Word was with God, and the Word was God." The Word was *theos*. In the middle it says "the Word became flesh." If we read the Prologue as having a chiastic structure—in which the beginning is recapitulated at the end (an *inclusio poetica*), with the high point in the middle—we would then expect a recapitulation of the line from the beginning of the Prologue. So in verse 18, it seems more likely that the proper reading is "only-begotten God," because the first verse uses "God."

We can conclude here a very simple thing. The one God is the Father of the Logos, the One whose Logos He is. The one God is the Father of the only-begotten Son; the Son is the *monogenes*, the only-begotten Son, of the Father (*para patros*). The Son is the only-begotten from the Father. So the Father is the one God. Nevertheless, this Logos, this only-begotten Son, is called *theos* here. He is called *theos* in the first verse and in the variant reading in verse 18. Here we have two places where the word *theos* or "God" is clearly applied to the Son and not to the Father.

Some scholars will point out that in both verse 1 and verse 18, no definite article is used with *theos*. It says "the Word (*ho logos*) is *theos*"; it doesn't say *ho theos*. This led some scholars to think you can call the Logos *theos*, which is God, but you really can't call Him *the* God, *ho theos*, because in both cases here in the Prologue, there is no definite article.

So the claim would be, "Yes, He's God, but he is not *the* God, because *the* God is His Father, and He is God because He is God's Son." That would be a classical, patristic way to explain things. That is in fact how we would understand it.

However, we have one more text that is critical, from John 20. If you consider John 21 as a later addition, as many do, the original text would end with 20:31: "but these [things] are written that you may believe that Jesus is the Christ, the Son of God, and that believing you may have life in his name." If we take that verse as the end of the Gospel—and it does read like an ending—and read the whole Gospel chiastically, I would say the center of the Gospel would be Jesus' confession that "before Abraham was, I Am" (8:58), a clear confession of divinity.

At the end of the Gospel, Jesus risen from the dead appears and shows Himself to the apostles. Thomas is not there. Thomas says that unless he sees Him, he will never believe. Then we have what I believe is the poetic inclusion of the entire Gospel that recapitulates the Prologue. Thomas sees the risen Christ, and He tells him, "Put your finger here, and see my hands; and put out your hand, and place it in my side; do not be faithless, but believing" (20:27).

Thomas's reply is extremely important. It is the only place in the entire New Testament where someone addresses Jesus as God, with a definite article (*ho theos*), and calls him "Lord God," *adonai eloheinu*, which is the name for God in the Old Testament. When Jesus tells Thomas to do this, "Thomas answered him, 'My Lord and my God!'" (v. 28).

In Greek, it says Thomas answered and "*eipen avto* (said to Him) *ho kyrios mou kai ho theos mou* (the Lord of me and the God of me)." Definite articles in both instances: *ho kyrios mou kai ho theos mou*, "the Lord and the God." There we have Jesus unequivocally addressed as God.

If we had only this sentence, and it was canonized by the Church from the beginning, we could certainly say that Eastern Orthodox Christians—classical, catholic, believing Christians through the ages—confess Jesus as God: the God, the God who is His Father.

St. Paul generally speaks about "the God" being the Father of Jesus, and Jesus being the Lord and the Savior. However, in 2 Peter 1:1, we find the same kind of expression Thomas used: "the God of us and the Savior of us, our Lord Jesus Christ" ("our God and Savior Jesus Christ," RSV). In Titus 2:13, St. Paul writes, "The great God and our Savior, Jesus Christ" ("our great God and Savior Jesus Christ," RSV). In 1 Timothy 1:1, he writes, "the command of God the Savior of us and Christ Jesus, the hope of us" ("by command of God our Savior and of Christ Jesus our hope," RSV).

These texts are translated and used liturgically as, "Our great God and Savior, Jesus Christ," or "Our great God and our Savior, Jesus Christ, our hope." For example, at the end of Vespers and Matins we say, "Glory to Thee, O Christ, our God and our hope."

The expression "Christ, our God" is used in Christian Liturgy, certainly Eastern Orthodox Christian Liturgy, very often. For example, in the Great Litany, we say, "Let us commend ourselves and each other and all our life to Christ, our God." And at the end of the service we say, "Glory to Thee, O Christ, our God and our hope."

But even when we call Jesus "the Lord," we remember that we also call God the Father "the Lord," and we also remember that the name for the Most High God, who is the Father of Jesus, is "the Lord." So the terms "the Lord" and "God" are applied in Scripture both to God the Father and to the Son. The Father is Lord; the Father is God. The Son is Lord; the Son is God. The Father is I Am; the Son is also I Am. These names are applied to Jesus the Son in exactly the same way they are applied to God.

If we want to be a little more technical, though, we can say that in the three examples above there is a grammatical issue, because they could as easily be translated with commas: "to our great God, and our Savior Jesus Christ"; "to the God of us, and to the Savior of us, our Lord Jesus Christ"; "a command of God, the Savior of us, and of Jesus Christ, our hope." It doesn't necessarily mean that the "great God and Savior" and "our great God and Savior, Jesus Christ," mean one and the same person, namely, Jesus. It could be "our great God," meaning God the Father, and "our Savior, Jesus Christ."

Perhaps we can simply say that it can be translated either way, and that it doesn't really matter that much, because it is a very clear teaching of the New Testament—by what Jesus says and does, and how he calls Himself, and what he says about Himself, and how the people call Him, and how He relates to God the Father, and in what is written about Him by the evangelists and the apostles—that He is really divine. So there is absolutely nothing wrong with saying that Jesus is God.

Here we want to be careful, though, because Jesus is not God the Father. We must always make that distinction, and we must also make the point strongly that the One God is not the Father, Son, and Holy Spirit, all together somehow as one Person. There is one divine nature, but there are three Persons or hypostases. There is one Divinity, but there are three who are divine: the Father, the Son, and the Spirit. And they are prayed to in the Divine Liturgy of St. John Chrysostom and St. Basil as three "Thous": "Thou and Thine only-begotten Son and Thy Holy Spirit."

Two other occurrences in Scripture should be mentioned. In Hebrews 1 the writer refers to a quotation from the Psalms where the Son is called "God." The author of Hebrews is insisting that the Son of God is not an angel, He is not a creature, He is ever-existing with God the Father, and He is the One by whom all things came to be. To support this, the author cites Psalm 45:6–7(44:7–8):

> Your divine throne endures for ever and ever.
> Your royal scepter is a scepter of equity;
> you love righteousness and hate wickedness.
> Therefore God, your God [the Father], has anointed you
> with the oil of gladness above your fellows.

However one interprets this text, one thing is clear. The entire New Testament says that Jesus sits on the same throne as God the Father. That throne is eternal, it is divine, it is God's throne, and Jesus does not sit on another throne, He sits on the same throne. He is co-enthroned. He sits at the Father's right hand, which means He has the same glory, dominion, honor, and majesty that God has, forever. This shows that He is truly divine.

One more text is often cited with regard to this issue—the famous hymn in Philippians 2:5-11, which begins, "Have this mind among yourselves, which is yours in Christ Jesus," or, literally, "Think this way among yourselves, as you think in Christ Jesus."

The text continues, "*hos en morphe theou hyparchon* (who in form of God subsists—is subsisting, is existing)." The RSV translation says, "who, though he was in the form of God." Many people say, "Well, that's very clear: He is divine." Others say, "No, it just means He is in the image of God, as Adam was." But that doesn't seem likely at all, because the hymn recorded here in Philippians—which most people think is a pre-existing liturgical hymn— continues to say, "did not count equality with God [*isa theo*] a thing to be grasped." Now, no Adam or creature can be called *isa theo*, equal to God.

Furthermore, He "emptied himself, taking the form of a servant, being born in the likeness of men." He took on the form of a slave, *morphen doulou*. He is in the form of God (*morphe theou*), and in His incarnation He takes on the form of a slave (*morphe doulou*). He takes on a form He didn't have before. He had a divine form—He was in the form of God; now He has on the form of slave, a bonded slave. Then it says, "*en homoiomati anthropon genomenos* (becoming in likeness of man)."

Of Adam, Genesis says he was in the likeness of God. Now, here it says that this one, who was in the form of God, is now taking the likeness of man. Just the opposite is happening, so to speak. Adam is found in the likeness of God, but this one, who is in the form of God and is *isa theo* (equal to God), is now found "in the likeness of men." He becomes like man. Then it says, "And being found *schemati hos anthropos* (as a man) he humbled himself and became obedient unto death, even death on a cross."

This has been classically interpreted to mean that Jesus is divine; He is equal to the Father. He is *theos*, just as God the Father is *theos*. Nevertheless, throughout the New Testament the Father is usually *ho theos,* and Jesus is *theos*. But Jesus can also be addressed as *ho theos*, as Thomas did.

In summary, the title *theos* and even *ho theos*, in some sense, is perfectly applicable to Jesus Christ. The one God is His Father, but as the divine Son, He is God, and even can be prayed to as "our God, my God," in an absolutely acceptable, legitimate, biblical, true way.

CHAPTER 8

Jesus the

WORD OF GOD

In the Gospel of John, Jesus is called "God's Word" or "the Word of God." Note the use of the definite article: *the* Word.

Jesus is not called "the Word of God" in the Gospels of Matthew, Mark, or Luke, nor in the writings of St. Paul. In those writings, He is certainly the Word itself incarnate, meaning that in His life, He fulfills the words of God as the unique, personal Word of God, but He is not called "the Word." He is called "the *Son* of God." To see what is said about Jesus being "the Word of God," we must go to the opening verses of the Gospel of John.

"In the beginning was the Word [Logos], and the Word was *pros ton theon* [with God or accompanying God]. And the Logos was God." The Logos is called *theos.* And this one, He "was in the beginning *pros ton theon* [together with God]; all things were made through him, and without him was not anything made that was made." Then, St. John writes that in Him, the Logos, "was life, and the life was the light of men," and that this light "was coming into the world" (John 1:4, 9). This is the first absolutely indisputable affirmation that the Word of God exists, that this Word is divine, that all things came to be through this Word, and that the life and light of God and of all things was in this Word.

In contemplating this, the Holy Fathers teach that God Almighty is never without His Word. The Word is not Him, but there never was a time when there was no Word of God.

As St. Athanasius the Great said, God is never *alogos,* or wordless. One cannot contemplate God and His self-revelation without also contemplating

His Word, because the Word *is* the one through whom God reveals Himself. When God speaks, it is this Word that is speaking.

The fourth-century heretic Arius and those who followed him said that the one God existed at first without His Word, and then somehow God created a Word for Himself. This is absolutely unorthodox, and absolutely incomprehensible—not only when we contemplate the Scriptures, but when we think of how God Himself must be.

Already in John, the Word of God is identified with the Son of God (John 1:14). The Son of God and the Logos of God are exactly the same Person. In that sense, "Son of God" and "Logos of God" are synonymous. Yet they are different names, and they connote different realities. They are deeply interrelated, and they cannot be separated, but there is nuance and distinction between them.

Father Dumitru Stăniloae, a Romanian Orthodox theologian of the twentieth century who was persecuted violently and imprisoned by the Communists, said the second Person of the divine Trinity is called "Son," "the Son of God," because God is *love*. And if God is love, He must express Himself perfectly in another Person and share His total being with that other Person. And therefore He *does* do that, and that Person is called His Son, and that is the One who was born of the Virgin Mary on earth as the man Jesus. He is the Son of God.

When Fr. Stăniloae was contemplating this expression, he said the reason that this same second Person of the Godhead, the one who is named the Son, is also named "the Word," "the Logos," is that God is *truth*.

Because God is the ultimate reality, His Son is called the Word. Because God is love, this Word is called His Son.

John 1 continues by saying this Logos was in the world, but the world did not know Him (v. 10). This does not refer to the Incarnation and to Jesus of Nazareth. The Holy Fathers interpret this as meaning that, in the very act of creation, the Word of God was present in all things. Some of the Church Fathers state that there is *a* word (*logos*) of God in everything that exists, and that word is what makes that thing what it is. It makes a human being a human being. It makes a tree a tree, a dog a dog, a star a star. According to these Fathers, there is a multiplicity of *logoi*; there are numerous words of God.

Therefore, the true light and Logos of God is in the world, but people do not recognize the presence of God in creation because they refuse to glorify God and purify their hearts so as to see Him (see Rom. 1:20–21). Humanity is in darkness, blinded by its own fallenness, and it passes on that darkness and blindness to its children. St. John continues:

> He came to his own home, and his own people received him not. But to all who received him, who believed in his name, he gave power to become children of God; who were born, not of blood nor of the will of the flesh nor of the will of man, but of God. (John 1:11–13)

Most of the Church Fathers would see this text as referring not to the Incarnation, but to the fact that God chose Israel and that they didn't receive Him. He gave His *Torah*, which in Hebrew is called "His word." In Hebrew, the expressions we translate as *law, precept, commandment, statute,* and *ordinance* are all "words," and they are all the expression of God in His commandments that He gave to the people of Israel.

A beautiful hymn sung on Holy Friday says, "Israel, my firstborn son, did not receive Me." This is a hymnographic reference to John 1:11. He came to His own, but most of His own did not receive Him. As many as did receive Him were given power to be called His sons.

John 1:14, many believe, is what makes Christianity, Christianity: "And the Word became flesh and dwelt among us." The Greek verb, *eskenosen*, literally means "tabernacled among us." The tabernacle, and later the temple, in the Old Testament was where God dwelt. St. John continues, "The Word became flesh, and He tabernacled among us." He lived as the Tabernacle of God among us.

"We have beheld His glory." That is a technical term, in Hebrew, for the glory of God dwelling in the tabernacle. The glory was in *Him* now. "The glory as of an only-begotten from a father." Jesus is showing the glory of God as an only-begotten, which means that no other exists that can do this. Here is the identification of the Logos of God with the Son of God.

"This only-begotten of the Father," St. John writes, "is full of grace and of truth. And of His fullness we have received grace instead of grace," or "one grace upon another," infinitely (John 1:14, 16).

The last verses of the prologue say, "For the law was given through Moses, but grace and truth came through Jesus Christ. No one has seen God at any time. The only begotten Son, who is in the bosom of the Father, He has declared Him" (John 1:17–18). Thus again the Logos, the only begotten Son, and Jesus Christ are identified as the very same Person.

In the Book of Revelation, Jesus Himself is called "the Word of God." In 19:11–13, the seer, John, says:

> Then I saw heaven opened, and behold, a white horse! He who sat upon it is called Faithful and True, and in righteousness he judges and makes war. His eyes are like a flame of fire, and on his head are many diadems; and he has a name inscribed which no one knows but himself. He is clad in a robe dipped in blood, and the name by which he is called is The Word of God.

It says, "He is clad in a robe dipped in blood." He is the Crucified One, and He is called the Word of God.

This reality of the crucified Word of God is reflected in many church hymns. For example, on every Sunday and major feast day, this hymn, attributed to the Emperor St. Justinian the Great, is sung during the first part of the Divine Liturgy:

> Only-begotten Son *and Word of God*, You who exist immortal and who for our salvation willed [deigned] to be incarnate of the holy Theotokos and ever-virgin Mary and without changing [remaining divine], You became man and were crucified, O Christ our God, trampling down Death by death. You are one of the Holy Trinity, glorified together with the Father and the Holy Spirit: save us.

In this hymn, Jesus is called the Son and the Word of God. Here, as in the Gospel of John, the Logos of God became flesh from the holy Theotokos.

The fifth tone in the *Oktoechos* for Sunday says, "The Word eternal [or without a beginning], together with the Father and the Spirit, is born of a Virgin for our salvation." This hymn makes several theological points. One is that the Logos and the Spirit have no beginning in time. They are always together in the very existence of God the Father Himself, who is not God without them. The Godhead is the Father *and* the Son *and* the Holy Spirit.

We should also affirm that the Son and the Spirit find their origin *in* the Father, eternally. St. Gregory the Theologian would say "timelessly": their origin does not belong to time and space; it is something within the Divinity.

The ninth ode of the canon read at Matins on great feast days states that the faithful will "enjoy the festivities of God, and of our Master, Christ, in the banquet of immortality"—that is, the Divine Liturgy—"in the upper chamber, with uplifted minds"—meaning in the very presence of the Kingdom of God—"where we receive the exalted words of the Word." Jesus, being the *Word*, gives to everyone the *words of God*, that is, all the different self-expressions of God.

Not only is the Word of God begotten timelessly from the Father, He was born in time for our salvation, taking flesh from the Virgin Mary. But what did it mean for the Word to become flesh? The late-fourth-century heretic Apollinarius taught that Jesus had no *nous*—in other words, no mind, no spirit. The Word of God was all of His spiritual content, and the body was the fleshly content. In other words, according to Apollinarius, Jesus was not a true human being. St. Gregory the Theologian, among others, firmly opposed this new teaching as something abhorrent, not found in Scripture, and contrary to the teaching of the Church. In opposition to Apollinarius, St. Gregory wrote the famous line: "What is not assumed is not healed." So the Word of God, by becoming human, took not only human flesh, but also a human mind, a human soul, a human will, and a human spirit.

St. John's Gospel asserts that there is a cosmic logos that is in all things, and that it is this logos that gives energy and life to reality. Some scholars say that St. John is drawing on a purely Hellenistic concept, one that does not belong to the Hebrew tradition and is therefore under suspicion. But few would hold this perception anymore. When we read the Gospel of John in the light of the Old Testament Scriptures, we see that "the Word of God" is in the Old Testament from the very beginning. *Logos* is simply the Greek translation of the Hebrew *davar*.

In the Old Testament, God is always acting by His Word and also by His Spirit. St. Irenaeus of Lyons said, "God has two hands." One hand is His Word, and the other hand is His Spirit. One is the *davar Yahweh*, and the other is the *ruach* or the *pnevma theou*, the Spirit of God. And God never works with one hand. The Word is always vivified by the Holy Spirit, and the Holy Spirit is always bearing the Word.

If we look at the act of creation, God creates the world by His Word, through the Spirit. God *speaks*: "Let there be light," and there was light (Gen. 1:3). God creates through His speech, through His act. He created the world by His Word and by His Spirit. Psalm 33(32):6 says, "By the Word of the Lord the heavens were made, and all their host by the *breath* of His mouth." *Breath* is a synonym for *Spirit*. In Job, the Holy Spirit is called "the breath of the Almighty" (Job 32:8; 33:4). It is this *breath* that makes alive the Word of God.

If we keep reading the Old Testament, we see that the Law of God and the *Torah* are called the word of God and are considered to be inspired. The Holy Spirit inspires both the word of God and the understanding of this word.

In the Prophets, it says, "the word of the Lord came to [Elijah]" (1 Kings/ 3 Kingdoms 17:2), "the word of the Lord came to Isaiah" (Is. 38:4), "the word of the Lord came to Ezekiel" (Ezek. 1:3). When the Prophets receive the word of God, it happens by the indwelling of the Holy Spirit, and they speak the word.

I used to jest with my Jewish friends, saying, "We think you believe in the Holy Trinity. You just don't want to admit it."

They would say, "Oh no! There is no Trinity. There is one God, the Lord."

I would say, "Hey, wait a minute. Don't you believe that God has a Word? Is the *devar Yahweh* not divine? Is it not with God from all eternity?"

They would say, "Of course, of course." The Orthodox Jews would even say the Law of Moses was pre-eternal, that it preexisted its expression in the laws that were written down in the Scriptures. They would say the Word of God is vivified by the *ruach Yahweh*, by the breath of the Lord.

I would say to them, "You see? You believe in the one God, *Yahweh Elohim*, you believe in the *devar Yahweh*, and you believe in the *ruach Yahweh*, and you believe that they are always all together. Well, so do we!" Thus, we see the Holy Trinity already in the Old Testament.

In the final covenant, Christians have the outrageous belief that the Messiah, Jesus of Nazareth, is, in fact, that very Word in human flesh. This belief is found in the theological Gospel of St. John: "And the Word became flesh and dwelt among us, full of grace and truth" (John 1:14). Thus, Jesus is the Word incarnate, and as the Word incarnate, He speaks the words, He delivers the Word, and He is vivified by the Holy Spirit.

All human beings were created to be words of God, by the Holy Spirit dwelling in them, so that they could be revelations of God. In human beings, this happens by grace and faith. In Jesus, it is by nature. This is the Christian faith: Jesus Christ is the Word of God in human flesh. And therefore He makes the *logoi*, the words, known.

Christians should never say to Muslims, "You have the *Quran* and we have the Bible." Instead, we should say, "You believe that the *Quran* is the Word of God. We believe that a *Person* is the Word of God: Jesus of Nazareth."

Do not let anybody think that the Word of God for Christians is the Bible. *It is not.* The Holy Scriptures in the Bible *testify* to the Word, but the Word is Jesus Christ.

As we've been saying, in Hebrew, the expression "the word" does not refer simply to a spoken word or a concept, like the *logos* in Greek philosophy. The word *davar* means "act," and it means "thing." Thus, we could say that the Word of God is God's act. The Word of God is God's *thing*. And every time God speaks, He acts. We might say He does His thing.

The living God speaks; the living God acts. This is truly amazing to contemplate.

There is a wonderful story about a holy man of the Hasidic Jewish tradition named Zusya. Zusya understood the Word of God perfectly, although he had never read it because he was illiterate. But he had never heard it either. Then how could he know the Word of God perfectly? The story says that every time he was in the synagogue, when the reader said, "Thus says the Lord," Zusya went into ecstasy. He was so amazed by the fact that God would *speak* that he never heard the reading. But everybody said Zusya knew the Law of God and the Torah better than anybody, because he heard it in mystical ecstasy and in silence.

The Word of God comes out of the silence of God and leads back *into* the silence of God. St. Ignatius of Antioch wrote, "Whoever sees Jesus as the utterances of God hears also His silence" (see Ignatius' *Letter to the Ephesians,* 15). And St. Basil the Great says, "When we read and hear the

Scriptures, we hear not only the words, we hear the silence out of which they come and into which they lead us."

This is the reason the ultimate revelation of Jesus as the Word of God comes when He hangs silent and dead as a corpse upon the Cross. "Let all mortal flesh keep silent and in fear and trembling stand" (from the Cherubic Hymn on Holy Saturday). In that resounding silence, one hears the Word of God, and that Word *acts*. It comes inside, it inspires, it purifies. That is the Word that Jesus Himself is.

When we think of Jesus as the Word, we should not think simply of speech. And, once again, we should not think of the Bible as God's Word. In some sense, yes, the Bible is the Word of God, but as St. Maximus the Confessor would say, "The Bible is the Word of God incarnate in human words," just as in the cosmos, the Word of God is incarnate in created forms. But Jesus of Nazareth is the Word of God Himself, perfectly, in the flesh, and that is why all His words are, in fact, "words of the Word."

When Orthodox believers see, hear, touch, and taste Jesus, and see how He acts, we are confessing Him as the unique Word of God, who is also the only begotten Son, the Wisdom, and the Power.

Jesus is the Word of God. He is God's ultimate speech, God's ultimate revelation of Himself, God's ultimate act, and God's ultimate and final thing. The embodiment of God in the Commandments becomes flesh and lives the human life as Jesus of Nazareth, the great "I Am," and God's very Son.

CHAPTER 9

Jesus the

WISDOM OF GOD

J esus is God's Wisdom—in Hebrew, the *chokhmah,* or in Greek, the *sophia,* of God. If we had no biblical texts to tell us this, it would still follow that if Jesus is the Word of God, the Son of God, the *Logos,* He must also be the Wisdom of God, because where God's Word is, there is God's Wisdom also.

According to the whole *skopos* or function of Scripture, particularly in what is called the "Wisdom literature" of the Old Testament (Psalms, Job, Proverbs, Ecclesiastes, Song of Songs, Wisdom of Solomon, and Wisdom of Sirach), human beings are called to pursue wisdom; it is what we should desire more than anything else. It is more precious than gold and sweeter than honey (Psalm 19[18]:10; 119[118]:103). The worst possible condition someone can be in is to be a *fool*—"The fool says in his heart, 'There is no God'" (Psalm 14[13]:1; 53[52]:1).

Wisdom has a special character and meaning in the Bible. It is not simply factual knowledge. It is insight into the very nature of things. It is the knowledge of the *logos* or inner principle of reality, whereby we know the significance of things and their relationship to everything else. Through wisdom, we know their proper use, and know it vitally, in life itself. We could say wisdom is a kind of practical application of knowledge.

God is wise. Scripture says about God's created things, "In wisdom hast thou made them all" (Psalm 104[103]:24). The Wisdom literature even personifies Wisdom. In Proverbs, Wisdom speaks in the first person:

> "Ages ago I was set up,
> at the first, before the beginning of the earth.

When there were no depths I was brought forth,
when there were no springs abounding with water.
Before the mountains had been shaped,
before the hills, I was brought forth;
before he had made the earth with its fields,
or the first of the dust of the world.
When he established the heavens, I was there,
when he drew a circle on the face of the deep,
when he made firm the skies above,
when he established the fountains of the deep,
when he assigned to the sea its limit,
so that the waters might not transgress his command,
when he marked out the foundations of the earth,
then I was beside him, like a master workman [*demiurgos*, the one by
    whom and through whom God acts];
and I was daily his delight,
rejoicing before him always,
rejoicing in his inhabited world
and delighting in the sons of men.
And now, my sons, listen to me:
happy are those who keep my ways.
Hear instruction and be wise,
and do not neglect it.
Happy is the man who listens to me,
watching daily at my gates,
waiting beside my doors.
For he who finds me finds life
and obtains favor from the Lord;
but he who misses me injures himself;
all who hate me love death." (8:23–36)

This is a hypostatization (or personalization, personification) of Wisdom in the writings of the Old Testament. Because *chokhmah* is feminine in Hebrew, Wisdom is presented as *she*: "I loved her and sought her from my youth, / And desired to take her as a bride for myself; / And I became a lover of her beauty" (Wisdom of Solomon 8:2). When Wisdom is spoken of in the Bible, the feminine form is used.

Proverbs 9 says:

Wisdom has built her house,
she has set up her seven pillars.
She has slaughtered her beasts, she has mixed her wine,
she has also set her table.
She has sent out her maids to call
from the highest places in the town,
"Whoever is simple, let him turn in here!"
To him who is without sense she says,
"Come, eat of my bread
and drink of the wine I have mixed.
Leave simpleness, and live,
and walk in the way of insight." (vv. 1–6)

Some have considered Wisdom to be a feminine element in God, a kind of divine feminine, seeing *Sophia* as a feminine counterpart to the masculine *Logos*. Yet we never draw theological conclusions from the gender of nouns in any language. The word for *spirit*, for example, is feminine in Hebrew and Aramaic, masculine in Latin, and neuter in Greek.

There is no masculine and no feminine in God at all. God is God. God is not like anything in creation. God is beyond being. God, and all that belongs to God, all His qualities—His wisdom, His love, His truth, His power, His glory, His splendor, His peace—are not like anything else. Nothing is comparable to these divine attributes, in heaven or on earth.

Jesus of Nazareth is a man, not a woman, but it is the teaching of Scripture and the Eastern Orthodox tradition that Jesus Christ is the hypostatic Wisdom of God Himself. Jesus is the personification of absolutely every divine quality, and so, too, of God's Wisdom. Metaphorically, we seek that Wisdom who is Jesus as a bride, as a beautiful beloved. We want Wisdom to dwell in us, we want to become wise, and the Wisdom we desire in the human form is Jesus Christ the God-man.

St. Athanasius says exactly the same thing about Wisdom that he says about the *Logos*: he had said that one cannot think of God as *alogos*, without Word, and likewise one cannot think of God as *asophos*, without Wisdom. In the Bible—the Psalms, the Proverbs, Ecclesiastes, the Wisdom of Solomon—Wisdom is always with God. It "abides with His throne," to use Sirach's expression (see Wisdom of Sirach 1:6). God does everything by His

Wisdom. God is truth; therefore Wisdom is always in the divine activity. That God created all things through His Wisdom, St. Paul would say, shows clearly that God creates everything by Christ, in exactly the same way as the Old Testament speaks about the divine Wisdom.

St. Athanasius says that when we read about Wisdom in Holy Scripture, we have to keep two things in mind: the divine, eternal, uncreated Wisdom that is the Wisdom of God Himself; and Wisdom as expressed in creation. We can *see* God's Wisdom in all that exists. If we contemplate the stars and the moon and the plants and the animals and the trees, we see a revelation of the very Wisdom of God in all of these things, as well as of His power, His beauty, His truth, His glory, and His splendor.

The Arians said, "The Logos is a creature, the Son of God is a creature, and therefore the Wisdom of God is a creature." They used the text of Proverbs, "the Lord created me at the beginning of His work, the first of His acts of old" (Prov. 8:22), to say, "You see? The first creative act of God was to create Wisdom. Then God used His Wisdom as an instrument, as a kind of *demiurgos* through which He did all of His activities. Wisdom is like a tool in the hand of God."

Yet when the Bible uses such terms as *create* or *fashion* or *form* or *make*, these are different words used in different ways. A clear and accurate distinction between "coming forth from God," "abiding with God," and "being in God," and then "being created *by* God as a creature," was only formulated when the Fathers were fighting the Arian and Eunomian heresies in the fourth century.

Words like *proceeded from* or *abided in* or *born of* or *begotten of,* the Holy Fathers say, testify to the fact of that which is *not* created, which is ever-existing. The term *to make* would then be considered to signify an act of God's will. The Nicene Creed makes this distinction when it speaks about Jesus being "begotten, not made."

Jesus is the Wisdom that God fashioned for humanity from before the foundation of the world, revealed in the world in human form, but that very Wisdom itself existed before the mountains had been shaped, before the hills, before He made the earth with its fields, before there was any dust in the world. When He established the heavens, that Wisdom was already there, and that Wisdom is the very Wisdom of God Himself. Wisdom is "the fashioner of all things." The Wisdom of Solomon says, "[I learned] whatever is hidden and whatever is visible. / For wisdom, the artisan of all things, taught me" (Wisdom of Solomon 7:21).

Scripture also speaks about "the Spirit of Wisdom." Isaiah, prophesying about Jesus, says, "And the Spirit of the Lord shall rest upon him, the spirit of wisdom and understanding, the spirit of counsel and might, the spirit of knowledge and the fear of the Lord" (11:2). This sort of language about the Holy Spirit—the *ruach* of God, the breath of God—pervades Scripture. Just as we cannot think of God without His Spirit, we cannot think of God without His Wisdom.

The Spirit is the Spirit of the Word, but also the Spirit of Wisdom—the living, existential, vital aspect of Wisdom itself. Without the Spirit, there is no Word, no Wisdom, no truth, and no life. Wisdom of Solomon 7 says:

> So in herself, wisdom is a spirit that is rational,
> Holy, only-begotten, manifold, subtle, easily moved, clear,
> Undefiled, manifest, invulnerable, loving what is good, keen,
> Unhindered, beneficent, man-loving, steadfast, unfailing,
> Free from worry, all-powerful, all-surveying,
> And penetrating all spirits that are rational, pure, and most subtle.
> For wisdom moves from one place to another
> More easily than motion itself,
> And because of her purity, she penetrates all things.
> So she is the exhalation of the power of God
> And the emanation of the pure glory of the Almighty;
> Therefore nothing defiled enters her.
> For she is the radiance of eternal light,
> A spotless mirror of the operative power of God
> And the image of His goodness. (vv. 22–26)

It even speaks about the Spirit that dwells within Wisdom being the Holy Spirit: "Who has known Your counsel, / Unless You have given him wisdom / And sent him Your Holy Spirit from on high?" (9:17).

All these things relating to Wisdom in the Old Testament are, in the New Testament, clearly applied to Jesus Christ. St. Paul writes:

> For I want you to know how greatly I strive for you, and for those at
> Laodicea, and for all who have not seen my face, that their hearts may
> be encouraged as they are knit together in love, to have all the riches of
> assured understanding and the knowledge of God's mystery, of Christ, in
> whom are hid all the treasures of wisdom and knowledge. (Col. 2:1–3)

The passage that has preeminence in the Church's understanding of Jesus as
God's Wisdom is in 1 Corinthians 1: "For Christ did not send me to baptize
but to preach the gospel, and not with eloquent wisdom, lest the cross of
Christ be emptied of its power" (v. 17). St. Paul says his teaching is not by
human wisdom, like that of a rhetorician.

In Galatians, he says this gospel is not his, but God's, and what he imparts
from God—including the wisdom and knowledge of God—is from God and
not from human beings (see Gal. 1:11 and following). The Cross, however, is
the revelation of God and of all God's qualities, including Wisdom. Here in
1 Corinthians, he continues:

> For the word of the cross is folly to those who are perishing, but to us
> who are being saved it is the power of God. For it is written,
>   "I will destroy the wisdom of the wise,
>   and the cleverness of the clever I will thwart."
> Where is the wise man? Where is the scribe? Where is the debater of
> this age? Has not God made foolish the wisdom of the world? For since,
> in the wisdom of God, the world did not know God through wisdom,
> it pleased God through the folly of what we preach to save those who
> believe. For Jews demand signs and Greeks seek wisdom, but we preach
> Christ crucified, a stumbling block to Jews and folly to Gentiles, but to
> those who are called, both Jews and Greeks, Christ the power of God
> and the wisdom of God. For the foolishness of God is wiser than men,
> and the weakness of God is stronger than men. (1:18–25)

In the same way God's power is revealed through weakness, His Wisdom
is revealed through the foolishness and the scandal of the Cross. In Christ
crucified, we see the Wisdom of God revealed.

Then, at the end of that same chapter, the Apostle says:

> But God chose what is foolish in the world to shame the wise, God
> chose what is weak in the world to shame the strong, God chose what

is low and despised in the world, even things that are not, to bring to nothing things that are, so that no human being might boast in the presence of God. He is the source of your life in Christ Jesus, whom God made our wisdom, our righteousness and sanctification and redemption. (1:27–30)

The Apostle's message of Christ crucified *is* the expression of that Wisdom. Thus he says:

When I came to you, brethren, I did not come proclaiming to you the testimony of God in lofty words or wisdom. For I decided to know nothing among you except Jesus Christ and him crucified. And I was with you in weakness and in much fear and trembling; and my speech and my message were not in plausible words of wisdom, but in demonstration of the Spirit and of power, that your faith might not rest in the wisdom of men but in the power of God.

Yet among the mature we do impart wisdom, although it is not a wisdom of this age or of the rulers of this age, who are doomed to pass away. But we impart a secret and hidden wisdom of God, which God decreed before the ages for our glorification. None of the rulers of this age understood this; for if they had, they would not have crucified the Lord of glory.

But, as it is written,
"What no eye has seen, nor ear heard,
nor the heart of man conceived,
what God has prepared for those who love him,"
God has revealed to us through the Spirit. (1 Cor. 2:1–10)

He says we have received not the spirit of this world, but the Spirit which is from God, which according to Scripture *is* the Spirit of Wisdom, the Spirit of Truth, the Spirit of Life, by which we understand the gifts bestowed on us by God. We impart this in words taught not by human wisdom but by the Spirit, interpreting spiritual truths to those who possess the Spirit. He ends that whole chapter by saying simply, "We have the mind of Christ" (v. 16).

The Eastern Orthodox Church has no doubt at all that the Wisdom of God is Jesus. A hymn from the Paschal service says, "O Christ the great and holy Pascha, *O Wisdom*, Word, and Power of God, allow us to partake of You more perfectly in the never-ending day of Your Kingdom."

On Holy Thursday, the day of the Lord's Mystical Supper in church, one whole ode of the canon speaks to Jesus as Wisdom. It says in the Book of Proverbs that Wisdom has built a home for herself, has set her table, and that Wisdom becomes food for the faithful, offering bread and wine (9:1–5). When we participate in the Holy Eucharist, we are eating and drinking the Wisdom and the Word of God. In Communion, Wisdom comes into us and acts in us. That Wisdom is Jesus Christ Himself.

In the liturgical services, every time we call out, "Wisdom! Let us attend!" we are calling people to focus on Christ, to focus on the Gospel, to focus on His Person, which, according to St. Paul, is the embodiment of the very Law of God in which Wisdom is found.

Proverbs 9:1 says, "Wisdom has built her house" or her temple. The Eastern Orthodox tradition has been bold enough to identify this with the Theotokos. Mary is often called "the temple of Wisdom" or "the throne of Wisdom."

The great cathedral in Constantinople was always called Holy Wisdom: *Hagia Sophia*. Sometimes we read in books that it was dedicated to "St. Sophia," but that is not what it means; *Sophia* here means Christ, God's Holy Wisdom.

Christ is Wisdom incarnate. In ancient Christianity, according to the Scripture and the tradition of the Church in interpreting that Scripture, the Wisdom that is given to us, that we can understand and know and experience, is Jesus Christ.

Jesus Christ, being God's Wisdom, God's Power, God's *Logos*, God's Truth, and God's Son, expresses, actualizes, and realizes for us the uncreated Wisdom of God Himself, in His human life on the planet Earth. We confess our Lord Jesus Christ as truly and genuinely the Wisdom of God the Father Himself.

CHAPTER 10

Jesus the

ICON OF GOD

The word *icon* (in Greek, *eikon*) simply means "image." *Eikon* is the exact word used in the Greek version of Genesis when it speaks about human beings being created "in the image and according to the likeness of God." Genesis 1 states:

> Then God said, "Let us make man [human, *anthropos*] in our image [*eikon*], after our likeness; and let them have dominion over the fish of the sea, and over the birds of the air, and over the cattle, and over all the earth, and over every creeping thing that creeps upon the earth." So God created man in his own image, in the image of God he created him; male and female he created them. (vv. 26–27)

It is a Christian teaching that all human beings are made in the image and likeness of God. How that is understood varies.

Of all the creatures that exist in all of creation, only the human is said to be made according to the icon and the likeness of God. Angels are not. Angels are like God; *El*, a Hebrew name for God, is in the names of angels— Michael ("noble like God"), Gabriel ("power of God"), Raphael ("healing of God"), Salathiel ("asked of God"). As their names reveal, the angels reflect God's reality, but so does every created thing—trees, plants, animals—they all reflect, in created form, something that is of God.

Of all God's creatures, human beings have the central place, because the human person, male or female, has all the elements of created order and reflects, in a created way, qualities that belong only to God.

Our bodies are made of matter. We grow like plants and are vivified like animals, but what makes us different from the plants and the animals is that we have self-consciousness. We have freedom, and we can choose to do good. We have the possibility of intelligence and wisdom. We can act. We can be prophetic, priestly, pastoral, and creative. We have the qualities of a *nous*, a mind, and a spirit, a *pnevma*.

As St. Gregory of Nyssa says, we were created to govern, to care as God cares. God gives all of creation to human beings, and they function as sons of God, caring for the things of God, including the angelic realm. St. Paul wrote that we will sit on thrones judging the angels (1 Cor. 6:3). We are certainly called to rule over the demons, to cast them out, and not to let them touch us. In the liturgical texts, Mary, Jesus' mother, is said to be "more honorable than the cherubim and beyond compare more glorious than the seraphim." In Hebrews, it says that God is not concerned with angels, but with human beings (see Heb. 2:16).

All the qualities that belong perfectly and essentially to God—power, beauty, care, kindness, forgiveness, love, wisdom—are shared with us. We are to be, by grace and by God's good will, everything God is by nature. A human being is a creature with a commandment to be divine.

We have a structure that allows us to actualize this. The thinking quality, the speaking quality, the governing quality, the acting quality, the creative quality: all these qualities that other beings do not have allow us to *act* like gods. Jesus says, "He called them gods to whom the word of God came" (John 10:34–35), quoting the Psalm, "I say, 'You are gods'" (82[81]:6).

Part of that structure is that we are persons who can live in communion. Many in the Church have taught that humanity is a multitude of hypostases, or persons, having the same human nature and the ability to relate to one another through the qualities that make us human.

We see the Godhead as three hypostases, having one and the same nature, having the same qualities and energies of activity, and forming an absolute, perfect communion of one life, one mind, one heart, one action, and one will.

Each of the billions of human beings is a unique hypostasis, a unique person, a unique "I am," who has the same human nature as all the other human beings. When humanity is operating properly, when there is no sin or corruption, then human beings really are of one mind, one heart, one will, and one body.

We claim this about the Church, even though we complain that the Church is often not this way. In the Liturgy we pray, "And grant us, O Lord, that with one mind and one heart we may partake of the one bread and the one cup of Christ, and form one body." St. Ignatius of Antioch defined the Church as an *henosis agapes kai pistes*—a union of love and faith.

Each individual person, according to some writers, images the Trinity. If the one God is Father—I Am—and Logos, and Spirit, we can say that a human being is a person—an "I am"—and has a *logos* and a spirit of being. God's Logos and His Spirit are so perfect that they are distinct hypostatic instances of divinity. As a creature, my *logos* and my spirit cannot be perfect, but in the order of creation, I can express myself. I can be logical—*logikos*—and I can breathe and live and be energetic—being filled with the spirit. This is the human being's structure.

This all is expressed in different ways, by different ancient and modern thinkers. In my own opinion, the reason we have bodies is due to the multiplicity of the divine energies and operations and splendors that exist with God. I think that is why we, and not the angels, are said to be in the image and likeness of God, because we can express our holiness, our goodness, our truth, mirroring God, even in a bodily manner, which an angel by nature cannot do.

Matter is energetic. Not one cell in my body existed in me seven years ago. My body is actually a cluster of incredibly dynamic, microscopic movements. It is a kind of energetic field and an expression of being human—and, of course, the divine energies of God are also there.

St. Augustine thought being made in the image and likeness of God was expressed in a human being as memory, understanding, and will. For him, *memoria* is a consciousness of oneself, an ability to retain one's thoughts.

For some Fathers, *image* and *likeness* were simply two ways of saying the same thing, just a way of affirmation by repetition found often in the Bible. That would be my own preference. However, some Fathers liked to make a distinction between *image* and *likeness*. They would say that image, *imago*, is our structure as human beings, which can never be totally destroyed. On the basis of the image, we have existence—the existential actualization of that image—which is called *likeness*.

The image is given, and then, on that image, we either grow in divine likeness—from one degree of glory to another, becoming more and more like Christ—or we corrupt that image and mar it. We can use that same structure to destroy ourselves, to grow more and more unlike God. The likeness can be destroyed, and the image can become more and more obscured. When we are functioning properly, our growth in divine likeness is unending because God is infinite.

The Apostle Paul said, "But we all, with unveiled face, beholding as in a mirror the glory of the Lord, are being transformed into the same image from glory to glory, just as by the Spirit of the Lord" (2 Cor. 3:18, NKJV). Our person—unveiled and beholding the glory of the Lord as in a mirror—is changed into the same image, from glory to glory.

The writing attributed to St. Dionysius the Areopagite says that human beings do three things when they actualize themselves as being made in the image and likeness of God. First, they imitate God; the word in Greek is *mimesis*. Then they attain a resemblance, a *homoiosis*. Finally, they achieve a participation or a communion with God. We can do these things because we are made in the image and likeness of God.

The teaching of the Apostle Paul is that the image and likeness according to which we are made is Christ Himself. "And even if our gospel is veiled, it is veiled only to those who are perishing. In their case the god of this world has blinded the minds of the unbelievers, to keep them from seeing the light of the gospel of the glory of Christ, who is the likeness [*eikon*] of God" (2 Cor. 4:3–4).

The New Testament is very clear that the image and the likeness of God, according to which we are created, is Jesus Christ Himself. When Genesis says that humanity, male and female, is made in the image and likeness of God, it means we are created in the image and likeness of God, *who is Christ*.

We do not just say "in the image and likeness of Christ" because that is not what Scripture says. It says we are created in the image of God, who is Christ. We are created to have the same relationship, the same understanding, the same communion, the same imitation of God that Christ has. He has it by nature, as the eternal, divine Son of God who has become man as Mary's child, and He gives that possibility to us—to have it by grace and by faith. We are not made in the image of Christ; we are created to be godlike in the same way that Christ is godlike.

We must also mention a passage from Colossians:

> . . . giving thanks to the Father, who has qualified us to share in the inheritance of the saints in light. He has delivered us from the domin- ion of darkness and transferred us to the kingdom of his beloved Son, in whom we have redemption, the forgiveness of sins. He is the image [*eikon*] of the invisible God, the firstborn of all creation. (Col. 1:12–15)

The incarnate Christ, who images God from all eternity within the Trinity as the divine Son—now the God-man on earth—is for us the image of the invisible God.

St. John does not use the term *eikon*, but it does say in the prologue of his Gospel that no one has *seen* God at any time, but the only begotten Son who dwells in the bosom of the Father. It also says, "and we *beheld* His glory, the glory as of the only begotten of the Father, full of grace and truth" (John 1:14, NKJV). The verb *to see* requires an object—something for us to see, an image.

The Holy Fathers often use the terms *archetype* and *image*, saying that God the Father is the archetype and Christ is the icon.

Fr. Dumitru Staniloae said that Jesus Christ is the *Logos* because God is the truth, and Christ is the *eikon*, icon, or image, because God is beauty. How beautiful God is! The truth of God, the goodness of God, the power of God, and the presence of God are shown to us in Christ.

In John 12, Jesus does many signs, yet the people do not believe in Him, and Jesus makes reference to the prophecy of Isaiah (John 12:38): "Lord, who has believed our report, and to whom has the arm of the Lord been revealed?" Then He quotes Isaiah again, saying, "He has blinded their eyes and hardened their heart, / lest they should see with their eyes and perceive with their heart, / and turn for me to heal them" (12:40).

In the Bible, the heart is the organ of sight. In the Sermon on the Mount, Jesus says, "Blessed are the pure in heart, for they shall see God" (Matt. 5:8).

In the Liturgy, the prayer the priest reads before the Gospel reading says, "Illumine our hearts, O Master, with the light of Your divine knowledge. Open our minds to the comprehension of Your Gospel. Let us *see*, hear, know, and understand."

John 12 continues:

> Isaiah said this because he saw his glory and spoke of him.
> Nevertheless many even of the authorities believed in him, but for fear of the Pharisees they did not confess it, lest they should be put out of the synagogue: for they loved the praise of men more than the praise of God.
> And Jesus cried out and said, "He who believes in me, believes not in me but in him who sent me. And he who sees me sees him who sent me. I have come as light into the world, that whoever believes in me may not remain in darkness." (vv. 41–46)

Thus, it is only when Christ the Light comes that people are able to see.

In John 14 this teaching is repeated. Jesus is speaking openly to His disciples about who He is, how He relates to the Father and the Holy Spirit, how He relates to believers, how He relates to the world, and while He is speaking of these things, in John 14:8, Philip says to Him, "Lord, show us the Father, and we shall be satisfied." Then Jesus says to Philip:

> Have I been with you so long, and yet you do not know me, Philip? He who has seen me has seen the Father; how can you say, 'Show us the Father'? Do you not believe that I am in the Father and the Father in me? The words that I say to you I do not speak on my own authority; but the Father who dwells in me does his works. Believe me that I am in the Father and the Father in me; or else believe me for the sake of the works themselves. (John 14:9–11)

Jesus is the image, the icon. When we look at Him, we see God. Also, of course, when we hear Him, we hear God. When we touch Him, we touch God. When we eat Him—His Body and Blood—we eat the body and blood of God. "*Pleroma theotes somatikos,*" St. Paul said: "the whole fullness of deity . . . bodily" (Col. 2:9). That which is bodily—embodied—can be seen.

This teaching is also in Hebrews:

God, who at various times and in various ways spoke in time past to the
fathers by the prophets, has in these last days spoken to us by *His* Son,
whom He has appointed heir of all things, through whom also He made
the worlds; who being the brightness of *His* glory and the express image
of His person . . . (1:1–3, NKJV)

In the Son, we truly behold the face of the Father. For this reason, some of
the symbolical icons of ancient Christianity, when they depict the Ancient
of Days, show the face looking exactly as the face of Jesus looks in icons,
because Jesus is the face of God.

He is the Icon of God—this is a title for Him, and this is the interpretation
of Scripture that secures the defense of the holy icons in church. We venerate
the icons of Christ and of the saints, who are made in the image and likeness
of God and who have expressed that image by faith in Jesus and through
His grace. We venerate icons because Jesus is the Icon of God, and that is
the only place we can see God; but even in those saints and holy people
who became Christlike by the Holy Spirit, we can see the face of God. Each
one of us is supposed to be a word and an icon of God. Each one of us is
supposed to show forth the divine beauty of the beautiful archetype, who is
God Himself.

And we see God Himself in the face of Jesus Christ. Jesus Christ *is* the
Icon of the invisible God (see Col. 1:15). The light of the glory of God that
shone from God on the mountain to Moses in the Old Testament, St. Paul
says, now shines upon us from the Person of the Lord, who is the image, the
likeness, and the Icon of God Himself.

CHAPTER 11

Jesus the

POWER OF GOD

In the Greek language, there are several different words for *power*, and there are different nuances or connotations of the word *power* in English. If we read the New Testament in English, often we'll see the word *power*, but we cannot always catch the nuance except by discerning the context where the word is used.

The word in its usual sense denotes a kind of force. That word in Greek would be *dynamis*. In Greek, *dynamis* comes from the same root as the word meaning "possible," *dynatos*. When Scripture says that all things are possible to God, the word used is *dynatos*, and He is the *o dynatos*, the powerful or the possible one.

Another Greek term that is often translated "power" is *exousia*. That term means "power" in the sense of authority. For example, in Matthew 28:18, when the risen Christ says, "All authority in heaven and on earth has been given to me," the word there is *exousia*. It is the kind of power a king would have over his subjects or a ruler over his slaves.

When Scripture says that Jesus has power over the living and the dead, the word is *exousia*, authority. Often, Jesus is said to be speaking "as one with authority," as in Matthew 7:29: "for he taught them as one who had authority, and not as their scribes."

A couple of other words can be translated "power." *Kratos* can mean "strength" or "power"; that is the root of words like *Pantocrator*, the Almighty One. *Kratos* probably would be best translated as "might."

There's also the word *ischyros*, which means "strong." In the Trisagion, we sing *agios ischyros,* "holy and strong," or "holy strong one"—usually rendered in English as "holy mighty." The adjective *ischys* means "strong" or "mighty," and the verb *ischyo* means "to be able" or "to have the strength to do something."

So we have four root words for power: *dynamis, exousia, kratos,* and *ischyros* or *ischys.* Here, however, we want to focus on the term *dynamis,* power in the sense of force. This is where we get our English word *dynamite,* which has great power. *Dynamis* is used as a title for Christ in 1 Corinthians 1:18–24:

> For the word of the cross is folly to those who are perishing, but to us who are being saved it is the power of God. . . . Has not God made foolish the wisdom of the world? For since, in the wisdom of God, the world did not know God through wisdom, it pleased God through the folly of what we preach to save those who believe. For Jews demand signs and Greeks seek wisdom, but we preach Christ crucified, a stumbling block to Jews and folly to Gentiles, but to those who are called, both Jews and Greeks, Christ the power of God and the wisdom of God.

The last phrase in Greek is, *Christon theou dynamin kai theou sofian*— literally, "Christ, God's power and God's wisdom." In that sentence, there is no definite article. It doesn't say "the" power of God or "the" wisdom of God.

Throughout Scripture and in the Church's prayer and liturgy, it is said that Christ is the hypostatic wisdom of God and even the hypostatic power of God. The power of God, or God's own power, is expressed perfectly in His Son. The powerful God expresses His power in His Son, who is His Logos, His Word, His image, His exact expression—who is everything that He is, not being Him.

Here we have a kind of theological principle that has been elaborated by the Church Fathers, such as Gregory the Theologian in his *Theological Orations,* along with many others. Everything that God is, is expressed in personified or hypostatic form in His Son, who is the Second Person of the Trinity, who becomes a man, the Man, Jesus of Nazareth. Jesus of Nazareth is both God and a real human being, really *anthropos,* the Man, having God's qualities and characteristics—God's *idiomata,* in other words

His properties, shown in personal form in the person of Jesus of Nazareth Himself.

St. Athanasius the Great, in his most famous treatise, *On the Incarnation of the Word of God,* stresses the fact that the Son and Word of God, His Wisdom, literally becomes flesh and becomes the man Jesus. The one God is the Father of Jesus, and who and what and how that one God is, is revealed on earth in the person of Christ. He is the Son of God in human form.

Athanasius would say that one God, the Father of Jesus, is the one, the only God there is. The oneness, the unity of God is shown forth in the one Son. There can only be one Son of God because there is only one God. Christ shows the unity of God. That means that if the one true living God is powerful, if He is omnipotent, the God to whom all things are possible in heaven and on earth, then the power of that all-powerful God for Christians is Jesus Christ.

Many times in the New Testament we see that Christ has that *dynamis,* that dynamite, so to speak. This is not power in the sense of having authority over creation or over life and death, not in the sense of mere strength, but in the sense of being powerful, *dynamis.* He not only has authority over demons, for example, but he has power to cast them out. He not only has authority over the winds and the waves, but he has the power to quiet them down. He not only has *authority* to forgive sins, but he has the *power* to forgive them.

This power of Jesus is spoken of in many places in the New Testament. One example that must come to mind is in Luke 8:40–48, the story of the woman who touches Him in the crowd when He is on His way to raise Jairus's daughter from the dead. This woman has had a hemorrhage, a flow of blood, for twelve years, suffered many things under many physicians and spent all she had, and has only grown worse.

She broke the taboo laws of her time by going out on the street when she was unclean because of the blood. She got into the crowd and heard about Jesus, and she thought, "Well, this is my chance." She went against all convention and just touched the hem of his garment, thinking, "If I just touch even His garments, I shall be made whole. I shall be healed." Literally, it says, "I shall be saved." The Gospel says she did that, and immediately the hemorrhage ceased. She felt in her body that she had been healed of her disease. She felt a kind of power come into her.

Jesus, perceiving in Himself that power, *dynamis*, had gone forth from Him, immediately turned around in the crowd and said, "Who touched My garments?" The disciples said to Him, "You see the crowd pressing around You, and yet You say, 'Who touched Me?'" He looked around to see who had done it. But the woman, knowing what had been done to her, came in fear and trembling, fell down before Him, and told Him the whole truth. He said to her, "Daughter, your faith has made you well. Your faith has saved you. Go in peace and be healed, be saved, of your disease."

The expression there is very important for our topic right now. He perceived that power had gone out of Him. In other words, that power is in Him. This is a very interesting case, because He doesn't lay on hands; He doesn't spit; He doesn't anoint. He doesn't say anything. The woman is totally anonymous, and she herself doesn't do anything but touch—not even Him, but His garment. Then He says, "I know that power went out from Me." He is a kind of incarnate, walking power.

Our understanding is that Jesus regulates that power. He knows when to show it, when not to show it, how to reveal it, when not to reveal it. Another example would be the Transfiguration, when Peter, James, and John are taken up on the mountaintop, and they see Him transfigured. They see all the energy, the splendor, the glory, and the light of God shining from Him. We can say that was always in Him, but He wasn't showing it. He was hiding it.

Jesus not only *has* power, but *is* power. The power He has is the power He is. The power He shows forth is the power that actually belongs to Him. It is His own.

In St. John's Gospel, He makes that point several times. When Pilate says, "I have the power to crucify You. I have the power to let You go," Jesus says, "You would have no power at all if it weren't given to you from above" (see John 19:10–11). He Himself also says specifically, "I have the power to lay down My life. I have the power to take it up again" (see John 10:18). He doesn't usually exercise that power in the way we think He could—simply by raising up a dead person like Lazarus, for example—but He has it. When He doesn't exercise it, it is because He chooses not to.

In the Gospel of John, Jesus says He does not even have to pray to God for that power. It is always His. He and the Father are one. The Father has given everything He is to Jesus. He really is what the Father is in His Sonship, and even in and through His humanity, because the Word became flesh, and the Son of God became the son of the Virgin and lived on earth.

When they want to take up swords when He is in the garden, He says, "Put those swords away. Don't you know I could call twelve legions of angels and wipe you all out if I wanted to?" (see Matt. 26:52–53). In fact, He didn't need to call twelve legions of angels; He could have just wiped them out Himself. As it says in 2 Thessalonians 2:8 and Revelation 19:15, He could have slain them by the breath of His mouth. Even His word is a powerful reality, a two-edged sword that cuts to the bones and marrow (see Heb. 4:12). Everything that Jesus is, is a power.

This reality of power is extended to all His other qualities. His wisdom is a power. His truth is a power. His light is a power. His glory is a power. Everything is filled with power, that very power that He Himself is, because Christ is God's power.

When we meditate on Christ as the power of God, we encounter this great paradox: The power of God is not a power of brute force. It's the power of love, truth, beauty, glory, wisdom, and peace. The paradox is that as St. Paul says, God's strength, God's power, is made perfect in weakness. In 2 Corinthians 12:7–10, he says that when he was praying for power over the thorn in his flesh, he asked God three times to take it away. God said, "My grace is sufficient for you, for my power is made perfect in weakness." Then the Apostle Paul says, "When I am weak, then I am strong."

We could apply this to Jesus Christ our Lord Himself. God shows through Jesus the power of His love, His truth, His wisdom, His glory. Jesus shows that power by becoming meek, lowly, and powerless, by identifying with those who are in the power of evil, in order to deliver them from that power.

In the crucified Christ, who is God's power, it is God's power that is being shown. When Christ is crucified and dies for us, that is God expressing His divine power. That is God using power as power ought to be used, to create life and not death.

As Mary says in the Magnificat, the ultimate power of God is when He looks at the abject poverty and powerlessness of His handmaiden, and becomes incarnate in her womb as a baby and becomes human. Jesus says, "Learn from me. I am *praÿs* —meek—and *tapeinos tei kardia* —powerless in heart, empty of power" (see Matt. 11:29). Jesus, though He has everything, became totally nothing; being rich, He became poor; being the wise one, He became a fool as far as this world is concerned. He emptied Himself, poured Himself out, divested Himself of His power.

Here, again, is the paradox: that this very divesting of power *is* the powerful act of God. That is why we can say that Jesus destroyed death by the power of God. The humiliation of Jesus in His self-emptying as the Suffering Servant of God is the expression of God's power. It is the way God's power acts. This is *o dynatos,* the Mighty One, showing His might by destroying death through the act of total humiliation, condescension, and love.

His is the power of love. He loves us to the end, and He takes on all our weakness and powerlessness. He gives up all His power.

Ultimately, He wants to reveal God's ultimate power, and that is the power of love that is stronger than death. He destroys death by dying and taking that death upon Himself. This is why not only do we say Christ is God's power; we say *Christos estavromenos,* Christ crucified, is the power of God and the wisdom of God. And the wisdom and the power of God go together.

CHAPTER 12

Jesus the

SON OF MAN

In the Gospels, Jesus always refers to Himself as the Son of Man. No one else in the four Gospels ever calls Him by that title (except once in John 12:34, where someone quotes it back to Him after He has said it of Himself). They call Him "Rabbi," "Lord," or "Master"; some even say, "You are the Son of God." But only He Himself calls Him "Son of Man."

Martin Hengel, a German scholar whom I regard as the best critical scholar of the Holy Scripture ever, writes in a book of essays on the New Testament and Christology that the title "Son of Man" is used 81 times in the four Gospels—14 times in Mark, 25 in Luke, 30 in Matthew, and 12 in John. It is not used by anyone else but Jesus, and He only uses it for Himself.

Since "Son of Man" is an Old Testament Hebrew expression, Martin Hengel says that to Greek speakers it was probably completely meaningless. It doesn't have an obvious meaning as do the titles "King," "Judge," "Lord," or "God." Martin Hengel called it a "veiled code word," a kind of Hebrew insider word for Jews. (That may explain why it is found most often in Matthew, because Matthew is considered to be the Gospel originally written for the Jewish Christians.) The term in Greek is *ho huios tou anthropou*, the Son of the Man, or *ho huios anthropou*, or simply *huios anthropou*. *Anthropos* means "human being," and *huios* means "son," a male child.

The fact that this term is used exclusively by Jesus leads Professor Hengel to conclude that this must have been a title Jesus gave to Himself. His followers of their own accord might give Him the title "Christ," or "Lord," or "God." But why would anyone give him the title "the Son of Man"? Certainly, for someone from the Greek-speaking world, it wouldn't make much sense. Another point is that when the New Testament refers to the Old Testament places where the expression "Son of Man" is used, such as Psalm 79(80) and Daniel 7, the New Testament author wants to show that in fact the term has to be applied to Jesus, and this is probably why Jesus was using the term Himself.

Later in the New Testament, though, when the apostles preach about Jesus, they never preach about Him as the Son of Man. He is preached as the Son of God, as Lord, as Christ, as Savior, but not as Son of Man. In the Orthodox Liturgy there are also almost no prayers addressed to Jesus as Son of Man.

To me it seems pretty clear what the reason for this is. Jesus speaks about Himself as the Son of Man, but what He wants from those who hear Him is to confess Him as the Son of God; as the Lord, *kyrios*; as the Christ. He asks the disciples, "Who do you say that I am?" Peter does not say, "You are the Son of Man"; he says, "You are the Christ, the Son of the Living God." And Jesus says, "Right. Flesh and blood has not revealed this to you, but my Father, who is in heaven" (see Matt. 16:15–17).

The expression "Son of Man" is found in the Old Testament. It can be used simply to mean a man, a human being. But it seems that already in the Old Testament the expression "like a Son of Man," or "the Son of Man," has the connotation that this is *the* man: when *that* man comes, the one who has that title, then you know he is the man we are looking for. So when Jesus is referring to Himself as Son of Man, He is saying, "I am the Man you are all looking for; I am the One; I am the human being, there is no other."

One particular text in the Prophets is likely the main reason that title is so significant. This text is in Daniel 7:13:

> I saw in the night visions,
> and behold, with the clouds of heaven
> there came one like a son of man,
> and he came to the Ancient of Days
> and was presented before him.

"Ancient of Days" is a title for God. In Isaiah 6 He is the One who sits upon the throne, to whom the angels are singing "Holy, holy, holy." Earlier, Daniel

7:9 describes how He looks and how He is vested, sitting on this judgment seat. That same figure appears in the Apocalypse. The One who sits upon the throne in the Apocalypse is certainly the One who sits on the throne in Isaiah, and the One who's sitting on this throne as the Ancient of Days in Daniel.

Verse 14 continues:

> And to him was given dominion and glory and kingdom,
> that all peoples, nations, and languages should serve him;
> his dominion is an everlasting dominion,
> which shall not pass away,
> and his kingdom one
> that shall not be destroyed.

In Greek it says, "To Him belongs *he arhē*." *Arhē* means the beginning of everything. Revelation will say the Son of Man is the *arhē kai telos*, the Alpha and the Omega, the Beginning and the End, which God Himself is. Also there is given to Him *ke timē*, honor, *he vasilia,* the kingdom, and *pantes he laoi,* all the peoples, all the nations; and all these peoples and nations and languages and tribes are going to serve Him. His dominion will be an everlasting dominion which will not pass away, and His kingdom shall never be destroyed.

This is why Jesus uses the expression "Son of Man" for Himself—because He is that Son of Man, and He wants people to recognize Him as such. He wants people to recognize Him as the One who was presented to God Himself—who is His Father, the Ancient of Days, the One from everlasting. He wants them to understand that He, together with the Father, receives all the glories and honors that belong to the Father.

In the Book of Revelation, those honors that are given to Him, together with God the Father, are multiplied even more than in the Book of Daniel. When He is sitting on the throne and everyone falls down before Him, what they offer to Him is glory, honor, power, blessing, thanksgiving, and worship. All of these things are offered to Him who sits upon the throne together with God, who in the language of the Book of Revelation is called the Lamb. He is identified in Revelation 1:13–14 as the Son of Man, by reference to Daniel:

"and in the midst of the lampstands one like a son of man, clothed with a long robe and with a golden girdle round his breast; his head and his hair were white as white wool, white as snow; his eyes were like a flame of fire." The description sounds like the Ancient of Days, but the one described is called the Son of Man. He is the first and the last, the One who was dead and is alive again; He is the "Amen" of God.

Thus, Jesus in the New Testament is identified with the Son of Man in Daniel. That is why Jesus Himself uses that expression. He is that Man that is talked about. He is the One who appears.

I would like to amplify this point by using two other Old Testament texts that are very familiar to Orthodox Christians. One of them is from Daniel 3—the story of Shadrach, Meshach, and Abednego, whose Hebrew names are Hananiah, Azariah, and Mishael—the three youths in the Babylonian furnace. These three young boys absolutely refused to worship the golden idol Nebuchadnezzar built, so they were thrown into the fire. But they danced in the flames and were not burned, and they praised and blessed God from the midst of the flames.

> Then King Nebuchadnezzar was astonished and rose up in haste. He said to his counselors, "Did we not cast three men bound into the fire?"
> They answered the king, "True, O king."
> He answered, "But I see four men loose, walking in the midst of the fire, and they are not hurt; and the appearance of the fourth is like a son of the gods." (3:24–25)

In the Christian tradition, that fourth person is Christ. He is the One whom God sends. And of course that prefigures the descent of Jesus, the Christ, into Hades, into the fiery furnace, to raise up all those who are dead. Even though it says the fourth looks similar to a Son of God, it says there are four *andres* in the fire—four men. So He clearly appears as a man. That is important for us, because Daniel is a very important prophecy for the Christian faith.

The second example should be familiar to Orthodox Christians from the Liturgy. When the Trisagion Hymn is sung during a hierarchical Divine Liturgy, it is sung in this way: "Holy God, Holy Mighty, Holy Immortal, have mercy on us," three times. Then the deacon or priest shouts, "Power!

(*Dynamis!*)" Then this part is sung even louder. In the middle of this, the bishop comes out with his candlestick and cross, faces the people, and says a line from Psalm 80(79):14–15: "Turn again, O God of hosts! Look down from heaven, and see; / have regard for this vine, the stock which thy right hand planted." He says only that line, but this is how the Psalm continues:

> They have burned it with fire, they have cut it down;
> may they perish at the rebuke of thy countenance!
> But let thy hand be upon the man of thy right hand,
> the son of man whom thou hast made strong for thyself!
> Then we will never turn back from thee;
> give us life, and we will call on thy name!
> Restore us, O Lord God of hosts!
> let thy face shine, that we may be saved! (vv. 16–19)

The vine is saved by the Son of Man, whom the Lord has made powerful for Himself and has put on His right hand. This is very important.

In the Gospel of Mark, when Jesus is undergoing His Passion and being interrogated in front of the high priest, the high priest says to Him, "Are you the Christ, the Son of the Blessed?" Jesus says, "I Am." That is a powerful expression, because "I Am" is the divine name that was given to Moses. Then He says, "You will see the Son of man seated at the right hand of Power, and coming with the clouds of heaven" (Mark 14:61–62).

No Jew who knew the Scriptures could hear that sentence without thinking of Daniel and the Son of Man coming on the clouds in power, in God's power, in the power of the Ancient of Days. This also has to evoke Psalm 110(109):1: "The LORD says to my Lord, 'Sit at My right hand.'" To be at the right hand is to be in power. The Son of Man is the one who is seated at the right hand of Power, coming on the clouds of heaven.

For the Jews, the Son of Man was the Son of God, and therefore the Anointed, the Christ, the Chosen, the Righteous, the Holy One, the Lord—and, therefore, God Himself in human flesh. So His interrogators said, "Are You the Son of God, then?" And He said to them, "You say that I am." And they said, "What further testimony do we need? We have heard it ourselves, from His very own lips."

Jesus calls Himself the Son of Man, and the scribes and the elders and the high priest, knowing the Scripture, know exactly what He means. The Gentiles later on had to learn what it meant. But a Jew knew that the expression "the Son of Man" is tantamount to "the Messiah"; it is tantamount to being God's Son; it's tantamount to being the One who sits on the throne and who receives all honor, glory, dominion, majesty, blessing, power, and thanksgiving.

"Son of Man" is what Jesus calls Himself, and it is the only thing He calls Himself. But once He is confessed, once that Son of Man comes, then He is to be given all glory, honor, and worship, as the Christ, the Lord, the Savior, the Man at the Father's right hand, the One who sits enthroned with Him, God's very own Son and God Himself, in human flesh. All of this is contained in the expression, "the Son of Man."

Jesus keeps calling Himself this in order that we would confess Him for who He truly is: our Lord, our Savior, our Christ, God's Son, God's Logos, God's Wisdom, God's Power, God's Icon, and indeed, God from God, God Himself in human flesh. This is Jesus of Nazareth, who called Himself always, and without exception, Son of Man.

CHAPTER 13

Jesus the

MAN

In the Holy Scriptures, Jesus appears as a man. He preaches in the temple as a boy, and then, as a grown man, He asks to be baptized. There can be no doubt that He is an *anthropos*, a human being. Those in His hometown synagogue ask, "Is not this the carpenter, the son of Mary and brother of James and Joses and Judas and Simon?" (Mark 6:3).

Right from the beginning, there were questions about His humanity: "What sort of man is this, that even winds and sea obey him?" (Matt. 8:27). He is doing things no mere man can do and saying things no mere man can say. Nevertheless, He is certainly a man.

There are texts in which He is simply called "the Man" or "a man." Probably the most memorable is John 19, where Pontius Pilate has Jesus brought out and presented to the people on the judgment seat. After Jesus is scourged and mocked, Pilate goes out again and says to the people:

> "See, I am bringing him out to you, that you may know that I find no crime in him."
> So Jesus came out, wearing the crown of thorns and the purple robe. Pilate said to them, "Behold the man!" (John 19:4–5)

There are several paintings of Jesus standing bound, dressed in a purple garment with the crown of thorns on His head, called *Ecce Homo*—"Behold the Man."

Also in John 9, when the man born blind is healed and the leaders of the people are questioning him, they say, "How were your eyes opened? Who did this?" The blind man answers, "The man called Jesus" (see vv. 10–11).

In John 7:46, the leaders of the Jews send officers to arrest Jesus, but they return empty-handed, saying, "No man ever spoke like this Man!"

In Acts 17:31, St. Paul says to the men of Athens, "He has fixed a day on which he will judge the world in righteousness by a man whom he has appointed." Here the term used is not *anthropos*, "human being," but *anēr*, which means "a male."

First Timothy 2:5–6 says, "For there is one God, and there is one mediator between God and men, the man Christ Jesus, who gave himself as a ransom for all." We believe that all human beings who by faith and grace are one in Christ can also be mediators for one another before God, but there is *the one* Mediator between God and human beings, *the Man,* Christ Jesus.

As we already mentioned, people were puzzled about Jesus: What manner of human being is He? No one ever spoke like this Man, did what He did, or claimed what He claimed.

In the Gospels, when people bow down to worship Jesus, *never once* does He say, "Stand up; I'm just a man *like you.*" We never find that in the text because, although he is a real human being, He is *not* a human being just like the rest of us.

Jesus is an authentic, real, perfect human being, but He is not *merely* a human being. He is the human being that the Son of God has become.

This is put powerfully in John 1:1, 14: "In the beginning was the Word, and the Word was with God, and the Word was God. . . . And the Word became flesh and dwelt among us, full of grace and truth; we have beheld his glory, glory as of the only Son from the Father."

That is clearly said also in Philippians 2:5–8:

> Have this mind among yourselves, which is yours in Christ Jesus, who, though he was in the form of God, did not count equality with God a thing to be grasped, but emptied himself, taking the form of a servant, being born in the likeness of men. And being found in human form he humbled himself and became obedient unto death, even death on a cross.

Hebrews 2:9 says Jesus "was made lower than the angels, crowned with glory and honor because of the suffering of death, so that by the grace of God he might taste death for every one." It says that He is not ashamed to call human beings His brethren, meaning that He became human exactly as we are.

In Greek it says that since the children—meaning human beings, children of God—share in flesh and blood, "He Himself partook of the same." We are flesh and blood, and He shared of the same that, through death, He might destroy death and the devil (Heb. 2:11–15).

He became like us in every respect *except sin.* In the Orthodox Christian understanding of humanity, to be a human being is not to be a sinner. Sometimes people say, "If you're a real human being, you have to be a sinner, because all human beings are sinners." This is not true. When we sin, we ruin our humanity. Perfect humanity is not sinful, so we cannot say that if Jesus did not sin, then He is not really human.

Many questions can be raised about these texts. C. S. Lewis said that if the man Jesus said and did what He said and did as recorded on the pages of Scripture, then He must be either the Lord, or a liar, or a lunatic. Another way this has been put is, "He is either mad, bad, or God." The atheist Richard Dawkins would say, "Well, maybe He was just genuinely mistaken." If that is the case, however, then He really was a lunatic.

Another objection that is raised is, "Maybe He never even said those things. Maybe all of this was just made up. Maybe the authors who wrote the Gospels put all these words in His mouth and made up all these events." Some people say Jesus never even existed.

We would certainly say that Matthew, Mark, Luke, and John *are* the literary works of their respective authors, that they are stylized, that certain things may be conflated. I would say, personally, that it is not particularly impious or incorrect to say that passages like the Sermon on the Mount in Matthew or the catechetical oration in John 13—17 are compilations of Jesus' sayings. It is not absolutely necessary to believe all those things were said on that occasion, and we know they were not said in that form because the different Gospels report them differently, based on memories transmitted orally.

Yet it is certainly the case for Orthodox Christianity that Jesus the Man really existed, and He really said and did things that led people to question who He was and what He did. It is certainly the case that some people, *even*

His own brethren in Mark's Gospel, thought He was "beside Himself," that He had lost His mind (3:21). Also, we know that, according to the Scripture, He was actually killed for making Himself out to be God, being a man (see John 19:7).

It is a Christian conviction that everything applied to God in the Scripture is applied to *the Man,* the male human being, Jesus. That is why Jesus is claimed to be "perfect God and perfect man."

This is the first part of the Nicene-Constantinopolitan Creed: "And I believe in one Lord, Jesus Christ, the only-begotten Son of God, begotten of the Father before all ages, Light from Light, true God from true God, begotten, not created, *homoousios tō Patri*"—of one very same nature, being, substance, essence, divinity, and reality with the Father—"who for us human beings and for our salvation came down from heaven, was incarnate of the Holy Spirit and the Virgin Mary, and became a human being."

The doctrinal statement has been clearly formulated that the Man Jesus Christ is not only divine, with the same divinity as God the Father, but He is *human* the way we are human. There is a double consubstantiality. He is consubstantial with the Father, and He is consubstantial with all human beings. He is perfect God and perfect Man.

What does *perfect* mean? It means, first of all, metaphysically or ontologically perfect. Everything and whatever God is, Jesus is; and everything and whatever humans are, Jesus is.

The heretic Apollinarius said that Jesus did not have a human soul, that He was just an enfleshed *Logos,* God acting through a body. St. Gregory the Theologian, in his famous letter to Cledonius the Presbyter (Epistle 101), wrote, "What is not assumed is not healed. What the Logos has not taken up is not saved." If there were any element of humanity that Jesus did not actually have and experience, that element of humanity would not be united to the Godhead and would not be saved. Thus, Jesus assumed everything. He became everything we are so that we can become everything He is. That is what Gregory the Theologian meant by *perfect man*: whole, complete, lacking nothing.

Saying Jesus is a human being also means He is a particular human being in a particular time and place, with a particular culture, a particular language, particular physical features, and so on. If one is a real human being, one is limited. One learns things as a human being, with a human brain. As a man, Jesus was not omniscient. He was not omnipresent. Yet, as a man, in history, through His Jewish, first-century humanity, He could pronounce forgiveness of sins. He could raise the dead. He could heal the blind. He could do wonderful, divine actions like calming the wind and walking on water, but He did all this *as a Man,* in His humanity.

Thus, Jesus could not, for example, speak English. Now, one could say, "Well, God could have infused in Him the knowledge of English." Perhaps God could have; perhaps He could have infused it in anybody if He wanted to (although English did not even exist in Christ's time). It does not seem very likely, but in any case, if Jesus was really human, then He was also ignorant of many things. He did not know the theory of relativity. He never read Charles Darwin. He did not know the *Baghavad Gita.* Maybe He even thought the earth was flat; who knows? He was a first-century, real human being.

Some might claim, "Well, if you take Gregory the Theologian's teaching 'What is not assumed is not healed,' women are not saved, because Jesus was male," or "Eating spaghetti was not saved because Jesus never ate spaghetti." That is simply ridiculous. To become a human being, it is necessary to become a particular human being. Jesus was a Jew, not a Gentile. He was first-century, not twentieth-century. He was a male human being, not a female human being. Yet He was a *real* human being, so all human beings, whether they are male or female, are saved by Him, because the humanity of a man and a woman is exactly the same humanity. We all share in the same humanity, which is the humanity that Jesus had, albeit He had it in Jewish, first-century, male (and not female) form.

Some might say, "Well, if Jesus never had sex, then sexuality is not saved." Again, for our understanding, that is complete nonsense. Jesus was a human being; He was a male; and He had all the usual male parts. There are plenty of human beings who never had sex and are no less human for that fact. Having sex is not necessary to be a real human being, just as one does not have to eat Chinese food to be a real human being. Rather, one has to be sexual—in other words, one must be a man or a woman. We have to be sexual *in a sane manner,* and we believe that Jesus was, as were many of the saints—

in contrast to most of us. We certainly believe Jesus was fully human.

Hebrews says Jesus was tempted as we are tempted. He became like His brethren in *every respect*: "For we have not a high priest who is unable to sympathize with our weaknesses, but one who in every respect has been tempted as we are, yet without sin" (4:15).

When we say Jesus was tested in every way we are, this does not necessarily refer to specific details. Jesus was not tempted to look at sex on a computer, for example. He did not have a computer. When it says He was tempted in every respect, it does not necessarily mean, I think, that He experienced temptation in every single possible way in which every human being who ever lived has been tempted.

I think Jesus most likely was never tempted to sexual sin because He was God incarnate and in communion with God the Father. When a person is in communion with God, His temptations are different from those of a person who is not. Similarly, saints are tempted differently and tested differently by the devil and by other people than, say, lechers.

It is true, however, that as a first-century Jew, the incarnate Son of God who is the Messiah was tempted in every possible way. The synoptic Gospels of Matthew, Mark, and Luke illustrate how Jesus was tempted by the devil in the wilderness to change the stone to bread, to jump off the top of the temple, to worship demons, and so on. These temptations were attempts to persuade Him not to be the Messiah, to get Him to bypass the Cross, to get Him to be a different kind of teacher from the one God wanted Him to be. Later, in the Garden of Gethsemane before His crucifixion, Jesus would say to God the Father, "My Father, if it be possible, let this cup pass from me; nevertheless, not as I will, but as thou wilt" (Matt. 26:39). He was certainly tempted *in His humanity* not to be the Man God wanted Him to be.

Sometimes people will say, "Well, if He is God incarnate, then temptation is nothing! He's God, He can just dismiss it, just like that!" That is not our teaching because, if the Incarnation is real, then He had to struggle with all these trials and temptations in His humanity, with His human brain, His human will, His human passions, and His human heart.

And He *does* do that, He does know what it is to be tried. He can sympathize with us. He can co-suffer with us. He can take our suffering on

Himself, because He was in this world and He knew what it is like to be in this world of sin and death. As a matter of fact, He knew better than anyone, because He was crucified, He was killed, He was totally rejected.

Perfect man means He has every attribute of what it means to be human—morally as well. From His fetal form inside Mary's womb until He breathed His last upon the Cross, Jesus never did evil. He never gave in to the devil. He achieved all of that as a man. And it was not magic. With God, there is never magic. If God could have saved the world magically, He would not have had to take on the sin of the world. We believe that He could only save the world by incarnation, crucifixion, resurrection, and glorification.

C. S. Lewis said (paraphrased), "All I am in private life is a literary critic and historian, that's my job. And I am prepared to say on that basis if anyone thinks the Gospels are either legend or novels, then that person is simply showing his incompetence as a literary critic. I've read a great many novels and I know a fair amount about the legends that grew up among early people, and I know perfectly well the Gospels are not that kind of material" (see *Christian Reflections,* p. 209).

We believe the Jesus described on the pages of the Gospels is the real Jesus. The Gospels sometimes recount his story in different forms, but we are convinced that Jesus was not honestly mistaken, nor was He a liar, nor was He a mythical creation. He really lived, and really said and did the things the Scriptures say He said and did.

We affirm that Jesus of Nazareth is a real *anthropos*. He is the Man, *Jesus,* who is a man in exactly the same way that we are human beings. However, what makes Jesus unique and our Lord and Savior is that He is not a mere mortal man. He *became* like his brethren, but His Father is God, and His mother is Mary, and He is truly divine and truly human. The divinity of Christ is revealed through and in His humanity.

Therefore, when we picture Jesus standing at the judgment seat before Pontius Pilate, clothed in a purple robe of mockery, a crown of thorns upon His head, bearing the marks of scourging and spitting and ridicule, with a reed stuck in his bound hands as a mockery of His kingship, and Pilate says of Him to the crowd, "*Idou ho anthropos—Ecce homo—*Behold the man! Behold the human being!" we say, "Yes, He is really and truly *the Man.*"

CHAPTER 14

Jesus the

LAST ADAM

The New Testament contrasts the Adam of Genesis with Jesus Christ, the final Adam. The first Adam is from earth, and the second Adam—the last Adam—is from heaven.

Genesis relates how man, *anthropos*, was fashioned from the dust and was given the name *Adam*, or *Adama,* which in Hebrew means "earth." Then God breathed His own Spirit, His own life, into this earth creature, and he became a living soul. The life of this human being, his soul, is rational. It is self-conscious, free, and intelligent. Unlike the souls of animals and plants, this human soul can make moral choices because it is made in the image of God.

In the Scripture, God fashions the woman, Eve, out of the rib of man. She is taken from man's substance, and God fashions her very particularly. Then Adam, the earth creature, looks upon her and says, "This at last is bone of my bones / and flesh of my flesh" (see Gen. 2:23). The two become one flesh, one reality (v. 24). When Adam had lived 230 years, he became the father of a son in his own likeness, whom he named Seth (5:3).

The first humans lived in Paradise, and their life was to be a joyful and beautiful life. They were to govern the earth. They were to spread Paradise by following the commandments of God. St. Paul says in Romans 1 that humanity was made from the dust to offer God glory and thanksgiving, and if man would do this, then he would see the power and divinity of God in all that exists; then everything would be perfect and in harmony (see vv. 20–22). Adam and Eve would reproduce, and their children would carry on this divine and godly life by obeying God, proving their love for Him by offering Him praise, honor, and thanksgiving.

That was the intention, but it did not happen that way. Many different mythologies have imagined an innocent first condition of human beings, but the Genesis story does not give us that vision at all. God creates the man and the woman, He puts them in this paradisiacal garden, and He gives them a commandment. He allows them to eat or commune from the Tree of Life, which symbolizes living forever in communion with God. Yet in the story there is another tree, the Tree of the Knowledge of Good and Evil, whose existence generally means that already the possibility of evil exists. Human beings can taste of sin, and that is symbolized in the story by the eating from or participation in this Tree of the Knowledge of Good and Evil.

Then, of course, there is the serpent, which in Sunday school class simply stands for the devil. However, I think that, in a more accurate interpretation, the serpent would stand for human wisdom, the wisdom of this world—a spirit that is earthly and psychic, or unspiritual or merely animal, and can become demonic and destructive.

We believe this is a theological story meant to give us an understanding of humanity. The dogmatic point of the story is this: Humanity sins from the beginning. There is no record in the Bible of any happy, perfected holy life in Paradise. Eve listens to the serpent and is tempted to sin. This sin is likely symbolized by eating the fruit of the Tree of the Knowledge of Good and Evil.

In the Bible, knowledge is not theoretical. When one knows something, one knows it by experience. The verb *to know* is the verb for sexual intercourse in the Bible. Partaking of—that is, experiential knowledge of—the Tree of the Knowledge of Good and Evil means intercourse with evil, apostasy, and turning against God.

In Paradise, God tells Adam, "You may freely eat of every tree of the garden; but of the tree of the knowledge of good and evil you shall not eat, for in the day that you eat of it you shall die" (Gen. 2:16, 17). This did not mean Adam and Eve would die an instantaneous death the minute the fruit was eaten, but rather that if they transgressed the commandment, they would become mortal and bring death into the world.

"The wages of sin *is* death" (Rom. 6:23). Those who break communion with God bring death upon themselves. Humanity sins and becomes mortal. Then life becomes a struggle, full of toil. The earth is cursed because of sin, and humanity now eats only by the sweat of its brow. Now there is enmity between creation and man—the ground brings forth thistles and the serpents bite. Also, there is now enmity between the man and the woman. They no longer experience a communion of love. Her recourse is to her husband, and he rules over her (see Gen. 3:16–20).

In Romans 5:12–14, St. Paul makes this contrast between the original Adam and Christ.

> Therefore as sin came into the world through one man and death
> through sin, and so death spread to all men because all men sinned—sin
> indeed was in the world before the law was given, but sin is not counted
> where there is no law. Yet death reigned from Adam to Moses, even over
> those whose sins were not like the transgression of Adam, who was a
> type [a figure] of the one who was to come.

Whether or not this one man, Adam, was literally a unique individual, the theological point here is that there is a man who sins, and when he sins, his progeny inherit that brokenness, and they sin also. Then death spreads to all of humanity because all human beings, ultimately, have sinned.

This verse has caused trouble in Christian history. It was translated into Latin as the equivalent of "and so death spread to all men, *in whom all men sinned.*" One can read this either as "*in death* all people sinned" or "*in Adam* all people sinned," but either way, that was a mistranslation. In the West, St. Augustine came to believe we all had somehow preexisted in that original Adam, and in that one Platonic idea of man, we all had sinned and were, therefore, born guilty.

That text was conflated with Psalm 51(50):5, which says, "Behold, I was brought forth in iniquity, / and in sin did my mother conceive me." This only means we are born and conceived in a mortal and sinful world. However, the Jerusalem Bible and the New Revised Standard Version actually translate it as "I was born a sinner, a sinner from my mother's womb," or "I was born guilty." No baby is born into this world guilty, as a sinner. However, every baby born in this world is brought into a world where sin already reigns, where death already reigns, and where perishability and mortality exist. This is no fault of the baby. It is a result of our legacy from Adam.

We could say that humanity as a whole has sinned, but we should be very careful. We become guilty or personally culpable only by what we ourselves do. A lot of human beings, and certainly little children, can do things that are sinful, but they are not culpable. They have inherited their humanity from their parents and imitate them. They also get their DNA, brain chemistry, and bodies from their parents. We even get our *nephesh*—Hebrew for "life and being"—from our parents. We are made in their image and likeness, according to Genesis 5:3.

In Romans 5:14, the Apostle Paul says this original Adam, who with Eve sinned even before the Law of Moses, was a *typos* (a type) of the One who was coming, Christ. In other words, the original Adam was a potentiality. He had a task, but he, together with Eve, failed. Therefore, a new Adam was needed, a real Adam, an Adam who would give life. There had to be a Man who would not die because He has not sinned. There had to be a new human being. "A human being according to Adam" is what St. Paul calls the old human being, which is cursed, sinful, diseased, under the power of demons, and bound for a tomb. There had to be a second human being who could bring a godly life, who could restore Paradise.

Romans 5 continues:

> But the free gift is not like the trespass. For if many died through one man's trespass, much more have the grace of God and the free gift in the grace of that one man Jesus Christ abounded for many. And the free gift is not like the effect of that one man's sin. For the judgment following one trespass brought condemnation, but the free gift following many trespasses brings justification. (vv. 15–16)

The trespass of Adam brought destruction and judgment upon all, but the free gift of God in Jesus Christ, following many trespasses already committed, makes human beings righteous.

> If, because of one man's trespass, death reigned through that one man, much more will those who receive the abundance of grace and the free

gift of righteousness reign in life through the one man Jesus Christ.

Then as one man's trespass led to condemnation for all men, so one man's act of righteousness leads to acquittal and life for all men. For as by one man's disobedience many were made sinners, so by one man's obedience many will be made righteous. Law came in, to increase the trespass; but where sin increased, grace abounded all the more, so that, as sin reigned in death, grace also might reign through righteousness to eternal life through Jesus Christ our Lord. (vv. 17–21)

(Here we see one of St. Paul's ideas, that when we have laws and commandments and we go against them, we are more culpable than when we don't have the law.)

In those verses, the word *one* is used about ten times: one man, one man's transgression, one man's righteousness. This comparison is between the original Adam and Jesus Christ. Luke 3:38 says Adam was made to be God's son. Adam, however, sinned and brought death, and put us under the devil's power. Jesus Christ does just the opposite. He glorifies, thanks, and is obedient to God His Father. He does not commune with the knowledge that comes by eating from the Tree of the Knowledge of Good and Evil. He never tasted transgression; therefore, He can never taste corruption.

Jesus Christ certainly did die, but He dies voluntarily. He takes on the curse of Adam, as we sing in church, to restore the fallen image. He comes to restore Adam, to reopen the gates of Paradise. He comes so that we can again commune of the Tree of Life, which is His Cross. We eat from the Tree of Life, which is His broken Body and shed Blood on the Cross, and He Himself will be the new and final Adam, who will finally establish Paradise in God's Kingdom throughout all the world. All who have died in Adam will be made alive in Christ (see 1 Cor. 15:22). All who sinned, following and imitating Adam and dealing with Adam's nature, will again be allowed to live with God. Thus, the real Adam is Jesus.

Who, then, is the real Eve? The Church Fathers say that when we read Genesis from the point of view of Christ's Crucifixion and Resurrection, we can understand what is really being taught there. They ask: Why does God Almighty fashion Eve, who is named the mother of the living, from Adam's substance when he is in a deep sleep? Then they answer: When the real

Adam, Jesus, is put into the deep sleep of death on the Cross, out of His side, where it was pierced with a spear, there comes forth blood and water. The Fathers interpret the blood and water as signifying the Church. The water is baptism, and the blood is the life of God, that very Blood of Christ that is given to us in the Eucharist. The Fathers like to say that God fashions His Church from the side of the dead Jesus. We become the Bride of Christ.

The Church, then, becomes the real mother of the living. St. Cyprian of Carthage says one cannot have God as Father unless one has the Church as mother. The Church is described in the New Testament, also, as the Bride of Christ, the one with whom Christ becomes one flesh. The Church is made of sinful people who are accursed and dead, whom Christ raises up, glorifies, and forgives in love. When we love Christ and become one flesh with Him, we become the new Eve. Whereas in Genesis the woman is taken out of the man, in the New Testament, the man is taken out of a virgin woman.

The Holy Fathers also identify Mary as the new Eve. She is the symbol of the Church. Mary is the antitype of Eve in the Genesis story. The original Eve is supposed to be the helpmate of Adam, but she leads him into sin after listening to the serpent. Mary does exactly the opposite. She listens to the Holy Spirit and to the Archangel Gabriel. Whereas the first Eve disobeyed, Mary says, "Let it be to me according to your word" (Luke 1:38). Whereas the original Eve breaks the commandment, Mary says, "My soul magnifies the Lord, / and my spirit rejoices in God my Savior" (1:46–47). The hymns for Dormition say of her, "You were translated to life, O mother of life." Thus, Mary and the Church are conflated as the new Eve, the Bride of Jesus Christ, who leads man not into sin, but into Paradise.

In 1 Corinthians 15:20–22, St. Paul says:

> But in fact Christ has been raised from the dead, the first fruits of those who have fallen asleep. For as by a man came death, by a man has come also the resurrection of the dead. For as in Adam all die, so also in Christ shall all be made alive.

The apostle goes on to speak about the resurrection of the dead, revealing that the last enemy to be destroyed is death itself (v. 26).

> So is it with the resurrection of the dead. What is sown is perishable,
> what is raised is imperishable. It is sown in dishonor, it is raised in glory.
> It is sown in weakness, it is raised in power. It is sown a physical body, it
> is raised a spiritual body. (vv. 42–44)

What is sown is the original apostasy of Adam, and the raising is the resurrection of the spiritual Body of Christ.

> Thus it is written, "The first man Adam became a living being"; the last
> Adam became a life-giving spirit. But it is not the spiritual which is
> first but the physical, and then the spiritual. The first man was from the
> earth, a man of dust; the second man is from heaven. (vv. 45–47)

The first Adam is an earthly Adam, a mud-born Adam, but the real Adam, Jesus Christ, is a heavenly Adam. He came down from heaven, as the Nicene-Constantinopolitan Creed says, and became human. He became *the* Man. In the language of St. Paul, the first Adam is earthly, psychic, and devilish. The final Adam is heavenly, spiritual, and divine.

First Corinthians 15 continues:

> As was the man of dust, so are those who are of the dust; and as is the
> man of heaven, so are those who are of heaven. Just as we have borne
> the image of the man of dust, we shall also bear the image of the man of
> heaven. (vv. 48, 49)

At the Orthodox baptismal service, when the person to be baptized is being anointed with oil before being submerged in the water, the priest prays, "Let him be recreated according to the image of his Maker. Let him put on Christ and be clothed with the new man."

The Apostle Paul says in Galatians, "as many of you as were baptized into Christ have put on Christ" (3:27). In Ephesians 4, he says:

> Put off your old nature which belongs to your former manner of life and
> is corrupt through deceitful lusts, and be renewed in the spirit of your
> minds, and put on the new nature, created after the likeness of God in
> true righteousness and holiness. (vv. 22–24)

This same contrast is made in Colossians 3:

Put to death therefore what is earthly in you: fornication, impurity, passion, evil desire, and covetousness, which is idolatry. On account of these the wrath of God is coming. In these you once walked, when you lived in them.

But now put them all away: anger, wrath, malice, slander, and foul talk from your mouth. Do not lie to one another, seeing that you have put off the old nature with its practices and have put on the new nature, which is being renewed in knowledge after the image of its creator. (vv. 5–10)

Some Russian Orthodox crosses have little images of the spear and the sponge, and then, at the bottom, a mountain and a skull. By the foot of the Cross are the Slavonic letters corresponding to "GG," which stand for "Mount of Golgotha," the Place of the Skull (see Matt. 27:33). Just above the skull are the Slavonic letters corresponding to "GA," which stand for *glava Adama*, "the head of Adam." Thus, when Jesus is on the Cross, His blood goes down from the Place of the Skull onto the very skull of Adam in order to raise him up, to forgive him, to make him divine again.

On these same crosses, there is also this very mysterious inscription—four Slavonic letters corresponding to "MLRB." I did not know what that meant when I was a student, so I asked Father John Meyendorff, who knew everything of that sort. He said it stands for the Slavonic words *mesto lobnoye rai byst'*—"the Place of the Skull has become Paradise." This is the ultimate reversal. Adam was in Paradise, and he made it the pit of death. Christ is on Golgotha, and He transforms the pit of death into Paradise.

The first Adam, with his Eve, is a type of the one to come. The final Adam, Jesus Christ, with His Eve, the Church—symbolized by His mother, the first of believers—is the fulfillment of that type. As St. Paul would say, the first was a shadow. The second was the reality, and the ultimate reality is in Christ. When we think about Adam, we should not think about that muddy earth creature who ruined everything from the beginning. We should think of the true Adam, the second Adam, the last Adam, the Man from heaven, Jesus Christ our Lord. That is why, among the names and titles of Jesus in Holy Scripture, we find the second Man, *devteros anthropos*, the second Adam, and *eschatos* Adam, the last Adam.

CHAPTER 15

Jesus the

TEACHER

We first encounter Jesus on the pages of the Scriptures as a teacher, a rabbi. Early in St. John's Gospel, Jesus is called "'Rabbi' (which means Teacher)" (1:38). When He begins to collect followers in the Scriptures, they are called "disciples," which means students or pupils.

The Gospel of Mark says that after John the Baptist was arrested, Jesus came into Galilee, preaching the gospel of God and saying, "The time is fulfilled, and the kingdom of God is at hand; repent, and believe in the gospel" (1:15). Then, after He chose Peter and Andrew, and James and John, the sons of Zebedee, to follow Him, they went to Capernaum and immediately, on the Sabbath, Jesus entered the synagogue and taught (1:21).

The synagogue is the place of teaching. It was a place where Jews assembled—*synagogoi*, "came together"—for the sake of *Torah*, which means "instruction."

Jesus taught not only on mountaintops and by seashores, but in the synagogue. He even taught in the Jerusalem temple. In John's Gospel, after He was arrested, brought before the high priest, and questioned about His teaching, Jesus said, "I have spoken openly to the world; I have always taught in synagogues and in the temple, where all Jews come together; I have said nothing secretly" (18:20).

Jesus gathered His first disciples from John the Baptist, who was also a teacher. John the Baptist, standing with two of his disciples, looked at Jesus and said, "Behold the Lamb of God!" The two disciples heard him say this, and they followed Jesus (John 1:36–37). When Philip and Nathanael were called, Nathanael said to Jesus, "Rabbi, You are the Son of God! You are the King of Israel!" (John 1:49).

Jesus had many disciples, but not all the disciples were apostles. An apostle, *apostolos* in Greek (meaning "sent one"), is a disciple who is sent on a mission. Yet an apostle must begin as a disciple. A Christian, first and foremost, is a disciple, a student; and Christ Jesus, for Christians, is first of all their Teacher, the one who gives them the gospel of God.

Jesus is identified as the *Logos*, the very Word itself; so the Word of God that He teaches is, in some sense, Himself. Yet Jesus insists that His teaching is not His own, that He received it from God the Father (see, for example, John 12:49). When the people are astonished at His teaching, they say that He teaches "as one who had authority" (Mark 1:22).

Archbishop Demetrios, the present ranking archbishop of the Greek Orthodox Archdiocese of America, wrote a very good commentary on Mark entitled *Authority and Passion*. He wrote that, in Mark, there is an apocalyptic clash between the truth of God and the falsehood of this world, between God and the demons. Jesus is in the midst of controversy over what He teaches from the very beginning, and that controversy is because of not only *what* He teaches, but *how* He teaches, because He speaks "as one who had authority, and not as the scribes" (Mark 1:22). Archbishop Demetrios says that teaching with authority was what led to the Passion, to His suffering, death, and rejection.

This rejection of Jesus happens throughout the Gospels. In Mark, His relatives come to Him, even with His mother, and they think He has gone crazy. They try to get Him to come home. They think He is teaching incredible things (see 3:21, 31–35).

Others said He was a devil, or was possessed by the devil, and that He was blaspheming the Law, misleading the people, and desecrating the temple (see Mark 3:22). They said what He was teaching was not acceptable.

His disciples believed His teaching. They believed it was from God—He did not make it up. Throughout John, Jesus says, "My will is not My own will. I do the will of My Father in heaven. My works are not My own works. I do the works of My Father in heaven who sent Me. My words are not My words; they are the words of the Father who sent Me" (see John 5—7).

John says Jesus heard these words from God before He was even born, that Jesus was with God in the beginning, and everything that He has, He has from God. His very divinity is from the Father. He is begotten of the Father eternally, before all ages. All that He is teaching He received from God, face-to-face (see John 1:1–18; 8:37–59).

The Gospels often make a comparison and contrast between Jesus and Moses. Moses was taught by God. Moses went into the holy place, God instructed him, and he gave God's commandments to the people. They were not Moses' commandments; they were from God.

But, as Hebrews 3 says, Moses learned from God as a servant, as a creature. Jesus learns from God as a Son. The Son is far greater than the servant. The servant serves in the name of the Master, but the Son Himself *is* the Master over the house (3:5–6).

Hebrews begins with these words:

> In many and various ways God spoke of old to our fathers by the prophets; but in these last days he has spoken to us by a Son, whom he appointed the heir of all things, through whom also he created the world. He reflects the glory of God and bears the very stamp of his nature, upholding the universe by his word of power. When he had made purification for sins, he sat down at the right hand of the Majesty on high. (1:1–3)

The Gospel in which Jesus is most formally presented as the Teacher sent from God is Matthew. In fact, we can say that Matthew's Gospel *is* the Christian *Torah*, the Christian Law. Matthew is divided into five teaching sections; Moses' Law is given in five books, the *Pentateuch*. Matthew makes a conscious comparison and contrast between Moses and Jesus: Moses as the quintessential teacher of the Jews, the receiver of the Law; and Jesus as the Messianic Teacher, the one who says, "And do not be called teachers; for One is your Teacher, the Christ" (Matt. 23:10, NKJV).

In the infancy narratives at the beginning of Matthew, Jesus is already compared and contrasted to Moses. Jesus is born in Bethlehem, in Judah. He is the governor who comes to govern His people. When He is born, Joseph and Mary go off into Egypt, and then they have to come back from Egypt.

God also called Moses out of Egypt, and the people were led out of Egypt. Jesus is baptized in the Jordan River, which Moses was not able to cross. Joshua, whose name in Greek is Jesus, crossed it.

When Jesus began to teach, He went about all Galilee, teaching in their synagogues, and preaching the gospel of the Kingdom, and healing every disease and every infirmity of the people (4:23). These three things always go together: the teaching, the preaching, and the healing.

In the same way that the Ten Commandments are the central part of the Mosaic Law, the Sermon on the Mount in Matthew 5—7 is the central instruction of the New Moses, who is Jesus Christ. Jesus goes up onto the mountain and, after He sits down, His disciples come to Him (5:1). The mountain evokes the memory of Moses, for in those days, a teacher sat while his disciples stood and listened.

The Sermon on the Mount ends with, "And when Jesus finished these sayings, the crowds were astonished at his teaching, for he taught them as one who had authority, and not as their scribes" (7:28–29). In Luke's Gospel, Jesus is already in the temple among the teachers when He is twelve years old, and they are astonished at His learning. Now, He is a thirty-year-old man, announcing the Kingdom of God and teaching astonishing things with authority. Here ends the first part or "book" of Matthew's Gospel.

Afterward, Jesus comes down from the mountain. The crowds follow Him, and He goes around teaching. He calls Matthew, the tax collector, and tells him to follow Him. He does miracles, healing every form of epilepsy, lunacy, paralysis, blindness, dumbness, lameness—and at the same time He is teaching.

He calls the twelve disciples and then sends them out, making them apostles. He also gives them authority over unclean spirits and charges them to go teach that the Kingdom of heaven is at hand. He tells them they will not be the ones speaking and teaching, but the Spirit of God will speak through them. Therefore, they should not think ahead of time what they are going to say (10:5–20). In John 17:8, Jesus says He is giving them the words the Father has given Him, so that they would announce those very words. "And when Jesus had finished instructing his twelve disciples, he went on from there to teach and preach in their cities" (Matt. 11:1).

In the Sermon on the Mount, Jesus is interpreting: "It was said to the men of old . . . but I say to you . . ." Afterward, He both interprets the Scripture and fulfills that Scripture in His own behavior. In the Sermon on the Mount, He says, "He who does [these things] and teaches them shall be called great in the kingdom of heaven" (5:19). We do them first, and then we teach them.

Jesus gave His second section of instruction to His twelve disciples only, but in His third section of instruction, He goes about teaching in the cities— teaching them all, healing them all—and giving to them the mysteries of the Kingdom of heaven. However, He gives the mysteries in a mysterious manner—through parables. "The disciples came and said to him, 'Why do you speak to them in parables?'" (Matt. 13:10). He answers:

> And he answered them, "To you it has been given to know the secrets
> of the kingdom of heaven, but to them it has not been given. . . . This
> is why I speak to them in parables, because seeing they do not see, and
> hearing they do not hear, nor do they understand. With them indeed is
> fulfilled the prophecy of Isaiah." (vv. 11–14)

Many people think a parable is a story to make things clear, but in fact, a parable is meant to mystify the hearer. Those who have a pure heart will catch the meaning; those whose hearts are not right will not understand it. In the same way, His works will not convince them either.

Here the third section or book of Matthew comes to a close.

> And when Jesus had finished these parables, he went away from there,
> and coming to his own country he taught them in their synagogue,
> so that they were astonished, and said, "Where did this man get this
> wisdom and these mighty works? Is not this the carpenter's son? Is not
> his mother called Mary? And are not his brothers James and Joseph and
> Simon and Judas? And are not all his sisters with us? Where then did
> this man get all this?" And they took offense at him.
>   But Jesus said to them, "A prophet is not without honor except in his
> own country and in his own house." And he did not do many mighty
> works there, because of their unbelief. (Matt. 13:53–58)

After this, Jesus begins the fourth section of His teaching, when He teaches in the synagogues of Galilee and also in various other places and in various ways. He says in the Gospels that when the people do not hear Him, it would be better even for Sodom and Gomorrah than for them on the Day of Judgment, because the final Messianic Teacher has come (Matt. 10:15; 11:24).

In this part of Matthew, Jesus asks His disciples, "Who do the people say that I, the Son of Man, am?" They give various answers, such as, "You are John the Baptist, raised from the dead," or "You are one of the prophets, returned." Then Jesus asks, "Who do *you* say that I am?" In Matthew, Simon Peter says, "You are the Christ, the Son of the living God" (see 16:13–16).

Then Jesus begins to teach them that He has to be crucified. He also teaches that *they* will have to suffer. *They* will have to take up their own crosses and be afflicted because of Him. Nevertheless, He says, "some standing here will not taste death before they see the Son of man coming in his kingdom" (see 16:21–28). By this, Jesus refers to the Transfiguration and the Resurrection.

After this comes a section of ethical and moral teaching: How many times should we forgive? Should we give tribute to Caesar? The Jewish leaders are trying to catch Him in His words.

Then Matthew 19:1–2 gives another conclusion: "Now when Jesus had finished these sayings, he went away from Galilee and entered the region of Judea beyond the Jordan; and large crowds followed him, and he healed them there." After this, He contacts the leaders of the Jewish people.

This is the fifth section or book of Matthew, and it takes place in Judea. It illustrates the clash between Jesus and the leaders of the Jewish people. Now Jesus begins to question those who question Him. He also begins to speak about the end of the world—the ultimate clash between earthly and heavenly authorities. In addition, He teaches about the great commandments of love. He also addresses the issue of His identity, asking the Jewish leaders, "What do you think about the Christ? Whose Son is He?" (22:42). Here He identifies Himself with the Lord, quoting the Psalm: "The LORD said to my Lord, / "Sit at my right hand, / Till I put thy enemies under thy feet" (109[110]:1). "If David thus calls him 'Lord,' how is he his son?" (Matt. 22:45).

Then Jesus addresses the Pharisees' teaching. He says, "The scribes and the Pharisees sit on Moses' seat; so practice and observe whatever they tell you, but not what they do; for they preach, but do not practice" (23:1–3). He calls them serpents, a brood of vipers, hypocrites, and blind guides. And a few chapters later: "When Jesus had finished all these sayings, he said to his disciples, 'You know that after two days the Passover is coming, and the Son of man will be delivered up to be crucified'" (26:1–2). Because of His teaching, He is put to death.

Jesus' twelve apostles will themselves become teachers. At the end of Matthew, Jesus says:

> All authority in heaven and on earth has been given to me. Go therefore
> and make disciples of all nations, baptizing them in the name of the
> Father and of the Son and of the Holy Spirit, teaching them to observe
> all that I have commanded you; and lo, I am with you always, to the
> close of the age. (28:18–20)

This is often called the Great Commission: "*You* become teachers of all the nations." The Christian Church is a congregation that includes teaching.

After the very first sermon was given on Pentecost, and people came to believe, the believers "devoted themselves to the apostles' teaching," which is the teaching of Christ (Acts 2:42). As the Father sent Christ, so Christ sends the apostles to teach.

St. Paul writes, "teach what befits sound doctrine" (Titus 2:1). Since the earliest days of the Church, some have had a particular *charisma*, or a gift of the Holy Spirit, to be teachers. St. Paul says this in Romans (see 12:6–8), in 1 Corinthians (see 12:28), and in Ephesians (see 4:11): "Some should be apostles, some prophets, some evangelists, some pastors and teachers."

There are those who, to this day, have the particular charisma of teaching. The Holy Fathers are teachers; they teach the doctrine, the theology, and the dogmas. The bishops are teachers. They are consecrated at the Liturgy with the Holy Gospel over their heads, and in the olden days, the bishops always had to appear in public carrying the Gospel book. This is why, on all the icons of bishops, they are carrying a Gospel book—because their task was to teach the gospel.

St. Paul writes that the elders—the presbyters—are worthy of special honor, especially those who persevere in teaching (1 Tim. 5:17). James says, "Let not many of you become teachers, my brethren, for you know that we who teach shall be judged with greater strictness" (James 3:1). (I am always aware of this when speaking on the radio and as a professor at a theological seminary.)

Not everyone is called to teach, but everyone is called to learn. Before one can become a teacher, one has to be a disciple. One has to be a catechumen—one who listens to the catechesis of the one who teaches in the name of the Lord.

Christ remains our Teacher. He teaches through the bishops—the charismatic teachers—and the Holy Fathers and saints of the Church. The teaching of God remains with us by the Holy Spirit, the Spirit of truth, who guides us into all truth, and brings to remembrance everything Christ Himself has done (John 16:13).

Jesus says the Holy Spirit "will take what is mine and declare it to you" (John 16:14). Then, in the next chapter, Jesus prays for those who continue in the words He, the Rabbi sent from God, teaches them (v. 20).

In the Holy Scriptures, the very first title of Jesus as Messiah is *Rabbi*, that is, "Teacher." He begins as a teacher. He teaches His disciples; He teaches His twelve apostles; He teaches the crowds; He teaches in Galilee; He teaches in Judea. He is the quintessential Teacher.

As Jesus said, "But you are not to be called rabbi, for you have one teacher, and you are all brethren" (Matt. 23:8).

CHAPTER 16

Jesus the

PROPHET

One of the titles for Jesus as the Messiah is *the* Prophet. He is the final prophet, the last prophet.

What is a prophet? Most people think prophets are those who predict the future, and that very often is the case. When prophets are inspired by God, they do say what is going to befall the people, especially if the people do not repent.

However, the term *prophet* is deeper and wider than that. God's prophet is the one upon whom God's Spirit dwells—not the elemental spirits of the universe or the evil spirits, but the *Ruach Yahweh*, the Spirit of the Lord. The prophet is filled with the Spirit in order to proclaim the Word of the Lord. According to Hebrews 4:12, "the word of God is living and active, sharper than any two-edged sword, piercing to the division of soul and spirit, of joints and marrow." The word spoken by the prophets is powerful because the Spirit of God rests upon them. St. John of Damascus says God never speaks without breathing, and He never breathes without speaking.

The holy prophets, being inspired by the Word of God, proclaim the word of God. They proclaim the truth. They proclaim what God does, wants, says, and commands. The prophets are not opposed to the Law of Moses; they proclaim the word of God enshrined in the Law. In fact, Moses is considered to be among the first of the prophets. When we commemorate Moses liturgically, he is called the prophet and God-seer, the one who speaks God's words.

Neither are prophets opposed to teachers, scribes, and priests. In fact, some of the prophets were priests, such as Ezekiel. The priests and teachers are also inspired, prophetic servants of God.

In the Bible, the prophets always call people to follow God's Law. They are always calling people, even the priests themselves, to do their jobs according to the will of God, to make right offerings to the Lord, in the right spirit, and not to go after idols. The true prophets rebuke the false prophets, and there are always false prophets, false teachers, and corrupted priests.

These rebukes may use fiery words, as in Jeremiah 5:

> An appalling and horrible thing
> has happened in the land:
> the prophets prophesy falsely,
> and the priests rule at their direction;
> my people love to have it so,
> but what will you do when the end comes? (vv. 30–31)

> "For from the least to the greatest of them,
> every one is greedy for unjust gain;
> and from prophet to priest,
> every one deals falsely.
> They have healed the wound of my people lightly,
> saying, 'Peace, peace,'
> when there is no peace.
> Were they ashamed when they committed abomination?
> No, they were not at all ashamed;
> they did not know how to blush." (Jer. 6:13–15)

Jeremiah 23 expounds more fully concerning the false prophets:

> Concerning the prophets:
> My heart is broken within me,
> all my bones shake;
> I am like a drunken man,
> like a man overcome by wine,
> because of the Lord
> and because of his holy words.
> For the land is full of adulterers;
> because of the curse the land mourns,
> and the pastures of the wilderness are dried up.

Their course is evil,
and their might is not right.
"Both prophet and priest are ungodly;
even in my house I have found their wickedness,"
says the Lord. (vv. 9–11)

"Do not listen to the words of the prophets who prophesy to you, filling
you with vain hopes; they speak visions of their own minds, not from
the mouth of the Lord. They say continually to those who despise the
word of the Lord, 'It shall be well with you'; and to every one who
stubbornly follows his own heart, they say, 'No evil shall come upon
you.'" (vv. 16–17)

"I have not sent the prophets, yet they ran;
I did not speak to them, yet they prophesied." (v. 21)

"Behold, I am against the prophets, says the Lord, who use their tongues
and say, 'Says the Lord.' Behold, I am against those who prophesy lying
dreams, says the Lord, and who tell them and lead my people astray by
their lies and their recklessness, when I did not send them or charge
them; so they do not profit this people at all, says the Lord.

   "When one of this people, or a prophet, or a priest asks you, 'What is
the burden of the Lord?' you shall say to them, 'You are the burden, and
I will cast you off, says the Lord.'" (vv. 30–33)

The Old Testament makes an appeal to true and proper prophecy. In the
Book of Numbers, there were two men in the camp named Eldad and
Medad.

   Now two men remained in the camp, one named Eldad, and the other
   named Medad, and the spirit rested upon them; they were among those
   registered, but they had not gone out to the tent, and so they prophesied
   in the camp. And a young man ran and told Moses, "Eldad and Medad
   are prophesying in the camp."
      And Joshua the son of Nun, the minister of Moses, one of his chosen
   men, said, "My lord Moses, forbid them."
      But Moses said to him, "Are you jealous for my sake? Would that all
   the Lord's people were prophets, that the Lord would put his spirit upon
   them!" (Num. 11:26–29).

In Deuteronomy 18, Moses teaches that God will raise up a Prophet in the last day:

> "The Lord your God will raise up for you a prophet like me from among you, from your brethren—him you shall heed—just as you desired of the Lord your God at Horeb on the day of the assembly, when you said, 'Let me not hear again the voice of the Lord my God, or see this great fire any more, lest I die.'
>
> "And the Lord said to me, 'They have rightly said all that they have spoken. I will raise up for them a prophet like you from among their brethren; and I will put my words in his mouth, and he shall speak to them all that I command him. And whoever will not give heed to my words which he shall speak in my name, I myself will require it of him." (vv. 15–19)

In other words, that word will condemn and judge those who do not hear the Prophet.

In the New Testament, we see that the Prophet spoken of by Moses is Jesus. We see this in the Gospel of John. When John the Baptist comes out preaching and teaching and baptizing the people, the leaders of the Jews come to him and question him about what he is doing and why. They ask, "Who are you?"

> He confessed, he did not deny, but confessed, "I am not the Christ." And they asked him, "What then? Are you Elijah?" He said, "I am not." "Are you the prophet?" And he answered, "No." (John 1:20–21)

At the time, the idea was that Elijah was going to be the forerunner of the Messiah. In the Synoptic Gospels, when the disciples ask Jesus if Elijah is supposed to be His forerunner, Jesus speaks to them about John the Baptist. In Matthew 11, Jesus says, "For all the prophets and the law prophesied until John; and if you are willing to accept it, he is Elijah who is to come" (vv. 13–14).

Elijah means "the man of God." St. John Chrysostom said:

> John the Baptist is the man of God, the Elijah, who comes as the Forerunner for Jesus into His kenotic Crucifixion in the form of a slave. John the Baptist is the Forerunner of Jesus, even into Hades. He is the

one who announces that Christ is the Lamb of God who comes to take upon Himself the sin of the world.

John says, "I am not *the* Prophet." The Messiah is *the* Prophet. The Lord Jesus Christ, the Son of God who suffered for us, He is *the* Prophet. John bore witness to Christ, and Jesus says there is a testimony that is even greater than that of John the Baptist—the testimony of God the Father and of the Holy Spirit. It is also Jesus' own testimony by His own words and deeds. Yet Jesus insists that John is the greatest of the prophets. Among the regular prophets, John is the greatest and the last. No one born of woman, according to Jesus, is greater than John the Baptist (Matt. 11:11).

The expressions "a prophet" and "the Prophet" are used several times in John. In John 6:14, where Jesus multiplies the loaves, the people see the sign He has done and say, "This is truly the Prophet who is to come into the world."

The Samaritan woman says, "Sir, I perceive that You are a prophet" (John 4:19). When the man blind from birth is asked who healed him, he says, "The Man called Jesus." Then they ask what he thinks of this Jesus, and he says, "He is a prophet" (John 9:11–17).

In John 7:40–41, Jesus has been speaking about living water. "When they heard these words, some of the people said, 'This is really the prophet.' Others said, 'This is the Christ,'" which amounts to the same thing.

The Muslims proclaim that the final and ultimate prophet is Mohammed. They think Jesus is a prophet, one of the greatest prophets before Mohammed, but only a prophet. He is one who is anointed by God, who is filled with the spirit, who speaks the word of God. In the Koran, Jesus is even born of a virgin, but not crucified, because, according to Muslims, God's prophet cannot suffer a degrading, humiliating death.

We Christians say the final prophet who is merely human is John the Baptist, and even that greatest of prophets dies a violent death in the Christian tradition. Jesus, however, is the Son of God. He is *the* messianic, anointed Prophet.

The Book of Acts articulates this very specifically. Peter says in his sermon at Solomon's Porch, "And now, brethren, I know that you acted [killing

Jesus] in ignorance, as did also your rulers" (Acts 3:17). This echoes Jesus, when from the Cross He cried out, "Father, forgive them, for they know not what they do" (Luke 23:34).

Peter continues, "But what God foretold by the mouth of all the prophets, that his Christ should suffer, he thus fulfilled" (Acts 3:18). All that the prophets have said is fulfilled in Jesus. In his Gospel, Luke says that when Jesus was raised from the dead, He opened the minds of the apostles to understand that He had to be crucified and suffer before entering into His glory, and to understand how everything in the Law, the Psalms, and the Prophets is about His Crucifixion and glorification (see Luke 24:44–45).

Peter later references Deuteronomy 18, saying,

> "Moses said, 'The Lord God will raise up for you a prophet from your brethren as he raised me up. You shall listen to him in whatever he tells you. And it shall be that every soul that does not listen to that prophet shall be destroyed from the people.' And all the prophets who have spoken, from Samuel and those who came afterwards, also proclaimed these days. You are the sons of the prophets and of the covenant which God gave to your fathers, saying to Abraham, 'And in your posterity shall all the families of the earth be blessed.' God, having raised up his servant, sent him to you first, to bless you in turning every one of you from your wickedness." (Acts 3:22–26)

In the King James Version of Scripture, wherever it says *ho prophetes*, "the Prophet," the translators write "*that* Prophet." Jesus is *that* Prophet. He is *the* Prophet. He is the divine-human, theandric Prophet. He is not even numbered with the prophets in the usual listing. There are no other lords or teachers or prophets or kings or judges who are even like Him. All of them are fulfilled in Him. He is the Word incarnate, and being the Word incarnate, He is *that* Prophet, that One Moses spoke about, the unique, final One.

Those who are baptized into Christ and receive the Holy Spirit by chrismation are also made to be prophets. Christians believe the saying of Moses, "Would that all the Lord's people were prophets!" (Num. 11:29), is fulfilled with the coming of the Messiah. Nevertheless, in the Christian community, there are some members who have the particular gift or charisma of prophecy, just as there are some who have the particular gift of healing or teaching. The New Testament even mentions these prophets—the daughters of Philip, for example (Acts 21:9).

In 1 Corinthians 12—14, there is an issue regarding teaching, because the Corinthians are an ecstatic community, manifesting phenomena such as speaking in tongues which are similar to those exhibited by the false prophets in the Old Testament. Sometimes the spirit at work is not the Spirit of God, and they need to be checked. They need to have a person like St. Paul guiding them in the variety of their gifts to make sure they are gifts of God.

In 1 Corinthians, St. Paul speaks about the particular gift of prophecy. He says the Holy Spirit is given for various purposes: the utterance of knowledge according to the Spirit, faith according to the Spirit, gifts of healing of the one Spirit, the working of miracles, the ability to distinguish between spirits, and prophecy (see 1 Cor. 12:8–10). When there is an argument about these gifts—which are the best and what is most important—Paul says in 1 Corinthians 13 that the only important thing is love. We could have all these gifts, but if we do not have love, we are nothing. In 1 Corinthians 14 he says the gifts are for the edification, encouragement, and consolation of the Church, and love should be the aim.

Nevertheless, he says,

> And God has appointed in the church first apostles, second prophets, third teachers, then workers of miracles, then healers, helpers, administrators, speakers in various kinds of tongues. Are all apostles? Are all prophets? Are all teachers? Do all work miracles? Do all possess gifts of healing? Do all speak with tongues? Do all interpret? (1 Cor. 12:28–30)

Obviously not. But the more excellent way is the way of love. He goes on to say, "Make love your aim, and earnestly desire the spiritual gifts, especially that you may prophesy. For one who speaks in a tongue speaks not to men but to God; for no one understands him, but he utters mysteries in the Spirit. On the other hand, he who prophesies speaks to men for their upbuilding and encouragement and consolation" (1 Cor. 14:1–3).

This is what the real prophetic gift is—edification or building up: not tearing down, not factiousness, not separating. St. Paul was very concerned that a lot of these charismatics were separating from the Church; they were causing trouble.

In the Sermon on the Mount, Jesus says, "On that day many will say to me, 'Lord, Lord, did we not prophesy in your name, and cast out demons in your name, and do many mighty works in your name?' And then will I declare to them, 'I never knew you; depart from me, you evildoers!'" (Matt. 7:22–23). God can give His Spirit to people to prophesy, to cast out demons, and to do miracles, and they might be lost because they are not doing those things out of the love of God.

Nevertheless, St. Paul says to the Thessalonians, "Do not quench the Spirit, do not despise prophesying, but test everything; hold fast what is good, abstain from every form of evil" (1 Thess. 5:19–22). This is how we understand who the Prophet is. The Prophet is the God-inspired one, who pronounces and proclaims the Word of God for the sake of edifying, upbuilding, encouraging, exhorting, consoling, and comforting God's people.

The Prophet is Jesus. He gives the Spirit to those who are baptized in His name—the name of the Father and the Son and the Holy Spirit. He gives the Spirit to those who believe in Him and obey Him, and they become a company, a prophetic people. That very same Spirit is given to some people in particular, to be prophets of the Lord; but Jesus Christ the Lord is the Messianic Prophet, the ultimate Prophet, the Prophet different from all other prophets. For all Christians, there is only one who is that Prophet, *the* Prophet. That one is Jesus of Nazareth, the Christ who suffers.

CHAPTER 17

Jesus the

GREAT HIGH PRIEST

J esus is *the* Priest, the great High Priest. The teachers, prophets, kings, and priests all over the world, and from all religions, prefigure and typify Him. He perfects, fulfills, and accomplishes everything Himself. He is the High Priest who offers the perfect sacrifice—His own flesh and blood, which He offers, as the Liturgy of St. John Chrysostom says, "for the life of the world."

In the Gospels, Jesus is never explicitly called "priest" or "high priest." Nevertheless, it is clear that Jesus' self-offering on the Cross is a sacrificial, high-priestly offering. It is the ultimate offering which ransoms all creation from sickness, sin, the power of the devil, and death itself. It is the great redemption, the great buying back of creation by God Himself in the Person of His Son, in order to reconcile all things with God so that God could fill all things with Himself, and that there could be absolute peace and unity between God and His creatures.

This teaching is explicit in Hebrews. Jesus fulfills all the priestly sacrifices of the Old Testament and offers the sacrifice once and for all (see Heb. 7:27), the eternal offering to God that effects an eternal salvation.

In Genesis, offerings were sacrificed to God. Cain kills Abel because it is written that Cain's sacrifice was not acceptable to God, but Abel's offering was. Some people think the reason behind that was not so much the *content* of the offerings, but the *spirit* in which they were offered. For an offering to be acceptable, it has to be an offering of love, given from a contrite and humble heart with thanksgiving to God.

When Abraham returned from his victory over the kings, he was visited, in the King's Valley, by Melchizedek, the king of Salem or "peace," who brought out an offering of bread and wine. Melchizedek was a priest of God Most High. He blessed Abraham and said, "Blessed be Abram by God Most High, / maker of heaven and earth; / and blessed be God Most High, / who has delivered your enemies into your hand!" (Gen. 14:19–20).

In the New Testament, Jesus is called "a priest for ever, / after the order of Melchizedek" (Heb. 7:17, citing Ps. 110[109]:4)—not the Levitical priesthood of the Mosaic Law, but the new priesthood of Melchizedek. The offering of Melchizedek was bread and wine, which is the offering of Jesus at the Mystical Supper when He takes bread and says, "This is My Body, broken," and takes the cup of wine and says, "This is My Blood, shed." In the New Covenant, Christians, together with Jesus Christ, offer to God Jesus Christ's own flesh and blood in the form of bread and wine.

Genesis 22 tells a terrifying story. God commands Abraham to sacrifice his only son, one born in Abraham and Sarah's old age, the one through whom all the families of the earth were supposed to be blessed. Human sacrifice was practiced in Canaan in those days, but God forbade any kind of human sacrifice. This was a test for Abraham. Does God's servant really trust Him? Is he ready to do *anything* God asks? The story of Abraham's offering of Isaac, which is read at the vigil of Pascha, shows not only that Abraham obeyed God, but that he trusted Him.

Moriah, where God tells Abraham to go, means "God provides." When they are going there, Abraham says to Isaac, "God will provide the lamb," but there is no lamb. The lamb is Isaac, the *only* son of Abraham from his wife, Sarah.

God sees Abraham's faith and does *not* allow him to sacrifice his only son, but provides a ram to be put in his place. Virtually all the classical ancient Christian traditions of this story say that ram typifies Jesus. Jesus becomes not only the Paschal Lamb, he becomes the Lamb—the fulfillment—of *all* the sacrifices offered in the Old Covenant.

When Jesus, *God's* only Son, is led to the Mount of Calvary and hung upon the tree of the Cross, God does allow Him to die. In Luke 22:43, an angel comes to comfort Jesus in Gethsemane *before* His Passion, but when Jesus is offered up by the Father and offers Himself up, no angel comes.

God Himself does what He *does not* require of Abraham, the paradigmatic believer. God gives us His Son to die for our sins, that by His blood, by His life, the whole world might be saved.

Jesus is put in the place of Isaac and of all of us. This is the very heart of the Christian gospel, that God's Son is born into the world in order to offer Himself to the Father on our behalf, to become the living Sacrifice, to redeem the world. As St. Gregory the Theologian says, "One drop of His blood recreates the whole creation."

Some people find the story of Abraham and Isaac absolutely outrageous. The "new atheists" like Richard Dawkins and Christopher Hitchens cite this story to show how awful, cruel, and ridiculous religion is, that God would ask a human being to sacrifice his son. Yet God has that right. All things belong to Him. *We* belong to Him; *nothing* is our own. We should be ready to offer Him anything He asks. The story of Abraham and Isaac shows clearly, however, that God in fact *does not* ask the sacrifice of our children; He forbids that. It is *God* who sacrifices *His* own Son. That is the point.

The Old Testament spells out a whole sacrificial system connected to the tabernacles in the wilderness and then the temple in Jerusalem. At the time of the Passover, the paschal lamb was sacrificed. The blood was given to God. The lamb was eaten as a sign of communion with God, and the people were led out by God. Jesus is the Paschal Lamb who offers Himself.

The Levitical code mentions all kinds of sacrifices and offerings: grain sacrifices, cereal sacrifices, lambs, goats, bulls, whole-burnt offerings, holocausts, praise offerings, thank offerings, guilt offerings, peace offerings, and sin offerings. There are offerings for purification after touching blood, touching death, giving birth, emitting semen. Joseph and Mary came to the temple and made the offering according to the Law after Jesus was born.

These offerings are to make reconciliation with God under two different types of conditions. One is the offering when a person has sinned, when he or she is guilty and offers whatever is prescribed in order to be delivered from that guilt, to be made one with God again.

The other is when a person comes in contact with the holiness of God, as in blood or childbirth or death, because it was thought that God Himself was present in these things. When a creature and a sinner comes in contact with those actions of God, according to the Law the person is rendered unclean and has to make a sacrificial offering. That was even the case when the priests were in the temple offering the incense and the sacrifices, or when they were touching the holy books. They had to offer a sacrifice to be made clean. They were being cleansed from holiness, so to speak.

Alas, often the priests were corrupted. They polluted the sacrifice and the sanctuary; they sinned against God. Fr. James Bernstein says in his book *Surprised by Christ* (Conciliar Press/Ancient Faith Publishing, 2008) that he was so surprised as he read the Scriptures of the Old Testament to find that *most* of the time, the people of God were unfaithful, sinning, and following their own mind. They were irrevocably God's chosen people—to them was given the Law, from them the prophets arose, and from them according to the flesh came the Christ. By and large, however, the priests were corrupting the sanctuary, the pastors were neglecting the sheep, and it was really bad news.

The *good* news of the gospel is that God so loves the world that He sends His only-begotten Son to be the great High Priest. We hear of this in great detail in Hebrews:

> Therefore he had to be made like his brethren in every respect, so that
> he might become a merciful and faithful high priest in the service
> of God, to make expiation for the sins of the people. For because he
> himself has suffered and been tempted, he is able to help those who
> are tempted. Therefore, holy brethren, who share in a heavenly call,
> consider Jesus, the apostle and high priest of our confession. (Heb.
> 2:17—3:1)

> Since then we have a great high priest who has passed through the
> heavens, Jesus, the Son of God, let us hold fast our confession. For we
> have not a high priest who is unable to sympathize with our weaknesses,
> but one who in every respect has been tempted as we are, yet without
> sin. Let us then with confidence draw near to the throne of grace, that
> we may receive mercy and find grace to help in time of need. (Heb.
> 4:14–16)

> For every high priest chosen from among men is appointed to act on
> behalf of men in relation to God, to offer gifts and sacrifices for sins. He
> can deal gently with the ignorant and wayward, since he himself is beset

with weakness. Because of this he is bound to offer sacrifice for his own sins as well as for those of the people. And one does not take the honor upon himself, but he is called by God, just as Aaron was.

So also Christ did not exalt himself to be made a high priest, but was appointed by him who said to him,

"Thou art my Son,
today I have begotten thee";

as he says also in another place,

"Thou art a priest for ever,
after the order of Melchizedek."

In the days of his flesh, Jesus offered up prayers and supplications, with loud cries and tears, to him who was able to save him from death, and he was heard for his godly fear. Although he was a Son, he learned obedience through what he suffered; and being made perfect he became the source of eternal salvation to all who obey him, being designated by God a high priest after the order of Melchizedek. (Heb. 5:1–10)

Hebrews 7 says that once Jesus offers Himself in sacrifice to God as a great High Priest, He does so according to the order of Melchizedek, who became a priest not through a legal requirement concerning bodily descent, like Aaron, but by the power of an indestructible life, by the choice of God Himself. The former priests were many in number. This priesthood of Christ is only one. The sacrifice is only one. It is made once and for all. It is absolutely holy, blameless, unstained, separated from sinners, exalted above the heavens.

Hebrews says that Jesus, as *this* kind of High Priest, has no need to offer sacrifices daily, first for His own sins and then for those of the people, because He is sinless and offered up Himself *once for all* (Heb. 7:27). The Law appoints men in their weaknesses as high priests, but the word of the oath, which came after the Law, appoints a Son who had been made perfect forever. The oath is the promise of God that the one High Priest would come, whose sacrifice would be all-embracing, ultimate, and never to be repeated.

Once that sacrifice is made on the Cross, Hebrews 9:24 tells us that Jesus entered into the heavens, into the sanctuary not made by human hands. According to the author of Hebrews, the tabernacle holy place and the temple holy place, where the priests of the Old Testament went, was only a shadow (in Greek, *skia*), a prefiguration of the heavenly sanctuary. It is prophesied in Jeremiah that the days will come when there will be a new covenant with the house of Israel and the house of Judah, and this covenant will not be made in the blood of goats and bulls but in the blood of the Messiah Himself (see Jer. 31:31–34, LXX 38:31–34).

One of the psalms also says that God does not want sacrifices and offerings. "Sacrifices and offerings thou hast not desired, / but a body hast thou prepared for me" (Heb. 10:5, quoting Ps. 40[39]:6). He gives this body to His Messiah, and it is this risen Body of Christ with His flesh that enters into the very presence of God, there to intercede on our behalf, "thus securing an eternal redemption" (Heb. 9:12).

He is in the presence of God now, having sacrificed His body, having given Himself to God; and He will appear again from heaven. He will appear to us in order to raise us from the dead and take us to be where He Himself is.

> But when Christ had offered for all time a single sacrifice for sins, he sat down at the right hand of God, then to wait until his enemies should be made a stool for his feet. For by a single offering he has perfected for all time those who are sanctified. And the Holy Spirit also bears witness to us; for after saying,
>
> > "This is the covenant that I will make with them
> > after those days, says the Lord:
> > I will put my laws on their hearts,
> > and write them on their minds,"
>
> then he adds,
>
> > "I will remember their sins and their misdeeds no more."
>
> Where there is forgiveness of these, there is no longer any offering for sin.
>
> Therefore, brethren, since we have confidence to enter the sanctuary by the blood of Jesus, by the new and living way which he opened for us through the curtain, that is, through his flesh, and since we have a great priest over the house of God, let us draw near with a true heart in full assurance of faith, with our hearts sprinkled clean from an evil conscience and our bodies washed with pure water. Let us hold fast the confession of our hope without wavering, for he who promised is faithful. (Heb. 10:12–23)

Jesus is our High Priest. In Him, we also become priests. "To him who loves us and has freed us from our sins by his blood and made us a kingdom, priests to his God and Father, to him be glory and dominion for ever and ever. Amen" (Rev. 1:5–6). Revelation 20:6 says, "Blessed and holy is he who shares in the first resurrection! Over such the second death has no power, but they shall be priests of God and of Christ, and they shall reign with him a thousand years."

We become priests of God and Christ when we are baptized. We are anointed with the Spirit, to be prophets and priests.

> But you are a chosen race, a royal priesthood, a holy nation, God's own people, that you may declare the wonderful deeds of him who called you out of darkness into his marvelous light. Once you were no people but now you are God's people; once you had not received mercy but now you have received mercy. (1 Pet. 2:9–10)

> So put away all malice and all guile and insincerity and envy and all slander. Like newborn babes, long for the pure spiritual milk, that by it you may grow up to salvation; for you have tasted the kindness of the Lord.
>
> Come to him, to that living stone, rejected by men but in God's sight chosen and precious; and like living stones be yourselves built into a spiritual house, to be a holy priesthood, to offer spiritual sacrifices acceptable to God through Jesus Christ. (1 Pet. 2:1–5)

St. Paul says the same thing in Romans 12:1: "I appeal to you therefore, brethren, by the mercies of God, to present your bodies as a living sacrifice, holy and acceptable to God, which is your spiritual worship."

Those words are used in the Orthodox Divine Liturgy, where we, as priests, offer ourselves, together with Christ our High Priest, to God. We offer Him our bodies to be broken and our blood to be shed. The Holy Spirit comes upon us, and our bodies become the very Body of Christ. The Church becomes the very Body of Christ, and our blood is our life; the life of God lives in us. This is what happens when we celebrate the Divine Liturgy.

Jesus is not *punished* in our place on the Cross. Jesus is *offering Himself* to God, in our place and *with us* on the Cross. He is offering Himself, even in the most horrible conditions—being rejected, spit upon, mocked, and beaten. He is a perfect, innocent sacrifice, and His life belongs to God. *God sacrifices Him to Himself* on the Cross.

This is how the priest prays at the Divine Liturgy: "For You, O Lord Christ, are the one who offers, the one who is offered, the one who receives the offering, and the very offering itself, that is distributed to the faithful people for Holy Communion."

Jesus is the perfect High Priest who offers the perfect sacrifice, who makes the perfect redemption, and once and for all takes us into the holy sanctuary of the presence of God Himself to receive grace and glory at the altar of God in heaven. We become priests with Him, provided that we suffer with Him and offer ourselves to God with Him, out of love for God and for our neighbor, as the perfect offering in perfect innocence.

We cannot do this by ourselves, because we are sinners. No amount of blood from goats and bulls and calves is going to effect that redemption. Only the perfect offering of the perfect High Priest can do this. We have that High Priest: Jesus Christ. We are to offer ourselves to God together with Him in order to reign with Him in the presence of the Holy of Holies above the heavens.

CHAPTER 18

Jesus the

KING

The issue of kingship is central in the Holy Scriptures. In the Old Testament, we see that God Himself is King over His people. Several psalms speak of the Lord *reigning*. One is Psalm 93(92): "The Lord reigns [or "is King"]; he is robed in majesty" (v. 1). We sing part of this psalm at Vespers on Saturday nights:

> The Lord reigns; he is robed in majesty;
> the Lord is robed, he is girded with strength.
> Yea, the world is established; it shall never be moved;
> thy throne is established from of old;
> thou art from everlasting.
> The floods have lifted up, O Lord,
> the floods have lifted up their voice,
> the floods lift up their roaring.
> Mightier than the thunders of many waters,
> mightier than the waves of the sea,
> the Lord on high is mighty!
> Thy decrees are very sure;
> holiness befits thy house,
> O Lord, for evermore. (vv. 1–5)

This psalm is connected to a group of psalms with the same beginning: "The Lord reigns." These psalms and others, in the New Covenant, are applied to the Lord Jesus Christ and connected with the issue of judgment:

> But the Lord sits enthroned for ever,
> he has established his throne for judgment. (Ps. 9:7)

Arise, O God, judge the earth;
for to thee belong all the nations! (Ps. 82[81]:8)

Say among the nations, "The Lord reigns!
Yea, the world is established, it shall never be moved;
he will judge the peoples with equity." (Ps. 96[95]:10)

O sing to the Lord a new song,
for he has done marvelous things!
His right hand and his holy arm
have gotten him victory [or *salvation*]. (Ps. 98[97]:1)

He has remembered his steadfast love and faithfulness
to the house of Israel.
All the ends of the earth have seen
the victory of our God. (Ps. 98[97]:3)

Yet God my King is from of old,
working salvation in the midst of the earth. (Ps. 74[73]:12)

The Lord reigns; let the peoples tremble!
He sits enthroned upon the cherubim;
let the earth quake!
The Lord is great in Zion;
he is exalted over all the peoples.
Let them praise thy great and terrible name!
Holy is he!
Mighty King, lover of justice,
thou hast established equity;
thou hast executed justice
and righteousness in Jacob.
Extol the Lord our God;
worship at his footstool!
Holy is he! (Ps. 99[100]:1–5)

I will sing of loyalty and of justice;
to thee, O Lord, I will sing. (Ps. 101[100]:1)

But thou, O Lord, art enthroned for ever;
thy name endures to all generations. . . .
The nations will fear the name of the Lord,

and all the kings of the earth thy glory.
For the Lord will build up Zion,
he will appear in his glory. (Ps. 102[101]:12, 15–16)

The people of Israel want to have a king; they want to be like other people.
God originally says to them, "I *am* your King. You are *not* like other people.
Other people may have kings or princes or rulers and judges, but *I* am your
King, *I* am your ruler, I am your shepherd, I am your governor." These terms,
shepherd and *pastor*, in the Old Testament, are synonymous with *king*.

Samuel judges Israel all the days of his life, but when Samuel becomes old
and makes his sons to be judges over Israel, the people object:

> Then all the elders of Israel gathered together and came to Samuel at
> Ramah, and said to him, "Behold, you are old and your sons do not
> walk in your ways; now appoint for us a king to govern us like all the
> nations." But the thing displeased Samuel when they said, "Give us a
> king to govern us." And Samuel prayed to the Lord. And the Lord said
> to Samuel, "Hearken to the voice of the people in all that they say to
> you; for they have not rejected you, but they have rejected me from
> being king over them. According to all the deeds which they have done
> to me, from the day I brought them up out of Egypt even to this day,
> forsaking me and serving other gods, so they are also doing to you."
> (1 Sam. 8:4–8)

God relents to the desires of the people and has Samuel anoint Saul as the first
king of Israel. Saul does not do well; he is depressed and difficult. Ultimately,
it is David who emerges as the paradigmatic king, and it is of David's seed
that the ultimate Anointed One of God will come, the one whose Kingdom
will have no end.

Throughout all the Books of Kings (1 and 2 Samuel included), there
are hardly any kings who are totally faithful to God. They were following
their own minds, worshiping idols, doing all kinds of horrible things. Even
David sins. Yet, though David may have done wickedness, adultery, murder,
he does not apostatize. After him, Solomon not only had many wives and
concubines and riches, but he was not faithful to God even in worship. Still,
he was chosen. Through David, Solomon, and their descendants would come
the Christ, who really is the King.

Psalm 89(88):3–4 says,

> Thou hast said, "I have made a covenant with my chosen one,
> I have sworn to David my servant:
> 'I will establish your descendants for ever,
> and build your throne for all generations.'"

These are two great promises of the Old Covenant: God promises Abraham that in his *seed*—and St. Paul insists in Galatians that should be singular: in *one* of Abraham's descendants—*all* the nations will be blessed. Then there is the promise to David about his descendants: "One of the sons of your body / I will set on your throne" (Ps. 132[131]:11).

In the New Testament, there is the following:

> Now when Jesus was born in Bethlehem of Judea in the days of Herod
> the king, behold, wise men from the East came to Jerusalem, saying,
> "Where is he who has been born king of the Jews? For we have seen his
> star in the East, and have come to worship him." (Matt. 2:1–2)

This is exactly the charge made against Jesus when He is crucified and nailed to the Cross as King of the Jews.

The English writer Dorothy L. Sayers wrote a play about Jesus called *Born to be King*. In it, she makes the point that Jesus *is* the King—not only the King of the Jews, but the King of Glory, whose throne is established in the heavens. *He* is the Lord who reigns. *He* is the one who arises and judges the earth. *He* is the one to whom God says, "Sit at my right hand, / till I make your enemies your footstool" (Ps. 110[109]:1). All this applies to Jesus.

As Dorothy Sayers says, Jesus of Nazareth is the only one who was born in order to die, and He enters His glory and His kingship *by suffering*, by dying. This is presented already in the first chapters of Matthew, because immediately after His birth, Herod tries to kill Him.

The four Gospels end with the Passion of Christ. He is executed in the most vile, degrading way a human being—and particularly a Jew—can possibly die: outside the walls of Jerusalem, at the hands of Gentiles, among thieves, rejected by His own people, abandoned by everyone. This is what the King does: He gives His life for His people, and *all* human beings are His people.

We see the same theme in the infancy narrative of Luke. Luke does not use the term *king*, but he does make an exact reference to Old Testament prophecy, where the angel says to Mary:

> "Do not be afraid, Mary, for you have found favor with God. And behold, you will conceive in your womb and bear a son, and you shall call his name Jesus. He will be great, and will be called the Son of the Most High; and the Lord God will give to him the throne of his father David, and he will reign over the house of Jacob for ever; and of his kingdom there will be no end." (1:30–33)

One of the thieves who is crucified with Jesus says to Him, "Lord, remember me when You come into Your Kingdom" (Luke 23:42, NKJV). That can also be translated, "Remember me when You come into Your king*ship*," into Your reign.

The gospel is the gospel of the Kingdom of God. This theme is presented from the very beginning of all four Gospels. John the Baptist says, "Repent, for the kingdom of heaven is at hand" (Matt. 3:2), and then he announces the coming of Jesus. When *Jesus* begins preaching, He says the same words as John: "*Metanoite* [change your mind; change your way of seeing reality], for the kingdom of heaven is at hand," the Kingdom is coming (Matt. 4:17).

Jesus' first teachings are all about the Kingdom. His first parables are the parables of the Kingdom: the Kingdom of heaven is like this, the Kingdom of heaven is like that. Jesus came forth in order to announce the Kingdom of God, the Kingship of God. He says things like, "Truly, I say to you, whoever does not receive the kingdom of God like a child shall not enter it" (Mark 10:15). When Matthew writes about the Last Judgment, Christ is enthroned and all the peoples of the world gather in front of Him like subjects before the throne of their king (Matt. 25:32).

In the Passion narratives, the theme of kingship becomes very specific. At the Last Supper before the Passion, Jesus speaks about not eating and drinking again with His disciples until they eat and drink again in the Kingdom of God, when the Kingdom comes (see Matt. 26:29). Jesus is put to death for claiming to be the King. They mock him as a king, putting a crown of thorns on His head and clothing Him in a purple cloak. They put a reed into His hand, to mockingly symbolize a scepter. They ridicule and shame Him, saying He is claiming to be a king, claiming even to be God's Son.

When they are asking Him questions, He says to them, "Let Me ask *you* a question: When the Messiah comes, whose Son is He going to be?" They say, "David's," because they know He has to be the Son of David; He has to be the King from David's line. Then Jesus says, "Why, then, does David call Him 'Lord,' when he says, 'The Lord said to my Lord, "Sit at My right hand until I put all the enemies beneath Your feet"'?" He sits on the throne of God Himself. This is considered blasphemous, that He would relate this verse to Himself (see Matt. 22:41–46).

In Matthew, Mark, and Luke, what actually causes the high priest to go totally wild and say, "This Man has to die," is when Jesus refers to a verse in the Book of Daniel about the Son of Man coming on the clouds with all the angels in the whole power and glory of God Himself (see Dan. 7:13; Matt. 26:64; Mark 14:62; Luke 22:69). That is the language of reigning, and that is what gets Him crucified.

In John, which is the theological Gospel, Jesus' Crucifixion is symbolically presented like enthronement. In John, Jesus is "lifted up" (3:14; 8:28; 12:32). The lifting up on the Cross is connected to the lifting up and being enthroned at the right hand, in power in heaven. The psalm, "Extol the Lord our God; / worship at his footstool! / Holy is he!" (99[98]:5)—or *it*, meaning the footstool is holy—is applied to the Cross of Christ. When Jesus is nailed to the Cross, this is the sign of His *glory*.

When the Passion begins in John, Jesus says:

> "Now is my soul troubled. And what shall I say? 'Father, save me from this hour'? No, for this purpose I have come to this hour. Father, glorify thy name." Then a voice came from heaven, "I have glorified it, and I will glorify it again."
>
> The crowd standing by heard it and said that it had thundered. Others said, "An angel has spoken to him."
>
> Jesus answered, "This voice has come for your sake, not for mine. Now is the judgment of this world, now shall the ruler of this world be cast out; and I, when I am lifted up from the earth, will draw all men to myself." He said this to show by what death he was to die. (12:27–32)

For this reason, on the crucifixes in Orthodox churches the title "King of the Jews" is not written, but instead "The King of Glory."

In John, Pontius Pilate brings Jesus out and sets Him on the judgment seat.

> He said to the Jews, "Behold your King!" They cried out, "Away with him, away with him, crucify him!" Pilate said to them, "Shall I crucify your King?" The chief priests answered, "We have no king but Caesar." Then he handed him over to them to be crucified.
>
> So they took Jesus, and he went out, bearing his own cross, to the place called the place of a skull, which is called in Hebrew Golgotha. There they crucified him, and with him two others, one on either side, and Jesus between them. Pilate also wrote a title and put it on the cross; it read, "Jesus of Nazareth, the King of the Jews." Many of the Jews read this title, for the place where Jesus was crucified was near the city; and it was written in Hebrew, in Latin, and in Greek. The chief priests of the Jews then said to Pilate, "Do not write, 'The King of the Jews,' but, 'This man said, I am King of the Jews.'" Pilate answered, "What I have written I have written." (John 19:14–22)

So He is killed as King. This is fitting and proper, because the king must do two things. He must be ready to sacrifice himself unto death for his people. Jesus does that. Also—and this is the whole point of the king—he must destroy the people's enemies.

In the New Covenant, the enemies of God are not the nations; they are not people. The enemies of God are sin, not the sinners. The King gives His life for the sinners. The enemies that Christ as the King has to destroy are sin, disease, injustice, impurity, and evil. As the Apostle Paul says, "The last enemy to be destroyed is death" (1 Cor. 15:26). The King has to die, because that is how He is victorious. This is the gospel.

The king destroys the enemies, and destroys them by dying, as in the words of the Paschal troparion: "Christ is risen from the dead, trampling down death by death, and upon those in the tombs bestowing life." This theme is also expressed in the Paschal psalm, "Let God arise; let His enemies be scattered. Let those who hate Him flee from before His face. As smoke vanishes, so let them vanish, as wax melts before the fire" (Ps. 68[67]:1–2). He rises from the dead. As the prokeimenon for Holy Saturday says, "Arise, O Lord, and judge the earth" (Psalm 82[81]:8). Arise, O Lord, and be enthroned at the right hand of the Father. Arise, O Lord, and reign over all creation.

On Palm Sunday, Jesus enters Jerusalem before the Passion as a King, fulfilling the prophecy:

> Lo, your king comes to you;
> triumphant and victorious is he,
> humble and riding on an ass,
> on a colt the foal of an ass. (Zech. 9:9)

John 12:16 says that only after He was raised and glorified did the disciples remember that prophecy about Jesus. The prophecy was fulfilled in Jerusalem, the city of the great King David.

In Revelation, Jesus Christ is seated on the throne with God. God is called "Him who sits on the throne," but it always says, "Him who sits on the throne *and the Lamb*," Jesus Christ (Rev. 5:13).

> "They will make war on the Lamb, and the Lamb will conquer them, for he is Lord of lords and King of kings, and those with him are called and chosen and faithful." (Rev. 17:14)

All the kings of the earth will have to bow down and worship the King of kings and the Lord of lords. This is both He who sits on the throne and the Lamb: "The kingdom of the world has become the kingdom of our Lord and of his Christ, and he shall reign for ever and ever!" (Rev. 11:15). Again,

> "Worthy is the Lamb who was slain,
> to receive power and wealth and wisdom
> and might and honor and glory and blessing!" (Rev. 5:12)

Those words sound very much like the Book of Daniel, where the Son of Man is enthroned together with the Ancient of Days (see Dan. 7:9–14).

Jesus of Nazareth *is* the King, the Son of David who sits upon the throne forever, but that King is the Son of God who has become human in order to die for His subjects, to be raised and glorified, and to sit together on His throne with His Father, as He did from before the foundation of the world.

This is the Christian worldview. God's Son, the Lord, the Christ, has to be the King, and the King has to be the Savior. These various names and titles express the same reality. *God* is our King before the ages. *He* has established salvation in the midst of the earth. But He *makes* the salvation in the Person of His Son, who has become Mary's child, Jesus of Nazareth, and *He* is the King.

As St. Athanasius said in his letters to Serapion, "You have the Lord God who reigns; the *Basilevs*, the King of God's Kingdom is Christ; and the Kingship itself is the power of the Holy Spirit." The King, personally, of the Kingdom of God is Jesus of Nazareth, and the power of His Kingship is the very Spirit of God, who is the power of truth, the power of life, the power of beauty, and the power of God Himself.

At the beginning of the Divine Liturgy, the priest says, "Blessed is the Kingdom of the Father and of the Son and of the Holy Spirit." It is the *Son* of God, Jesus, who is personally our King.

CHAPTER 19

Jesus the

GOOD SHEPHERD

Synonymous with *vasilevs,* or "king," is the Biblical term *poimen,* "shepherd." In the Bible, the kings of Israel are called the shepherds of Israel.

In the same way that God alone is the King, according to Scripture, God alone is the Shepherd.

> Give ear, O Shepherd of Israel,
> thou who leadest Joseph like a flock!
> Thou who art enthroned upon the cherubim, shine forth! . . .
> Stir up thy might,
> and come to save us! (Ps. 80[79]:1–2)

Psalm 79(78):13 says, "Then we thy people, the flock of thy pasture, / will give thanks to thee for ever; / from generation to generation we will recount thy praise." The people identify themselves as the flock of God, and God shepherds them.

Psalm 23(22):1 says, "The Lord is my shepherd." The Greek of the Septuagint, however, does not say, "The Lord is my shepherd." It says, "The Lord *shepherds.*" The Lord does the act of shepherding.

The same thing happens with *shepherd* as with *king.* God is the King, but there are human beings who are appointed to be kings, and they are supposed to reign and rule according to God, who is *the* King. Most often in the Scripture, human kings fail to do this. When the Old Testament speaks about the shepherds, it is speaking about the kings. The kings are supposed to be shepherding the flock, but they do not. They abuse, abandon, and betray the flock. They are false shepherds, false kings. Jeremiah 23:1–5 says:

> "Woe to the shepherds who destroy and scatter the sheep of my pasture!" says the Lord. Therefore thus says the Lord, the God of Israel, concerning the shepherds who care for my people: "You have scattered my flock, and have driven them away, and you have not attended to them. Behold, I will attend to you for your evil doings, says the Lord. Then I will gather the remnant of my flock out of all the countries where I have driven them, and I will bring them back to their fold, and they shall be fruitful and multiply. I will set shepherds over them who will care for them, and they shall fear no more, nor be dismayed, neither shall any be missing, says the Lord.
> "Behold, the days are coming, says the Lord, when I will raise up for David a righteous Branch, and he shall reign as king and deal wisely, and shall execute justice and righteousness in the land."

Ezekiel says exactly the same thing (see Ezek. 37:22, 24). God says not only that He is against the shepherds, but that He Himself is going to rescue the sheep *from* the shepherds. He is going to care for the sheep *against* the shepherds.

It is not for nothing that David was a shepherd-boy and then became the shepherd of all God's people. He came from Bethlehem and built Jerusalem, the City of Peace. Jerusalem has great symbolic resonance for the Christian faith. Jesus brings us to the New Jerusalem, the heavenly Jerusalem, not a Jerusalem on the map.

The prophecy of Micah says,

> But you, O Bethlehem Ephrathah,
> who are little to be among the clans of Judah,
> from you shall come forth for me
> one who is to be ruler [*hegoumenos*] in Israel. (Mic. 5:2)

All this is fulfilled in Jesus. He says:

> "Truly, truly, I say to you, he who does not enter the sheepfold by the door but climbs in by another way, that man is a thief and a robber; but he who enters by the door is the shepherd of the sheep." (John 10:1–2)

That expression—"Most assuredly, I say to you," or in the King James Version, "Verily, verily," or in other languages, "Amen, amen"—is a peculiarity of the teaching of Jesus in the New Testament. He says *amen* twice to emphasize that this is not negotiable, and whether one agrees or not is beside the point.

The gate is the door of the pen where the sheep are kept. Only the shepherd enters by the door, and the gatekeeper opens to the shepherd. "To him the gatekeeper opens; the sheep hear his voice, and he calls his own sheep by name and leads them out. When he has brought out all his own, he goes before them, and the sheep follow him, for they know his voice" (John 10:3–4). There is a profoundly intimate relationship between the shepherd and his sheep. The sheep know the shepherd's voice, and they won't follow the voice of a stranger.

The shepherd knows the sheep *by name*. This is very important, because in the Bible, when the name of something is known, so is its reality. The one who knows the name of something has a kind of control over it. That is why, when Moses asks God His name, God will not tell him (see Ex. 3:13–14). That is why we say in the Lord's Prayer, "Hallowed be Your *name*" (Matt. 6:9). That is why the Ten Commandments say, "You shall not take the name of the Lord your God in vain" (Ex. 20:7). We pray in the name of the Lord. When He says He knows the sheep *by name*, it means He knows who they are. He knows each one, in his or her uniqueness.

The shepherd brings out *his own*. They are his. They belong to him. If Jesus Christ is our Pastor, our Shepherd (which is the same word), then we belong to Him. We do not belong to ourselves. Christopher Hitchens and Richard Dawkins ridicule that; they say, "What kind of a religion is Christianity, where the people are called 'sheep,' where they follow another?" They consider that demeaning, but we do not. If we are creatures, we have a Creator. We are servants. We identify ourselves that way. We are proud of it. We have a Shepherd whose voice we know, who knows our names. He knows each one of us, and we, as individuals, have to know Him. We have to know His voice; we have to hear His voice.

Jesus says in the Gospel of John that the reason some people do not recognize Him is that they do not belong to Him. They belong to the devil. They are themselves their own rulers. If we are not ready to have God as our

Lord and Ruler and Shepherd, we will never know His voice. We will not follow Him. Instead, we will reject Him, ridicule Him, and crucify Him by our behavior.

"'A stranger they will not follow, but they will flee from him, for they do not know the voice of strangers.' This figure Jesus used with them, but they did not understand what he was saying to them" (John 10:5–6). This is a parable, and those who are not of God do not understand it. Those who are of God say, "Choose me, Lord. Let me be Yours," and they understand immediately what He is talking about.

The sheep *follow* the Shepherd. Where Jesus was speaking, in the Middle East, the shepherd has such an intimate relationship with his flock that they voluntarily follow after him. That is very important, because if we are going to identify ourselves as sheep with Jesus as our Shepherd, then we must follow Him voluntarily. Only the stubborn sheep run away. Then, of course, the shepherd goes after them. He goes after even the one that goes astray. He lifts him up, puts him on his shoulders, and brings him back (see Luke 15:4–7). But the obedient sheep do not follow out of constraint. They follow freely.

Once I heard a speaker say that, in the Middle East, shepherds will often ride donkeys, ringing a little bell and singing, and the sheep will follow obediently and in an orderly manner after the shepherd. The shepherd may have a crook, a staff, with which he can pull back one of the sheep who is straying, but he does not use that staff to hurt them. He uses it to protect them against wolves and other dangers. There is no compulsion, no beating. He does not push them into the pen; they follow him freely.

While this man was making this point, a person in the audience raised a hand and said, "Hey, wait a minute! I was once in that part of the world and I saw a man forcing the sheep into the pen, beating them in. What you're saying isn't true!"

The speaker said, "What you saw wasn't a shepherd. It was the butcher."

I will never forget that. The butcher beats the sheep into the pen and then butchers them. The shepherd does not butcher or beat them. He calls them by name, and they follow him freely. They are happy to be members of his flock.

The people Jesus spoke to did not understand all of this. "Then Jesus said to them again, "Truly, Truly [in other words, this is not negotiable], I say to you, I am the door of the sheep. All who came before me are thieves and robbers; but the sheep did not heed them" (John 10:7–8). In the Old Covenant, the shepherds were bad. They were not taking care of the flock, so the sheep did not follow them. The New Testament says shepherds of the flock must be shepherds the way Jesus is, not by compelling, not by tricking, not by exercising violence or force. The sheep should follow freely, voluntarily. The shepherding has to be done lovingly. Thieves and robbers do not behave that way.

Jesus continues:

> "I am the door; if any one enters by me, he will be saved, and will go in and out and find pasture. The thief comes only to steal and kill and destroy; I came that they may have life, and have it abundantly. I am the good shepherd. The good shepherd lays down his life for the sheep." (John 10:9–11)

True shepherds have to die for their flock, and Jesus does. The images Jesus uses for Himself are of one who is ready to die, who comes in order to die. Jesus continues:

> "He who is a hireling and not a shepherd, whose own the sheep are not, sees the wolf coming and leaves the sheep and flees; and the wolf snatches them and scatters them. He flees because he is a hireling and cares nothing for the sheep." (John 10:12–13)

In the Old Covenant, the kings and shepherds cared nothing for the sheep. Sad to say, this is also an accusation made against pastors of churches today. Pastors should ask themselves the question: "Am I a real shepherd? Am I ready to lay down my life for my sheep?"

Jesus says a second time, "I am the good shepherd; I know my own and my own know me" (John 10:14). Pastors need to know their parishioners. They have to know them *by name*. When St. Polycarp of Smyrna was going to be put to death for being a Christian bishop, he asked for one last wish, and they granted it to him. His last wish was that he could pray for his flock, and he prayed for every one of the members of his church *by name*. Jesus goes on:

"As the Father knows me and I know the Father; and I lay down my life for the sheep. And I have other sheep, that are not of this fold; I must bring them also, and they will heed my voice. So there shall be one flock, one shepherd." (John 10:15–16)

The usual interpretation of "other sheep" is the Gentiles—not just the people of Judah and Israel, but all the people of the earth, everyone who knows God's voice and wants to belong to God—they will belong to Jesus, and He will save them.

In Romans 10:20, the Apostle Paul quotes Isaiah 65:1, saying, "I have been found by those who did not seek me; / I have shown myself to those who did not ask for me." Jesus is the Shepherd of every human being, not just of Jews, but of everyone who ever lived and will yet live. The question remains whether *we* want to be members of His flock, or whether we are going to make fun of the imagery of being the sheep in the flock of Christ.

John 10 continues:

"For this reason the Father loves me, because I lay down my life, that I may take it again. No one takes it from me, but I lay it down of my own accord. I have power to lay it down, and I have power to take it again; this charge I have received from my Father."

There was again a division among the Jews because of these words. Many of them said, "He has a demon, and he is mad; why listen to him?" Others said, "These are not the sayings of one who has a demon. Can a demon open the eyes of the blind?"

It was the feast of the Dedication at Jerusalem; it was winter, and Jesus was walking in the temple, in the portico of Solomon. So the Jews gathered round him and said to him, "How long will you keep us in suspense? If you are the Christ, tell us plainly." Jesus answered them, "I told you, and you do not believe. The works that I do in my Father's name, they bear witness to me; but you do not believe, because you do not belong to my sheep. My sheep hear my voice, and I know them, and they follow me; and I give them eternal life, and they shall never perish, and no one shall snatch them out of my hand. My Father, who has given them to me, is greater than all, and no one is able to snatch them out of the Father's hand. I and the Father are one." (John 10:17–30)

Jesus also says that the Good Shepherd goes after the sheep that are straying, and that the angels in heaven rejoice more over one who is lost and brought back than over the whole flock (Luke 15:7).

After the Gospels, the imagery of the shepherd and the sheep continues. The last chapter of Hebrews says:

> Now may the God of peace who brought again from the dead our
> Lord Jesus, the great shepherd of the sheep, by the blood of the eternal
> covenant, equip you with everything good that you may do his will,
> working in you that which is pleasing in his sight, through Jesus Christ;
> to whom be glory for ever and ever. Amen. (Heb. 13:20–21)

Scripture says not only the "Good Shepherd," but the "great Shepherd." The expression "chief Shepherd" is also used, in the letters attributed to St. Peter. "For you were like sheep going astray, but have now returned to the Shepherd [*poimen*, "pastor"] and Overseer [*episcopos*, "bishop"] of your souls" (1 Pet. 2:25, NKJV). And later:

> So I exhort the elders among you, as a fellow elder and a witness of
> the sufferings of Christ as well as a partaker in the glory that is to be
> revealed. Tend the flock of God that is your charge, not by constraint
> but willingly, not for shameful gain but eagerly, not as domineering
> over those in your charge but being examples to the flock. And when
> the chief Shepherd is manifested you will obtain the unfading crown of
> glory. (1 Pet. 5:1–4)

Revelation 7 says the Lamb of God is on the throne, together "with Him who sits upon the throne," which is God the Father.

> After this I looked, and behold, a great multitude which no man could
> number, from every nation, from all tribes and peoples and tongues,
> standing before the throne and before the Lamb, clothed in white robes,
> with palm branches in their hands, and crying out with a loud voice,
> "Salvation belongs to our God who sits upon the throne, and to the
> Lamb!" (Rev. 7:9–10)

> "For the Lamb in the midst of the throne will be their shepherd,
> and he will guide them to springs of living water;
> and God will wipe away every tear from their eyes." (Rev. 7:17)

This is beautiful. The chief Shepherd becomes the Lamb, and the Lamb in the midst of the throne with God will be their Shepherd.

The Lord Jesus Christ, the King, is also the Shepherd, the great Shepherd, the chief Shepherd, the Good Shepherd, and He gives His life for the sheep. He knows the sheep; the sheep know Him. They follow Him voluntarily. He loves them. He knows their names. He protects them. He gives His life for them. Jesus of Nazareth, the Son of God, the Lord, the Christ, the King, the Teacher, the Prophet, the High Priest, is also the Good Shepherd.

CHAPTER 20

Jesus the

LAMB OF GOD

When Abraham is taking Isaac up to Mount Moriah, Isaac says, "Where is the lamb for a burnt offering?"

Abraham answers, "God will provide the lamb" (see Gen. 22:8). The Lamb that God provides is His own Son. God asks the father of faith, Abraham, to sacrifice his son, but then He does not allow him to do it; He sends His own Son as the Lamb to be sacrificed.

In the Passover story of Exodus 12, God leads the Israelites out of Egypt, freeing and delivering them. This is the prefiguration and the prototype of Pascha (Easter), the New Passover, the death and the Resurrection of Christ. The Apostle Paul writes:

> Do you not know that a little leaven leavens the whole lump? Cleanse
> out the old leaven that you may be a new lump, as you really are
> unleavened. For Christ, our paschal lamb, has been sacrificed. Let us,
> therefore, celebrate the festival, not with the old leaven, the leaven of
> malice and evil, but with the unleavened bread of sincerity and truth.
> (1 Cor. 5:6–8)

The Paschal lamb is Christ. It is His blood that saves us. When we are marked with His blood, as were the dwellings of the Israelites, the angel of death passes over. God delivers us, not from Egypt into the Promised Land, but, as we sing on Pascha, "from death to life, and from earth to heaven." When we sing the hymn, "O Pascha of beauty, the new Pascha, the Pascha of the Lord," that Pascha is Christ Himself.

The Passover Exodus was the center of the Old Testament faith. In the

Christian Church, the center of our faith is the New Pascha, the Pascha of Christ, which fulfills the Passover of the Jews. In the Gospel of John, the Passion of Christ takes place on the Jewish Passover, and it echoes all the *acts* of Passover, so that when the Passover lamb is being offered in the temple, Pilate is saying to the people, "Behold your King."

This imagery of a lamb is used throughout the Old Testament.

> He was oppressed, and he was afflicted,
> yet he opened not his mouth;
> like a lamb that is led to the slaughter,
> and like a sheep that before its shearers is dumb,
> so he opened not his mouth. (Is. 53:7)

At the Passion of Christ, Jesus remains silent. Pilate asks Him, "Won't You speak?" Jesus says, "I have told you everything. Why do you want Me to tell you more? I spoke openly in the temple. I didn't hide anything from anyone." Then, in the end, He remains silent. When Pilate asks, "What is truth?" Jesus remains silent (see John 18:19–24, 38).

When John the Baptist sees Jesus, he says, "Behold, the Lamb of God, who takes away the sin of the world!" (John 1:29). Sometimes this is translated, "who takes *upon Himself* the sin of the world." Then John's disciples leave John and follow the Lamb of God.

In the Orthodox tradition, the bread for the Holy Eucharist is called the Lamb. On this bread is a seal that says "ICXC NIKA," which is an abbreviation for *Iesous Christos Nika,* or "Jesus Christ, the Victor [or Conqueror]." The Book of Revelation refers to the victorious, conquering Christ as the Lamb of God. In the West, that bread is called the Host, which means "that which is offered in sacrifice."

In Acts 8, an angel sends Philip to the road going south from Jerusalem.

> Now when they had testified and spoken the word of the Lord, they returned to Jerusalem, preaching the gospel to many villages of the Samaritans.
>
> But an angel of the Lord said to Philip, "Rise and go toward the south to the road that goes down from Jerusalem to Gaza." This is a desert road. And he rose and went. And behold, an Ethiopian, a eunuch, a minister of the Candace, queen of the Ethiopians, in charge of all her

treasure, had come to Jerusalem to worship and was returning; seated in his chariot, he was reading the prophet Isaiah. And the Spirit said to Philip, "Go up and join this chariot." So Philip ran to him, and heard him reading Isaiah the prophet, and asked, "Do you understand what you are reading?" And he said, "How can I, unless some one guides me?" And he invited Philip to come up and sit with him. Now the passage of the scripture which he was reading was this:

"As a sheep led to the slaughter
or a lamb before its shearer is dumb,
so he opens not his mouth.
In his humiliation justice was denied him.
Who can describe his generation?
For his life is taken up from the earth."

And the eunuch said to Philip, "About whom, pray, does the prophet say this, about himself or about some one else?" Then Philip opened his mouth, and beginning with this scripture he told him the good news of Jesus. (Acts 8:27–35)

The Apostle Peter writes:

You know that you were ransomed from the futile ways inherited from your fathers, not with perishable things such as silver or gold, but with the precious blood of Christ, like that of a lamb without blemish or spot. He was destined before the foundation of the world but was made manifest at the end of the times for your sake. Through him you have confidence in God, who raised him from the dead and gave him glory, so that your faith and hope are in God. (1 Pet. 1:18–21)

Jesus is the Lamb without blemish or spot. The sacrificial lamb has to be innocent; it has to be pure. In the Old Testament, the prophets chastised the priests for offering afflicted animals. St. Gregory the Theologian even says it must be a *male* lamb, because a male lamb had to be offered as the Passover lamb.

In Revelation, the term *Lamb* is used almost thirty times.

And between the throne and the four living creatures and among the elders, I saw a Lamb standing, as though it had been slain, with seven horns and with seven eyes, which are the seven spirits of God sent out into all the earth; and he went and took the scroll from the right hand of

him who was seated on the throne. And when he had taken the scroll, the four living creatures and the twenty-four elders fell down before the Lamb, each holding a harp, and with golden bowls full of incense, which are the prayers of the saints; and they sang a new song, saying,
"Worthy art thou to take the scroll and to open its seals,
for thou wast slain and by thy blood didst ransom men for God
from every tribe and tongue and people and nation,
and hast made them a kingdom and priests to our God,
and they shall reign on earth." (Rev. 5:6–10)

The visionary sees a multitude of angels singing with a loud voice: "*Axion estin*: Worthy is the Lamb who was slain, to receive power and wealth and wisdom and might and honor and glory and blessing." And every creature on heaven and on earth and under the earth and in the sea was saying to Him who sits upon the throne *and* to the Lamb: "Blessing and honor and glory and might forever and ever." The four living creatures, who stand for the whole of the cosmic creation, say, "Amen." The presbyters, who stand for the Jews and the Gentiles—that is why there are twenty-four of them, twelve and twelve—fall down and worship (see Rev. 5:11–14).

Seven is the symbol of fullness, completion, and perfection. The Lamb's seven horns indicate full power. Seven eyes mean full knowledge. Seven spirits signify being full of life. The Lamb represents the total perfection God has sent to the earth. All the way through the Apocalypse, glory and honor and blessing and wisdom and power are given to Him who sits upon the throne—that is God—and to the Lamb, that is Jesus Christ.

Revelation 6 begins, "Now I saw when the Lamb opened one of the seven seals, and I heard one of the four living creatures say, as with a voice of thunder, 'Come!'"

Each of the seals is opened in succession until the sixth seal, where it says, "Then the kings of the earth and the great men and the generals and the rich and the strong, and every one, slave and free, hid in the caves and among the rocks of the mountains" (6:15). They call out from the mountains and the rocks, "Fall on us and hide us from the face of him who is seated on the throne, and from the wrath of the Lamb" (6:16).

Yet, just as there is the wrath of the Lamb, there is also the peace of the Lamb. The Lamb conquers only by goodness, love, truth, innocence, sinlessness, and purity. These, however, are experienced as wrath by sinners. They cannot endure it.

The seventh seal is the mystery of mysteries. If something is sealed seven times, there is no greater mystery than that. Before the seventh seal is opened, the visionary says the number of the seal was 144,000 (Rev. 7:4). This means the whole multitude of the saved: twelve times twelve thousand. This is not a literal number as in arithmetic, but a symbolic number.

> After this I looked, and behold, a great multitude which no man could number, from every nation, from all tribes and peoples and tongues, standing before the throne and before the Lamb, clothed in white robes, with palm branches in their hands, and crying out with a loud voice, "Salvation belongs to our God who sits upon the throne, and to the Lamb!" And all the angels stood round the throne and round the elders and the four living creatures, and they fell on their faces before the throne and worshiped God, saying, "Amen! Blessing and glory and wisdom and thanksgiving and honor and power and might be to our God for ever and ever! Amen."
>
> Then one of the elders addressed me, saying, "Who are these, clothed in white robes, and whence have they come?" I said to him, "Sir, you know." And he said to me, "These are they who have come out of the great tribulation; they have washed their robes and made them white in the blood of the Lamb." (Rev. 7:9–14)

The white robes symbolize their resurrected bodies. This is why, in church, the priests wear white robes underneath their vestments—and they should always be white, not red or gold or purple. The robes are washed white in the Blood of the Lamb.

> Then one of the elders addressed me, saying, "Who are these, clothed in white robes, and whence have they come?" I said to him, "Sir, you know." And he said to me, "These are they who have come out of the great tribulation; they have washed their robes and made them white in the blood of the Lamb.
>
> Therefore are they before the throne of God,
> and serve him day and night within his temple;
> and he who sits upon the throne will shelter them with his presence.

> They shall hunger no more, neither thirst any more;
> the sun shall not strike them, nor any scorching heat.
> For the Lamb in the midst of the throne will be their shepherd,
> and he will guide them to springs of living water;
> and God will wipe away every tear from their eyes [see Is. 49:10]."
> (Rev. 7:15–17)

The eighth chapter continues, "When the Lamb opened the seventh seal, there was silence in heaven for about half an hour" (Rev. 8:1). The ultimate mystery is totally silent.

In the twelfth chapter, all the evil people are overcome and conquered by the Blood of the Lamb and by the word of their testimony. It is the Lamb who conquers. Then in chapter 13:

> And all who dwell on earth will worship it, every one whose name has not been written before the foundation of the world in the book of life of the Lamb that was slain. If any one has an ear, let him hear. (Rev. 13:8–9)

The beast is worshiped by those whose names are not written in the Book of Life of the Lamb that was slain. The beast symbolizes Antichrist or antichrists. The word *antichrist* is not used in Revelation, but in 1 John 2:18; 2:22; 4:3; and 2 John 1:7, where John uses both the singular and the plural.

Revelation continues:

> Then I saw another beast which rose out of the earth; it had two horns like a lamb and it spoke like a dragon. (Rev. 13:11)

> Then I looked, and lo, on Mount Zion stood the Lamb, and with him a hundred and forty-four thousand who had his name and his Father's name written on their foreheads. (Rev. 14:1)

They sing a song before the throne. Then it says:

> It is these who have not defiled themselves with women, for they are chaste; it is these who follow the Lamb wherever he goes; these have been redeemed from mankind as first fruits for God and the Lamb, and in their mouth no lie was found, for they are spotless. (Rev. 14:4–5)

If anyone follows the beast and does evil, then the Lamb's presence causes torment to him. This is in Isaiah also, that when the Messiah appears, His glory and beauty will cause torment to those who are evil.

Revelation continues: "And they sing the song of Moses, the servant of God, and the song of the Lamb" (Rev. 15:3). Moses represents the Old Covenant, and the Lamb—Christ, the New Moses—represents the New. They sing:

> "Great and wonderful are thy deeds,
> O Lord God the Almighty!
> Just and true are thy ways,
> O King of the ages!
> Who shall not fear and glorify thy name, O Lord?
> For thou alone art holy.
> All nations shall come and worship thee,
> for thy judgments have been revealed." (Rev. 15:3–4)

Toward the end of the book, it says that all the wicked of the world will make war on the Lamb:

> "They will make war on the Lamb, and the Lamb will conquer them, for
> he is Lord of lords and King of kings, and those with him are called and
> chosen and faithful." (Rev. 17:14)

The end, in the Apocalypse, is called "the marriage supper of the Lamb" or even simply "the marriage of the Lamb."

> "Hallelujah! For the Lord our God the Almighty reigns.
> Let us rejoice and exult and give him the glory,
> for the marriage of the Lamb has come,
> and his Bride has made herself ready." . . .
> "Blessed are those who are invited to the marriage supper of the Lamb."
>   (Rev. 19:6–9)

The Church, the faithful, becomes the Bride of the Lamb. The New Jerusalem is the Bride of the Lamb. She comes down like a bride for her husband, who is the Lamb who was slain.

The Apocalypse ends by saying that He, the Lamb, conquers. He wipes away every tear. Those who are righteous reign with Him.

Then came one of the seven angels who had the seven bowls full of the seven last plagues, and spoke to me, saying, "Come, I will show you the Bride, the wife of the Lamb." And in the Spirit he carried me away to a great, high mountain, and showed me the holy city Jerusalem coming down out of heaven from God, having the glory of God, its radiance like a most rare jewel, like a jasper, clear as crystal. (Rev. 21:9–11)

Later the visionary says, "And I saw no temple in the city, for its temple is the Lord God the Almighty and the Lamb. And the city has no need of sun or moon to shine upon it, for the glory of God is its light, and its lamp is the Lamb" (Rev. 21:22–23). This is why Orthodox sing on Pascha: "Shine, shine, O New Jerusalem, for the glory of the Lord has arisen upon you!"

The water of life that flows through the city—the Holy Spirit—flows from the throne of God *and from the Lamb*. The Tree of Life in the city is watered and bears all fruit, and "There shall no more be anything accursed, but the throne of God and of the Lamb shall be in it, and his servants shall worship him" (Rev. 22:3).

They shall be in the New Jerusalem, which is the Bride of the Lamb, and they will be filled with light. It ends with the Lamb saying, "Surely I am coming soon," and the visionary praying, "Amen. Come, Lord Jesus!" (Rev. 22:20).

The Lord Jesus Christ is the Lamb of God the Father who sits upon the throne. He is glorified, and to Him is given honor, glory, dominion, majesty, power, and thanksgiving forever and ever. What is given to God who sits upon the throne also belongs to the Lamb.

This Son comes on earth to take the place of Isaac, to be the perfect Passover Lamb, to be the Lamb of God who does not open His mouth, to be the one who is sacrificed and dies.

By being the Lamb, He becomes the Shepherd. The Good Shepherd gives His life for the sheep by becoming a sheep. He saves His lambs by becoming the Lamb of God, taking their sins upon Himself in order to save them. Those who follow Him and who then conquer with Him have all the honor and glory and worship that belong to God Himself *and to the Lamb*.

To God and to the Lamb of God belong all power, dominion, and glory unto ages of ages. That victorious Lamb of God is our Lord Jesus Christ, who takes upon Himself the sin of the world, and who by doing so is glorified together with God His Father, receiving all the glory from the totality of creation. The Lamb of God was slain and is alive again, having been called from before the foundation of the world to redeem the world by His precious Blood. Jesus Christ is the Lamb of God.

CHAPTER 21

Jesus the

SERVANT OF THE LORD

Several times throughout the Scriptures, Jesus is called "the Servant of the Lord." In Biblical Greek, there are three words for *servant*. One is *doulos*, which means "a bonded slave." Philippians 2:7 says that, although Christ was in the form of God, He took on the form of a slave, *morphē doulou*.

Another word for *servant* in the Bible is *diakonos*, which means "someone who serves at tables." In Matthew 20:28, when Jesus says, "the Son of man came not to be served but to serve," the verb used is from *diakonia*.

The third biblical word for *servant* is *païs*, which can mean "a servant," but it can also mean "a child." When this term is used, the context is very important. Sometimes it is used interchangeably with the word meaning "son."

Jesus, of course, is the Son of God. That is a confession of faith about Him: "You are the Christ, the Son of the living God, the only-begotten Son, the firstborn Son." Also, the term for *son*, *huios*, cannot mean anything other than a biological or an adopted son.

The term *païs*, however, can mean "son"; it can also mean "child," or it can mean an "attendant" to a master. In the old movies set in the Middle Ages, the king would have his *boy*, who would serve him and take care of his horse and bring his clothes, akin to a valet. *Païs* has a softer connotation than *doulos*, which refers to someone who is bought and sold. It is more loving.

The hymns from the Book of Isaiah that are quoted in the New Testament referring to Jesus use the term *païs*.

In Acts, Peter and John go into the temple and are asked for alms by a crippled man. Instead of giving him money, they tell him, "In the name of Jesus Christ of Nazareth, walk" (Acts 3:6). The man is healed, and the people see him walking, praising God. They are astonished. Peter addresses the people, saying:

> "Men of Israel, why do you wonder at this, or why do you stare at us, as though by our own power or piety we had made him walk? The God of Abraham and of Isaac and of Jacob, the God of our fathers, glorified his servant [*païs*] Jesus, whom you delivered up and denied in the presence of Pilate, when he had decided to release him. But you denied the Holy and Righteous One, and asked for a murderer to be granted to you, and killed the Author of life, whom God raised from the dead. To this we are witnesses." (Acts 3:12–15)

Later he says, "God, having raised up his servant, sent him to you first, to bless you in turning every one of you from your wickedness" (Acts 3:26). *Païs* is used again here.

In Acts 4, Peter and John are again preaching. Now, David is called the *païs*, the child.

> "Sovereign Lord, who didst make the heaven and the earth and the sea and everything in them, who by the mouth of our father David, thy servant [*païs*], didst say by the Holy Spirit,
> 'Why did the Gentiles rage,
> and the peoples imagine vain things?
> The kings of the earth set themselves in array,
> and the rulers were gathered together,
> against the Lord and against his Anointed'—
> for truly in this city there were gathered together against thy holy servant [*païs*] Jesus, whom thou didst anoint, both Herod and Pontius Pilate, with the Gentiles and the peoples of Israel, to do whatever thy hand and thy plan had predestined to take place. And now, Lord, look upon their threats, and grant to thy servants [*douloi*] to speak thy word with all boldness, while thou stretchest out thy hand to heal, and signs and wonders are performed through the name of thy holy servant [*païs*] Jesus." (Acts 4:24–30)

Note the apostles call themselves *douloi* rather than *païs*. They do not call themselves by the same word they use for David and Jesus.

Four times in Acts, Jesus is referred to as the Servant of Yahweh. This comes from Isaiah, and the apostles quote it because they are speaking to Jews on the streets of Jerusalem. They are making the most central, shocking point that could possibly be made at that time in that place: that the Messiah everyone has been waiting for, the Son of God, the Messianic King, the great last Prophet, the Priest, is the Suffering Servant of Isaiah's prophecy. God the Father Almighty sends His only begotten Son, who is Light from Light and true God of true God, into this world to be His Servant.

Those songs in Isaiah are sometimes so startlingly clear that they are called the *protoevangelium*, the "first gospel," the first announcement that the Crucified One is the Lord and Christ, and that the Lord and Christ enters His glory by being afflicted.

Isaiah 41:8 says, "But you, Israel, my servant [*païs*], / Jacob, whom I have chosen." Israel is called "My *païs*," "My servant," "My child," "My boy." Jacob is called the chosen one, and Jesus is called "My Chosen" in the New Testament. Isaiah 41 continues:

> You whom I took from the ends of the earth,
> and called from its farthest corners,
> saying to you, "You are my servant [*païs*],
> I have chosen you and not cast you off";
> fear not, for I am with you,
> be not dismayed, for I am your God. (Is. 41:9–10)

Isaiah 42:1–4 says:

> "Behold my servant [*païs*], whom I uphold,
> my chosen, in whom my soul delights;
> I have put my Spirit upon him,
> he will bring forth justice to the nations.
> He will not cry or lift up his voice,
> or make it heard in the street;
> a bruised reed he will not break,
> and a dimly burning wick he will not quench;
> he will faithfully bring forth justice.
> He will not fail or be discouraged
> till he has established justice in the earth;
> and the coastlands wait for his law.

In Matthew 12, this is applied directly to Jesus (see Matt. 12:18–21). It says, "I have put My Spirit upon Him." That is the anointing and what makes Him the Christ. This Spirit is upon this *Païs*, according to Isaiah 42. He does not lift up His voice; He is very meek. He does not crush people; He comes to save people.

Isaiah continues:

> Thus says God, the Lord,
> who created the heavens and stretched them out,
> who spread forth the earth and what comes from it,
> who gives breath to the people upon it
> and spirit to those who walk in it:
> "I am the Lord, I have called you in righteousness,
> I have taken you by the hand and kept you;
> I have given you as a covenant to the people,
> a light to the nations,
> to open the eyes that are blind,
> to bring out the prisoners from the dungeon,
> from the prison those who sit in darkness." (Is. 42:5–7)

In Luke, Jesus reads these texts and applies them to Himself. In Luke 4, right at the beginning of His public ministry, Jesus goes into the synagogue on the Sabbath day, and they give him the Book of the Prophet Isaiah. He opens the book and reads from Isaiah 61:

> The Spirit of the Lord God is upon me,
> because the Lord has anointed me
> to bring good tidings to the afflicted;
> he has sent me to bind up the brokenhearted,
> to proclaim liberty to the captives,
> and the opening of the prison to those who are bound;
> to proclaim the year of the Lord's favor. (Is. 61:1–2)

Luke 4:20-21 says, "And he closed the book, and gave it back to the attendant, and sat down; and the eyes of all in the synagogue were fixed on him. And he began to say to them, 'Today this scripture has been fulfilled in your hearing.'"

So Jesus applies to Himself Isaiah's prophetic hymns about the Servant of God who is the light of the nations, who opens the eyes of the blind, who sets the prisoners free, who proclaims the acceptable year of the Lord, who preaches the gospel to the poor.

This line is applied in the *Magnificat* of Mary (Luke 1:46–55), which begins:

> "My soul magnifies the Lord,
> and my spirit rejoices in God my Savior,
> for he has regarded the low estate of his handmaiden."

The term for "handmaiden" in Greek is *doulē*, the word for a bonded slave, because Mary is a servant and mere human being. Lowliness is important when we think of the servant, because the *païs* is always humble, lowly, and meek. Jesus says, "Take my yoke upon you, and learn from me; for I am gentle and lowly in heart" (Matt. 11:29).

The *Magnificat* continues:

> "For behold, henceforth all generations will call me blessed;
> for he who is mighty has done great things for me,
> and holy is his name.
> And his mercy is on those who fear him
> from generation to generation.
> He has shown strength with his arm,
> he has scattered the proud in the imagination of their hearts,
> he has put down the mighty from their thrones,
> and exalted those of low degree;
> he has filled the hungry with good things,
> and the rich he has sent empty away.
> He has helped his servant Israel,
> in remembrance of his mercy,
> as he spoke to our fathers,
> to Abraham and to his posterity for ever."

The Greek text here quotes the first verse of the Song of the Servant in Isaiah 42:1, "Behold my servant, whom I uphold." The *Magnificat* says, "He has helped [or "upheld"] His servant Israel." Then Isaiah says, "my chosen, in whom my soul delights; / I have put my Spirit upon him." In Greek, where it says, "He has upheld His servant Israel," *païs* is used. Mary calls herself *doulē*, but Jesus is *païs*, because it is a quotation from Isaiah.

"In remembrance of his mercy, as he spoke to our fathers, to Abraham and to his posterity [or "seed"] forever." Jesus is the Seed. The Israel in the Magnificat, the servant, is, in fact, Jesus. When it says, "He upheld His servant Israel," it means He upheld Jesus. In that sense, Jesus *is* the whole of Israel. That is a clear New Testament teaching: The whole of Israel, all of the people of God, the chosen, the beloved, the holy, are brought to the conclusion of this *one Person*, Jesus of Nazareth, who is this Servant: "Behold my servant, whom I uphold, / my chosen, in whom my soul delights."

Jesus is the Suffering Servant of Isaiah 42, and as we have already seen, it is on Him that the Spirit is placed; it is He who brings forth righteousness from the nations; He who opens the eyes of the blind; He who brings the prisoners out of the dungeons; He who brings those in darkness into light; He who is not failing; He who is not discouraged; and He who does not cry out or lift up His voice. He does not break a bruised reed; He does not quench the dimly burning wick, as it says about Jesus in Matthew's Gospel.

This is the Lord, and this is the *new thing*. Isaiah says, "Behold, the former things have come to pass, / and new things I now declare" (Is. 42:9). We will sing a new song, and this new song will be about the Servant of God, who is Jesus of Nazareth.

In Isaiah 43, 44, 45, and 49, the same thing occurs again. Isaiah 43 says:

> "You are my witnesses," says the Lord,
> "and my servant whom I have chosen,
> that you may know and believe me
> and understand that I am He.
> Before me no god was formed,
> nor shall there be any after me.
> I, I am the Lord,
> and besides me there is no savior." (Is. 43:10–11)

Isaiah 44 says:

> "But now hear, O Jacob my servant,
> Israel whom I have chosen!

Thus says the Lord who made you,
who formed you from the womb and will help you:
Fear not, O Jacob my servant,
Jeshurun whom I have chosen.
For I will pour water on the thirsty land,
and streams on the dry ground;
I will pour my Spirit upon your descendants,
and my blessing on your offspring." (Is. 44:1–3)

It is really worth reading Isaiah 40—53, and even to the end of the book. These chapters in particular prophesy the Suffering Servant. Chapter 49 says:

And now the Lord says,
who formed me from the womb to be his servant,
to bring Jacob back to him,
and that Israel might be gathered to him,
"I will give you as a light to the nations,
that my salvation may reach to the end of the earth." (Is. 49:5–6)

The New Testament applies the Servant songs of Isaiah to Jesus of Nazareth, our Lord and Christ, who is the Servant of Yahweh, the Servant of the Lord. In the second sermon given in Christian history, and in the prayer the Apostles John and Peter make when they are delivered from prison, this is how He is addressed: as *the Servant of the Lord.*

Everyone who heard this knew what the Apostles were talking about. This afflicted, Crucified One, this one they heard about in Isaiah—this is the Son of God. This is the Savior, the Redeemer, the Reconciler, the one who heals our diseases. This is the Light to the Nations. This is the Anointed One upon whom the Spirit dwells.

Jesus is the Servant of the Lord. He is the Lord Himself who becomes the Servant, so that, through His servitude, we may reign with Him as kings and lords in God's Kingdom, and as sons of God.

CHAPTER 22

Jesus the

SUFFERING SERVANT

The last hymn about the Servant of the Lord in Isaiah 52—53 is important because it is so controversial. Why is it that the death of Jesus on the Cross saves us? How is it that, through this act, everything is made right and we are allowed, by faith in Christ crucified, to become ourselves the righteousness of God? We will never, perhaps, be able to explain it fully.

This text is often interpreted to mean that God Almighty is angry at the human race and that He has to punish them because of their sin, that the Law has been broken and the only way things can be restored and reconciled and redeemed is when a sufficient *punishment* is made. Therefore, many people think God is punishing His Son Jesus on the Cross, in our place.

I believe this is completely incorrect. There is another way of understanding this that has nothing to do with punishment. The very word *punishment* is never even found in the writings of the New Testament. I do not find it in the Holy Week services; I do not find it in the writing of the early Church Fathers. It is just not there.

In Romans, the Apostle Paul says we have to be righteous before God (see Rom. 2:13), but there is no one who is righteous. He says one Man's [Christ's] act of righteousness leads to our acquittal and life. By Jesus' act of righteousness before God, we are redeemed, reconciled, and given life (see Rom. 5:12–21). This is best summed up in 2 Corinthians: "For our sake he [God] made him [Jesus] to be sin who knew no sin, so that in him we might become the righteousness of God" (2 Cor. 5:21).

It does *not* say Jesus "became a sin offering," which sometimes people have added to the text. Jesus reveals the righteousness of God by actually being in the condition of sin, experiencing human sin, and being the *object* of the sins of the world.

In Hebrews, where Jesus' offering is compared to lambs and bulls, those lambs and bulls are not being punished for our sin. Their blood is a sign that we are offering our life to God, so that God's sacrificial action in us could avail to our salvation and healing. The blood of lambs and bulls cannot give us a new conscience before God. It cannot ultimately make things right.

Hebrews says that Jesus, in His self-offering and through His blood, makes things right eternally. God put Him in the position of sin, and so all that comes from sin—on the one hand the wrath of God, on the other hand death—comes onto Jesus when He is on the Cross. And this act is an act of perfect righteousness. According to Hebrews, this act of Jesus once and for all reconciles us to God. It frees us from our sin. It destroys death.

Christ, as a Man, is everything God wants from men, and God does not want our punishment. Christ being tortured is not what redeems us, but rather it is His righteousness that does. This perfect righteousness makes everything right. By faith in Jesus and by grace, we can become righteous.

This last Servant Song begins at Isaiah 52:13: "Behold, my servant shall prosper, / he shall be exalted and lifted up, / and shall be very high." This Servant of Yahweh will act prudently, will do the right thing. Therefore, He shall be exalted and lifted up. The Gospel of John speaks of Jesus being "lifted up," both on the Cross and into the heavens. In a sense, in the New Testament, those are the same thing. When Jesus is exalted upon the Cross, He enters into His glory, at the right hand of God the Father.

The Servant of Yahweh shall be over all things. In the New Testament, He is called the Most High. One of the names of God in the Old Testament was *El Shaddai*, which means "the Most High."

The passage continues:

> As many were astonished at him—
> his appearance was so marred, beyond human semblance,
> and his form beyond that of the sons of men—
> so shall he startle many [or "all"] nations;
> kings shall shut their mouths because of him;

for that which has not been told them they shall see,
and that which they have not heard they shall understand. (Is. 52:14–15)

Jesus said to His disciples, "many prophets and kings desired to see what you see, and did not see it, and to hear what you hear, and did not hear it" (Luke 10:24). They were hearing and seeing the great mystery of God revealed in front of their very eyes. The gospel of Jesus shocks everybody. It was not the generally accepted idea about how God would act through His Messiah, that He would be a Suffering Servant marred beyond human form.

Isaiah prophesies, "Who has believed what we have heard? / And to whom has the arm of the Lord been revealed?" (Is. 53:1). These words are quoted in John, when Jesus is speaking about being lifted up from the earth and all looking upon Him whom they have pierced (see John 12:38–41). Jesus continues, saying God Himself is blinding the eyes and shutting the ears that people would not understand. Yet God only hardens the hearts of people who do not open their hearts to Him. Then the presence of God is experienced as wrath and not as mercy. The wrath of God is a sign of His love for us, but when we resist that love, it is experienced as wrath.

Isaiah continues:

> For he grew up before him like a young plant,
> and like a root out of dry ground;
> he had no form or comeliness that we should look at him,
> and no beauty that we should desire him.
> He was despised and rejected by men;
> a man of sorrows, and acquainted with grief;
> and as one from whom men hide their faces
> he was despised, and we esteemed him not. (vv. 2–3)

Nobody sees anything great in Him. In the RSV annotated version, it says *rejected* could also be translated *forsaken*, which makes us think of Jesus' words from the Cross: "My God, my God, why hast thou forsaken me?" (Matt. 27:46). *Sorrows* can be translated *pains*, and *grief* as *sickness*, so the verses could be read, "He was despised and forsaken by men, a Man of pains, and acquainted with sickness."

Isaiah continues:

Surely he has borne our griefs
and carried our sorrows;
yet we esteemed him stricken,
smitten by God, and afflicted. (Is. 53:4)

He carries our sorrows, our sicknesses, our pains. He is smitten by God; He is afflicted, and that is how we see Him. The description is so vivid one would think Isaiah was looking at the Cross of Christ and describing it. In John, Jesus says, "Your father Abraham rejoiced that he was to see my day; he saw it and was glad" (John 8:56). He rejoices because Jesus is raised and glorified, and God reconciles the world through His bearing our griefs and carrying our sorrows—not only the sorrows we ourselves bear, but those that are put upon Him by us.

Isaiah continues:

But he was wounded for our transgressions,
he was bruised for our iniquities;
upon him was the chastisement that made us whole,
and with his stripes we are healed. (Is. 53:5)

Here the preposition *for* is crucial. In the Septuagint, it is *dia*: "for" or "by." We might say, "He was wounded *due to* our transgressions, and bruised *due to* our iniquities." Chastisement does not necessarily mean punishment. Chastening is a way of cleansing, of healing, and even of instructing. Scripture tells us that God chastens those whom He loves (see Prov. 3:12; Heb. 12:6).

There is no retributive justice here. We suffer because we sin. Jesus takes this on Himself. He bears the griefs, carries the sorrows, is smitten and afflicted by God, and is wounded. All of this is because of our transgressions.

We are the ones who do it, not only to ourselves and to each other, but we do it to *Him*. The human race is nothing but sorrow, affliction, grief, pain, and ultimately corpses. As the old Latin saying goes, "Man is a wolf to man." We are destructive; we consume one another; we all die together in pits like beasts. Even in the best societies, there is extortion, greed, lying, stealing, perversion, oppression of the poor, inequality, and injustice. And we suffer because of them.

Isaiah says that God's Servant bears all these things for us, because of us. He enters into all of our world, for us and for our salvation. It is not that God is torturing Him or punishing Him; rather, He enters into the torturing and the punishment that we inflict upon each other and upon ourselves.

Hebrews says, "if we sin deliberately after receiving the knowledge of the truth," that is, after baptism, after chrismation, after receiving Holy Communion, "there no longer remains a sacrifice for sins" because we have rejected the very means of redemption and reconciliation God has given us (Heb. 10:26). That is why Hebrews 6 says those who apostatize or fall away crucify the Lord again. We sinners cause the suffering of the Suffering Servant of the Lord, described by Isaiah in this prophecy. His suffering is because of us and for us.

We believe the Incarnation and suffering of Jesus Christ was the only way we could be made whole, which in Greek means being saved. There is no other way than by God's Servant becoming a Man and suffering death.

Isaiah continues:

> All we like sheep have gone astray;
> we have turned every one to his own way;
> and the Lord has laid on him
> the iniquity of us all. (Is. 53:6)

He has put Him in the situation in which we now find ourselves because of our iniquity. The Lord sent Him into the world so that He could become it, experience it, and therefore reconcile it to God by this way. F. D. Morris said in *The Doctrine of Sacrifice*, "There is no righteousness without sacrifice." Any righteous human being is righteous because he loves and gives his life to the other. God Himself is righteous because He sacrifices Himself for us. The great proof of the righteousness and the love of God is that He comes and sacrifices His own Son.

The former TV personality Phil Donahue was a Roman Catholic, but he lost his faith and wrote a horrible book, *Donahue*, wherein he said, "Christianity is stupid. If God is such a great, loving God, why didn't He come and suffer Himself? Why does He send His Son?"

St. Athanasius would answer: Because all things are made through His

Son. The Creator of all has to be the Redeemer of all; and if God creates through His Son, He has to redeem through His Son. St. Athanasius also said that, in some sense, it is more shocking that God would sacrifice His Son. Any father would rather die himself than sacrifice his son. It is part of the startling character of Christianity that the Son of God, who is the Servant of Yahweh, bears the iniquities of us all.

Isaiah continues:

> He was oppressed, and he was afflicted,
> yet he opened not his mouth;
> like a lamb that is led to the slaughter,
> and like a sheep that before its shearers is dumb,
> so he opened not his mouth. (v. 7)

Before Pilate and the high priests, Jesus remains silent. He has said everything He had to say. His silence is more eloquent than words at this point. In simplicity and innocence, He offers Himself in total silence.

Isaiah continues,

> He was taken from prison and from judgment,
> And who will declare His generation?
> For He was cut off from the land of the living;
> For the transgressions of My people He was stricken. (v. 8, NKJV)

Jesus was put in prison, and He was brought out of prison. The line "Who will declare His generation?" makes one think of Melchizedek, and of Jesus' countrymen saying, "when the Christ appears, no one will know where he comes from" (John 7:27). One could say He comes from Bethlehem or Nazareth, but it is God who begot Him. "Cut off from the land of the living" is a biblical expression that means He is dead.

> And they made his grave with the wicked
> and with a rich man in his death,
> although he had done no violence,
> and there was no deceit in his mouth. (v. 9)

Usually, this is interpreted as referring to His Crucifixion between the two thieves and His execution as an evildoer. The Jewish religious leaders said

He was a blasphemer of God, an offender against the Law, a destroyer of the temple, and a deceiver of the people. They even said He was a Samaritan and had a devil, that He did miracles and healings by Beelzebul.

"With a rich man in his death" is usually interpreted to refer to Joseph of Arimathea's tomb, because Joseph was very rich. "He had done no violence, and there was no deceit in his mouth": He was perfectly innocent. He harmed no one and deceived no one.

> Yet it was the will of the Lord to bruise him;
> he has put him to grief;
> when he makes himself an offering for sin. (v. 10)

He gives His life as a sin-offering. Those who crucify Him think they are doing it to Him, but He is doing it Himself, because otherwise He could not save the world. Then Isaiah says:

> He shall see his offspring, he shall prolong his days;
> the will of the Lord shall prosper in his hand;
> he shall see the fruit of the travail of his soul and be satisfied;
> by his knowledge shall the righteous one, my servant,
> make many to be accounted righteous;
> and he shall bear their iniquities. (vv. 10–11)

The Lord will prosper Him, and the Lord will see the fruit of all this. Christ will see it. The whole world will see it. The kings will shut their mouths because they are all going to see it: that this Suffering Servant of the Lord is exalted on high and saves the multitude, all the nations who come to Him.

Isaiah concludes:

> Therefore I will divide him a portion with the great,
> and he shall divide the spoil with the strong;
> because he poured out his soul to death,
> and was numbered with the transgressors;
> yet he bore the sin of many,
> and made intercession for the transgressors. (v. 12)

"He was numbered with the transgressors": this means *us*. We are all transgressors, and He became one of us. He bore the sins of the multitude, of all of us, and He lives to make intercession for the transgressors. St. Paul says, "For there is one God, and there is one mediator between God and men, the man Christ Jesus" (1 Tim. 2:5).

St. John says that if we say we have no sin, we are liars and we make God a liar (1 John 1:8–10). There is no one who is righteous. Only Yahweh's Servant, Jesus Christ, is the Righteous One. It is by *His* righteousness that we are redeemed, saved, made whole, liberated, sanctified, glorified, and made alive forever.

The debt we owe God is our righteousness. We must be righteous, but we are not. The Servant of Yahweh is righteous, and that is why His suffering and His death saves us.

Jesus, the Servant of God, was stricken for us, bearing our sin. He suffered because we torture Him ourselves. Every time we sin, we put Him on the Cross. The Savior of the world is the Servant, the boy, the child, of the God of Abraham, Isaac, and Jacob. He is God's Son, the Suffering Servant, the Lord Jesus Christ Himself, our Savior and our Redeemer.

CHAPTER 23

Jesus the

RIGHTEOUS ONE

In his last chapter on the Suffering Servant, Isaiah also calls Jesus the Righteous One. "By his knowledge shall the righteous one, my servant, / make many to be accounted righteous; / and he shall bear their iniquities" (Is. 53:11).

First John also calls Jesus the Righteous One:

> My little children, I am writing this to you so that you may not sin; but if any one does sin, we have an advocate with the Father, Jesus Christ the righteous; and he is the expiation for our sins, and not for ours only but also for the sins of the whole world. And by this we may be sure that we know him, if we keep his commandments. (1 John 2:1–3)

If we look up *righteousness* or *righteous* or *the right* in a concordance, we will see how very many times it is used in the Bible. In the original languages, it is used even more, because sometimes the words for *righteous* and *righteousness, dikaios* and *dikaiosynē,* are translated "upright," "just," and "justice." Instead of being called the Righteous One, Jesus is sometimes called the Just One. *Justification* is the verb for "being made righteous," and the whole of Pauline theology, especially in Romans 4 and 5, is about how human beings are made righteous and share in the righteousness of God, by grace through faith.

God Almighty Himself is called the Righteous One, so to call Jesus "the Righteous" is to use the same term as the term for God. Similarly, Jesus is called the Holy One, and God alone is holy. Righteousness and holiness belong to Jesus by nature. *We* become righteous and holy through Jesus Christ by the *grace* of God, but Jesus has the very righteousness of God Himself, by *nature*.

In Scripture, there is some ambiguity about righteousness because, on the one hand, "there is no one who is righteous, no, not one" (see Ps. 14[13]:3); God alone is righteous. Nevertheless, on the other hand, Scripture does speak about the holy ones and about the righteous. Jesus said, "I have not come to call the righteous, but sinners to repentance" (Luke 5:32). Luke 2 says that Simeon and Anna were righteous according to the Law. In Scripture, *righteous* describes those who keep the precepts of the Law of God.

When we use the terms *just* or *justice* or *justification*, we think of the law, and in a sense that is correct: one who keeps the law is just. *Justification* often becomes, in people's minds, being put right according to the law. In the Beatitudes, "Blessed are those who hunger and thirst for justice" could lead one to think of social justice. Therefore, the question is: Is *justification* a legalistic, juridical term or not? It is, on some level, because the Law is simply the ordinances, the statutes. *Dikaiomata*, "statutes," means that which is according to *dikaiosynē*, "justice" or "righteousness."

However, I think the term *dikaiosynē* is more a metaphysical term than a juridical one. *Dikaiosynē* means living according to the reality of the way things actually are, as they have been ordered and established and created by God. The laws of God are prescriptions that people should live according to reality. Therefore, when something is *made righteous* or *put right* or *justified*, it means that it is aligned up rightly. One could even say it is according to truth.

Jesus, the Righteous One, is the one who lives according to the way things really are, as coming from God. When He justifies or makes righteous, He restores to reality. Human beings, when they are made righteous, are made to be what they really are. It has to do with a person's very being, not just a person's activity. Righteous*ness* is the reality of things being the way they really are and as they ought to be from God.

Justification is making things the way they ought to be, doing what one owes or what one ought to do. There is a connection between *owe* or *ought* and *debt* in relation to righteousness. If things are not right, we pay the debt or we do what ought to be done, and then things are made right.

The Lord's Prayer says, "Forgive us our debts as we forgive our debtors." We could say, "Forgive us or set us free from having to pay off *what we owe* or how we *ought* to be, as we forgive and let go the people who are not toward *us* the way they *ought* to be." When a debt is paid, things are made right. They are made to be the way they are supposed to be.

When Jesus, as the Righteous One, *does* righteousness, He pays the price or the debt. That brings us to the concept of redemption or atonement. If we redeem something, it means we have paid the price to make things right. It is always a costly act and very often a sacrificial one.

There is only one way to make things right, and that is to be right ourselves. When Jesus makes sinners righteous, He does it by being righteous, and His righteousness is proved by the sacrifice of His own life and His own blood on the Tree of the Cross when He is crucified.

The Crucifixion of Christ makes things right. When He dies on the Cross, He does the perfect act of righteousness as the Righteous One, acting according to the commandments of God. He keeps the *dikaiomata*, the ordinances and the statutes, and everything is then made right; everything is harmonious, the way it ought to be.

Jesus is the Righteous One, the one who puts things right. We believe that, in and through Him, *our* lives can be made right, can be straightened out, and can be put back together, becoming the way they *ought* to be.

To meditate further on this, read the Psalter. The Book of Psalms is a textbook on who the righteous are, how they live, and what happens to them. I went through my Septuagint Psalter and counted that the words *righteous*, *unrighteous*, or *righteousness* are used over 150 times in the 150 psalms.

Psalm 1:5–6 says:

> Therefore the wicked will not stand in the judgment,
> nor sinners in the congregation of the righteous;
> for the Lord knows the way of the righteous,
> but the way of the wicked will perish.

Psalm 1 begins, "Blessed is the man / who walks not in the counsel of the wicked," the wicked being the unrighteous. Also, it does not say *human being* here, but *man*, a male human being. This led the Church Fathers to say that whenever we hear the term *the righteous man*, we should think of Christ. Everything in the Psalter that is applied to *the righteous man* belongs to Jesus Christ par excellence. Jesus is the only one who, by every thought, word, and deed, by every movement of His being, truly puts into practice what is right.

There are righteous people, but they possess no righteousness of their own; if they are righteous, it is only because of their faith and obedience and the grace of God. There are people who reach very high levels of righteousness. The best example of this is the Theotokos, who we believe never sinned unto death. Her soul magnified the Lord; her spirit rejoiced in God her Savior. She was a handmaiden. She was empty of everything; she had nothing but God. She was full of grace. Everything she had, she had by her faith in God and her obedience to God: "Let it be to me according to your word," she tells the Archangel Gabriel (Luke 1:38).

Some Protestants object to the way we talk about the Virgin Mary. Some students left my classroom and slammed the door because I said, "The Virgin Mary is perfectly righteous by the grace of God." The Church Fathers teach that Mary, while she might have had some little weaknesses, never had any unrighteousness. She lived according to the Law and the commandments of God with every breath, with every thought, with every deed.

They say, "How can this be?" Our response is very simple: No human being is righteous by nature—in other words, we are not righteous by ourselves. St. Athanasius the Great said that if we look at ourselves, what we really are is nothing but *phthora*, "corruption," and *ouk ōn*, "nothing." We are just wind, a breath in the night, a piece of flesh, a bunch of dust. We are *nothing* without God, and we are certainly not righteous. Yet, with God, by divine grace, a person can truly become righteous.

Psalm 2 ends with "Blessed are all who take refuge in him" (v. 12). First Peter says, "he trusted to him who judges justly" (1 Peter 2:23). God executes righteous judgment; and human beings, if they are in communion with God and keep His commandments, also judge rightly.

Psalm 4 says, "Hear me when I call, O God of my righteousness!" (v. 1, NKJV) and "Offer the sacrifices of righteousness, / And put your trust in the LORD" (v. 5, NKJV). This is what Jesus did. The sacrifice of Jesus on the Cross was the sacrifice of righteousness spoken about in the psalms.

Psalm 7:8 says, "Judge me, O Lord, according to my righteousness / and according to the integrity that is in me." Who can say such a thing? Here, we believe the words of the psalms are the words of Jesus. Jesus could say this to God the Father because He [Jesus] is innocent and just. When people bowed down before Jesus and recognized Him as the Righteous One, the Chosen One, the Son of David, the Son of God, Jesus never said, "Don't say that," because He would be lying if He said that. He said, "You're right. That's Me."

The psalm continues, "O let the evil of the wicked come to an end, / but establish thou the righteous" (see Ps. 7:9). Jesus Himself is totally directed by God. He never does or says anything except under the direction of God. He says, "My food is to do the will of him who sent me, and to accomplish his work," and that is the work of righteousness (John 4:34). He has come "to fulfill all righteousness" (Matt. 3:15).

Psalm 11(10) in the Septuagint says, "The Lord tries [tests] the righteous and the ungodly, and he that loves unrighteousness hates his own soul [his own life]" (Ps. 11[10]:5, NKJV). Jesus was tested and tempted in every possible way in order to help us who are tested and tempted (see Heb. 2:18). The New Testament says no one can enter God's kingdom without being tested, so we are always tested toward our righteousness.

Psalm 11(10):7 says, "For the Lord is righteous, he loves righteous deeds; / the upright shall behold his face." Psalm 15(14):1–2 (NKJV) says:

> Lord, who may abide in Your tabernacle?
> Who may dwell in Your holy hill?
> He who walks uprightly,
> And works righteousness,
> And speaks the truth in his heart.

St. Benedict says the monastic life is simply to put this into practice.

Psalm 17(16) begins:

> Hear a just cause, O Lord; attend to my cry!
> Give ear to my prayer from lips free of deceit!
> From thee let my vindication come!
> Let thy eyes see the right! (v. 1)

It ends, "As for me, I will see Your face in righteousness; / I shall be satisfied when I awake in Your likeness" (v. 15, NKJV). At the end, the righteous person appears in righteousness before the face of God.

Psalm 18(17):20 speaks of personal righteousness: "The Lord rewarded me according to my righteousness; / according to the cleanness of my hands he recompensed me." God deals with us according to our works, and those works have to be righteous.

Psalm 23(22):1–3 mentions "the paths of righteousness."

> The Lord is my shepherd, I shall not want;
> he makes me lie down in green pastures.
> He leads me beside still waters;
> he restores my soul.
> He leads me in paths of righteousness
> for his name's sake.

Psalm 34(33) says:

> The eyes of the Lord are toward the righteous,
> and his ears toward their cry. (v. 15)

> Many are the afflictions of the righteous;
> but the Lord delivers him out of them all.
> He keeps all his bones;
> not one of them is broken.
> Evil shall slay the wicked;
> and those who hate the righteous will be condemned.
> The Lord redeems the life of his servants;
> none of those who take refuge in him will be condemned. (vv. 19–22)

Jesus is the Righteous One, and His afflictions are many. In this world, the righteous suffer. Yet the New Testament applies verse 20—"He keeps all his bones; / not one of them is broken"—directly to Jesus. When Joseph of Arimathea asked for the body of Jesus after His Crucifixion, the soldiers were about to break His legs, since that was the practice at the time in order to hasten death. But they found that He was already dead and there was no need to break His bones.

Psalm 35(34):27–28 (NKJV) says:

Let them shout for joy and be glad,
Who favor my righteous cause;
And let them say continually,
"Let the LORD be magnified,
Who has pleasure in the prosperity of His servant."
And my tongue shall speak of Your righteousness
And of Your praise all the day long.

"My tongue" means "my words": "the words of my mouth will be about Your righteousness and Your praise." Our rejoicing is in the righteousness the Lord God gives us. Many other verses from the Psalter teach of righteousness and the righteous. Psalm 37(36) says:

He shall bring forth your righteousness as the light,
And your justice as the noonday. (v. 6, NKJV)

Better is a little that the righteous has
than the abundance of many wicked. (v. 16)

I have been young, and now am old;
yet I have not seen the righteous forsaken
or his children begging bread. (v. 25)

The righteous shall possess the land,
and dwell upon it for ever.
The mouth of the righteous utters wisdom,
and his tongue speaks justice. (vv. 29–30)

Psalm 92(91):12 says, "The righteous flourish like the palm tree."
Hebrews applies Psalm 45(44):6–7 to Jesus Christ:

Your throne, O God, *is* forever and ever;
A scepter of righteousness *is* the scepter of Your kingdom.
You love righteousness and hate wickedness;
Therefore God, Your God, has anointed You
With the oil of gladness more than Your companions. (NKJV)

The list goes on and on, and I would encourage everyone to read the Psalms daily and note the use of the words *righteousness* and *justice*, for example in Psalm 58(57):

Do you indeed speak righteousness, you silent ones?
Do you judge uprightly, you sons of men?
No, in heart you work wickedness;
You weigh out the violence of your hands in the earth. (vv. 1–2, NKJV)

The righteous will rejoice when he sees the vengeance;
he will bathe his feet in the blood of the wicked.
Men will say, "Surely there is a reward for the righteous;
surely there is a God who judges on earth." (vv. 10–11)

The only Righteous One is Jesus, and if we are righteous at all, it is only because of the grace and power of God within us. Jesus Christ *is* the Righteous One, and He came *to make us righteous*, godlike. The Lord alone is righteous, but when we believe in Him, when we give our life to Him, when we sacrifice ourselves together with Him, when we strive to keep His commandments, then His very righteousness becomes our own, and that is the meaning of our life.

As our Savior, God saves us by communicating to us His righteousness. When Jesus lies dead in the tomb on Great and Holy Friday, Psalm 119(118) is read over Him, because that whole psalm is about the righteous person who is righteous because he keeps the commandments of God. This is why it is applied to Jesus par excellence. He *lives* because He keeps the commandments of God, and thus He becomes the Righteous One. He keeps the *dikaiomata*, the statutes or the ordinances, of God Himself.

On the Cross, Jesus makes everything *right*, and He communicates this rightness and righteousness to every single one of us. All that remains is for us to accept or reject it.

CHAPTER 24

Jesus the

JUDGE

Sometimes when the Scripture uses the verb *judge*, another term is used, such as *vindicate* or *advocate*, as on behalf of the servant—a servant calling on God's judgment. God *vindicates* the righteous, the meek. He *vindicates* those who want what is just and true and good. He *judges* the whole world.

The verb *to judge* can also be translated as *to condemn*. Jesus taught us not to judge anyone, and that by the measure with which we judge, He will judge us. That does not mean we do not discern things. Being merciful does not prohibit calling people to account for their behavior, but the teaching of Holy Scripture is against condemning people.

In the Old Covenant, God is just in all His judgments. The three holy youths in the fiery furnace say, "O God, You are just in *all* that You have done for [or to] us" (Dan. 3:27 LXX). The claim of Holy Scripture is that, at the end of the world, every single human being will actually cry out to God, "You are just in all that You have done for [or to] us."

God does not want to condemn anyone. As Ezekiel says, "As I live, says the Lord God, I have no pleasure in the death of the wicked, but that the wicked turn from his way and live" (Ezek. 33:11). All the chastening of His people is to get them to repent. It is ultimately an act of mercy. "The LORD *is* merciful and gracious, / Slow to anger, and abounding in mercy" (Ps. 103[102]:8, NKJV). That sentence is found in the Law of Moses, in the Prophets, in the Psalms—throughout the Scriptures.

One of the prokeimena of Vespers says, "Save me, O God, by Your *name*

[Your presence, Your being], and judge me by Your might" (Ps. 54[53]:1). The people pray to God to be judged. Anyone who loves truth and reality and goodness wants the judgment to come from God, because God can be trusted to judge justly. They will say, "Arise, O God, judge the earth" (Ps. 82[81]:8). This also is expressed throughout the Scriptures.

Psalm 82(81):1 says, "God has taken his place in the divine council; / in the midst of the gods he holds judgment." God is judging over all the false gods, the gods of the nations. The psalm continues, "How long will you judge unjustly / And show partiality to the wicked?" (v. 2), because the kings and the rulers of this earth often judge unjustly. The Scriptures say justice cannot come from anyone but God Himself.

> "Give justice to the weak and the fatherless;
> maintain the right of the afflicted and the destitute.
> Rescue the weak and the needy;
> deliver them from the hand of the wicked."
> They have neither knowledge nor understanding,
> they walk about in darkness;
> all the foundations of the earth are shaken.
> I say, "You are gods,
> sons of the Most High, all of you." (Ps. 82[81]:3–6)

In Jesus Christ, we all become christs. We all become sons of God. We are made, as the Holy Fathers say, to be by grace everything God is by nature.

In John 10, Jesus quotes Psalm 82(81) in defense of His own divinity. He says, "I and the Father are one," and the people pick up stones to stone Him for blasphemy "because you, being a man, make yourself God." Jesus replies, "Is it not written in your law, 'I said, you are gods'? If he called them gods to whom the word of God came (and scripture cannot be broken), do you say of him whom the Father consecrated and sent into the world, 'You are blaspheming,' because I said, 'I am the Son of God'?" (John 10:34–36).

Psalm 82(81) continues, "Nevertheless, you shall die like men, / and fall like any prince" (v. 7). Because of our wickedness, we die. Another translation might be: "O princes of the earth, you will fall, as all people fall." God alone does not fall, and the Son of God does not fall. He takes on the sin of the world, but He is vindicated.

The psalm concludes: "Arise, O God, judge the earth; / for to thee belong all the nations" (v. 8). God judges the world, and He seats the Son of God on the throne to judge the whole world, and all those who are together with Him sit on thrones with Him, judging the whole world. Jesus says to the disciples, "Truly, I say to you, in the new world, when the Son of man shall sit on his glorious throne, you who have followed me will also sit on twelve thrones, judging the twelve tribes of Israel" (Matt. 19:28).

One thing is taught very clearly in Acts. Peter says:

> "Truly I perceive that God shows no partiality, but in every nation any one who fears him and does what is right is acceptable to him. You know the word which he sent to Israel, preaching good news of peace by Jesus Christ (he is Lord of all), the word which was proclaimed throughout all Judea, beginning from Galilee after the baptism which John preached: how God anointed Jesus of Nazareth with the Holy Spirit and with power; how he went about doing good and healing all that were oppressed by the devil, for God was with him. And we are witnesses to all that he did both in the country of the Jews and in Jerusalem. They put him to death by hanging him on a tree; but God raised him on the third day and made him manifest; not to all the people but to us who were chosen by God as witnesses, who ate and drank with him after he rose from the dead. And he commanded us to preach to the people, and to testify that he is the one ordained by God to be judge of the living and the dead. To him all the prophets bear witness that every one who believes in him receives forgiveness of sins through his name." (Acts 10:34–43)

The Creed says, "And He will come again with glory to judge the living and the dead, and of His Kingdom there will be no end." So also in the Book of Acts, Jesus Christ is the Judge of the living and the dead.

What did Jesus teach about judgment? It is important to be careful. He sometimes uses the term *judge* as a synonym of *condemn*. He says, "Don't condemn anyone," that's God's business. The Apostle Paul says:

> Beloved, never avenge yourselves, but leave it to the wrath of God; for it is written, "Vengeance is mine, I will repay, says the Lord." No, "if your enemy is hungry, feed him; if he is thirsty, give him drink; for by so doing you will heap burning coals upon his head." (Rom. 12:19–20)

Jesus is making the same point. Yet in St. John's Gospel, He makes it very clear that His judgment is according to what He says and does. In John 12, He says:

> "If any one hears my sayings and does not keep them, I do not judge him; for I did not come to judge the world but to save the world. He who rejects me and does not receive my sayings has a judge; the word that I have spoken will be his judge on the last day. For I have not spoken on my own authority; the Father who sent me has himself given me commandment what to say and what to speak." (John 12:47–49)

Whether we accept it or reject it, that is going to be the judgment. He says the same thing in John 8:15–16: "You judge according to the flesh, I judge no one. Yet even if I do judge, my judgment is true, for it is not I alone that judge, but I and he who sent me."

He says the same thing in John 3:

> For God sent the Son into the world, not to condemn the world, but that the world might be saved through him. He who believes in him is not condemned; he who does not believe is condemned already, because he has not believed in the name of the only Son of God. And this is the judgment, that the light has come into the world, and men loved darkness rather than light, because their deeds were evil. For every one who does evil hates the light, and does not come to the light, lest his deeds should be exposed. But he who does what is true comes to the light, that it may be clearly seen that his deeds have been wrought in God." (John 3:17–21)

The Fathers say that, at the end of the ages, if there are those who do not love God, then the very presence of that light is a judgment upon them.

In John 5, Jesus says:

> "Truly, truly, I say to you, he who hears my word and believes him who sent me, has eternal life; he does not come into judgment, but has passed from death to life.
>
> "Truly, truly, I say to you, the hour is coming, and now is, when the dead will hear the voice of the Son of God, and those who hear will live. For as the Father has life in himself, so he has granted the Son also to

have life in himself, and has given him authority to execute judgment, because he is the Son of man." (John 5:24–27)

God gives Jesus the authority to execute judgment because He is the Son of Man. The Son of God and the Son of Man is the same Son, but the nuance here is important, because some people say, "Who is God to judge me? God doesn't know my affliction."

The whole point of Christianity is this: The Son of God became a man. He is the Son of Man, who takes upon Himself the sin of the world. *He* bore the affliction. *He* was rejected, ridiculed, nailed to the Cross. *He* was speared in the side, and *He* was dead and buried in a tomb. It is because of *this* that He has the authority to execute judgment.

We call the Cross of Christ "the balance beam of judgment." It has a right hand and a left hand, and when you stand in front of that Cross, that is the judgment. However, it is a judgment by *non*-judgment. Jesus judges by showing mercy and taking the judgment upon Himself, and suffering all of our sins in His own body of flesh on the Tree of the Cross. It is our sin that put Him on the Cross. *That* is the judgment. Then the Lord continues:

> "Do not marvel at this; for the hour is coming when all who are in the tombs will hear his voice and come forth, those who have done good, to the resurrection of life, and those who have done evil, to the resurrection of judgment. I can do nothing on my own authority; as I hear, I judge; and my judgment is just, because I seek not my own will but the will of him who sent me." (John 5:28–31)

God's judgment through Jesus is absolutely just because it is an act of mercy, which then turns into a judgment. As He hears, as He sees, so He judges. He is simply pronouncing the verdict we have put upon ourselves.

Matthew 25:31–46 contains the parable of the Last Judgment, which is one of the most frightening parts of Holy Scripture. St. John Chrysostom said, "What kind of a judgment is this?" There is no judge nor jury, no trial nor advocate. There are no lawyers nor plea bargaining. No case is put forth, neither is there any evidence or demonstration. He said, "What kind of a judgment is it? It is a kind of judgment that the just Judge does," that God does through His Son, Jesus.

He merely becomes Himself: hungry, thirsty, naked, sick, in prison, wounded, homeless, and dead in this world. He identifies with everyone who is these things, and then He says, "Your judgment is: How did you act to them? Did you love them with the love that God commands? Did you express this love in concrete actions?"

First John 3:18 says, "Little children, let us not love in word or speech but in deed and in truth." We do not love in words; we love in *work*, in acts, and in truth. The Psalms, the Prophets, Romans, and Revelatiosn all say that, on the Day of Judgment, we will be judged by our *works*.

As the song says in 2 Timothy:

> If we have died with him,
> we shall also live with him;
> if we endure,
> we shall also reign with him;
> if we deny him,
> he also will deny us;
> if we are faithless,
> he remains faithful—
> for he cannot deny himself. (2 Tim. 2:11–13)

If we deny Him, He will deny us. He will send us into the fire that we ourselves have prepared with the devils. Being faithful to Himself, God judges with righteous judgment, which means He does not judge at all. He sends His Son to save the world, and that constitutes the judgment.

St. Symeon the New Theologian said a person might say, "I was sick myself; I couldn't go visit the sick. I was poor myself; I couldn't help the needy. I was naked myself; how could I share my clothes? Does that mean I'm going to hell?" He would answer, saying, "Absolutely not, because this parable has to do with loving in acts." Jesus names those acts that are normally capable of being done by people, but the real point is the love.

That is why Jesus, in the Sermon on the Mount, says, "Not everyone who says to me, 'Lord, Lord,' shall enter the kingdom of heaven." When the Day of Judgment comes, not everyone who says, "I accept Jesus as my Savior" will enter the Kingdom, but "he who does the will of my Father who is in heaven" (Matt. 7:21). The will of the Father is that we would love, that we would show mercy, that we would be kind, that we would do good to the measure that we are capable of doing and share the measure we are capable of sharing: our resources, our time, our strength. *That* is what God wants from us, and that is the judgment.

Jesus says, "On that day [meaning the Day of the Lord, when Christ comes again in glory, judging the whole of creation] many will say to me, 'Lord, Lord, did we not prophesy in your name, and cast out demons in your name, and do many mighty works in your name?'" We could even say, "I spoke on Ancient Faith Radio in Your name. I went to church in Your name. I belonged to the philanthropy club in Your name. I gave ten dollars to the orphans in Your name." Then Jesus will say to them, "I never knew you; depart from me, you evildoers" (Matt. 7:22–23).

Why? Because those acts can be done without love. They can be done not to the glory of God or for the good of the neighbor. They could be done for one's own glory, so people would praise us. This profits us nothing.

St. Paul, in 1 Corinthians, says:

> If I speak in the tongues of men and of angels, but have not love, I am a noisy gong or a clanging cymbal. And if I have prophetic powers, and understand all mysteries and all knowledge, and if I have all faith, so as to remove mountains, but have not love, I am nothing. If I give away all I have, and if I deliver my body to be burned, but have not love, I gain nothing. (1 Cor. 13:1–3)

That is the judgment. Jesus brings the love of God to the world. He comes to save, not to judge, not to condemn, but His bringing of that love to the world *is* the judgment. So we believe, according to Scripture, that in the end, when we have to stand before Him, that will be the judgment, and we will pronounce the verdict ourselves, because as He sees, He will judge, and His judgment is just.

Jesus Christ did not come to condemn us. In 1 Timothy, St. Paul says that the Lord "desires all men to be saved and to come to the knowledge of the truth" (1 Tim. 2:4). God is not a Nebuchadnezzar who would burn people in the furnace of hell. The Orthodox Church does not teach a material hellfire. God loves, and He appears, and He brings mercy. This is the judgment: that light is shining in the darkness, but some people choose darkness, because their deeds are evil.

When we think of Jesus as the Judge, we must ask ourselves, "Where do we stand?" At every Divine Liturgy, we pray for "a good defense at the dread judgment seat of Christ." He is raised and glorified, and His Cross is the balance beam of judgment. We will stand before it, and He will look at us, and He will pronounce what we ourselves have decided, according to what we ourselves have done. Jesus is the Judge, and what a marvelous Judge He is! He judges by showing mercy, and He asks us to show mercy, too: "Blessed are the merciful, for they shall obtain mercy" (Matt. 5:7). If we are not merciful, that judges us. If we are not loving, if we do not love light, if we do not love truth, that judges us.

Jesus is the truth. He is the light. He is the life. He is raised and glorified. He is the Judge. As Chrysostom said, however, He is not a Judge like a judge in an earthly court of law. There is no jury and no prosecutor or defender; there is just Him, sitting on the throne, the One who was crucified, pronouncing the judgment that we ourselves have pronounced through our deeds. As He sees, He judges, and His judgment is just.

Jesus is the Judge of the living and the dead, and He judges in the same way He saves: by what He has suffered and by the mercy of God that He brings to us, His people.

CHAPTER 25

Jesus the

LIGHT OF THE WORLD

According to St. John the Theologian, "God is light and in him is no
darkness at all" (1 John 1:5). The Apostle Paul writes to Timothy that
God is "the King of kings and Lord of lords, who alone has immortality and
dwells in unapproachable light, whom no man has ever seen or can see" (see
1 Tim. 6:15–16).

This light is connected with God Himself, but when this light comes into
the world, it brings judgment, because everything is seen clearly. In this
light, we are shown for who we are.

Alongside the imagery of light is the imagery of vision, of things becoming
clear. In the Scriptures, darkness is connected with evil, ignorance, and
death. The pit of Sheol is in darkness, whereas God dwells in unapproachable
light.

This imagery of light and darkness exists in nearly all cultures. Anyone
who reflects on life in this world comes to those images of light and
darkness, of clear vision and blindness. Light is also life-giving. Where there
is darkness, there cannot be life.

Genesis 1 says, "In the beginning God created the heavens and the earth.
The earth was without form and void [LXX, *invisible*]; and darkness was
upon the face of the deep" (vv. 1–2). In Scripture, antithetical to the presence
of God is the image of deep darkness. "And the Spirit of God was moving
over the face of the waters."

These are the first words from the mouth of God in Scripture: "And God
said, 'Let there be light'; and there was light. And God saw that the light was

good; and God separated the light from the darkness. God called the light Day, and the darkness he called Night. And there was evening and there was morning, one day" (vv. 2–5).

There are various theories of what the original created light was, but it certainly was not the light of the sun. According to Genesis, the sun and the stars and moon only come into being on the fourth day. Some people think this indicates a kind of spiritual realm, God dwelling in this unapproachable light, surrounded by all the heavenly hosts. Some people think it was a kind of primal energy from which all other things came, or a created spiritual world that became the foundation for the material world, which would need the light in order to exist. This light, however, is not the uncreated light of God. The Holy Fathers say it is a created form of what exists in uncreated form in God, something no one can comprehend or explain.

I once met a young Orthodox woman who was a doctoral student in physics. She was very moved by the fact that, in the Scriptures, the first thing brought into being is light. She believed light is somehow the prime creature, without which nothing else can be. She told me that light is the only constant in the universe. Weight, measurement, sound, time, and so forth act differently in what physicists call different frames of reference. There is a definite relativity of time and space in the created universe, but light acts the same way everywhere. It is a foundational measure of the created order.

Like Genesis, St. John's Gospel begins at the beginning. "In the beginning was the Word, and the Word was with God, and the Word was God. He was in the beginning with God; all things were made through him, and without him was not anything made that was made. In him was life, and the life was the light of men" (John 1:1–4). Light and life are connected. Jesus says: "I am the light of the world" (John 8:12). "The light shines in the darkness, and the darkness has not overcome it" (John 1:5). The light always defeats the darkness. Darkness, by definition, is the absence of light.

John the Baptist, St. John says, "was not the light, but came to bear witness to the light. The true light that enlightens every man was coming into the world. He was in the world, and the world was made through him, yet the world knew him not. He came to his own home, and his own people received him not" (John 1:8–11).

This light that enlightens every person became flesh and dwelt among us, full of grace and truth, and "we have beheld his glory, glory as of the only Son from the Father" (v. 14). That term, *glory*, or *doxa* in Greek, is the name for the divine splendor, the magnificent light of God Himself, the light in which God dwells, the Light that God Himself is.

The Holy Fathers speak about the divine light being so bright that it could be called darkness. They called it "luminous darkness" or the "divine darkness which is filled with light." It is so superabundantly light that we cannot even speak about it except by using a symbol of darkness.

In the Old Testament, Moses entered into that light, that luminous cloud on the mountaintop. In Exodus, when Moses is coming down from the mountain, his face is shining with the light, and they have to put a veil over his face because people could not look at him (see Ex. 34:29–35).

In the synoptic Gospels, at the Transfiguration, Jesus goes up on Mt. Tabor with Peter, James, and John and is transfigured, shining with the uncreated light. The disciples see Him, but they have to hide their faces (see Matt. 17:1–9; Mark 9:2–10; Luke 9:28–36).

These passages show the real, divine light that is in the world, a light that human beings can actually experience. We can know it and see it, and as creatures we can participate in it. The mystical saints, when speaking of this light, name it Jesus. If there are holy and righteous people anywhere who have pure hearts and seek the true God, God in His mercy may reveal to them His divine light. We, as Christians, would say it is Jesus Christ they see. The others may not know it is Jesus, but we do.

This glory St. John speaks about—"we have beheld his glory" (John 1:14)— is the uncreated splendor of God that Moses, Elijah, and Isaiah in the temple saw in the Old Testament. It is the light St. Paul saw when he was struck down on the road to Damascus. This light of God, we Christians confess, is hypostatically, personally, Jesus Christ. Not only does this light shine from Jesus' face in the Transfiguration, but in St. John's Gospel Jesus says, "I am this Light." Jesus Christ is the Light and the source of light.

The Psalms also speak of the divine light. Psalm 36(35):9 says, "For with thee is the fountain of life; / in thy light do we see light."

Psalm 27(26):1 says, "The Lord is my light and my salvation; / whom shall

I fear?" We use this verse at baptisms, when a person becomes illumined.

Psalm 119(118):105 says, "Thy word is a lamp to my feet / and a light to my path." This light and this lamp are identified with Christ.

The light of God overcomes physical and spiritual blindness. When Jesus is healing people to show that He is the Messiah, He illumines them, He opens their eyes so they can see the light.

In the prophecy of Isaiah, the messianic figure is called the light of the nations: "I will give you as a light to the nations, / that my salvation may reach to the end of the earth" (Is. 49:6). The Gentiles will be in His light. As Isaiah says, "And nations shall come to your light, / and kings to the brightness of your rising" (Is. 60:3).

In Revelation, Jesus is the light of the New Jerusalem. "And the city has no need of sun or moon to shine upon it, for the glory of God is its light, and its lamp is the Lamb" (Rev. 21:23). In Hebrews, Jesus is called the radiance of the Father's glory (Heb. 1:3).

In John 8:12, Jesus says, "I am the light of the world; he who follows me will not walk in darkness, but will have the light of life." Light is not only vision and truth and judgment, but it is life.

He said earlier in John that light is not accepted by people who love darkness (see John 3:19–21). The blasphemy against the Holy Spirit that cannot be forgiven (see Matt. 12:32; Mark 3:29) is to see the light and prefer darkness; to see the truth and to prefer falsehood; to see what is beautiful and glorious and to prefer what is ugly, perverse, and corrupted.

Isaiah says, "Woe to those who call evil good / and good evil, / who put darkness for light / and light for darkness, / who put bitter for sweet / and sweet for bitter!" (Is. 5:20). There is no hope for them, because when the light shines and people do not want it, what can God do? That light, according to Orthodox theology, is the torture of hell. If you love the light, however, you become light yourself, the way the saints have become light.

There is a story about St. Innocent, when he was a bishop, visiting his parishes in Alaska. One day, one of the priests said to him, "I don't understand hell. I don't understand how God could punish people."

Outside the window was an ice-covered field. Everything was bright and sparkling white because the sun was shining on it. St. Innocent said, "Before I answer you, Father, why are you covering your eyes?"

"Your Grace," he said, "I am sitting by the window here, and the light is shining on the snow and the ice, and it is shining into my eyes."

St. Innocent asked, "Why don't you pull the shade down over the window?"

The priest said, "Oh, forgive me, Your Grace, but I do not have a shade. There is no way I can block out that light."

St. Innocent said, "There is your answer, Father. That is hell."

Jesus said in the Sermon on the Mount, "You are the light of the world. . . . Let your light so shine before men, that they may see your good works and give glory to your Father who is in heaven" (Matt. 5:14, 16).

We Christians are supposed to be the light of the world. If we are baptized, we are illumined. We should be walking around shining as Christ Himself is shining with the light of God, and people should see us and give glory to God. If there is any light among human beings, Christ is that light.

In John 9, Jesus meets a man blind from birth. He has spent his whole life in physical darkness. Jesus' disciples ask Him:

> "Rabbi, who sinned, this man or his parents, that he was born blind?"
> Jesus answered, "It was not that this man sinned, or his parents, but
> that the works of God might be made manifest in him. We must work
> the works of him who sent me, while it is day; night comes, when no
> one can work. As long as I am in the world, I am the light of the world."
> (John 9:2–5)

He comes to the blind man and gives him the light. He opens his eyes so that he may see. At the end of that beautiful event, Jesus says, "For judgment I came into this world, that those who do not see may see, and that those who see may become blind" (John 9:39). The light comes into the world and illumines those who wish to see, but it judges those who prefer darkness.

Some of the Pharisees near Him heard what He said. They ask Jesus, "Are we also blind?" Jesus says to them, "If you were blind, you would have no guilt; but now that you say, 'We see,' your guilt remains" (John 9:40–41). If they had not seen what He did, they would have no culpability, but since they saw the works of Christ and did not believe in Him, their guilt remains.

Later, Jesus says, "The light is with you for a little longer. Walk while you have the light, lest the darkness overtake you; he who walks in the darkness does not know where he goes. While you have the light, believe in the light, that you may become sons of light" (John 12:35–36).

Jesus was referring to Himself as "the light." He said "the light is with you for a little longer" because He was going to be crucified. When He was crucified, the light of the sun was hidden, and as the Prophet Amos said, there was darkness at noon (see Amos 8:9). Everything was plunged into darkness on that day, according to the imagery of the Scriptures.

Jesus continues:

> "He who believes in me, believes not in me but in him who sent me.
> And he who sees me sees him who sent me. I have come as light into the
> world, that whoever believes in me may not remain in darkness. If any
> one hears my sayings and does not keep them, I do not judge him; for I
> did not come to judge the world but to save the world." (John 12:44–47)

He judges the living and the dead as God's light. This light comes, and in it, we reveal what we really are, and God pronounces judgment and puts a seal on what we really are. The question is: Are we children of the light or children of darkness?

St. Paul bears witness to this in his letters. In 2 Corinthians 3 and 4, he says that if Moses had to cover his face because the splendor of God was upon him in the Old Covenant, what greater splendor is there in the dispensation of righteousness and salvation?

Paul writes that the New Covenant surpasses the Old Covenant as the owner of the house surpasses the slave who works in it. "What once had splendor [the Old Covenant] has come to have no splendor at all, because of the splendor that surpasses it. For if what faded away came with splendor, what is permanent must have much more splendor" (2 Cor. 3:10–11). He is speaking about the coming of Christ.

He says that Christians are very bold, unlike Moses, who had to veil his face. In Christ, Christians "beholding the glory of the Lord, are being changed into his likeness from one degree of glory to another" (2 Cor. 3:18).

In contrast, this is what St. Paul says about those who do not know God and those Jews who rejected Christ:

> In their case the god of this world has blinded the minds of the
> unbelievers, to keep them from seeing the light of the gospel of the glory
> of Christ, who is the likeness of God. . . . For it is the God who said, "Let
> light shine out of darkness," who has shone in our hearts to give the
> light of the knowledge of the glory of God in the face of Christ. (2 Cor.
> 4:4–6)

St. Paul says in Ephesians:

> For once you were darkness, but now you are light in the Lord; walk as
> children of light. . . . Take no part in the unfruitful works of darkness,
> but instead expose them. For it is a shame even to speak of the things
> that they do in secret; but when anything is exposed by the light it
> becomes visible, for anything that becomes visible is light. (Eph. 5:8–14)

As the psalm says, which we sing in the Doxology, "In Your light we see light" (Ps. 36[35]:9).

Ephesians continues: "Therefore it is said, 'Awake, O sleeper, and arise from the dead, / and Christ shall give you light'" (Eph. 5:14). The light that Christ gives us is the Light that He *is*.

St. John the Theologian also uses that imagery of light. He says:

> Yet I am writing you a new commandment, which is true in him and in
> you, because the darkness is passing away and the true light is already
> shining. He who says he is in the light and hates his brother is in the
> darkness still. He who loves his brother abides in the light, and in it
> there is no cause for stumbling. But he who hates his brother is in the
> darkness and walks in the darkness, and does not know where he is
> going, because the darkness has blinded his eyes. (1 John 2:8–11)

Light is inseparable from love. We Christians are supposed to be light-bearers. We are supposed to have that very Light that Christ Himself is, because He enlightens every man who comes into the world. He wants to enlighten us. We were baptized to be illumined.

We know that those who keep God's commandments, who love God and give themselves to Him completely, become light. In their famous conversation, Nikolai Motovilov could not even look at St. Seraphim of Sarov. It was said that people could not look at St. Anthony the Great either. Nevertheless, they were drawn to look. This always happens when the splendor and the glory of God is present. This light attracts you, and at the same time it judges you. When you are in this light, you know that you are a sinner. Nevertheless, this light is so beautiful and glorious. God will give it to anyone who desires it in the least way.

This light, in its divine, uncreated form, is Jesus Christ. He is personally that light. He comes into the world, and, being in the world, He is the Light of the World. Christ is the divine light—the light of truth, the light of life, the light of love—that illumines anyone, anywhere.

CHAPTER 26

Jesus, the

SUN OF RIGHTEOUSNESS

Let us meditate on two images from Scripture. One is an expression from Malachi: "But for you who fear my name the sun of righteousness shall rise, with healing in its wings. You shall go forth leaping like calves from the stall" (Mal. 4:2). In the hymnology of the Church, Jesus is identified with "the Sun of Righteousness."

This Sun of Righteousness, however, is also connected to other images. One is simply the image of the Day, that is, the Day of the Lord, the *Yom Yahweh*, or in Greek, the *Kyriaki Imera*, the Lord's Day. It is also connected with the imagery of the dawn, or as it is translated in the King James Version, "the Dayspring from on high."

This phrase occurs in the Gospel of Luke, in the song of Zechariah, the father of John the Baptist. When John is born, Zechariah sings the song that is called the *Benedictus*:

"Blessed be the Lord God of Israel,
for he has visited and redeemed his people,
and has raised up a horn of salvation for us
in the house of his servant David." (Luke 1:68–69)

"And you, child, will be called the prophet of the Most High;
for you will go before the Lord to prepare his ways,
to give knowledge of salvation to his people
in the forgiveness of their sins,
through the tender mercy of our God,
when the day shall dawn upon us from on high

to give light to those who sit in darkness and in the shadow of death,
to guide our feet into the way of peace." (vv. 76–79)

In Greek and Slavonic, east and west are connected with the rising and setting of the sun. The literal reading of Zechariah's hymn would be: "whereby will visit us the rising of the sun," or simply, "the East [or Orient] from on high." The rising of the sun comes from below the horizon, but this is the rising that comes from on high.

Jesus is called not only the Sun of Righteousness, but also the Dawn, the Dayspring, the Orient, or the beginning of the day. Dawn, day, and sun are all connected in a package of images referring to Jesus Christ.

Malachi 4 says, "the sun of righteousness shall rise, with healing in its wings." Here is the image of the sun and of rising, but we need to read the previous chapter to get the whole picture. Malachi 3 says:

> "Behold, I send my messenger to prepare the way before me, and the Lord whom you seek will suddenly come to his temple; the messenger of the covenant in whom you delight, behold, he is coming, says the Lord of hosts. But who can endure the day of his coming, and who can stand when he appears? For he is like a refiner's fire and like fullers' soap." (Mal. 3:1–2)

Here, God is called a fire. Hebrews says, "for our God is a consuming fire" (Heb. 12:29). We see the image of fire with Moses and the burning bush in Exodus and on Pentecost in Acts, where the Holy Spirit comes as tongues of fire. Jesus says in the Gospel of Luke, "I came to cast fire upon the earth; and would that it were already kindled!" (Luke 12:49).

The sun in the sky also symbolizes Christ, the Sun of Righteousness. It warms and illumines, but it also burns as a fire.

Malachi says this one who is coming comes like a refiner's fire. A refiner's fire burns out impurities. The same imagery is used in 1 Corinthians, describing the Day of Judgment as like a burning fire. St. Paul writes, "each man's work will become manifest; for the Day will disclose it, because it will be revealed with fire, and the fire will test what sort of work each one has done" (1 Cor. 3:13). The divine fire burns up all our sins and iniquities, and purges and cleanses us so that we may enter God's Kingdom totally purified.

Malachi 3 continues, "They shall be mine, says the Lord of hosts, my special possession on the day when I act, and I will spare them as a man spares his son who serves him" (Mal. 3:17). There will be a judgment between the righteous and the wicked, between the one who serves God and the one who does not serve God.

> "For behold, the day comes, burning like an oven, when all the arrogant and all evildoers will be stubble; the day that comes shall burn them up, says the Lord of hosts, so that it will leave them neither root nor branch. But for you who fear my name the sun of righteousness shall rise, with healing in its wings. You shall go forth leaping like calves from the stall. And you shall tread down the wicked, for they will be ashes under the soles of your feet, on the day when I act, says the Lord of hosts." (Mal. 4:1–3)

This is a prophecy of the coming of Christ. Jesus Christ is the Sun of Righteousness and the day. The term *Sun of Righteousness* is also used in the Liturgy. It occurs in the main hymns for the Nativity of Christ, for the Nativity of the Theotokos, and for the Meeting of the Lord in the temple. It also occurs in the services for Theophany, for the Synaxis of St. John the Baptist on the day after Theophany, and for the Dormition of the Theotokos, in the canon.

This is how the main hymn of the Nativity of Christ begins:

> Your Nativity, O Christ our God,
> has shone to the world the light of knowledge.
> For by it, those who worshiped the stars were taught by a star
> to adore You, the Sun of Righteousness,
> and to know You, the Orient from on high.

When we reflected on the Nativity of Christ before, we pointed out how the liturgical celebration of the Birth of Christ in the Christian Church was assigned to the very day of the birth of the Invincible Sun, the physical sun in the sky that the pagans were worshiping. Because of this, the troparion of Christmas is a polemic against paganism. It is saying that what is really to be celebrated today is not the birth of the physical sun, but the Nativity of Christ our God.

"Your Nativity, O Christ our God, has shone to the world the light of knowledge." It is Christ's Birth that brings the spiritual light to the world—not the physical light, but the light of God. "For by it, those who worshiped the stars were taught by a star." In Matthew, the Magi from the East are brought by a star to the place where Jesus is born. Those who were stargazers and astrologers are now taught by a star "to adore You," to worship You, Jesus Christ, "the Sun of Righteousness, and to know You, the Orient from on high." That is from Zechariah's hymn. The Orient, the Dayspring from high, has visited us.

Isaiah prophesied, saying, "The people who walked in darkness / have seen a great light; / those who dwelt in a land of deep darkness, / on them has light shined" (Is. 9:2), and "Arise, shine; for your light has come" (Is. 60:1). This light has come and visited us "to give light to those who sit in darkness and in the shadow of death, / to guide our feet into the way of peace" (Luke 1:79), as Zechariah sang. Christ is the Sun of Righteousness, and He is the Orient from on high.

The main hymn for the nativity of Christ's mother, Mary, is understandably patterned after that for the Nativity of Jesus.

> Your nativity, O Virgin, has proclaimed joy to the whole universe.
> The Sun of Righteousness, Christ our God, has shone from you,
>   O Theotokos.
> By annulling the curse He bestowed a blessing.
> By destroying death, He has granted us eternal life.

On the festival of the Meeting of the Lord in the temple, the same imagery is used. We sing to Mary on that day when she comes to the temple with her newborn Baby:

> Rejoice, O Virgin, Theotokos, full of grace.
> From you shone the Sun of Righteousness, Christ our God,
> enlightening those who sat in darkness [Is. 9:2].
> Rejoice and be glad, O righteous elder [Simeon],
> for you accepted in your arms the Redeemer of our souls,
> who grants us the resurrection.

Mary and Simeon are asked to rejoice because the Sun of Righteousness, who shone from Mary, is enlightening those who sat in darkness. Simeon, when he held Jesus in his arms, made a song, too:

> "Lord, now lettest thou thy servant depart in peace,
> according to thy word;
> for mine eyes have seen thy salvation
> which thou hast prepared in the presence of all peoples,
> a light for revelation to the Gentiles,
> and for glory to thy people Israel." (Luke 2:29–32)

On Theophany, when the water is blessed, the priest reads a long prayer by St. Sophronius, the Archbishop of Jerusalem. It says, "Today, the Sun that never sets has risen, and the world is filled with splendor by the light of the Lord. Today, the moon shines upon the world with the brightness of its rays. Today, the glittering stars make the inhabited earth fair with the radiance of their shining."

Christ, the Sun that never sets, has come. The same prayer says, "Today, Paradise has opened to men, and the Sun of Righteousness shines down upon us." The prayer then ends with "Light of Light, true God of true God," as we find also in the Nicene Creed.

This imagery is also used in the Matins service for Theophany. The kontakion says:

> Today, You have appeared in the universe,
> and Your light, O Lord, has shone upon us,
> who with knowledge sing Your praises.
> You have come. You are manifested.
> You are the Light that no human being can approach.

Then the *ikos* goes like this:

> Upon Galilee of the Gentiles,
> upon the land of Zebulon and the land of Naphtali, as the prophet said,
> a great Light has shone, even Christ our God.
> To those that sat in darkness, a bright dawn has appeared as lightning
>   from Bethlehem.
> The Lord born from Mary, the Sun of Righteousness,
> sheds His rays upon the whole inhabited world.

Come then, naked children of Adam,
let us clothe ourselves in Him that we may warm ourselves.
You who are a protection and veil to the naked,
a light to those in darkness.
You have come. You have shone forth.
You are the Light that no human being can approach.

Here again, He is called, simply, the Sun of Righteousness. The same thing takes place on the Synaxis of St. John the Baptist. The canon of Matins says:

O John, you have come as the voice of the Word,
and as the morning star, you have arisen, O Forerunner,
plainly announcing the coming of the Sun of Righteousness.

Then the *ikos* says:

Unto him that was in black darkness [Adam, who had fallen]
a Light has risen that shall never be put out.
There is no more night for him. All is day.
For his sake, the hour has now come round to the break of day
for it is written, it was the cool of evening when he [Christ] was hidden
    in the earth.
He who fell at evening [Adam] has found the brightness [Christ] that
    raises him up.
He is released from gloom, and has come to the Dawn
that is made manifest and gives light to all.

John the Baptist is said to have gone into Hades to preach the coming of Christ, who, shining with brightness, entered the darkness of Hades like the dawn of the new day. Because He is all day, there is no night and no darkness in that place anymore. When we contemplated Jesus the Light, we saw in the Book of Revelation that, in the coming Kingdom of God, there is no sun. God Himself is the light. The Lamb is the radiance. Christ is the lamp. They enlighten the whole of creation in the coming Kingdom that we Christians are expecting.

The canon at Matins for the Dormition of the Virgin Mary says:

The apostles assembled from the ends of the earth to minister to you,
    O Virgin.

> You are the swift cloud from whom the Most High God, the Sun of
>   Righteousness,
> shone forth upon those who were in the darkness and the shadow of
>   death.

Mary was dying, and the apostles were assembled to minister to her from whom the Sun of Righteousness had shone forth to those who were in darkness.

There is one song that most committed church people know because it is sung at marriages and at ordinations: "Rejoice, O Isaiah, for a virgin is with child and shall bear a Son, Emmanuel, both God and Man, and Orient is His name." That comes, again, from Zechariah's hymn in Luke. The Orient shall arise, "whom, magnifying, we call the Virgin blessed."

One last comment about the imagery of day: In the Holy Scriptures, the Day of the Lord has a double meaning, as is often the case in the Bible. It is the Day of Judgment. It is not a day filled with light, but a dark day for sinners. For example, Isaiah says:

> Wail, for the day of the Lord is near;
> as destruction from the Almighty it will come!
> Therefore all hands will be feeble,
> and every man's heart will melt,
> and they will be dismayed.
> Pangs and agony will seize them;
> they will be in anguish like a woman in travail.
> They will look aghast at one another;
> their faces will be aflame.
> Behold, the day of the Lord comes,
> cruel, with wrath and fierce anger,
> to make the earth a desolation
> and to destroy its sinners from it.
> For the stars of the heavens and their constellations
> will not give their light;
> the sun will be dark at its rising
> and the moon will not shed its light.
> I will punish the world for its evil,
> and the wicked for their iniquity;

> I will put an end to the pride of the arrogant,
> and lay low the haughtiness of the ruthless. (Is. 13:6–11)

The prophecy of Amos contains the same theme:

> Woe to you who desire the day of the Lord!
> Why would you have the day of the Lord?
> It is darkness, and not light;
> as if a man fled from a lion,
> and a bear met him;
> or went into the house and leaned with his hand against the wall,
> and a serpent bit him.
> Is not the day of the Lord darkness, and not light,
> and gloom with no brightness in it? (Amos 5:18–20)

However, as regards the Day of the Lord, we must affirm a paradox. It is not only a day of darkness, but also a day of light, a day of splendor, and a day of victory. It is a day of life for those who want God, who adore God, and who worship God.

There is a famous story of the Desert Fathers Joseph and Lot, wherein the one said to the other, "What should I do, Father?"

The other said, "What do you do?"

"Well, I say my prayers, I read my psalms, I keep my fast, I try to love the brethren."

The other man said to him, "Oh, you do very well, that is good, keep it up." Then he looked at him and lifted up his hands, and his fingers became like ten flames, and he said, "If you will, you can become all flame."

When the Sun of Righteousness enters into the world and casts fire on the earth, that fire is a torment to those who do not love it, but it is all joy for those who do. Those who love it become all fire, all light. They are filled with the light and the fire of Jesus Christ, the Son of God, the Sun of Righteousness, and then they live in that day without evening that has no darkness and no death—the day when the Sun is shining and will never set.

Thus, we give glory to God and sing to Him, "Rejoice, rejoice, O Christ our God. Your Nativity has shone upon the world the light of wisdom, for You are the Sun of Righteousness."

We can even sing to the prophets, as we do during the services of ordination and marriage, "Rejoice, Isaiah, a virgin is with child and shall bear a Son, Emmanuel, both God and Man, and Orient is His name; whom magnifying, we call the Virgin blessed."

Our Lord Jesus Christ is the Sun of Righteousness, and He is the Orient from on high.

CHAPTER 27

Jesus the

WAY

In the Gospel of John, Jesus gives His discourse at the Last Supper. Scholars think this is a compilation of words of Jesus that were brought together into one discourse in this context, similar to the way the Sermon on the Mount was constructed in Matthew. The discourse starts in John 13 and goes all the way through John 17. In some sense, this is the foundation of all Christian *theologia*, in the technical sense of the word *theologia*—theology, which means "speech about God." It is a discourse about Jesus: who He is, how He relates to the one God and Father, and who God is and how He relates to Jesus. Then Jesus explains about the Holy Spirit proceeding from the Father, being sent into the world through Jesus. So this is the first Trinitarian discourse.

In John 13—14, Jesus says His hour has come:

> "Where I am going you cannot follow me now; but you shall follow afterward." Peter said to him, "Lord, why cannot I follow you now? I will lay down my life for you." Jesus answered, "Will you lay down your life for me? Truly, truly, I say to you, the cock will not crow, till you have denied me three times. Let not your hearts be troubled; believe in God, believe also in me. In my Father's house are many rooms; if it were not so, would I have told you that I go to prepare a place for you? And when I go and prepare a place for you, I will come again and will take you to myself, that where I am you may be also. And you know the way [*hodos*] where I am going." Thomas said to him, "Lord, we do not know where you are going; how can we know the way?" Jesus said to him, "I am the way, and the truth, and the life; no one comes to the Father, but

by me. If you had known me, you would have known my Father also; henceforth you know him and have seen him." (John 13:36—14:7)

This expression, *the way*, has an implication of going somewhere. In modern Greek, *hodos* is an avenue, a street. Jesus is the Way, so, if one is with Jesus, one is going to where Jesus is. Jesus says many times in the Gospels, "Follow Me." This means, "Go where I am going and I will lead you somewhere." He also speaks about the sheep following the shepherd.

What Jesus was talking about in John was that He was going to die, to go the way of the Cross. He was going to be raised from the dead and then go into the realm of God His Father. This way is the way of death, but it is also the way of vindication, resurrection, and glorification.

In Hebrews, St. Paul writes of the "new and living way":

> Therefore, brethren, since we have confidence to enter the sanctuary by the blood of Jesus, by the new and living way which he opened for us through the curtain, that is, through his flesh, and since we have a great priest over the house of God, let us draw near with a true heart in full assurance of faith, with our hearts sprinkled clean from an evil conscience and our bodies washed with pure water. (Heb. 10:19–22)

This "way," in Hebrews, is the entry into the heavenly Jerusalem. Jesus is saying to the Apostles, "You're going to go the way of the Cross, too." He said, "If any man would come after me, let him deny himself and take up his cross and follow me" (see Matt. 16:24; Mark 8:34; Luke 9:23).

In John, Jesus says if you are following Him, you will do the works that He does. "Truly, truly, I say to you, he who believes in me will also do the works that I do; and greater works than these will he do, because I go to the Father" (John 14:12). Through these works, a Christian announces the Kingdom of God, shows His power, and even does His wonders. Ultimately, however, it means that, in doing the will of God, we die. This way is the way of the Cross, the way of doing God's will instead of our own, the way of suffering.

Jesus says the disciples will follow Him along this way. They say, "We don't know the way!" And then, it is unique to Jesus, among all the teachers on earth, that He does not say, "I will show you the way." Instead, He says,

"I am the Way. I am the Way, the Truth, and the Life" (see John 14:6). This is radically, uniquely Christian.

St. Nicholas Cabasilas says, in *The Life in Christ*, that Jesus is not only the beginning and the end, but also the inn along the way. He is the One who feeds us and cares for us and clothes us as we travel along this road, this way that He Himself *is*.

This imagery of "the way" is also in the Old Testament. In the whole of the Law, the Psalms, and the Prophets, the imagery of walking is used. Genesis says that Enoch (Gen. 5:24) and Noah (Gen. 6:9) walked with God. Abraham walked with God (see Gen. 17:1). The image of the way on which people must walk goes back to the beginning of Scripture.

Sometimes combined with the imagery of walking we find the imagery of standing and sitting. If you are standing or sitting in the right place, you are with God. If you are walking in the right direction, you are with God.

Metropolitan Kallistos Ware, in *The Orthodox Way*, tells this story. A monk was sitting very still, praying. Some people discovered him and said to him, "What are you sitting there for, doing nothing?" He replied, "Actually, sir, I'm on a journey."

Psalm 84(83):5 (NKJV) says, "Blessed *is* the man whose strength *is* in You, / Whose heart *is* set on pilgrimage." You can travel on the way while sitting still. There is a sense in which, in order to walk in this way, you have to know how to sit still and how to stand fast.

In Exodus, Moses has just led the Israelites out of Egypt, and they start murmuring against him, saying, "We should have stayed where we were." Moses replies, "Fear not, stand firm, and see the salvation of the Lord, which he will work for you today; for the Egyptians whom you see today, you shall never see again. The Lord will fight for you, and you have only to be still" (Ex. 14:13–14).

The Psalms often speak about the way: walk in the way; the way of salvation; the way of light; the way of peace; the way of the Lord; don't walk the crooked path, walk the level path. Psalm 1:1 says:

> Blessed is the man
> who walks not in the counsel of the wicked,

> nor stands in the way of sinners,
> nor sits in the seat of scoffers.

These images—walking, standing, sitting—in a sense all mean the same thing.

In the verse above, the word for *man* is *anēr*—a male human being. Surely everyone has to walk not in the counsel of the ungodly, but in my opinion, when the Scriptures use the term *anēr* or the expression *Son of Man* (whether capitalized or not), they are referring to Jesus.

The psalm verse means, "There will be that Man who walks not in the counsel of the ungodly, who never stands in the way of sinners or sits in the seat of scoffers." That is Jesus, the totally sinless one, whose way is the way of truth, the way of life, the way of righteousness, the exalted way. Jesus shows us the way by *being* the Way.

The Buddhists hold that Buddha showed people the way, but Buddha said, "I'm not God. You all have this Buddha nature." The Buddha is a teacher, but that is all he is. *You* have in you exactly what Buddha had in him. Jesus is not that kind of a teacher. He is the Teacher who is Himself the Truth.

In Deuteronomy 30:15–16, Moses says to the people:

> "See, I have set before you this day life and good, death and evil. If you obey the commandments of the Lord your God which I command you this day, by loving the Lord your God, by walking in his ways, and by keeping his commandments and his statutes and his ordinances, then you shall live and multiply, and the Lord your God will bless you in the land which you are entering to take possession of it."

Isaiah 2:3 says:

> "Come, let us go up to the mountain of the Lord,
> to the house of the God of Jacob;
> that he may teach us his ways
> and that we may walk in his paths."

The same thing is in Jeremiah:

> Thus says the Lord:
> "Stand by the roads, and look,

and ask for the ancient paths,
where the good way is; and walk in it,
and find rest for your souls." (Jer. 6:16)

In Jeremiah 32, God says, "I will give them one heart and one way, that they may fear me for ever, for their own good and the good of their children after them. I will make with them an everlasting covenant" (Jer. 32:39–40).

The gospel is constantly called "the Way," particularly in Acts. That is the name for the Christian faith: the way of salvation, the way of life, the way of God. The Christian Church is *the Way*. Before St. Paul is converted, Acts says:

> But Saul, still breathing threats and murder against the disciples of the
> Lord, went to the high priest and asked him for letters to the synagogues
> at Damascus, so that if he found any belonging to the Way, men or
> women, he might bring them bound to Jerusalem. (Acts 9:1–2)

He was given permission to persecute them even unto death, to utterly demolish them.

In Acts 16:17, after he is converted, a slave girl is following Saints Paul and Silas and crying out, "These men are servants of the Most High God, who proclaim to you the way of salvation."

Acts 18 says there was "a Jew named Apollos, a native of Alexandria," who was in Ephesus when Saints Priscilla and Aquila were there.

> [Apollos] had been instructed in the way of the Lord; and being fervent
> in spirit, he spoke and taught accurately the things concerning Jesus,
> though he knew only the baptism of John. He began to speak boldly in
> the synagogue; but when Priscilla and Aquila heard him, they took him
> and expounded to him the way of God more accurately. (Acts 18:25–26)

In the next chapter, St. Paul is visiting Corinth. "And he entered the synagogue and for three months spoke boldly, arguing and pleading about the kingdom of God; but when some were stubborn and disbelieved, speaking evil of the Way before the congregation, he withdrew from them, taking the disciples with him" (Acts 19:8–9).

Later on, Paul defends himself before the Jewish people in Jerusalem, citing his credentials in Judaism, how he was instructed by Gamaliel and well-educated "according to the strict manner of the law of our fathers, being zealous for God as you all are this day." Then he says, "I persecuted this Way to the death, binding and delivering to prison both men and women" (Acts 22:3–4).

In Acts 24, Paul says, "But this I admit to you, that according to the Way, which they call a sect, I worship the God of our fathers, believing everything laid down by the law or written in the prophets," (v. 14). "But Felix, having a rather accurate knowledge of the Way, put them off" (v. 22).

Nowadays, people speak about many ways and many paths. *Vedānta*, which is a teaching that comes out of the Hindu tradition, says it does not matter which way you follow, because they all end up in the same place. To put it technically, according to *vedānta*, there is a "transcendental unity of all *dharma*." (*Dharma* is difficult to translate because it has multiple meanings, but it relates to both the order of the universe and the right way of living.)

There are some who hold that Judaism, Islam, Buddhism, and Christianity are all "valid ways." They would say there are other ways that are not valid, but they would declare all the so-called "great religions of the world" to be "valid ways." They would say there are different windows, but the light that shines through them all is the same light.

Do we think that is true? The answer, very clearly according to Holy Scripture, is no, it is not true. Christians hold that there is only one Way, and this has to be taught and proclaimed. That Way is Christ Himself. We preach Christ crucified, who is *the* Way. We employ the definite article.

Christ is the fulfillment of all ways. If there are other ways people have found while hungering and thirsting for wisdom or light or peace or compassion or truth or reality, the end of their longing is Jesus Christ. He is the Way, the Truth, the Light, and the Life: come to Him! You will reach your destination.

However, our Holy Fathers say there are righteous people among the Gentiles. Take the case of the Roman centurion Cornelius in Acts 10. He was "a devout man who feared God with all his household, gave alms liberally to the people, and prayed constantly to God" (Acts 10:2). Cornelius had an active and fruitful faith in God, even though he was a Gentile, not a Jew.

204 ✠ THE NAMES OF JESUS

He then has a vision in which an angel tells him to call for St. Peter to come and instruct him on what to do. He does so, and when Peter arrives and learns the whole story, the apostle says, "Truly I perceive that God shows no partiality, but in every nation any one who fears him and does what is right is acceptable to him" (Acts 10:34–35).

The earliest Christian Fathers say the truth of God is sprinkled and spread out among all human beings; it is accessible to everyone. If any person hungers and thirsts for righteousness—whatever his or her particular situation and faith—God will try to meet that desire, to the measure of the person's capacity. If anyone is in light, then God is enlightening him. If anyone loves his neighbor truly and does good, then that love and goodness come from God.

God acts where and how He can in whomever He can, in individuals and in communities. He is merciful, gracious, and long-suffering. He wants to reveal Himself. In His conversation with Nicodemus, Jesus said:

> "He who comes from above is above all; he who is of the earth belongs to the earth, and of the earth he speaks; he who comes from heaven is above all. He bears witness to what he has seen and heard, yet no one receives his testimony; he who receives his testimony sets his seal to this, that God is true. For he whom God has sent utters the words of God, for it is not by measure that he gives the Spirit; the Father loves the Son, and has given all things into his hand. He who believes in the Son has eternal life; he who does not obey the Son shall not see life, but the wrath of God rests upon him." (John 3:31–36)

Thus, since Christianity follows the Way of Him who comes from heaven, Jesus Christ the God-Man, it is not merely "one of many paths that lead to God." It is God's revelation of Himself, not the product of human reasoning and invention.

If anyone follows a path that leads to God, whether he knows it or not, that path is Jesus. Jesus says, "no one comes to the Father, but by me" (John 14:6). If a person really does have communion with the one true God, it is always by way of Jesus Christ, by the power and indwelling and operation of the Holy Spirit. We see a Trinitarian dimension to all experience that is valid and true.

Christianity is not one of many windows; it is *the* window, and the light coming in through this window is Christ. Some people say, "Who do you think you are to be so exclusive and to make such a claim?" Well, that is our faith. We believe that what is good, true, beautiful, and holy is perfectly incarnate in human form in only one Person who ever lived on the planet Earth, and that is Jesus of Nazareth, the incarnate Son of God, born of the Virgin Mary.

When Father Sophrony Sakharov was young, although he was a baptized Christian, he left Christianity, became involved with Asian religions, and began meditating and following the practices of those religions. After a while, however, he realized that he had turned his back on the light, on the peace, on the wisdom, on the proper way, the true way, and the only way. Then he returned to Christianity as a penitent. All his life, he agonized over the fact that he had denied, for a time, the one and only Lord Jesus Christ.

Fr. Sophrony said (I paraphrase), "Wasn't there light there in what I went into? Yes, it is possible there to find some peace, some joy, some light, some wisdom, and some truth. Yes, that is true, but for *Christians* to go there, for those who have already been baptized and have participated in Holy Communion, for *them* to go there, then they are only being led there by the devil." One of the most pernicious tricks of Satan is to say to people, "It's all the same! Choose the one you want! Decide for yourself what is true!"

Christians do not make their own truth; rather, they submit to the Truth, to Jesus Christ. We know to what we are submitting. He is one to whom we should surrender ourselves wholly and without condition or reserve.

He is the Way, and we give ourselves completely and totally to *His* way, which is the way of the Cross. His way is the way of suffering and death. His is the way of self-emptying. His is the way of perfect love for God, perfect love for our neighbors, and perfect love for our enemies. We follow in His way. We follow the way He shows us. We follow the Way that He is.

CHAPTER 28

Jesus the

TRUTH

L et us think about what Jesus means when He says, "I am . . . the truth" (John 14:6). We have to remember what we said about the Way and the Light: Jesus does not say, "I will *show* you the truth" or "I will *tell* you the truth." Certainly, He is full of grace and truth, and the truth is in Him. "And the Word became flesh and dwelt among us, full of grace and truth" (John 1:14).

He shows the truth, He speaks the truth, and He even argues with the leaders of the people that what He is saying is the truth (John 8). Jesus says even His words bear witness to the fact that He is the Son of God. Yet, the truth He speaks is the Truth that He is. He *is* the Truth, personally, hypostatically.

When we think of Jesus *being* the Truth, we remember that the teaching of the Holy Scriptures and the whole witness of God's people Israel is that the God of Abraham is the *true God*. Only Yahweh is God, *Adonai Eloheinu*. No other god is God.

Even the Muslims would agree with this, because they also claim that this God of Abraham is the only god. Muslims also say Mohammed was the last prophet and he comes to tell the final truth, but Christians say, "No, *Jesus* is the final Prophet, the very Word of God incarnate in human flesh, and *He* is full of grace and truth. There is no truth that goes beyond *Him*." Christians insist, to Jews and Muslims and everyone, that Jesus Christ *is* the Truth of the true God.

Our Church Fathers like to play with this. They would say the Truth of the true God is personally, hypostatically, Jesus Christ. Likewise, the Life of the living God, the Wisdom of the wise God, and the Power of the powerful God *are* Jesus Himself. St. Athanasius the Great, for example, frequently speaks in this way. He would even say the King of God's Kingdom and the kingship thereof is Christ. Furthermore, the Spirit of Truth, the Spirit of Wisdom, the Spirit of Peace (the Truth, Wisdom, and Peace of God also being Christ) is the Holy Spirit.

Christ is the Truth of the true God, and the Holy Spirit is the Spirit of Truth. This teaching about the Truth—Jesus saying, "I am the truth" (John 14:6), or in effect, "The truth is revealed in Me"—is connected to the true God. The Hebrew Scriptures insist there is no god but God. Other gods are not gods at all; they are false and untrue. They are projections of the human mind and imagination; they are not real; they are not God.

More than thirty times in Isaiah, God says, "You are My witnesses, that you may know and believe Me and understand that I am the Lord, and beside Me there is no other." Ezekiel says sixty times that God is doing the things He does "that you may know" He is God and there is no other. "When this comes, then you will *know* that I am the Lord."

Knowing is connected with truth, because when you know something, you are intimately acquainted with its truth and reality. Jesus said, "and you will know the truth, and the truth will make you free" (John 8:32). If you are not in the truth, you are enslaved to falsehood. When Jesus says He is the Light, He means that those who do not know Him as the Light are enslaved to darkness. They are still in darkness; they do not know the Light and cannot see. A synonym for *to know* in the Scriptures is *to see*. Jesus is the One who says He is the Truth, the One who is dependable, the One who enables us to see.

When we think of *truth*, we remember also that Pontius Pilate asked Jesus, "So you are a king?" And Jesus answered, "You say that I am a king. For this I was born, and for this I have come into the world, to bear witness to the truth. Every one who is of the truth hears my voice" (John 18:37).

In the next verse, Pilate says to Him, "What is truth?" and Jesus remains silent because He is standing right in front of Pilate, and if Pilate cannot see that Jesus is the Truth, there is nothing Jesus can say that will convince him. Jesus is this Truth, and it is the Truth that the true God *is*.

If we examine the word *truth* in Hebrew, Greek, Latin, and even Slavonic, we can learn more. Truth, in Hebrew, is *emet*. It connotes "that which is dependable, not shifting." That is why the metaphor of God as a rock is connected with the teaching of God as the true God. Isaiah chastises the people: "For you have forgotten the God of your salvation, / and have not remembered the Rock of your refuge" (Is. 17:10). Hannah sings, "There is none holy like the Lord, / there is none besides thee; / there is no rock like our God" (1 Sam. 2:2).

The Psalter uses that imagery all the time:

> The Lord is my rock, and my fortress, and my deliverer,
> my God, my rock, in whom I take refuge,
> my shield, and the horn of my salvation, my stronghold. (Ps. 18[17]:2)

> To thee, O Lord, I call;
> my rock, be not deaf to me,
> lest, if thou be silent to me,
> I become like those who go down to the Pit. (Ps. 28[27]:1)

The Old Testament teaches that the true God is faithful. He is the only one who is there. All the other ones are not God at all.

Some direct translations from Hebrew to English translate *emet* as "faithfulness" (see, for example, Prov. 14:22 RSV). That is a very important meaning of the word *true*. In English we say, "He is my true friend," which does not simply mean he is a real friend, but that he is faithful. We say, "I'm true to my word," which means "I am faithful to what I say." Fidelity is connected with truth. One of the main characteristics of God in the Holy Scriptures is that He is faithful. That is the meaning of *truth* in Semitic languages generally.

In Latin, the word for truth is *veritas*, which has this same meaning. With *veritas* comes the connotation of something being dependable, faithful, and loyal. We say *veritable*, meaning something that is provable. It is a sure thing, beyond any doubt.

In the Septuagint, *emet* is often translated into Greek as *alētheia*: "true" in the sense of "dependable," or etymologically, "uncovered." When you know the truth, it means you see reality directly, because it is revealed and connected with knowledge. You know what something is because you can see it. It is no longer covered.

The Slavonic term is *istina*, which comes from the verb meaning "it is being," connoting that truth is the reality of things, not how we imagine them to be. Imagination, then, is the great enemy of truth. If we follow "the vain imaginations of our own heart," as we pray in the Church prayers, then we are not in truth; we are in falsehood.

God is dependable, faithful, real, and true, but the devil is a liar and completely undependable. He says things, but they are not true. You cannot count on him. The devil covers up and obscures the truth; that is why he is connected with darkness. The devil distorts reality; he does not want us to see things as they really are. He lies to us about himself because he wants to make us think he is wise, good, and true. He lies about God, about us, about creation, about Jesus. He lies to us about everything.

Once, I said to my professor of theology, Serge S. Verhovskoy, "Professor, what do you think is the worst possible sin?"

He said, "My dear, it's very clear, according to the Holy Scriptures and all the saints, that the worst sin of all is the lie. The most perverse lie we can possibly utter is the lie about ourselves and the lie about God. When we lie about God, we are lying about ourselves, and when we are lying about ourselves, we are lying about God." These two things are connected.

If you know the truth of God, you will know the truth about yourself. This is very important because we can mouth truths. We can talk about the Holy Scriptures being the inspired words of God in human words. We can say all kinds of things, but when we say those things, if we are in delusion about ourselves, whatever we say has no power. That is what St. Paul means when he writes of those who hold the truth in unrighteousness. We can hold the truth, but if we are unrighteous ourselves, we cannot even know what we are talking about, although, verbally, our words may be true. In other words, we may speak of Christ, the Truth, but if our hearts are far from Him, we do not know Him in truth.

We could say the words "Christianity is the truth" but not participate in the vital existential reality of what that means. When this happens, we show that we have no knowledge of God or of ourselves. St. Isaac of Syria says a person who comes to know the truth about himself is greater than a person who has raised the dead, because if you do not know the truth about yourself, then nothing is real for you.

If I am in total falsehood, making up my world and making up God, then I am in the hands of the devil, who is a liar, and I become a liar myself. If we ourselves are liars, the Bible and the Fathers of the Church teach, then we will distort reality in every conceivable way, from the reality of created things to the reality of God, even going so far as to make up our own Jesus.

Christ Himself said there will be people who say, "Christ is here; Christ is there" (see Matt. 24:26–28). Do not go there. It is not real. The demons themselves can appear as angels of light (see 2 Cor. 11:14) to lead people astray, to think they are in the truth, and they are not in the truth at all.

This is very scary. How do we know we are not in delusion but are in the truth? We may not really *know*; we just pray and invoke the Holy Spirit, the Spirit of Truth, to lead us and guide us into all truth. When we are thinking of Jesus Christ as *the Truth*, we remember He said He would send us the Spirit of Truth to guide us into all truth.

Jesus said,

> "If you love me, you will keep my commandments. And I will pray the Father, and he will give you another Counselor, to be with you for ever, even the Spirit of truth, whom the world cannot receive, because it neither sees him nor knows him; you know him, for he dwells with you, and will be in you." (John 14:15–17)

"The world" here means the fallen world, which cannot recognize what is truth.

> "But when the Counselor comes, whom I shall send to you from the Father, even the Spirit of truth, who proceeds from the Father, he will bear witness to me; and you also are witnesses, because you have been with me from the beginning. . . .When the Spirit of truth comes, he will guide you into all the truth." (John 15:26–27; 16:13)

God the Father is the true God; the Son is the Truth, the Logos, the Word incarnate; and the Holy Spirit is the Spirit of Truth, who guides us into all truth.

St. Paul tells the Corinthians that where the Holy Spirit is, there is freedom (2 Cor. 3:17). The Spirit of Truth makes us free; otherwise, we are trapped.

This truth is given to us to *know*. We can know the Truth, we know the true God, we can know Christ as Truth; and we can know all this through the Spirit of Truth, and therefore confess the Holy Spirit *as* the Spirit of Truth.

How does that work? Scientists know how to measure things, how to produce mathematical formulas about how things work, and they can draw conclusions. They can hope they are really in the truth and are not messing up the realities they are observing, but then, scientists can invite people to *verify*.

If a person says, "I will never believe the Earth is round," even with endless proofs, that person will not believe even the proofs because he does not want to know the truth. We must want to know the truth. We have to hunger and thirst for it.

If we hunger and thirst for the divine truth of the gospel, what do we have to do? The Scriptures are clear. We have to want it, to seek it, and to be ready to pay the price to have it. We will know the truth if we love one another as Jesus has loved us, if we take up our cross and follow Him, if we try to be meek and merciful, patient, peaceful, peace-making, pure in heart, and poor in spirit. When we strive to do these things, we can come to know the Truth.

"Blessed are the pure in heart, for they shall see God" (Matt. 5:8). If your heart is not pure, you will not see God, just as if you do not look through a microscope, you will not see whatever you have under the microscope. As Jesus said, if your deeds are evil, you will not see. "For every one who does evil hates the light, and does not come to the light, lest his deeds should be exposed" (John 3:20). "The eye is the lamp of the body. So, if your eye is sound, your whole body will be full of light; but if your eye is not sound, your whole body will be full of darkness. If then the light in you is darkness, how great is the darkness!" (Matt. 6:22–23). When our deeds are good and when we seek the glory of God and the good of our neighbor, then we will see because we will have come to the Light, to Christ.

Jesus promises that if we keep His commandments, beg God that we might do so, and repent when we do not, then we will know the Truth, and no one will be able to disabuse us of it. We can truly know spiritual truth, but we do not come to know this truth in the same way we come to know material reality or natural science, because we are not dealing with created things but with that which is uncreated and eternal.

St. John, in his first letter, is writing to all Christians. He says, "But you have been anointed by the Holy One, and you all know" (1 John 2:20). He is writing to us as people who *do* know the truth. "I write to you, not because you do not know the truth, but because you know it, and know that no lie is of the truth" (1 John 2:21).

"For I greatly rejoiced when some of the brethren arrived and testified to the truth of your life, as indeed you do follow the truth. No greater joy can I have than this, to hear that my children follow the truth" (3 John 3—4).

If we are Christians, we have to be the children of God who are following the truth. We have to put the truth into practice by living according to Christ's commandments, by living according to the Truth. We must love our enemies, bless those who curse us, pray for those who abuse us. We must decide to do good and not curse or lie or be angry. We must live purely and truly, living as true human beings in the ethical sense: dependable, responsible. We must keep our word.

A person who does these things will come to know the truth and, being convinced of it, will come to know the true God, despite whatever doubts and failures occur along the way.

We have to be lovers of truth. If we have that desire, then we will come to see that Jesus Christ is indeed the Truth, that He is not lying when He says, "I am the Truth." If we keep saying to Him, "What is truth?" like Pontius Pilate, He will stand there silently and say, "Look at Me and *you* decide. How many instructions can I give you so that you may *know*? The rest is up to you now. If you want to know, you will see. Seek and you will find."

Our conviction, and that of the Church in all her history, is that Jesus Christ is the Truth. As Christians, we believe all truth is Christian. It belongs to us, to the Church, and through the Church, God has given it to everybody. Mathematical, scientific, biological, archaeological, theological, philosophical, musical—whatever kind of truth there is, we believe that the heart, meaning, and significance of it is given to us by the Lord Jesus Christ.

He reveals the truth about everything, but we have to love that truth to know what it is. St. Paul wrote to the Philippians:

> Finally, brethren, whatever is true, whatever is honorable, whatever is just, whatever is pure, whatever is lovely, whatever is gracious, if there is any excellence, if there is anything worthy of praise, think about these things. (Phil. 4:8)

Alexander Solzhenitsyn, a Russian writer of our own time, said, "Let us at least try not to lie. Let us at least respect the truth—of science, mathematics, art. Let us be people of truth." If that is our intention, then we will see that Christ is the Truth. He holds everything together. He gives meaning to all things. He is indeed the source of the truth of all things because He is the one by whom, for whom, and toward whom all things are made.

The truth is in Jesus, and He is the truth about everything: God, human beings, the created world. Jesus Christ is Himself, personally and hypostatically, the Truth. That is our conviction and the teaching of the Church. Jesus is not only the truth *about* everything, but He also has given Himself to us so He could be *our* truth also. Our truth can be Christ Himself who is the Truth. Then we will not be deceived, but will have life in us because the Truth is life-giving, and without the Truth, we are dead.

CHAPTER 29

Jesus the

LIFE

In Holy Scripture, the term *life*, like the term *death*, is used in many different ways. First, there is biological life. The term *biological* comes from the Greek word *bios* for "life" or "living." *Biological* has to do with living things, both animals and plants.

The term *animal* comes from the Latin *anima*, which means "soul." In Hebrew, the term for "life" is *nephesh*, which also means "breath, being vivified, acting, and living." It is translated in the Greek Scriptures as *psyche*, which means "soul," and this complicates the issue.

Plants and animals are living things, and they can die. The same thing is true about human beings. Genesis 2:7 says, "Then the Lord God formed man of dust from the ground, and breathed into his nostrils the breath of life; and man became a living being." Human beings are animals in the sense that we are alive, but we are also spiritual. We can think, speak, act, will, choose, know, and do *good*. Because we have that kind of life, that freedom, we can also think, speak, act, will, choose, know, and do *evil*. We can turn our back on the God who made us. Therefore, we are capable of dying.

The Wisdom of Solomon says God did not make death for human beings (see WSol. 1:13). God's intention was that human beings, made in His image and likeness, would reign over the cosmos and would be able to govern and take care of the animals and plants. If human beings were what God created them to be, they would never die; they would have the Holy Spirit in them. Therefore, for human beings, biological death is a tragedy.

When someone dies, people may say the deceased "had a good, long life," but this sidesteps the tragedy. The person is dead! When people die, we weep. We say, "No! This is alien." We sing, as St. John of Damascus says, "Why are we wedded unto death?" Why did God give us, as the poet Wordsworth says, "intimations of immortality," only to know that, as it says in the psalm, we die like any beast (see Ps. 49[48]:20)?

You might have a long life without much suffering. You might have many children. You might even say, "Well, that's about as good as it gets." Yet this way of thinking does not address the critical questions: Why should we grow old in the first place? Why should we die, even if we have a peaceful death or, as they say nowadays, "a death with dignity"? I have been a priest for forty-six years, and I have seen all kinds of deaths, from babies born dead to hangings. I have cut down three people who have hanged themselves. Death is not dignified; it is ugly and repulsive. Literally, it stinks.

Some people avoid confronting the horrible reality of death by saying, "Well, that's just how it is, and if you have a long, good, and happy life, you just disappear afterwards. Your sorrows are over, and that's as good as it gets." Some people say, "You have a soul in you, and when you die, your body rots, but your soul goes off to contemplate eternal realities in some purely spiritual, heavenly world." That is Platonism, basically, and in some sense, it is also Hinduism and Buddhism. However, that is not at all the biblical teaching.

At the time of Jesus, there was a lot of debate among the people of Israel over whether or not there is a resurrection of the dead. The Pharisees believed in resurrection. They also believed that human beings are living souls. Spirit, soul, and body, according to the Scriptures as the ancient Christians understood them, all go together. When those things disintegrate, you die.

In the priest's prayer book, there is a prayer for "the separation of soul and body," which is read for those who are dying. No Christian would ever say, "It is good that we die. The soul is now liberated from the accursed flesh." That is Platonism again. Even when people speak of a "return to God" or "going home," those are not biblical expressions at all, in my opinion.

Earth is our home. Christians believe that God will raise the dead and recreate the cosmos, and we are going to live in that recreated order forever and ever—with the billions of galaxies, and all the trees, plants, and animals.

216 NAMES OF JESUS

This is where we belong. The Kingdom of God is not of this world, but this world is created to be the Kingdom of God.

In the time of the New Testament, the Pharisees were opposed by the Sadducees. They did not believe in resurrection, the immortality of the soul, an afterlife, or in rewards or punishment after death. They would say, "When you are dead, you are dead, and that's it."

The Acts of the Apostles says, "But when Paul perceived that one part [of the council accusing him] were Sadducees and the other Pharisees, he cried out in the council, 'Brethren, I am a Pharisee, a son of Pharisees; with respect to the hope and the resurrection of the dead I am on trial!'" (Acts 23:6). The minute he says, "I am on trial for the resurrection of the dead," the Jews start fighting among themselves about whether there is a resurrection.

Human beings are not supposed to die and lose the power of keeping ourselves alive. According to Holy Scripture, if you keep the commandments of God, if you glorify, thank, and love God, He will keep you alive forever.

In the symbolical language of Genesis, there are two trees in the garden of Paradise, where Adam and Eve were living. There is the Tree of Life, which symbolizes participation in God and keeping His commandments, and there is also the Tree of the Knowledge of Good and Evil. The day you touch that tree or taste of it, you die. Touching or tasting of the Tree of the Knowledge of Good and Evil seems to mean you give yourself over to sin; you do not love God, and you follow your own mind and listen to the serpent, which stands for earthly wisdom and the devil.

St. Paul puts it very starkly: "The wages of sin is death" (Rom. 6:23). We know that we should live, yet we die like any beast because our relationship with God is skewed; it has been broken.

As Orthodox Christians understand the Scriptures, if you do not sin, you cannot biologically die; you can keep yourself alive. In Genesis, however, it is very clear: Humanity sins and dies and returns to the earth, and life becomes full of pain and suffering. Therefore, God has to redeem what He made.

Biological life can be equated with everlasting life, because everlasting life has to be biological life. We believe in the resurrection of the body—a physical resurrection. It is the life for which God created us, the life that will literally never end—enduring not simply to length of days, but unto ages of ages.

Understanding it this way, biological life for a human being is to keep the commandments of God and to love God with all our mind, soul, heart, and strength; to love our neighbors as ourselves; and to do no evil. If we did that, we would live forever. Biological life would become everlasting life.

Eternal technically means "without time." Only God is eternal, timeless, without beginning. Creatures, on the other hand, have their beginning in time. Their existence is in time. They are not perfect but developing.

Rather than use the term *eternal*, Scripture speaks of *everlasting* life, a life without end. When we think of time in the sinful world, it is as an enemy. We grow older, we get sick, and we die. It does not have to be that way, however. There can be a time when our life is fuller and deeper and more and more alive, forever! That is the Christian view of what it means to be a human being—an unending growth of life.

When Jesus says He gives *eternal life*, He means we can have that life right now. St. Paul says, "When Christ who is our life appears, then you also will appear with him in glory" (Col. 3:4). Both St. Paul and St. John call Jesus *the Life*. He is the Life of everything that lives.

Metropolitan Tryphon Turkestanov said, "Darwin couldn't have been all bad if he was interested in *life*. Whether Darwin knew it or not, he was interested in Christ because Christ is Life." You cannot be interested in life and not, ultimately, be interested in Christ. Certainly, the opposite also is true: If you are interested in Christ, you are interested in life. Even in this world, Christ gives us the possibility to transform death into an act of life, to shatter death, to enter into everlasting life, and to take possession of the coming Kingdom, in which all things will be made alive again.

"For the Son of man came to seek and to save the lost," Jesus said (Luke 19:10). He is the Savior of all created things, of the entire cosmos, not just of human beings.

When Christ says, "I am the life" (John 14:6), He is saying that biological life is a gift from God. Wherever we see any kind of life, we see Christ there. St. Paul says in Acts, quoting Hellenistic philosophers who came to the same conclusion, "in him we live and move and have our being" (Acts 17:28). Christ dwells in and vivifies everything that exists on the earth. "The heavens are telling the glory of God; / and the firmament proclaims his handiwork" (Ps.

19[18]:1). Everything is filled with the glory and the power of God, and that is, hypostatically, Jesus Christ Himself, vivified by the Holy Spirit.

When we say Jesus is the Life, it means He is the content of everything that lives. The source of life, the beginning of life, the end of life, the meaning of life, the aim of life—every single one of them is Christ. He is the Life of life.

There is a distinction between simply existing or surviving and actually living. A person can be eating and drinking and actually be dead. C. S. Lewis, in *The Abolition of Man*, said if we lose that faculty within us that he calls the *tao* or the inner law or the spark of God, we are not living anymore. We are not even human anymore. We are nothing but a mind in matter.

Christ makes life more than biological or animal existence. He is God's image, and therefore He is the Life we are created to have.

Deuteronomy 30:19 says, "I have set before you life and death, blessing and curse; therefore choose life, that you and your descendants may live." If we choose goodness and truth and beauty, we are choosing life. Since Christ is the Life, not even biological death can destroy us.

Until the end of the ages, we human beings are still wedded unto biological death because we are still caught in this demon-riddled, death-bound world. Yet we are baptized and have died with Christ; we eat His Body, which is the Bread of Life, and drink His Blood, which is Life itself. In the Holy Scriptures, blood is a synonym for life. This is why, in the sacrificial system of the Old Testament, one could not touch the blood. When Jesus says, "Drink My blood" (see John 6:56), that is revolutionary language because the life was in the blood, and the life belonged to God.

The Psalms speak much of life, living, and divine life. We use this psalm verse at the beginning of Lent: "Seek God, and your soul will live" (Ps. 69[68]:32 LXX).

I would suggest that everyone read Psalm 119(118). It is the psalm Orthodox Christians read over the tomb of Christ on Holy Saturday and also at funerals. Read that psalm from this perspective, because that psalm is saying, "If you keep the commandments of God, you cannot die." The psalmist keeps saying, "I love Your law, because it gives me life." Enliven me, quicken me, because in Your commandments is life.

According to Scripture, the tragedy is that when you are biologically dead, you cannot praise God. "Can the dead praise You? Can they praise You from the pit? Can they praise You from Sheol?" (see Ps. 88[87]:10–12). That is why the Pharisees and the Lord Jesus Christ and the Apostle Paul and all Orthodox Christians hold that there must be a resurrection from the dead. We must be made alive again so that we can sing "Alleluia" to God.

In Christ, even if we die biologically, we cannot be killed. In John, Jesus says, "Truly, truly, I say to you, the hour is coming, and now is, when the dead will hear the voice of the Son of God, and those who hear will live" (John 5:25). Later, He says, "I am the resurrection and the life; he who believes in me, though he die, yet shall he live" (John 11:25). Christ has overcome death, and we who believe in Him have become victorious in Christ. In anticipation, in the Holy Spirit, we already experience the life which is life indeed. However, we still hope and pray that the Kingdom of God will come.

We do not know how the physical cosmos is going to act in the coming Kingdom. Some Church Fathers think that it will still be cyclical—there will be blossoms and plants and they will wither away and come back again, but there will not be anything tragic about it, since everything will be in constant restoration, and the souls and the bodies of human beings will never be separated again.

According to Scripture, we should never forget that people who do have a relatively painless life are obliged to help the people who are suffering. When a journalist said to Mother Teresa of Calcutta, "Well, *you* don't suffer, Mother Teresa," she said, "Christ my God suffered so that no one would suffer. He died so that no one would die. And if I have health, then I am obliged by my God to serve and to love and to help those who are suffering, who are dying."

Those who believe that Christ is the Life are obliged to enhance life, to protect life, to try to create a culture of life. Pope John Paul II called our present age in the West a "culture of death." We abort our unborn children. We take stem cells from babies. We have made biological life the be-all and end-all of reality. It seems that our only goal is to live as long as possible in this world in a peaceful and happy life. If that is our only goal, then we are really in the hands of the devil. If it is not a *holier* life that we seek, then what good is it? If we live without holiness or at least searching for holiness, we are not living, but spreading death.

If Christ is not there, life is not life. It is, as Shakespeare says, "full of sound and fury, signifying nothing." If we live truly, the life of the living God becomes our own. What makes life life is love. That is why the Scripture says love is stronger than death (see Song 8:6), because love is life itself.

Christ, who is Life, died on the Cross. He who is everything became nothing. When Life died, death was destroyed. Nothingness was transformed into everything. Through that act, everything is vivified, because that act is an act of love. Therefore, it is by nature life-producing. Christ will ultimately make life triumphant. As St. John Chrysostom says in the last line of his Paschal Homily, "Christ is risen, and life reigns." It says in Greek, "Christ is risen and life *lives*."

The Tree of Life is the Cross of Christ. That is why He is suspended on a tree. The Old Testament says that Wisdom is the Tree of Life (Prov. 3:18). If you know the Wisdom of God, then you are communing with Life, and that Wisdom makes you alive. Christ alone kept the commandments perfectly, and therefore He destroyed death by hanging on the Tree of Life. When we eat Christ's Body as the living bread and when we drink His Blood which is His life, then we are communing of the Tree of Life and of the Cross. The fruit of the Tree of Life is the broken Body and shed Blood of Jesus Christ. One of the last sentences of Revelation says, "Blessed are those who wash their robes, that they may have the right to the tree of life and that they may enter the city by the gates" (Rev. 22:14).

Christians believe that Christ is the Life. He not only speaks about life and shows life, but He is the Life. He said, "For the gate is narrow and the way is hard, that leads to life, and those who find it are few" (Matt. 7:14). Few there are who really want life, who want God, who want truth, who want beauty, but those who find it will have it. Jesus said, "I came that they may have life, and have it abundantly" (John 10:10), that their life may be life indeed.

When a young man asked Jesus about the commandments, He replied, "Do this, and you will live" (Luke 10:28). When the people are not following Him, He says, "Why don't you come to Me, that you may have life?" He gave Himself up for the life of the world. "For God so loved the world that he gave his only Son, that whoever believes in him should not perish but have eternal life" (John 3:16), and that Life is His Son, Jesus Christ.

CHAPTER 30

Jesus the

BREAD OF LIFE

I am the bread of life," Jesus says in the Gospel of John (John 6:35), after He performs the messianic sign of feeding the people with bread in the wilderness. He does not say, "I will give you bread," but "I am the bread."

The Jews at that time believed that, when God's Kingdom came, there would be no more hunger. This is a classical teaching of the Old Testament: God opens the eyes of the blind; God takes care of the widow and the orphan; God sets the prisoners free; God feeds those who are hungry. In this world are many hungering people who do not know the truth, but it is the Christian conviction that these things will be fulfilled in the age to come. In this life, we have a foretaste of the coming Kingdom in what Christ did when He was on earth. Those who belong to Christ are those who care for the poor, the orphans, and the widows. They do it because God does this for all of us, and He will do it in the age to come. In imitation of Christ, we have to feed those who are hungry when we can.

The miraculous feeding of the multitudes is related in all four Gospels, so it is very important. In the synoptic Gospels, there are two feedings.

After the second feeding, Jesus' disciples forgot to bring bread with them in the boat.

> And he cautioned them, saying, "Take heed, beware of the leaven of the Pharisees and the leaven of Herod." And they discussed it with one another, saying, "We have no bread." And being aware of it, Jesus said to them, "Why do you discuss the fact that you have no bread? Do you not yet perceive or understand? Are your hearts hardened? Having

eyes do you not see, and having ears do you not hear? And do you not remember? When I broke the five loaves for the five thousand, how many baskets full of broken pieces did you take up?" They said to him, "Twelve." "And the seven for the four thousand, how many baskets full of broken pieces did you take up?" And they said to him, "Seven." And he said to them, "Do you not yet understand?" (Mark 8:15–21)

Why did Jesus feed the multitudes twice? The best theory I have heard was by a Roman Catholic monk, a biblical scholar, who lives in Jerusalem. He said Jesus does it once in Gentile territory and once in Judaic territory, and that is a sign that He is the messianic Lord for the Gentiles as well as the Jews. This monk said that when the feeding of the five thousand had twelve baskets left over, that symbolized the Jews. And, in the feeding of the four thousand, the seven baskets left over symbolized the Gentiles. Seven, as a symbol of fullness, means the rest of humanity.

John 6 narrates the miraculous feeding:

After this Jesus went to the other side of the Sea of Galilee, which is the Sea of Tiberias. And a multitude followed him, because they saw the signs which he did on those who were diseased. Jesus went up on the mountain, and there sat down with his disciples. Now the Passover, the feast of the Jews, was at hand. (vv. 1–4)

People have come for the Passover from all regions. We remember the Passover in Exodus, how God gave the Israelites manna, bread from heaven, to eat. Now Jesus comes and spreads the table in the wilderness.

Lifting up his eyes, then, and seeing that a multitude was coming to him, Jesus said to Philip, "How are we to buy bread, so that these people may eat?" This he said to test him, for he himself knew what he would do. Philip answered him, "Two hundred denarii would not buy enough bread for each of them to get a little." One of his disciples, Andrew, Simon Peter's brother, said to him, "There is a lad here who has five barley loaves and two fish; but what are they among so many?" Jesus said, "Make the people sit down." Now there was much grass in the place; so the men sat down, in number about five thousand. Jesus then took the loaves, and when he had given thanks, he distributed them to those who were seated; so also the fish, as much as they wanted. And

when they had eaten their fill, he told his disciples, "Gather up the
fragments left over, that nothing may be lost." So they gathered them
up and filled twelve baskets with fragments from the five barley loaves,
left by those who had eaten. When the people saw the sign which he
had done, they said, "This is indeed the prophet who is to come into the
world!" (vv. 5–14)

After everyone has eaten and seen this miracle, Jesus leaves, having perceived
"that they were about to come and take him by force to make him king"
(v. 15). The disciples get into a boat to go across the lake without Him. Then
Jesus comes to them walking on the water.

The next day, the people who remained on the other side of the sea
saw that there had been only one boat and that Jesus had not entered the
boat when His disciples went away. Then it says, "However, boats from
Tiberias came near the place where they ate the bread after the Lord had
given thanks" (v. 23). This is a eucharistic overtone. In the Divine Liturgy,
in a dialogue with the congregation prior to Holy Communion, the priest
says, "Let us lift up our hearts, let us give thanks unto the Lord." It is the
Eucharist, *eucharistia,* "thanks."

The passage continues:

> So when the people saw that Jesus was not there, nor his disciples, they
> themselves got into the boats and went to Capernaum, seeking Jesus.
> When they found him on the other side of the sea, they said to him,
> "Rabbi, when did you come here?" Jesus answered them, "Truly, truly,
> I say to you, you seek me, not because you saw signs, but because you
> ate your fill of the loaves. Do not labor for the food which perishes,
> but for the food which endures to eternal life, which the Son of man
> will give to you; for on him has God the Father set his seal." Then they
> said to him, "What must we do, to be doing the works of God?" Jesus
> answered them, "This is the work of God, that you believe in him whom
> he has sent." So they said to him, "Then what sign do you do, that we
> may see, and believe you? What work do you perform? Our fathers ate
> the manna in the wilderness; as it is written, 'He gave them bread from
> heaven to eat.'" Jesus then said to them, "Truly, truly, I say to you, it was
> not Moses who gave you the bread from heaven; my Father gives you
> the true bread from heaven. For the bread of God is that which comes

down from heaven, and gives life to the world." They said to him, "Lord, give us this bread always." (vv. 24–34)

It is similar to what Jesus told His disciples after His conversation with the Samaritan woman:

> "I have food to eat of which you do not know." So the disciples said to one another, "Has any one brought him food?" Jesus said to them, "My food is to do the will of him who sent me, and to accomplish his work." (John 4:32–34)

The disciples did not understand Him. Jesus says in John 6:

> "I am the bread of life; he who comes to me shall not hunger, and he who believes in me shall never thirst. But I said to you that you have seen me and yet do not believe. All that the Father gives me will come to me; and him who comes to me I will not cast out. For I have come down from heaven, not to do my own will, but the will of him who sent me; and this is the will of him who sent me, that I should lose nothing of all that he has given me, but raise it up at the last day. For this is the will of my Father, that every one who sees the Son and believes in him should have eternal life; and I will raise him up at the last day."
>
> The Jews then murmured at him, because he said, "I am the bread which came down from heaven." They said, "Is not this Jesus, the son of Joseph, whose father and mother we know? How does he now say, 'I have come down from heaven'?" Jesus answered them, "Do not murmur among yourselves. No one can come to me unless the Father who sent me draws him; and I will raise him up at the last day. It is written in the prophets, 'And they shall all be taught by God.' Every one who has heard and learned from the Father comes to me. Not that any one has seen the Father except him who is from God; he has seen the Father. Truly, truly, I say to you, he who believes has eternal life. I am the bread of life. Your fathers ate the manna in the wilderness, and they died. This is the bread which comes down from heaven, that a man may eat of it and not die. I am the living bread which came down from heaven; if any one eats of this bread, he will live for ever; and the bread which I shall give for the life of the world is my flesh." (vv. 35–51)

Life is communion with God. Jesus is the one who makes this life possible. His own flesh is the Bread of Life.

> The Jews then disputed among themselves, saying, "How can this man
> give us his flesh to eat?" So Jesus said to them, "Truly, truly, I say to you,
> unless you eat the flesh of the Son of man and drink his blood, you have
> no life in you." (vv. 52–53)

That is a startling sentence, because every Jew knows one is not supposed
to touch the blood—that was forbidden by the Mosaic Law—but whenever
Jesus begins with "Truly, truly," it is not negotiable.

> "He who eats my flesh and drinks my blood has eternal life, and I will
> raise him up at the last day. For my flesh is food indeed, and my blood
> is drink indeed. He who eats my flesh and drinks my blood abides in
> me, and I in him. As the living Father sent me, and I live because of the
> Father, so he who eats me will live because of me." (vv. 54–57)

This teaching was difficult for even His disciples to understand. "Many of
his disciples, when they heard it, said, 'This is a hard saying; who can listen
to it?'" (v. 60), and they left Him. But those who kept following Him saw, at
the Last Supper, how He took bread and said, "This is My Body, which is
broken for you," and they witnessed His Passion, and then they understood.
We participate in Jesus' death and Resurrection by eating and drinking the
bread and the wine that are offered to God as the Christian sacrifice in the
new priesthood of the New Covenant. St. Paul says in Hebrews 7:17 that this
is the priesthood according to Melchizedek, who made the offering of bread
and wine (Gen. 14:18).

Sometimes people interpret "unless you eat the flesh of the Son of Man
and drink His blood, you have no life in you" to mean that those who have
never had Holy Communion cannot be saved because they have no life in
them. But Jesus is speaking to the Jews, who are supposed to know who He
is, and if they do not realize that He is the living bread that comes from
heaven, they have simply rejected their Messiah.

It was not just the Jewish leadership who rejected their Messiah, however,
but many of His own disciples left Him as well.

> After this many of his disciples drew back and no longer went about
> with him. Jesus said to the twelve, "Do you also wish to go away?"
> Simon Peter answered him, "Lord, to whom shall we go? You have the

words of eternal life; and we have believed, and have come to know, that you are the Holy One of God." (vv. 66–69)

Earthly bread is necessary, and God is the one who provides that bread, but, Jesus says, do not labor only for the food that perishes; labor for the living bread, the Bread of Life, that when you eat it, you never die. Jesus is not only bread as the Lamb of God who is sacrificed, but He is the bread as the Word, as teaching, as spiritual food.

Anyone familiar with the Holy Scriptures cannot fail to remember the words of the Prophet Amos:

> "Behold, the days are coming," says the Lord God,
> "when I will send a famine on the land;
> not a famine of bread, nor a thirst for water,
> but of hearing the words of the Lord.
> They shall wander from sea to sea,
> and from north to east;
> they shall run to and fro, to seek the word of the Lord,
> but they shall not find it." (Amos 8:11–12)

When Jesus began His earthly ministry, it says in Matthew, Mark, and Luke that He was driven into the wilderness, where He was tempted by the devil not to be the Messiah. Matthew says:

> And the tempter came and said to him, "If you are the Son of God, command these stones to become loaves of bread." But he answered, "It is written,
> > 'Man shall not live by bread alone,
> > but by every word that proceeds from the mouth of God.'"
> (Matt. 4:3–4)

Jesus refuses to be simply a giver of earthly bread. He is the Logos who comes from the mouth of God, and He is the Bread of Life. He came not just to provide for this earthly life that ends, but to give everlasting life.

During His temptation, Jesus quotes the Holy Scriptures. In each temptation He undergoes in the wilderness, the devil quotes Scripture, and Christ answers quoting another passage of Scripture. Martin Luther said, "Even the devil can quote Scripture to his advantage." As St. Hilary of

Poitiers said, "It's not in the reading, it's in the understanding."

Jesus quotes Deuteronomy:

> And he humbled you and let you hunger and fed you with manna,
> which you did not know, nor did your fathers know; that he might make
> you know that man does not live by bread alone, but that man lives by
> everything that proceeds out of the mouth of the Lord. (Deut. 8:3)

As the Russian Christian philosopher, Nikolai Berdyaev, said, "Bread for myself is a material problem; bread for my neighbor is a spiritual problem." It is a scandal that, in the twenty-first century, there are still hungry people on earth. We should be able to feed the whole world. *We* should be feeding the hungry.

Even that, however, is not our ultimate goal. In the Sermon on the Mountain, Jesus says, "Blessed are those who hunger and thirst for righteousness" (Matt. 5:6). Then, when He is teaching about prayer, He says:

> "Therefore do not be anxious, saying, 'What shall we eat?' or 'What
> shall we drink?' or 'What shall we wear?' For the Gentiles seek all these
> things; and your heavenly Father knows that you need them all. But
> seek first his kingdom and his righteousness, and all these things shall
> be yours as well." (Matt. 6:31–33)

Jesus says very clearly: Do not be anxious. We need to work, but should not worry; we need to trust God. As Psalm 37(36):25 says, "I have not seen the righteous forsaken / or his children begging bread." Some way or another, everything will work out; and Christians have to believe that.

Jesus said that, in our prayers, we should not pray for anything earthly— not for food, not for drink, not for clothing. The Holy Fathers are *violent* on this point. If you are a Christian, you do not pray for anything temporal, anything passing away. Sure, if you are hungry, you could say, "God, please provide some food." St. Peter wrote, "Cast all your anxieties on him, for he cares about you" (1 Peter 5:7). But we still have to add, "Your will be done." If God wants me to starve to death, I have to be ready to starve to death. That is terrifying, but it is true.

In the prayer life of the Christian, we pray for the eternal things, believing that, if we do that, God will provide as He knows. Why, then, does the Lord's

Prayer say, "Give us this day our daily bread?" Some interpretations say it means "give us what we need to keep us alive"—earthly and heavenly.

But that word is not *daily* in Greek. The Greek text says, *ton arton hēmon ton epiousion dos hēmin simeron* (Matt. 7:11). *Ton arton hēmon* means "the bread for us." *Ton epiousion* is a very strange phrase; nobody knows what it means because that phrase does not exist anywhere outside the Lord's Prayer. It is not even used in any other surviving classical Greek literature. Literally, *epi* and *ousia* mean "super-substantial" or "super-essential" bread. "Give us today the super-essential bread." In Luke 11, the same adjective, *epiousios*, is used.

I am convinced, following the Holy Fathers, that Jesus is not at all speaking about everyday bread here. He is not speaking about earthly food. *Epiousios* in Greek, according to those who know and follow the Semitic Fathers, such as St. Athanasius the Great and others, seems to mean "give us today the bread of the future age; give us today the bread of the age that is coming." The note in the Oxford Annotated Revised Standard Version says, "Give us today tomorrow's bread."

Here Jesus does not mean anything temporal or earthly. I think we have to conclude that, when the Lord's Prayer says, "Give us today the bread of the future age, the *real* bread, the super-substantial bread, the heavenly bread," it means Jesus Himself.

This is given to us now already in the Holy Eucharist. That is why we say the Lord's Prayer at the Divine Liturgy, just before we have Holy Communion. We pray that, with boldness and without condemnation, we may dare to call God "Father" and ask that He would give us the super-substantial Bread. The super-substantial Bread God the Father gives us is His own Son, Jesus Christ. Jesus said, "I am the Bread of Life. I am the living Bread that came from heaven. Seek *this* bread. Seek the Bread that I Myself am, because I, Jesus, the Messiah, the Son of God, the Incarnate Logos, I am the Bread of Life. He who eats *this* Bread will *never* die."

CHAPTER 31

Jesus the

RESURRECTION

Orthodox Christians believe that if Christ were not risen from the dead, there would be no Christianity. The only reason we have Christianity is that there were people who were absolutely convinced that Jesus of Nazareth, who was crucified, rose from the dead.

On Pentecost, Peter preaches:

"Men of Israel, hear these words: Jesus of Nazareth, a man attested to you by God with mighty works and wonders and signs which God did through him in your midst, as you yourselves know—this Jesus, delivered up according to the definite plan and foreknowledge of God, you crucified and killed by the hands of lawless men. But God raised him up, having loosed the pangs of death, because it was not possible for him to be held by it. For David says concerning him,

'I saw the Lord always before me,
for he is at my right hand that I may not be shaken;
therefore my heart was glad, and my tongue rejoiced;
moreover my flesh will dwell in hope.
For thou wilt not abandon my soul to Hades,
nor let thy Holy One see corruption.
Thou hast made known to me the ways of life;
thou wilt make me full of gladness with thy presence.'

"Brethren, I may say to you confidently of the patriarch David that he both died and was buried, and his tomb is with us to this day. Being therefore a prophet, and knowing that God had sworn with an oath to him that he would set one of his descendants upon his throne, he foresaw and spoke of the resurrection of the Christ, that he was not abandoned to Hades, nor did his flesh see corruption. This Jesus God raised up, and of that we all are witnesses. Being therefore exalted at the right hand of God, and having received from the Father the promise of the Holy Spirit, he has poured out this which you see and hear." (Acts 2:22–33)

The apostles were convinced that Jesus was risen, that He was glorified and seated at the right hand of the Father, because they believed the risen Christ had appeared to them.

The Gospels record appearances of the risen Christ to Mary Magdalene, to the apostles in the Upper Room, to Luke and Cleopas on the road to Emmaus, and to St. Paul. In 1 Corinthians 15, Paul says:

For I delivered to you as of first importance what I also received, that Christ died for our sins in accordance with the scriptures, that he was buried, that he was raised on the third day in accordance with the scriptures, and that he appeared to Cephas, then to the twelve. Then he appeared to more than five hundred brethren at one time, most of whom are still alive, though some have fallen asleep. Then he appeared to James, then to all the apostles. Last of all, as to one untimely born, he appeared also to me. For I am the least of the apostles, unfit to be called an apostle, because I persecuted the church of God. But by the grace of God I am what I am, and his grace toward me was not in vain. On the contrary, I worked harder than any of them, though it was not I, but the grace of God which is with me. Whether then it was I or they, so we preach and so you believed.

Now if Christ is preached as raised from the dead, how can some of you say that there is no resurrection of the dead? But if there is no resurrection of the dead, then Christ has not been raised; if Christ has not been raised, then our preaching is in vain and your faith is in vain. (1 Cor. 15:3–14)

We can quote from the Gospel of John the passage that is read at Orthodox funerals:

"Truly, truly, I say to you, the hour is coming, and now is, when the dead will hear the voice of the Son of God, and those who hear will live. For as the Father has life in himself, so he has granted the Son also to have life in himself, and has given him authority to execute judgment, because he is the Son of man. Do not marvel at this; for the hour is coming when all who are in the tombs will hear his voice and come forth, those who have done good, to the resurrection of life, and those who have done evil, to the resurrection of judgment." (John 5:25–29)

In John 11, Jesus says, "I am the resurrection and the life." He had gone to where His friend Lazarus was, who had been dead for four days.

> When Martha heard that Jesus was coming, she went and met him, while Mary sat in the house. Martha said to Jesus, "Lord, if you had been here, my brother would not have died. And even now I know that whatever you ask from God, God will give you." Jesus said to her, "Your brother will rise again." Martha said to him, "I know that he will rise again in the resurrection at the last day." Jesus said to her, "I am the resurrection and the life; he who believes in me, though he die, yet shall he live, and whoever lives and believes in me shall never die. Do you believe this?" She said to him, "Yes, Lord; I believe that you are the Christ, the Son of God, he who is coming into the world." (John 11:20–27)

For what purpose was Christ to come into the world? He came to suffer, thus fulfilling the Scriptures. In his letters to the Corinthians, St. Paul insists that Jesus suffered His Passion in accordance with the Scriptures; He is the Suffering Servant prophesied by Isaiah.

The other New Testament writers also became convinced that His Resurrection is according to the Scriptures. There are not many Old Testament texts about the Resurrection of the Messiah, and that leads some people to say, "Maybe a Suffering Servant was prophesied, but it never says the Messiah will be raised again." But the glorification, according to the reading of the Scriptures by the apostles, is "The LORD says to my lord: / 'Sit at my right hand, / till I make your enemies your footstool'" (Ps. 110[109]:1).

What did it mean in the Prophets that God's Kingdom would have no end? What did it mean that all the kings of the earth would stand as children of Abraham? St. Paul is very clear: To belong to Israel and to be a Jew in truth is a matter of faith and not a matter of flesh and blood. He says in 1 Corinthians, "flesh and blood cannot inherit the kingdom of God" (1 Cor.

15:50). There has to be a new creation, which can only take place if there is a death and a resurrection.

This is the reason the Resurrection of the Messiah was according to Scripture. Just as His suffering and death was according to Scripture, so did the Old Testament prophesy His vindication and glorification. The Holy One cannot see corruption in the tomb. Paul fought with his fellow Jews on this point because they did not understand the Scriptures that way. They thought Paul was mad.

If we look to the Old Testament, does it say anywhere that there would be a resurrection from the dead? In the Old Covenant, there were bodily resuscitations, people raised in the same way Jesus raised up Lazarus, the daughter of Jairus, and the son of the widow of Nain. But this was not the resurrection into the Kingdom of God; it was bodily resuscitation for more life in this fallen world. In the Old Testament, Elijah raised the son of the widow of Zarephath and Elisha raised up the son of the Shunammite woman. These prefigured Christ raising up the only son of a widow in Nain.

But does the Old Testament speak about a general resurrection from the dead? In Isaiah 26, the Canticle of Isaiah says:

> Thy dead shall live, their bodies shall rise.
> O dwellers in the dust, awake and sing for joy!
> For thy dew is a dew of light,
> and on the land of the shades thou wilt let it fall. (v. 19)

Hosea says:

> "I will deliver them out of the hand of Hades
> And will redeem them from death.
> Where is your penalty, O death?
> O Hades, where is your sting?" (Hos. 13:14 OSB)

Those lines are quoted by St. Paul in 1 Corinthians 15:54–55, and by St. John Chrysostom at the end of his Paschal Homily, which is read every year on Pascha and ends with, "Christ is risen and Death is destroyed. Christ is risen and Hades is harrowed."

In another passage in Hosea, the prophet says:

"Come, let us return to the Lord;
for he has torn, that he may heal us;
he has stricken, and he will bind us up.
After two days he will revive us;
on the third day he will raise us up,
that we may live before him." (Hos. 6:1–2)

This text is considered to be prophetic relative to Jesus, that He is killed on Friday; on Saturday, the second day, He revives us by lying dead in the tomb; and on the third day He appears, risen from the dead and raising all with Him. Matthew says that when Jesus was crucified and buried, some people in Jerusalem saw the bodies of the saints risen and walking around the city.

Christians read all the victory stories in the Old Testament as prefiguring the Resurrection of the Messiah. The greatest one is Pascha itself, the Passover exodus. In Egypt, the Israelites had no real life; they were slaves. But then God raised up Moses and led them out of Egypt, through the waters of the Red Sea, and into the desert. There they were fed with manna, bread from heaven, and given the commandments of God. Then, after the death of Moses, Joshua came to lead them; his name is the same as Jesus, and he took them across the Jordan River and into the Promised Land. All this is interpreted as a prefiguration of the death and Resurrection of Christ and the coming of the Kingdom of God, the kingdom of David that has no end.

All of these historical things—even if one calls them mythological—are salvific and victorious. *Salvation, victory,* and *healing* all translate the same word in Hebrew. They all prefigure the Resurrection of Christ. "Behold, I am doing a new thing," Isaiah prophesies (Is. 43:19). That is considered to be a prophecy of the resurrection of the dead. How can there be a new creation without the resurrection of the dead?

The story of the Patriarch Joseph is read as a prefiguration of the death and Resurrection of Christ. Joseph, the youngest and beloved child of Jacob, of Israel, is sold by his brothers into Egypt. They betrayed him and sold him because of envy. The New Testament says in all four Gospels that Christ was given up out of envy. In the story of Joseph (Genesis 37), his brothers dig a pit and bury him in the ground. They take his robe, prefiguring the robe of Christ, and then they decide, by divine Providence, not to kill him physically but to kill him in every other way by selling him as a slave into Egypt. Egypt represents being in the hands of the devil, being in bondage.

One of the Desert Fathers said Joseph was sold by his own humility. Joseph could have said to the slavers, "These are my brothers; they sold me," but he is silent; he lets himself be sold. He goes into the realm of the enemy, which prefigures the realm of death, and he becomes the ruler there.

The troparion of the Resurrection (in tone six) says that Christ overthrew and despoiled Hades, but was not tempted or tried by it. Joseph was not tempted by all the material power of Egypt. He was not tempted by the Egyptian woman who tried to seduce him. On the second day of Holy Week, we sing about these things in church.

Then Joseph's brothers come to Egypt. They are starving, and Joseph becomes their savior. The one they thought was dead was alive, reigning as a ruler. And he forgives the very brothers who betrayed him, just as Jesus forgives those who killed Him.

A few generations prior to these events in the life of Joseph, God tells Abraham to sacrifice his only son, Isaac (Genesis 22). Abraham is about to do as God commands until the Angel of the Lord stops him from killing his son, saying, "Do not lay your hand on the lad or do anything to him; for now I know that you fear God, seeing you have not withheld your son, your only son, from me" (Gen. 22:12). A ram is found and slain, and the son is saved. This is also considered to be a prefiguration of the death and Resurrection of Christ. He is the Lamb of God, prefigured by the ram who is slain.

The story of the Prophet Jonah also prefigures the Resurrection of Christ. Jonah is like a scapegoat; he dies for the other people. He says, "Throw me into the water and you guys will be okay" (see Jon. 1:12), and so they throw him into the water and he is swallowed by a whale. For three days and three nights, he is in the belly of the whale, and then the whale vomits him out and he goes to Nineveh to deliver God's message of warning to them. Then the people repent and are saved.

The entire Book of Jonah is read in church on Holy Saturday, and on Pascha we sing hymns referencing the story. The Canticle of Jonah (Jon. 2:2–9), which is the prophet's prayer to God from the belly of the whale, is a song of God's victory:

"I called to the Lord, out of my distress,
and he answered me;
out of the belly of Sheol I cried,
and thou didst hear my voice." (v. 2)

"I went down to the land
whose bars closed upon me for ever;
yet thou didst bring up my life from the Pit,
O Lord my God." (v. 6)

Also, in Matthew, Jesus Himself twice speaks of the "sign of Jonah" to point to His Resurrection. In Matthew 12, and again in chapter 16, He says:

"An evil and adulterous generation seeks for a sign; but no sign shall be given to it except the sign of the prophet Jonah. For as Jonah was three days and three nights in the belly of the whale, so will the Son of man be three days and three nights in the heart of the earth." (Matt. 12:39–40)

Another story prefiguring the Resurrection of Christ is that of the three young men in the fiery furnace, which is told more fully in the Septuagint version of the Book of Daniel. These three youths refused to worship the golden idol King Nebuchadnezzar had set up in Babylon and ordered everyone to worship. For refusing to obey the king's order, they were thrown into a fiery furnace and were supposed to perish there. The fiery furnace is a symbol of Sheol.

Yet, while they are still inside the furnace, a fourth figure appears inside. In astonishment, King Nebuchadnezzar says, "Did we not cast three men bound into the fire? . . . Behold, I see four men untied and walking in the midst of the fire, yet they are not destroyed; and the vision of the fourth is like the Son of God" (Dan. 3:91–92 OSB). The fourth man dances with the three youths in the flames and delivers them, and the three youths come out alive. This typifies the death and Resurrection of Christ, and how Christ, as the Son of God, enters into the pit of the fiery furnace of death and raises up all who are dead, and they come out alive. This story is read on Holy Saturday as well.

Another story, which is read at the very end of Matins on Great and Holy Saturday as the final act, is that of the dry bones from the Book of Ezekiel.

God says, "I will open your graves" (Ezek. 37:12). The first Christians read this in the light of the Resurrection of Christ. Israel is Jesus, and Jesus is raised from the dead, and He triumphs over all the enemies. All those stories are prefigurations of the death and Resurrection of Christ. The fact remains: God raised Jesus of Nazareth from the dead. Jesus is the Resurrection and the Life. The dead are raised, and they are raised because of Jesus.

Why does Jesus call Himself the Resurrection? Could God not have opened all the tombs without Him? Is it not possible for God to raise up the dead without the Passion of Jesus? The simple answer would be, "Sure He could, but what good would it do?" If it would just be a resuscitation into more life in this fallen world, where we would have to suffer and die again, then there would be no forgiveness of sins and no real healing. Death would not be destroyed in reality; we would still be caught in the cycle of death—that is, we would still be living with the things that brought about death in the first place.

The resurrection of the dead is not some kind of external miracle God performs. It is something that happens within humanity through the Man, Jesus. We believe every act of God is Trinitarian. Each is an act of God the Father, through the Son, by the Holy Spirit. The Son of God, the Word of God, the Wisdom of God, is the One who performs all God's activities toward creation and in creation, and that includes the redemption of the world.

When we think about Christ saying, "I am the resurrection and the life," we are saying God raises the dead by raising Jesus, and the power of that Resurrection is Jesus Himself. The paradox is, Jesus raises the dead by dying. He tramples down death by death. By emptying and humbling Himself, by becoming obedient even to the point of death on the Cross (see Phil. 2:8), He showed His power—the power that destroys death itself. And, through His Resurrection, Jesus made the whole creation new.

We must ask ourselves: Do we believe this? Do we believe that Jesus is the Resurrection and the Life? He said it: ""I am the resurrection and the life; he who believes in me, though he die, yet shall he live, and whoever lives and believes in me shall never die." (John 11:25–26), and "I will raise him up at the last day" (John 6:40).

CHAPTER 32

Jesus the

DOOR

In the Gospel of John, Jesus refers to Himself as "the door of the sheep." He says:

> "Truly, truly, I say to you, he who does not enter the sheepfold by the door but climbs in by another way, that man is a thief and a robber; but he who enters by the door is the shepherd of the sheep. To him the gatekeeper opens; the sheep hear his voice, and he calls his own sheep by name and leads them out. When he has brought out all his own, he goes before them, and the sheep follow him, for they know his voice. A stranger they will not follow, but they will flee from him, for they do not know the voice of strangers." This figure Jesus used with them, but they did not understand what he was saying to them.
>
> So Jesus again said to them, "Truly, truly, I say to you, I am the door of the sheep." (John 10:1–7)

Or it could also be translated: "I am the door of the sheep*fold*. I am the door of the flock, where the sheep are, where they are gathered together." Then He says:

> "I am the door; if any one enters by me, he will be saved, and will go in and out and find pasture. The thief comes only to steal and kill and destroy; I came that they may have life, and have it abundantly. I am the good shepherd. The good shepherd lays down his life for the sheep." (John 10:9–11)

Let us examine this imagery of the door. We have many doors in our churches: the doors on the icon screen, the doors into the temple itself, the doors into the church building. At the Divine Liturgy, when the doors of the nave are to be closed and only the faithful are to be present for the Holy Eucharist, the deacon says, "The doors, the doors! In wisdom, let us attend!"

The imagery of gates and doors is also used on the very first and very last pages of the Bible.

In Genesis, when humanity apostatizes from God through disobedience to the commandment not to eat of the fruit growing on the Tree of the Knowledge of Good and Evil, they are put out of Paradise and into the present world. It is then that the Scriptures speak of a gate, a kind of door.

An angel was stationed in front of the gates of Paradise, preventing entrance into Paradise until the saving work of Christ was accomplished. Christians reading Genesis would understand that Christ is the gate through which we can pass to enter again into Paradise and partake again of the Tree of Life (see Gen. 3:24). When Jesus says, "I am the Door," He is calling Himself the door to Paradise. By entering this door, we can live forever in communion with God.

Scripture uses the imagery of gates and doors in other ways as well. When the Hebrews were going through the desert, their encampment had a door through which only the righteous could enter, and when people violated the Law of God, they were put outside the camp, outside the gate. There were doors also on the tabernacle. Only the righteous—and of them, only those exercising the priestly ministry—were allowed to enter through these doors.

Then there was the door of the temple itself, the door facing east, through which passed the glory of the Lord. That gate was shut, and no one could enter through it because it was reserved for the Lord Himself. Thus, the kings and priests had to use the other door, the north door.

Then, of course, there were the gates of Jerusalem. Jesus was crucified *outside* the gate. The one who is Himself the Gate of the heavenly Jerusalem was cast out, along with the unrighteous and rejected. This happened so that He could become the Gate or the Door by which the unrighteous and rejected will then, being forgiven and redeemed, be able to enter into the heavenly, eternal Jerusalem.

Christ, as the Door and Gate, is prefigured throughout the Old Testament. Psalm 118(117), the paschal psalm, says, "I shall not die, but I shall live, / and recount the deeds of the Lord" (v. 17); "This is the day which the Lord has made; / let us rejoice and be glad in it" (v. 24); and "Blessed be he who enters in the name of the Lord!" (v. 26). When Jesus enters the city of Jerusalem as the King, He goes through the gate on Palm Sunday and then enters into the temple.

The same psalm also contains the imagery of the gate:

> Open to me the gates of righteousness,
> that I may enter through them
> and give thanks to the Lord.
> This is the gate of the Lord;
> the righteous shall enter through it. (vv. 19–20)

When we hear these verses, we think of the gates of Paradise, the gates of the temple, the gate of the holy of holies within the temple, the gates of Jerusalem, and, of course, the gates of the heavenly Kingdom, the heavenly Jerusalem.

The Book of Revelation describes the heavenly Jerusalem as being surrounded by a great, high wall having twelve gates, which are named after the angels. This is the heavenly model for the earthly temple in Jerusalem. There are four sides with three gates on each side, and twelve foundations. The twelve foundations are the twelve apostles of the Lamb. The gates of the heavenly Jerusalem are also continually open. "And its gates shall never be shut by day, and there shall be no night there" (Rev. 21:25). Thus, the heavenly Jerusalem is accessible. "The Spirit and the Bride say, 'Come'" (Rev. 22:17). Let everyone who can enter, come.

The Lord, by grace, opens up the gates of that Kingdom to all sinners if they will accept forgiveness, confess their sins, and glorify God. The gates are open, and they can enter if they wish to. There is not even a temple in the heavenly Jerusalem, "for its temple is the Lord God the Almighty and the Lamb" (Rev. 21:22).

Almost the very last line of the Bible says, "Blessed are those who wash their robes [or who do His commandments], that they may have the right to the tree of life and that they may enter the city by the gates" (Rev. 22:14). Outside those gates are the dogs, the sorcerers, the fornicators, the murderers, the idolaters, and everyone who loves and practices falsehood—all who have chosen not to repent. The imagery takes us right back to Genesis. Those who repent—the redeemed of the Lord—have the right, the privilege, and the boldness to approach the Tree of Life.

When we hear in Psalm 118(117), "Open to me the gates of righteousness, that I may enter through them *and give thanks to the Lord*" (v. 19), that is eucharistic language. *Eucharistein* in Greek means "to give thanks." In the week after Pascha, Bright Week, if we go into the church building, we will find that the royal gates and doors of the icon screen are open. This symbolizes the fact that, through Christ's Crucifixion and Resurrection, we now have access to the altar of God, as it says in Hebrews, and everybody enters in.

The psalm continues, "This is the gate of the Lord; / the righteous shall enter through it" (Ps. 118[117]:20). St. John, in his Gospel, says that gate is Jesus Himself, who does not only indicate the gate of salvation, the gate of righteousness, the gate of the Lord, the gate of the New Jerusalem, the gate of Paradise—he not only is the one who opens that gate—but He is the Gate.

Jesus says, "Truly, truly, I say to you, he who does not enter the sheepfold by the door but climbs in by another way, that man is a thief and a robber" (John 10:1). He is saying, "I am the only door there is. Any other door leads to perdition." And those doors are *broad* that lead to destruction.

But the Door that leads into God's Kingdom, into the Holy of Holies, is narrow, and few there be who find it (see Matt. 7:14). Jesus continues, "But he who enters by the door is the shepherd of the sheep" (John 10:2). So, as the Good Shepherd, He is the first one to walk through the door, the Door that He Himself *is*.

He is not only the Shepherd, he is not only the Door of the sheepfold, but He is also the sheep, the Lamb. He is everything! And truly, that *is* our conviction: that Jesus is everything. Anything you can name and think of, Jesus is. He is it, perfectly and hypostatically, and we have to follow Him through that Gate that He Himself is. He says, "If any one enters by me, he will be saved, and will go in and out and find pasture" (John 10:9).

We can reflect on a few other things, one of which is the teaching of the absolute uniqueness of Jesus. He is not one truth of many; He is *the* Truth.

He does not simply show the way to life; He is the Way and He is the Life. He does not just give the words; He is the Word. He is also the unique Gate. There are no other gates; He is the only Gate. If you are saved, you enter by Him.

Jesus says, "No one can come to the Father *except by Me*. No one can be saved *except by Me*. No one can enter into life and into light and truth *except by Me*." He is the One and the *only* One.

We Christians believe it is God's will, through His Son Jesus Christ and by the power and indwelling of the Holy Spirit, not only that we would have everything that God has, but that we would actually become everything that God is. God wills us human beings literally to participate in the life of God and become divine. This is a very bold teaching, but it is a clear Christian teaching that, by divine grace, we can become what Christ our God is by nature, and do the works that He does. Jesus said, "Truly, truly, I say to you, he who believes in me will also do the works that I do; and greater works than these will he do, because I go to the Father" (John 14:12). If Jesus is the Son of God, then all of us, male and female, can become adopted sons of God through Him. Those who believe in the Son of God have every gift and privilege of sonship.

We can say this about everything Jesus is. If Christ is the Door, by faith in Him and by God's grace, we, too, become doors. In Orthodox Christianity, we call Mary the gate of heaven. She is the gate by which Christ entered our world.

In Ezekiel, there is a prophecy concerning the ever-virginity of Mary:

> Then he brought me back to the outer gate of the sanctuary, which faces east; and it was shut. And he said to me, "This gate shall remain shut; it shall not be opened, and no one shall enter by it; for the Lord, the God of Israel, has entered by it; therefore it shall remain shut. Only the prince may sit in it to eat bread before the Lord; he shall enter by way of the vestibule of the gate, and shall go out by the same way." (Ezek. 44:1–3)

We use the imagery of a gate and a door for Mary as well as for Jesus, but in a different way. Jesus is the Door by nature; Mary becomes a door by the grace of God. The Holy Spirit comes upon her, the power of the Most High overshadows her, and she becomes the gate through which Christ enters the world.

She also functions, by her intercessions, as a gate through which we can enter into communion with her Son. We go by way of Mary into communion with Jesus, and then by way of Jesus into communion with God the Father. All this happens by the power of the Holy Spirit. Saints are doors that lead us to God. If you follow this saint or that saint, imitating their holiness, you will be led into the presence of God.

Each one of us is to be a gate for other people to enter into communion with God. This means we should not be obstacles. We should be open doors to God's Kingdom, inviting people to enter, and showing them how. We should not be like certain leaders of the Jewish people, of whom the Lord said, "But woe to you, scribes and Pharisees, hypocrites! because you shut the kingdom of heaven against men; for you neither enter yourselves, nor allow those who would enter to go in. . . . For you traverse sea and land to make a single proselyte, and when he becomes a proselyte, you make him twice as much a child of hell as yourselves" (Matt. 23:13, 15).

If you do not go through the Door yourself, you cease being a door. You become a dead end.

Christ is truly God and truly Man, and He calls us to become real human beings, to become gods by grace. We can never become God by nature, but we can become gods by grace. We can become sons of God, images of God, lights of God. We can become vessels of the grace of God. We can become pillars of the Wisdom of God. We can become bread of God that people can partake of and be nourished. And we can also become doors and gates.

We confess Jesus as the one and only Gate, the one and only Door. He is the one by which and through which we enter. He is the one who opens up the door that leads to life, the door of righteousness, the door of faith, the door of the Word of God, the door of Paradise, the door of the New Jerusalem, the door of the temple, the door of the Kingdom. He opens the Door; we pass through the Door; He is the Door.

CHAPTER 33

Jesus the

TRUE VINE

In a lengthy catechetical discourse given to His disciples at the Last Supper in the Gospel of John, Jesus calls Himself the True Vine.

Some people doubt the historicity of this discourse; they doubt that Jesus said the entirety of it at that particular time. I personally believe these are sayings of Jesus that come from the memory of the Church, from the apostles themselves. These sayings were probably put together in this extended discourse at the Supper for good evangelical and symbolical reasons.

John 15 begins, "I am the true vine, and my Father is the vinedresser" (v. 1), the one who takes care of the vine. In a sense, Jesus is saying that God His Father is nurturing Him, tending to Him as a vine keeper. Then He says, "Every branch of mine that bears no fruit, he takes away, and every branch that does bear fruit he prunes, that it may bear more fruit" (v. 2).

If there is a branch that does not bear fruit, God the Father cuts it away; but if it is a good, fruit-bearing branch, He prunes it—cuts it, lacerates it— that it might bear more fruit. This violent imagery about God's activity with us is common in Holy Scripture. God loves us with a severe, violent, divine love.

In Scripture, God is compared to a loving father who chastens his children. Hebrews says, "What son is there whom his father does not discipline?" (Heb. 12:7). If we are not disciplined by God, then we are not real children of God.

The loving God is the potter who smashes the vessel and refashions it with his own hands to make a vessel fit to bear the grace of God. He is a jeweler who refines the gold with fire, burning out all the impurities. He is also a lover who wounds the beloved. And so on.

Jesus continues in John, "You are already made clean by the word which I have spoken to you" (John 15:3). That sentence is very important: the Word of God scrubs us, cleanses us. Hebrews says, "For the word of God is living and active, sharper than any two-edged sword, piercing to the division of soul and spirit, of joints and marrow, and discerning the thoughts and intentions of the heart" (Heb. 4:12). Saint John Chrysostom says we go to church to hear the words of God and the Psalms so that God would cut out the malignant tumors that are in us—passions and sins.

Then Jesus says, "Abide in me, and I in you" (John 15:4). *Abide* can also mean "remain" or "dwell permanently." Earlier in this discourse, Jesus says He abides in God the Father, and God the Father abides in Him (see John 14:10). Therefore, He is the one through whom we abide in God.

"As the branch cannot bear fruit by itself, unless it abides in the vine, neither can you, unless you abide in me" (John 15:4). We cannot be fruit-bearing unless we are grafted into Him, the Vine.

The Apostle Paul also uses the imagery of grafting. In Romans, he speaks about the Gentiles being grafted into the vine of Israel and also urges them to note God's kindness and severity.

> You will say, "Branches were broken off so that I might be grafted in."
> That is true. They were broken off because of their unbelief, but you
> stand fast only through faith. So do not become proud, but stand in awe.
> For if God did not spare the natural branches, neither will he spare you.
> Note then the kindness and the severity of God: severity toward those
> who have fallen, but God's kindness to you, provided you continue in
> his kindness; otherwise you too will be cut off. (Rom. 11:19–22)

Israel is the original vine God planted, but that vine is ultimately one Person, Jesus of Nazareth. He becomes the sole Vine. The Gentiles are grafted to Israel and are therefore grafted to the Messiah so they can bear fruit.

Jesus continues, "I am the vine, you are the branches. He who abides in me, and I in him, he it is that bears much fruit, for apart from me you can do nothing" (John 15:5).

St. Augustine of Hippo said, "Jesus did not say, 'Without Me, you can do a little.' He said, 'Apart from Me, you are not able to do anything at all. You have no power, no strength to do anything.'"

But then Jesus says, "If a man does not abide in me, he is cast forth as a branch and withers; and the branches are gathered, thrown into the fire and burned" (John 15:6).

In the Gospel of Luke, Jesus tells the Parable of the Fig Tree:

> "A man had a fig tree planted in his vineyard; and he came seeking fruit on it and found none. And he said to the vinedresser, 'Lo, these three years I have come seeking fruit on this fig tree, and I find none. Cut it down; why should it use up the ground?' And he answered him, 'Let it alone, sir, this year also, till I dig about it and put on manure. And if it bears fruit next year, well and good; but if not, you can cut it down.'" (Luke 13:6–9)

But Jesus also curses the barren fig tree:

> In the morning, as he was returning to the city, he was hungry. And seeing a fig tree by the wayside he went to it, and found nothing on it but leaves only. And he said to it, "May no fruit ever come from you again!" And the fig tree withered at once. (Matt. 21:18–19)

Jesus told several parables about vineyards where the workers did not bring forth fruit, or they kept the fruits for themselves and did not give them to God and their neighbors. They were cast out. God took the vineyard away from them and gave it to those who would deliver the expected fruit.

John the Baptist, when he began preaching the coming of Jesus, used the same imagery.

> But when he saw many of the Pharisees and Sadducees coming for baptism, he said to them, "You brood of vipers! Who warned you to flee from the wrath to come? Bear fruit that befits repentance, and do not presume to say to yourselves, 'We have Abraham as our father'; for I tell you, God is able from these stones to raise up children to Abraham. Even now the axe is laid to the root of the trees; every tree therefore that does not bear good fruit is cut down and thrown into the fire." (Matt. 3:7–10)

246 ✠ THE NAMES OF JESUS

The Church Fathers play with that imagery. They say that fruit-bearing trees are very humble. They are bent over with branches close to the ground; their leaves serve to protect the fruit. Trees that do not grow fruit usually have beautiful leaves, and their branches reach quite high. But God is not interested in the leaves, but in the fruit. The Fathers go even further and say that our ascetical efforts—fasting, reading the Bible, keeping vigil, doing prostrations, going to church, singing the hymns, and saying the prayers—are all just leaves. These leaves are, of course, very important; but if you have only leaves, you are condemned, you are fruitless, you are good for nothing.

"If you abide in me, and my words abide in you," Jesus continues, "ask whatever you will, and it shall be done for you" (John 15:7).

Some people think we can ask God anything we want, and He will do it. According to the Scriptures, however, this is not true. We can only ask God for things we can ask in Jesus' name, and that does not mean we can simply tack on "in the name of Jesus, we ask this, O Lord." *In Jesus' name* means "according to Jesus, according to His teaching." It means, "whatever I can ask, as being grafted into Jesus, as being a branch of which He is the Vine." I can ask anything in *that* situation, and God will give it.

Jesus continues, "By this my Father is glorified, that you bear much fruit, and so prove to be my disciples" (John 15:8). In Matthew, Jesus says, "Thus you will know them by their fruits" (Matt. 7:20).

Those fruits are clearly stated in Galatians, although it is *fruit*, in the singular, because there are many fruits we could bear, but they are aspects of one and the same fruit. "But the fruit of the Spirit is love, joy, peace, patience, kindness, goodness, faithfulness, gentleness, self-control; against such there is no law" (Gal. 5:22–23). This is the fruit of the Holy Spirit; those are the elements that make us Godlike. That is what makes us like Christ; and the whole purpose of the Lord's coming is that we would have this fruit, that we would be grafted to Him, that we would abide in Him and He in us, and then these fruits would be produced.

Apart from Him, we cannot produce any of these fruits at all. There may be people who do not know anything about Christ, but if they have these realities in their lives—if they have real love, real joy, real peace, real kindness, real gentleness, real fidelity, real self-control—they have them because of the grace and Spirit of God.

If we are not bringing forth good fruit, we are bringing forth bad fruit. If we are not living and being vivified and being made fruitful by the Holy Spirit, then we are being vivified (or, rather, slowly killed), and even controlled and possessed, by the devil. There is no third option. It is either good fruit or bad fruit. It is either the Holy Spirit or the demons. It is either God or Satan.

Our Christianity can be proven only by the fruit of the Holy Spirit in our life, or, to be more humble, our laboring for that fruit, and our tears of repentance when we do not produce that fruit and we beg God not to cut us off. The term *anathema* literally means "to be cut off"—cut off from the True Vine, cut off from the Body of Christ—because one is not producing fruit; one is just a cancer on the Body.

The writers of the New Testament took this imagery of the vine from the Law, the Psalms, and the Prophets. Psalm 80(79) says:

> Thou didst bring a vine out of Egypt;
> thou didst drive out the nations and plant it.
> Thou didst clear the ground for it;
> it took deep root and filled the land.
> The mountains were covered with its shade,
> the mighty cedars with its branches;
> it sent out its branches to the sea,
> and its shoots to the River.
> Why then hast thou broken down its walls,
> so that all who pass along the way pluck its fruit?
> The boar from the forest ravages it,
> and all that move in the field feed on it. (vv. 8–13)

That vine is the people of Israel. God drove out the nations and planted them in the Promised Land. The Canaanites were driven out by God, who gave the land to His people.

After these verses comes this prayer:

> Turn again, O God of hosts!
> Look down from heaven, and see;

have regard for this vine,
the stock which thy right hand planted. (vv. 14–15)

When a bishop serves the Divine Liturgy, at the Trisagion he blesses the people and says those same words. We are the vine the right hand of the Lord God has planted; therefore, we are supposed to bring forth fruit.

The psalm continues, "They have burned it with fire, they have cut it down; / may they perish at the rebuke of thy countenance!" (v. 16). Then it proceeds with a promise, a hope: "But let thy hand be upon the man of thy right hand, / the son of man whom thou hast made strong for thyself!" (v. 17). That means Jesus. The psalm ends:

Then we will never turn back from thee;
give us life, and we will call on thy name!
Restore us, O Lord God of hosts!
let thy face shine, that we may be saved! (vv. 18–19)

Another example of the vine imagery is in Isaiah 5:

Let me sing for my beloved
a love song concerning his vineyard:
My beloved had a vineyard
on a very fertile hill.
He digged it and cleared it of stones,
and planted it with choice vines;
he built a watchtower in the midst of it,
and hewed out a wine vat in it;
and he looked for it to yield grapes,
but it yielded wild grapes.
And now, O inhabitants of Jerusalem
and men of Judah,
judge, I pray you, between me
and my vineyard.
What more was there to do for my vineyard,
that I have not done in it?
When I looked for it to yield grapes,
why did it yield wild grapes?
And now I will tell you
what I will do to my vineyard.

I will remove its hedge,
and it shall be devoured;
I will break down its wall,
and it shall be trampled down.
I will make it a waste;
it shall not be pruned or hoed,
and briers and thorns shall grow up;
I will also command the clouds
that they rain no rain upon it.
For the vineyard of the Lord of hosts
is the house of Israel,
and the men of Judah
are his pleasant planting;
and he looked for justice,
but behold, bloodshed;
for righteousness,
but behold, a cry! (Is. 5:1–7)

But then, six chapters later, this is written:

In that day the root of Jesse shall stand as an ensign to the peoples; him
shall the nations seek, and his dwellings shall be glorious. In that day
the Lord will extend his hand yet a second time to recover the remnant
which is left of his people, from Assyria, from Egypt, from Pathros,
from Ethiopia, from Elam, from Shinar, from Hamath, and from the
coastlands of the sea. (Is. 11:10–11)

Jesus is the Root of Jesse. This prophecy of Isaiah is alluded to in Matthew
2:23: "He shall be called a Nazarene." Many people think that means He
is going to be raised in Nazareth, but Nazareth is named after the word
nezer, which means "root" or "branch." Where it says "He shall be called a
Nazarene," it means that He will be the Branch, He will be the Vine, He will
be the one to whom we shall be grafted. He will be the one through whom
we can produce fruit. All this is quoted in the New Testament.

At the First Hour on Great and Holy Thursday, the day of the Last Supper,
we read from Jeremiah:

The Lord made it known to me and I knew;
then thou didst show me their evil deeds.

But I was like a gentle lamb
led to the slaughter.
I did not know it was against me
they devised schemes, saying,
"Let us destroy the tree with its fruit,
let us cut him off from the land of the living,
that his name be remembered no more." (Jer. 11:18–19)

Instead of God cutting off the fruitless branches, the evil people of the world are trying to cut down the stem God has planted. They are trying to cut down Christ. Oh, how did they not know that His name would be remembered forever!

At the end of that same reading from Jeremiah on Great and Holy Thursday are these words: "And after I have plucked them up, I will again have compassion on them, and I will bring them again each to his heritage and each to his land" (Jer. 12:15). The final word of the Lord is always the word of salvation, redemption, restoration, renewal, and of being grafted to the Vine again. That is our hope.

Jesus is the Vine, and apart from Him we can do nothing. But if we are grafted to Him, and His life—His Blood—flows through our veins, and we breathe by His own Holy Spirit, then we produce fruit. We even become vines ourselves; we become the vineyard God has planted.

When Jesus says, "I am the True Vine" and "I am the Vine, you are the branches," it means that we should be connected to Christ and that His life should be in us and our life should be in Him. Everything we ask for in this condition He will give to us, so that we may have the fruit of the Holy Spirit: love, peace, joy, patience, kindness, goodness, gentleness, fidelity, and self-control. This is what we should pray for.

CHAPTER 34

Jesus Our

PEACE

Peace, in the Holy Scriptures, is a very important reality. The Kingdom of God is identified with peace, the *shalom* of God, when all of creation will be at peace with God and itself. In the end, there will be a total peace, a restfulness.

Peace is not simply an absence of conflict, but a virtue, a content of divine life. Holy Scripture speaks not only about the peace of God, but about the God of peace. It also speaks about the peace of Jerusalem, the gospel of peace, the covenant of peace, the peacemakers, and the children of peace. At the time of Christ, people greeted one another with "Peace be to you." When they visited each other's homes, they would say, "Peace to this house."

The Apostle Paul defines the kingship of God as peace, joy, and righteousness in the Holy Spirit: "For the kingdom of God is not food and drink but righteousness and peace and joy in the Holy Spirit" (Rom. 14:17). For Christians, Christ is God's Peace. When He is born, the angels sing, "Glory to God in the highest, / and on earth peace among men with whom he is pleased!" (Luke 2:14), in the presence of the shepherds and of the newborn Christ.

In Ephesians, St. Paul writes about Christ as the Peace of Christians, the One who brought about peace between the Jews and the Gentiles:

> For he is our peace, who has made us both one, and has broken down
> the dividing wall of hostility, by abolishing in his flesh the law of
> commandments and ordinances, that he might create in himself one
> new man in place of the two, so making peace, and might reconcile
> us both to God in one body through the cross, thereby bringing the

hostility to an end. And he came and preached peace to you who were
far off and peace to those who were near; for through him we both have
access in one Spirit to the Father. (Eph. 2:14–18)

At Christmastime, we sing in church a section of Isaiah:

> The people who walked in darkness
> have seen a great light;
> those who dwelt in a land of deep darkness,
> on them has light shined.
> . . .
> For to us a child is born,
> to us a son is given;
> and the government will be upon his shoulder,
> and his name will be called
> "Wonderful Counselor, Mighty God,
> Everlasting Father, Prince of Peace."
> Of the increase of his government and of peace
> there will be no end,
> upon the throne of David, and over his kingdom,
> to establish it, and to uphold it
> with justice and with righteousness
> from this time forth and for evermore.
> The zeal of the Lord of hosts will do this. (Is. 9:2, 6–7)

Christians apply those words to Jesus. The prophecy also calls Him the
Father of the age to come, meaning He begets the coming age of cosmic
peace. Isaiah prophesies about this coming age of peace:

> The wolf shall dwell with the lamb,
> and the leopard shall lie down with the kid,
> and the calf and the lion and the fatling together,
> and a little child shall lead them. (Is. 11:6)

And, of the people living in that coming age, Isaiah prophesies:

> He shall judge between the nations,
> and shall decide for many peoples;
> and they shall beat their swords into plowshares,
> and their spears into pruning hooks;

> nation shall not lift up sword against nation,
> neither shall they learn war any more. (Is. 2:4)

> They shall not hurt or destroy
> in all my holy mountain;
> for the earth shall be full of the knowledge of the Lord
> as the waters cover the sea. (Is. 11:9)

Jesus' messianic title, *Prince of Peace*, means not only that He is the King whose kingship of peace will endure forever, but also that He is the source of all peace. He is the fountain from whom the peace comes, and He is the very Peace itself.

In Orthodox tradition, in Constantinople, there were several churches dedicated to the Lord Jesus Christ. The great church of that city was Hagia Sophia, which was not dedicated to St. Sophia, but to Christ as Holy Wisdom. But there was also a church called Hagia Irene, which was not dedicated to St. Irene, but to Christ as our Peace.

In the Holy Scriptures, Christ is also identified with Melchizedek (see Gen. 14:18–20), whose name means "king of righteousness" and "king of peace." This Melchizedek is a prefiguration of Christ.

Of the entire Old Testament, the line most often repeated in the New Testament is the first verse of Psalm 110(109): "The LORD says to my lord: / 'Sit at my right hand, / till I make your enemies your footstool.'" As the Apostle Paul says, "For he must reign until he has put all his enemies under his feet" (1 Cor. 15:25). All of the enemies of God have to be put under the feet of Jesus. The last enemy is death itself. Then God will be all in all, and the peace of God will reign throughout the whole of creation.

Psalm 110(109) continues:

> The Lord sends forth from Zion
> your mighty scepter.
> Rule in the midst of your foes!
> Your people will offer themselves freely
> on the day you lead your host
> upon the holy mountains.
> From the womb of the morning
> like dew your youth will come to you.

The Lord has sworn
and will not change his mind,
"You are a priest for ever
after the order of Melchizedek." (vv. 2–4)

Hebrews says:

> For this Melchizedek, king of Salem, priest of the Most High God, met
> Abraham returning from the slaughter of the kings and blessed him;
> and to him Abraham apportioned a tenth part of everything. He is first,
> by translation of his name, king of righteousness, and then he is also
> king of Salem, that is, king of peace. He is without father or mother
> or genealogy, and has neither beginning of days nor end of life, but
> resembling the Son of God he continues a priest for ever. (Heb. 7:1–3)

Jesus becomes a priest forever according to the order of Melchizedek; He is
appointed permanently and forever by God to make the perfect self-offering
that brings the peace of God to all creation. Complete fulfillment of this will
take place at Jesus' Second Coming.

For this reason, when we celebrate the Divine Liturgy, the priest blesses
the people with "Peace be to all"; the deacon says, "Again and again, in peace
let us pray to the Lord"; and we pray constantly for the peace from above, for
the salvation of our souls, for the peace of the whole world, for the welfare
of God's holy churches, for the union of all people. Then, when we actually
offer the bread and wine, which is what Jesus offered at the Last Supper and
which is prefigured in Melchizedek's offering of bread and wine, we say, "A
mercy of peace, a sacrifice of praise." This is the offering for peace.

In the levitical codes, there were thank offerings, praise offerings, peace
offerings, guilt offerings, and redemption offerings. Christ fulfills them all,
and they are all an offering for the peace of the whole world—in prefiguration
of and in response to the peace that was proclaimed at Christmas, and in
expectation of the peace that will reign in the coming age.

It is to be hoped that when we are in church, we are in that peace. Jesus
said in the Gospel of John, "Peace I leave with you; my peace I give to you;
not as the world gives do I give to you. Let not your hearts be troubled,
neither let them be afraid" (John 14:27). He gives the peace that passes all

understanding (see Phil. 4:7). The peace of God Himself, and the peace that God *is*, is Jesus Christ, and He makes peace through shedding His blood on the Cross.

A Christian must also become peace. We must be in this world the presence of God's peace. Our whole life we are striving to be at peace, to be witnesses to the covenant of peace, to be children of peace, and to be makers of peace. Jesus said, "Blessed are the peacemakers, for they shall be called sons of God" (Matt. 5:9). It says "sons" because women also have the status of sons in the final covenant. In Christ, there is neither male nor female, Jew nor Greek, slave nor free (see Gal. 3:26, 28), and all are to be at peace.

We are supposed to embody in our own flesh, as Jesus Christ did, all the virtues, splendors, powers, qualities, characteristics, and properties of God Himself, and the heart of them all is peace. Wisdom and peace go very closely together in Holy Scripture, because you cannot be at peace unless you are wise. *Sophia*, besides wisdom, has the additional connotation of everything being harmonious and at peace. Peace is also connected with poverty, because when you are full—and full of yourself—you are not at peace. But when you empty yourself and become a vessel of God's gracious presence, then you are a person of peace.

We can only become people of peace if we are at peace within ourselves. When the scribes accused Jesus of casting out demons by Beelzebub or Satan, Jesus said, "And if a house is divided against itself, that house will not be able to stand" (Mark 3:25). An individual person cannot be a house divided against himself. All the elements of our humanity—mind, soul, will, heart, speech, body, feelings, passions, emotions—must be at peace.

St. Seraphim of Sarov said the whole meaning of life is to acquire "the Peaceful Spirit." In Hebrew, it would be "the Spirit of Peace," the Holy Spirit. That is the foretaste, the pledge of the coming Kingdom of God, the Kingdom of Peace.

St. Seraphim said that if we acquire God's Spirit of Peace, thousands around us will be saved. But if we do not acquire the Spirit of Peace, then we are contributing to all the madness of hell that is around us. So the first thing we work for is our personal peace, and this is only possible by the action of God, the Lord Jesus Christ, and the Holy Spirit.

Jesus' disciples heard His teaching and wondered, "Who then can be saved?" But He answered, "With men this is impossible, but with God all things are possible" (see Matt. 19:23–26). With God, everything becomes possible. With His help, we can actually practice what Jesus teaches—we can be pure in heart, we can be peacemakers, we can bless those who curse us, we can share what we have, and we can love with the love of God, even in this corrupted world.

Jesus gives us that peace; He is that Peace. Then, to the measure that we are at peace, we bring peace to others. We can be icons of peace. We can be martyrs for peace. In the earliest stories of the martyrs, they peacefully forgave even the people who killed them. The first Christian martyr, St. Stephen, while being stoned, prayed, "Lord, do not hold this sin against them" (Acts 7:60). The martyrs died in peace, and we pray in the great litany in the Divine Liturgy for a peaceful ending to our life. We are supposed to be peaceful even in facing our own death, because we trust God that we will be with Christ, who is our peace.

But that peace comes only at the end. Until that time, we will encounter struggle and contradiction. When Jesus was presented in the temple as a little child, Simeon said to His mother,

> "Behold, this child is set for the fall and rising of many in Israel,
> and for a sign that is spoken against
> (and a sword will pierce through your own soul also),
> that thoughts out of many hearts may be revealed." (Luke 2:34–35)

Jesus is going to cause people to be at enmity with each other. They are going to argue and fight about Him; some are going to accept Him and some are going to reject Him, and then they are going to be at war with each other. We should not be so wrong as the newscasters who say, "Today the Christians are celebrating the birth of the Prince of Peace, but even still in the Holy Land, fourteen people were just blown up. Where is this peace that Christ said He was going to bring to the world?"

The Gospels never said there would be peace on earth before the Second Coming of Christ. Jesus told His disciples:

> "And you will hear of wars and rumors of wars; see that you are not
> alarmed; for this must take place, but the end is not yet. For nation will
> rise against nation, and kingdom against kingdom, and there will be
> famines and earthquakes in various places: all this is but the beginning
> of the birth-pangs." (Matt. 24:6–8)

Christians especially cannot expect to live in peace until the Lord's return,
for Jesus said, "They will put you out of the synagogues; indeed, the hour
is coming when whoever kills you will think he is offering service to God"
(John 16:2). There will be strife, particularly against those who are children
of peace. Yes, Jesus is the Prince of Peace, but that peace only comes in power
throughout the whole of creation at the end of the world.

Jesus says in Matthew:

> "Do not think that I have come to bring peace on earth; I have not come
> to bring peace, but a sword. For I have come to set a man against his
> father, and a daughter against her mother, and a daughter-in-law against
> her mother-in-law; and a man's foes will be those of his own household.
> He who loves father or mother more than me is not worthy of me; and
> he who loves son or daughter more than me is not worthy of me; and he
> who does not take his cross and follow me is not worthy of me. He who
> finds his life will lose it, and he who loses his life for my sake will find
> it." (Matt. 10:34–39)

In Luke 14 are probably some of the most terrifying words Jesus ever spoke:

> "If any one comes to me and does not hate his own father and mother
> and wife and children and brothers and sisters, yes, and even his own
> life, he cannot be my disciple. Whoever does not bear his own cross and
> come after me, cannot be my disciple." (vv. 26–27)

What is the meaning of that text? Is it a violation of peace? No; it is a
hyperbolic sentence, but it means nothing can stand in the way of our
serving Christ, the Prince of Peace. We have to be His disciples and take
up our cross and suffer with Him, in peace—not with enmity, hostility, or
retaliation, but with love, truth, joy, kindness, and mercy. These are our
weapons, according to the Apostle Paul. These are the weapons of peace, and
we are fighting the war of the Lamb of God, the Lamb of Peace.

That fight begins with the fight against our own self. We have to bring our own self into peace, and then we have to be at peace in our families, with our neighbors, with our enemies, and with everyone and everything. Some of our great saints even brought peace to the animal world. St. Seraphim, St. Gerasimus, St. Mary of Egypt, and others had the same peaceful relationship with animals that Adam had before he fell. This desire for peace extends to the angelic realm as well, that the demonic rebellion against God would end, so that the peace of God would encompass the entire creation. Christians must be witnesses of the peace of God until the Lord Jesus Christ returns.

Christ is our peace. Every possible kind of peace there is, Christ is. He wants to reign in peace, on earth as it is in heaven, so that His name would be sanctified, His will would be done, and there would be peace. As the beautiful line of Metropolitan Tryphon in the Akathist of Thanksgiving (or "Glory to God for All Things") states, "Glory to You, O God, who have given us Your Church as a refuge of peace in a hostile world." May our churches be communities of peace, and may we be martyrs, witnesses of peace in this world in which there is no peace, and which will become less and less peaceful as time goes on.

Already, even to attain a fleeting and imperfect earthly peace, many have filled themselves with drugs. People are experiencing more and more strife within themselves, within their families, and among their neighbors. If Christ is our peace, however, we will be at peace. The Kingdom of Peace will come. Let us beg God with all our heart and mind and soul and strength:

O Christ who is our peace, let us also, with You, be peace. Let us be presences of peace, individually and together as communities, witnessing to You.

CHAPTER 35

Jesus the

PARACLETE

When we say *Paraclete*, Christians almost always think of the Holy Spirit. That is because, in Jesus' final discourse with His disciples at the Last Supper in the Gospel of John, He speaks about sending the Holy Spirit. He calls Him *Paraclete*, saying, "And I will pray the Father, and he will give you another Counselor [Greek *Paraklētos*], to be with you for ever, even the Spirit of truth" (John 14:16–17).

The King James Version translates the Greek term *Paraklētos* here as "Comforter," while the New King James says "Helper." In 1 John 2:1, the term is applied to Jesus, but in the New King James and other versions it is translated as "Advocate."

Paraklētos is a word of many meanings. Besides "counselor," "comforter," "helper," and "advocate," it can also mean "consoler" or "encourager." As a noun, it could mean "encouragement" or "support." It could be the one who stands on behalf of or defends a person. It could be a kind of witness to a person's righteousness. A related word, *paraklēsis*, which is the name of a church service, in the Balkans is also the common name for a chapel.

In its meaning of "comfort" or "consolation," *paraklēsis* is used in 2 Corinthians 1 *ten times*:

> Blessed be the God and Father of our Lord Jesus Christ, the Father of mercies and God of all comfort, who comforts us in all our affliction, so that we may be able to comfort those who are in any affliction, with the comfort with which we ourselves are comforted by God. For as we share abundantly in Christ's sufferings, so through Christ we share abundantly

in comfort too. If we are afflicted, it is for your comfort and salvation; and if we are comforted, it is for your comfort, which you experience when you patiently endure the same sufferings that we suffer. Our hope for you is unshaken; for we know that as you share in our sufferings, you will also share in our comfort. (2 Cor. 1:3–7)

The first time Jesus speaks about sending the Holy Spirit from the Father in His name, this is what He says:

"If you love me, you will keep my commandments. And I will pray the Father, and he will give you another Counselor, to be with you for ever, even the Spirit of truth, whom the world cannot receive, because it neither sees him nor knows him; you know him, for he dwells with you, and will be in you." (John 14:15–17)

Jesus is saying, "I am the first one, and I'm going to send you another one." Then, a little later, He says:

Jesus answered him, "If a man loves me, he will keep my word, and my Father will love him, and we will come to him and make our home with him. He who does not love me does not keep my words; and the word which you hear is not mine but the Father's who sent me.

"These things I have spoken to you, while I am still with you. But the Counselor, the Holy Spirit, whom the Father will send in my name, he will teach you all things, and bring to your remembrance all that I have said to you." (John 14:23–26)

At the end of John 15, Jesus said that He came to fulfill all the Law, and yet they hated Him without a cause. He said, "He who hates me hates my Father also" (John 15:23). "But when the Counselor comes, whom I shall send to you from the Father, even the Spirit of truth, who proceeds from the Father, he will bear witness to me; and you also are witnesses, because you have been with me from the beginning" (John 15:26–27).

In Orthodox theology, we insist the Holy Spirit proceeds from the Father. The Son can *send* Him; He comes *through* the Son, but He proceeds from the Father. Western Christians changed the Nicene Creed to say the Holy Spirit proceeds from the Father *and the Son*. They added words to Holy Scripture. That is why we reject *filioque*, which means "and from the Son" in Latin.

Jesus uses the phrase "the Spirit of truth." We use that in the prayer, "O Heavenly King, *Paraklētos* (the Comforter), the Spirit of truth, who are everywhere present and fill all things, treasury of blessings, giver of life, come and abide in us."

In John 16, Jesus says He has to go away, and then He says:

> "But because I have said these things to you, sorrow has filled your hearts. Nevertheless I tell you the truth: it is to your advantage that I go away, for if I do not go away, the Counselor will not come to you; but if I go, I will send him to you. And when he comes, he will convince the world concerning sin and righteousness and judgment: concerning sin, because they do not believe in me; concerning righteousness, because I go to the Father, and you will see me no more; concerning judgment, because the ruler of this world is judged.
>
> "I have yet many things to say to you, but you cannot bear them now. When the Spirit of truth comes, he will guide you into all the truth; for he will not speak on his own authority, but whatever he hears he will speak, and he will declare to you the things that are to come. He will glorify me, for he will take what is mine and declare it to you. All that the Father has is mine; therefore I said that he will take what is mine and declare it to you." (vv. 6–15)

Now let us turn to 1 John 2:

> My little children, I am writing this to you so that you may not sin; but if any one does sin, we have an advocate with the Father, Jesus Christ the righteous; and he is the expiation for our sins, and not for ours only but also for the sins of the whole world.
>
> And by this we may be sure that we know him, if we keep his commandments. He who says "I know him" but disobeys his commandments is a liar, and the truth is not in him; but whoever keeps his word, in him truly love for God is perfected. By this we may be sure that we are in him. (vv. 1–5)

So here, Jesus is the Paraclete (here translated as "advocate").

Now let us think about this word and its various meanings. The word *advocate*, in many languages, means a lawyer, someone who defends us before the judge. And, in many languages, another word for *lawyer* is *counselor*. You can take counsel. You can bring in a counselor to help you, to defend you, to stand up for you when you are tried and tested, and to plead your cause when you are accused.

I think it would be better to translate *Paraklētos*, in John's Gospel, as "Counselor" or "Advocate" instead of "Comforter," for the Holy Spirit comes as an advocate, a counselor. A significant portion of St. John's Gospel has to do with legal language. The word for "bear witness" or "testify" is used almost a hundred times. The author was arguing against those who said, "Jesus is not the Son of God. He may be the Messiah, but He is not divine. He's just a man like the rest of us." In answer to this, in John's Gospel there are witnesses to Jesus that He is the Son of God.

Among the first witnesses to Jesus as God's Son is the Holy Spirit. That is why the Holy Spirit is called the *Paraklētos* four times, because He is sent from God in the name of Christ, and Christ sends Him from the Father to be a witness, like a defense attorney, to set forth the facts of the case, to guide people into truth, to help them understand who Jesus is, what He said, what it means for the world.

It is a comfort to have an advocate who will speak on your behalf. That is why the terms *comfort* and *consolation* can also be used. When we are in affliction and troubled, we have someone to stand up for us, to plead our cause. The advocate has the right to do so because he knows the truth and fulfills the law; he is trustworthy, and that is a great encouragement.

First John says very clearly that we are not supposed to sin. We are supposed to walk in the way Christ walked. But then it says, if any claim they are not sinners, they are liars and make God a liar, because everyone is a sinner, and therefore, everyone is in need of a paraclete. We need to have someone stand before the face of God on our behalf.

Our Advocate before the face of God is Jesus Christ. God's own Son is our Advocate with His own Father, who becomes our Father through Him.

St. Gregory the Theologian said, "How do we know the one true God? Jesus Christ reveals Him. Jesus Christ manifests Him. Jesus Christ testifies to Him. Jesus Christ is the one who makes Him known." If we have to stand before that true God, Jesus Christ is the Advocate.

Then St. Gregory asks, "But who stands on behalf of Jesus Himself? What happens when Jesus is attacked?" St. Gregory's answer would be the answer of St. John the Theologian, who says, "The Holy Spirit bears witness to Him." And that Holy Spirit, the Spirit of truth, is also given to us. The Holy Spirit even advocates on our behalf before Jesus. When we sin, when we fall short, then the Holy Spirit can come to us; He can cleanse us from all impurity; He can illumine us; He can guide us; He can pray within us, as St. Paul says. Then, having Christ as our Paraclete, and having the Holy Spirit as our Paraclete, we must become paracletes for the world. We have to become paracletes for one another. We have to advocate before each other and even before God for one another and the whole world.

The saints are advocates, comforters, counselors, consolers, encouragers, defenders, and testifiers on behalf of us sinners. The saints live to make intercession for us before God, and the main human advocate is the Theotokos. She not only prays, but she makes intercession. There is a little nuance there. We can pray for somebody to be healed, but when we *intercede* for someone, it means we stand on their behalf.

In ancient Christian tradition, St. Mary, the Mother of God, intercedes on our behalf especially at the moment of our death. At the moment when our soul goes into the presence of God, she is there, beseeching God on our behalf, asking the Lord to be merciful to us *for her sake*. All the saints do this.

In 1 Corinthians 14:3, the Apostle Paul says he begs everyone to seek the gift of prophecy, because the prophet brings *oikodomē*, "edification," and he brings *paramythia*, which is "exhortation" and "encouragement," but he also brings *paraklēsis*. A prophet is also a *paraklētos*. A prophet can say, "Thus says the Lord. This is the word of God," and can speak that word on our behalf; thus he is also a paraclete. In Exodus 32, Moses stood in the breach on behalf of the people of Israel when God wanted to crush them. Moses advocated for them, and God let the people off for the sake of Moses' intercession.

A prophet of the true God always advocates on behalf of the people against whom he prophesies. A true prophet not only preaches the Word of God to people, but he advocates with God on behalf of those people.

According to Holy Scripture, we cannot prophesy or pronounce the word of God over anyone for whom we are not willing, if necessary, to *die*. Jesus Christ is the great Paraclete because He *died* for us. The Holy Spirit is the

Paraclete because He identifies completely and totally with us; He becomes one Spirit with us.

In the Church, the bishops and the priests are supposed to be paracletes, to intercede and advocate before the face of God on behalf of the people. A spiritual father advocates on behalf of his spiritual children. Even biological parents advocate before God on behalf of their children.

Monks and nuns stand as advocates on behalf of all creation every single day. They take seriously that a Christian is supposed to advocate before God on behalf of the whole world.

We also advocate before one another. Friends are paracletes. True friends will advocate on behalf of their friends. They will console, comfort, and encourage the friend. They will counsel the friend; they will stand with the friend; they will stand on behalf of the friend. Every human being is called by God to be a *paraklētos*.

Christ is the Paraclete. The Holy Spirit is the Paraclete. All the saints, by faith and the grace of the Holy Spirit, become paracletes on behalf of the whole creation. That is what we do at the Divine Liturgy: We offer ourselves along with Christ, as the priest prays, "Your own of Your own we offer unto You on behalf of all and for all."

Thus, our task is to pray, to mediate, to intercede, to advocate, to be a counselor, to be a witness, in the light of God's Law, on behalf of all and for all. Hopefully everyone else will be my advocate before God, and the Holy Spirit and the Lord Jesus Himself will be our common Paracletes before the face of God the Father. This is our faith.

CHAPTER 36

Jesus Our

REDEEMER

In 1 Corinthians, St. Paul says:

> But God chose what is foolish in the world to shame the wise, God
> chose what is weak in the world to shame the strong, God chose what
> is low and despised in the world, even things that are not, to bring to
> nothing things that are, so that no human being might boast in the
> presence of God. He is the source of your life in Christ Jesus, whom
> God made our wisdom, our righteousness and sanctification and
> redemption; therefore, as it is written, "Let him who boasts, boast of the
> Lord." (1 Cor. 1:27–31)

The Scriptures teach that all divine acts come from the Father, but they are
done by and through the Son, and then they are completed, accomplished,
and perfected by the Holy Spirit.

The reverse is also true. When we cooperate with God, it is because the
Holy Spirit is in us and perfects our activity, and then through Christ, the
Son of God, we have communion with the Father. Thus, we have communion
with God through Christ, by the indwelling of the Holy Spirit.

The clear teaching of the Holy Scriptures is that God is the Redeemer.
God will redeem all things. In Job, there is a famous line, as sung in Handel's
Messiah, "I know that my Redeemer liveth" (see Job 19:25).

In the second part of Isaiah (chs. 40—66), that word, *Redeemer,* is used
many times. This part of Isaiah is often called the Old Testament gospel,
the *protoevangelium*, the part of the Old Testament that most clearly speaks
about what will happen when the Christ comes. Isaiah 41:14 says:

> Fear not, you worm Jacob,
> you men of Israel!
> I will help you, says the Lord;
> your Redeemer is the Holy One of Israel.

Isaiah 43:1–4 says:

> But now thus says the Lord,
> he who created you, O Jacob,
> he who formed you, O Israel:
> "Fear not, for I have redeemed you;
> I have called you by name, you are mine.
> When you pass through the waters I will be with you;
> and through the rivers, they shall not overwhelm you;
> when you walk through fire you shall not be burned,
> and the flame shall not consume you.
> For I am the Lord your God,
> the Holy One of Israel, your Savior.
> I give Egypt as your ransom,
> Ethiopia and Seba in exchange for you.
> Because you are precious in my eyes,
> and honored, and I love you,
> I give men in return for you,
> peoples in exchange for your life."

Redeemer is used together with *Savior.* "I, I am the Lord, / and besides me there is no savior" (Is. 43:11). "Thus says the Lord, / your Redeemer, the Holy One of Israel" (Is. 43:14). This occurs again and again:

> Thus says the Lord, the King of Israel
> and his Redeemer, the Lord of hosts:
> "I am the first and I am the last;
> besides me there is no god." (Is. 44:6)

All this speaks about Yahweh, the Lord God.

Later, there is a prophecy of the Messiah, using the same language of redemption and deliverance.

> Thus says the Lord,
> the Redeemer of Israel and his Holy One,

to one deeply despised, abhorred by the nations,
the servant of rulers:
"Kings shall see and arise;
princes, and they shall prostrate themselves;
because of the Lord, who is faithful,
the Holy One of Israel, who has chosen you." (Is. 49:7)

"I will make your oppressors eat their own flesh,
and they shall be drunk with their own blood as with wine.
Then all flesh shall know
that I am the Lord your Savior,
and your Redeemer, the Mighty One of Jacob." (Is. 49:26)

Isaiah 52:3–6 says:

For thus says the Lord: "You were sold for nothing, and you shall be
redeemed without money. For thus says the Lord God: My people
went down at the first into Egypt to sojourn there, and the Assyrian
oppressed them for nothing. Now therefore what have I here, says the
Lord, seeing that my people are taken away for nothing? Their rulers
wail, says the Lord, and continually all the day my name is despised.
Therefore my people shall know my name; therefore in that day they
shall know that it is I who speak; here am I."

In the New Testament, there are ten quotations from Isaiah 53 and thirty-
two allusions to Jesus offering Himself as the ransom, as the redemption
of God. That is how God redeems and ransoms His people, through His
Suffering Servant.

Isaiah 54:5–8 says this:

"For your Maker is your husband,
the Lord of hosts is his name;
and the Holy One of Israel is your Redeemer,
the God of the whole earth he is called.
For the Lord has called you
like a wife forsaken and grieved in spirit,
like a wife of youth when she is cast off,
says your God.
For a brief moment I forsook you,
but with great compassion I will gather you.

> In overflowing wrath for a moment
> I hid my face from you,
> but with everlasting love I will have compassion on you,
> says the Lord, your Redeemer."

The Scriptures constantly affirm that God is the Redeemer—the ransomer, the one who pays the price, the one who sets free.

Let us hear one more line from Isaiah:

> Whereas you have been forsaken and hated,
> with no one passing through,
> I will make you majestic for ever,
> a joy from age to age.
> You shall suck the milk of nations,
> you shall suck the breast of kings;
> and you shall know that I, the Lord, am your Savior
> and your Redeemer, the Mighty One of Jacob. (Is. 60:15–16)

In the New Testament, this language is all over the place. In Luke, for example, when John the Baptist is born and Zacharias's silence is broken, Zacharias is filled with the Holy Spirit and he prophesies:

> "Blessed be the Lord God of Israel,
> for he has visited and redeemed his people,
> and has raised up a horn of salvation for us
> in the house of his servant David,
> as he spoke by the mouth of his holy prophets from of old,
> that we should be saved from our enemies,
> and from the hand of all who hate us;
> to perform the mercy promised to our fathers,
> and to remember his holy covenant,
> the oath which he swore to our father Abraham, to grant us
> that we, being delivered from the hand of our enemies,
> might serve him without fear,
> in holiness and righteousness before him all the days of our life."
> (Luke 1:68–75)

When Jesus is born, Mary and Joseph take Him to the temple to redeem Him (Luke 2:22–24). According to the Law of Moses, all the firstborn belonged to

God, so when there was a firstborn son, the parents had to go to the priest and buy the son back by offering a sacrifice. When Jesus is brought there, He meets Simeon the elder and the old prophetess Anna: "And coming up at that very hour she gave thanks to God, and spoke of him to all who were looking for the redemption of Jerusalem" (Luke 2:38).

In Romans 3:21–26, St. Paul writes:

> But now the righteousness of God has been manifested apart from law, although the law and the prophets bear witness to it, the righteousness of God through faith in Jesus Christ for all who believe. For there is no distinction; since all have sinned and fall short of the glory of God, they are justified by his grace as a gift, through the redemption which is in Christ Jesus, whom God put forward as an expiation by his blood, to be received by faith. This was to show God's righteousness, because in his divine forbearance he had passed over former sins; it was to prove at the present time that he himself is righteous and that he justifies him who has faith in Jesus.

In 1 Corinthians 6:19–20, he writes, "Do you not know that your body is a temple of the Holy Spirit within you, which you have from God? You are not your own; you were bought with a price. So glorify God in your body."

In Matthew 20, and again in Mark 10, when James and John ask Jesus if they can sit on thrones with Him in His Kingdom, Jesus asks them, "Can you drink the cup that I drink? Can you be baptized with the baptism with which I am baptized?" In other words, "Can you die with Me? Can you suffer with Me?" They say, "We can," and He says, "You will." But then He rebukes them for thinking this way:

> "You know that the rulers of the Gentiles lord it over them, and their great men exercise authority over them. It shall not be so among you; but whoever would be great among you must be your servant, and whoever would be first among you must be your slave; even as the Son of man came not to be served but to serve, and to give his life as a ransom for many." (Matt. 20:25–28)

Jesus is the Redeemer who performs the act of redemption, but He is also the redemption itself, and the price of redemption. He redeems by His own blood, by His own life.

Purchased, bought with a price, redeemed by the blood, ransomed by the blood—what is the meaning of these things? The meaning is that Jesus' act of self-offering saves and redeems the people. From what does it save and redeem them? We are not redeemed from God, because it is not God who is holding us. We do not have to be released from punishment under the Law; that is not what it is all about. When St. Gregory the Theologian, in his paschal homily, says that we are bought with a price, he asks, "To whom is the price paid?"

There was an idea floating around then that we were redeemed from the devil. By sinning, we had given ourselves over to the devil, and the devil owned us because of our sin. In order that we could be released, God gave His Son to the devil as a payment.

It would be like an old-fashioned cowboy movie: The bad guys are holding the beautiful lady, and then the savior figure shows up—the good cowboy with the white hat—and he says to the bad guys, "Let her go; take me in her place."

In answer to this notion that we were redeemed from the devil, St. Gregory the Theologian says, in the old English translation, "Fie upon the outrage!" He says the devil was not holding us justly; he had tricked us. He is the deceiver. God sent His Son in the form of a Man to be crucified on the Cross and to deceive the devil. The devil thought he had taken a mortal man, but as St. John Chrysostom's paschal homily says, "The devil grasped Him, and he met God face to face." The deceiver was deceived, and through this divine deception we are liberated. But, Gregory the Theologian says, we should not think that God redeems us from the devil in the sense that He gives Christ to the devil as a payment for us. The devil has no rights over us. God cannot traffic with the devil on that level; that would be ridiculous.

Then how do we understand this language of *ransom, redemption, purchase,* and *bought with His blood*? St. Gregory gives the same answer St. Basil the Great gave. The Divine Liturgy of St. Basil says, "And He gave Himself as a ransom *unto death,* by which we were held captive, sold under sin." We are ransomed from death, which is the wages of sin. We are ransomed from the effect of our own sinfulness, which makes us mortal.

St. Leo the Great, the pope of Rome, in his twenty-eighth letter—the famous Tome of Leo to the Council of Chalcedon—said that Jesus is our Redeemer because He pays the debt "to our condition." Our condition is cursed, sinful, and dead. We are under the law of sin and death, as St. Paul says in Romans 8:2. Even if we are born into the world and have not committed a single sin, we are already in a sinful condition, subject to death and corruption. In that sense, we are in the hands of the devil.

God redeems us through Christ, whom He makes our Redeemer and our very redemption through His death on the Cross, because, in that one death, we are delivered from everything that enslaves us.

We are enslaved by the vain imaginations of our own hearts and minds. We are enslaved by our will, our passions, and our emotions. We are enslaved by our generation and by our DNA. We are enslaved by the humanity we have received from our forebears. We are enslaved by entertainment, pornography, sex, alcohol, drugs, food—all these things that do not let us really live a free life. All this is holding us. But then, as the Scriptures and the saints say, we even add to this our own will. We sin ourselves. We deceive ourselves. We are caught by our own egos. Therefore, we need to be saved from them. We need to be liberated from them. And the price has to be paid for our liberation.

Jesus, according to St. Paul, becomes sin for us (2 Cor. 5:21); He takes our place as the sinner. He is cursed according to the Mosaic Law, because it is written, "Cursed is everyone who hangs upon a tree" (see Gal. 3:13 and Deut. 21:23). He is cursed because He is put to death in mid-life at the hands of Gentiles. That is the truth of the substitution theory of atonement. He puts Himself in our place. He says, "Take Me."

But when darkness takes Him, because He is Light, the darkness is destroyed and we are delivered from it. We are ransomed by His righteousness, not by His being punished. When ugliness encounters Beauty, the Beauty delivers us from the ugliness. When anything impure comes in contact with the Pure, then the Pure is victorious. When Life itself dies, it is death that is destroyed. We are delivered from death by His life, from sin by His righteousness, from our state of being cursed by His blessedness. This is the blessed exchange. This is the teaching of Scripture.

It is the greatest price that can ever be imagined. It requires His suffering.

The blood of the Son of God in human flesh is necessary for this to happen. Why? Because, as the Psalms say, "What can we give in the redemption for our own life?" (see Ps. 49[48]). We have nothing to give; we are caught without means of escape. Someone else is going to have to free us, because we are caught by our own insanity, sickness, and death.

The church services for the Sunday of the Cross during Great Lent include a hymn which says that God took His Son like a pen and dipped Him in the blood like ink, and then He wrote our redemption papers in His own blood. When He effected that act, all the sins—the handwriting against us, as St. Paul said (Col. 2:14)—were ripped up, no longer being in force, because what was necessary to destroy their force was accomplished by Christ. Our condition was satisfied, so to speak.

This is how we understand Jesus as our Redeemer, and as Job said a long time ago, we know that our Redeemer lives (Job 19:25). Our Redeemer who lives is the Christ who was dead, because "He gave Himself as a ransom unto death, by which we were held captive," as the Divine Liturgy of St. Basil the Great says. Jesus descended into Hades and released all those who were held there, enslaved by death and by the power of the devil, and He raised us all up by doing everything that was necessary to effect our freedom, to pay the debt.

CHAPTER 37

Jesus the

FIRSTBORN

In the Holy Scriptures, Israel is called God's firstborn. Exodus 4:21–23 says:

> And the Lord said to Moses, "When you go back to Egypt, see that you do before Pharaoh all the miracles which I have put in your power; but I will harden his heart, so that he will not let the people go. And you shall say to Pharaoh, 'Thus says the Lord, Israel is my first-born son, and I say to you, "Let my son go that he may serve me"; if you refuse to let him go, behold, I will slay your first-born son.'"

This expression, *firstborn son*, is used throughout the Scriptures in a very particular way. Sirach 36:11 says, "Have mercy upon Your people called by Your Name, O Lord— / Upon Israel, whom You have likened to Your firstborn son" (OSB). Another translation would be, "whom You have named Your firstborn son."

In the Scriptures, the firstborn was the blessed one, the heir, the favored one. Thus, calling Israel the firstborn son meant that Israel, of all the peoples of the earth, was God's own son. The Second Book of Esdras connects the expression *firstborn son* with *the chosen*, *the elect*, and *the beloved*. The firstborn is the one who has preeminence over all the others.

On Great and Holy Friday, at the end of Matins, there is a verse that refers to Israel as "My firstborn son." The verse goes on to say that Israel did not fulfill that firstborn position as a people; Israel, the chosen, betrayed God.

God does not reject Israel as His firstborn son; the promise to Abraham, Isaac, and Jacob remains forever. Psalm 89(88) affirms that one of the seed of

Abraham will be the Firstborn, Israel, through whom all the nations of the earth will be called blessed. The psalm begins:

> I will sing of thy steadfast love, O Lord, for ever;
> with my mouth I will proclaim thy faithfulness to all generations.
> For thy steadfast love was established for ever,
> thy faithfulness is firm as the heavens.
> Thou hast said, "I have made a covenant with my chosen one,
> I have sworn to David my servant:
> 'I will establish your descendants for ever,
> and build your throne for all generations.'" (vv. 1–4)

Later it says:

> For thou art the glory of their strength;
> by thy favor our horn is exalted.
> For our shield belongs to the Lord,
> our king to the Holy One of Israel.
> Of old thou didst speak in a vision
> to thy faithful one, and say:
> "I have set the crown upon one who is mighty,
> I have exalted one chosen from the people.
> I have found David, my servant;
> with my holy oil I have anointed him;
> so that my hand shall ever abide with him,
> my arm also shall strengthen him.
> The enemy shall not outwit him,
> the wicked shall not humble him.
> I will crush his foes before him
> and strike down those who hate him.
> My faithfulness and my steadfast love shall be with him,
> and in my name shall his horn be exalted.
> I will set his hand on the sea
> and his right hand on the rivers." (vv. 17–25)

All this refers to the seed of David. The psalm continues, "He shall cry to me, 'Thou art my Father, / my God, and the Rock of my salvation'" (v. 26). This is one of the few places in the Old Testament where God is called *Father*.

Jesus regularly calls God *Father*. Jesus of Nazareth is God's literal Son. He will say, "You are my Father, my God, and the rock of my salvation," which also means *victory*. God is the rock who makes Christ the victor, who makes Him the Savior, who saves Him from death and makes Him the cause of salvation for everyone else through what He suffered. The psalm continues:

"And I will make him the first-born,
the highest of the kings of the earth.
My steadfast love I will keep for him for ever,
and my covenant will stand firm for him.
I will establish his line for ever
and his throne as the days of the heavens.
If his children forsake my law
and do not walk according to my ordinances,
if they violate my statutes
and do not keep my commandments,
then I will punish their transgression with the rod
and their iniquity with scourges;
but I will not remove from him my steadfast love,
or be false to my faithfulness." (vv. 27–33)

The psalm goes on to say how, at the present time, the wrath of God is upon the people, the crown is defiled in the dust, and the people have not been faithful to God, *although God keeps His covenant and remains faithful to them* to the very end. Toward the end of the psalm are these verses:

Thou hast removed the scepter from his hand,
and cast his throne to the ground.
Thou hast cut short the days of his youth;
thou hast covered him with shame. (vv. 44–45)

This psalm is a prophecy of Christ; it is *Jesus* who is being treated that way. Hebrews 1:8 makes an oblique reference to this, quoting Psalm 45(44):6:

But of the Son he says,
"Thy throne, O God, is for ever and ever,
the righteous scepter is the scepter of thy kingdom."

The scepter endures forever because of the promise and the covenant of God.

God's covenant is forever. No matter how unfaithful the people are, even though His wrath has to come upon them because of their sins and transgressions, nevertheless the covenant is *not* broken; and there *will* be that one Son of David who will cry out to God, "My Father, My God, the rock of My victory!" That one is the Firstborn.

In the Old Covenant, the firstborn belong to God. This includes the firstborn of all the beasts. The firstborn was the symbolical treasure of the people. That is why, when the Israelites are enslaved in Egypt, God slays the firstborn of the Egyptians. He slays the firstborn of the beasts and of the people, and so liberates His firstborn son, Israel.

In the Christian interpretation of the text, however, this takes place so that God's Firstborn can come into the world. Jesus Christ, as God's Firstborn Son and Heir, is crucified and raised to *save* all the firstborn who were enslaved and slain, including the firstborn in Egypt.

In fact, on the Feast of the Meeting of the Lord, one of the readings of the Old Testament says that an altar will be set up in Egypt (see Is. 19:19). The *Egyptian* people will set up an altar to the God of the Jews, and through the Jewish Messiah, the Egyptian people will themselves be saved.

In Matthew's Gospel, Jesus has to be taken into Egypt. The Copts are the descendants of the Egyptians who first accepted and glorified the God of Israel. They recognized that Israel the firstborn is now the Firstborn of Mary, Jesus, who was sacrificed in order to save *them*. He fulfilled the prophecy that from Israel would come the salvation of *all* the nations, thus reconciling the enmity between Jews and Gentiles that had existed for ages.

But the end of the age has come upon us with the coming of Christ, the Firstborn of all creation, the Firstborn of the dead, and the Firstborn of many brethren. St. Paul's Epistle to the Hebrews begins:

> In many and various ways God spoke of old to our fathers by the prophets; but in these last days he has spoken to us by a Son, whom he appointed the heir of all things, through whom also he created the world. He reflects the glory of God and bears the very stamp of his nature, upholding the universe by his word of power. When he had made purification for sins, he sat down at the right hand of the Majesty on high, having become as much superior to angels as the name he has obtained is more excellent than theirs.

> For to what angel did God ever say,
> "Thou art my Son,
> today I have begotten thee"?
> Or again,
> "I will be to him a father,
> and he shall be to me a son"?
> And again, when he brings the first-born into the world, he says,
> "Let all God's angels worship him."
> Of the angels he says,
> "Who makes his angels winds,
> and his servants flames of fire."
> But of the Son he says,
> "Thy throne, O God, is for ever and ever,
> the righteous scepter is the scepter of thy kingdom.
> Thou hast loved righteousness and hated lawlessness;
> therefore God, thy God, has anointed thee
> with the oil of gladness beyond thy comrades."
> And,
> "Thou, Lord, didst found the earth in the beginning,
> and the heavens are the work of thy hands." (Heb. 1:1–10)

Also in Hebrews 12, when the author is comparing Moses to Jesus, and the worship of Moses and the commandments of Moses to that which Jesus brings into the world in the final and everlasting covenant, he says to the Christians:

> But you have come to Mount Zion and to the city of the living God, the
> heavenly Jerusalem, and to innumerable angels in festal gathering, and
> to the assembly of the first-born who are enrolled in heaven, and to a
> judge who is God of all, and to the spirits of just men made perfect, and
> to Jesus, the mediator of a new covenant, and to the sprinkled blood
> that speaks more graciously than the blood of Abel. (Heb. 12:22–24)

We Christians enter into the Church, the assembly of the *firstborn* who are enrolled in heaven. We have all become firstborn.

We become firstborn by being grafted to Israel, the beloved and chosen of God. That happens through the flesh and blood of Jesus Christ, who is Himself exclusively God's Firstborn. He is God's chosen; He is God's beloved, and that is how He is spoken about in the New Testament. At the Baptism of Jesus, and at the Transfiguration, the voice of God the Father says, "This is My beloved Son. Listen to Him."

Sometimes in the New Testament, *firstborn* is identified with *only-begotten*. Not only is Jesus the "first-born among many brethren" (Rom. 8:29)—who are brethren by faith, not by biology—but He is the only Son of God. Israel was created to be God's son; Adam was created to be God's son; but neither fulfilled this role. So God sends His only begotten Son to be the New Adam, to be the real Israel as the chosen of God.

Jesus is the only one born of God; the others are born through faith. That is who He is as the messianic King, because no mere mortal man can be the messianic King. God the Father had to send His Son, begotten of Him before the ages. This is why Jesus, the Son of God, is born of a virgin.

We all become sons of God in Him. We all—including women, Gentiles, and slaves—have the status of "sons" in Him. Every single possible human being, by faith and grace, can become a son of God, have the *status* of a firstborn, and therefore be the heir of everything God Himself has, which is what God wants. He wants to give us everything He has and to allow us to become, by His grace and our faith, everything He is by nature.

In the New Testament, this is said in a more explicit way:

> We know that in everything God works for good with those who love
> him, who are called according to his purpose. For those whom he
> foreknew he also predestined to be conformed to the image of his Son,
> in order that he might be the first-born among many brethren. And
> those whom he predestined he also called; and those whom he called
> he also justified; and those whom he justified he also glorified. (Rom.
> 8:28–30)

God predestined, before the foundation of the world according to His foreknowledge, all things that exist. He predestined all those who believe in Him to be conformed to the image of His Son, so that all those who are elect, chosen, and saved—because they are ready to suffer with Christ, to keep His commandments, and to pay whatever price is necessary—will be conformed to the image of His Son, Jesus Christ.

St. Paul gives the reason for this: in order that He might be the Firstborn among *many* brethren. He is not simply the Firstborn in and of Himself, but *many brothers and sisters* will have the status of firstborn sons in and with Him.

In Colossians 1, Paul begins by speaking about how we may be strengthened in the gospel for all endurance and patience and joy,

> giving thanks to the Father, who has qualified us to share in the inheritance of the saints in light. He has delivered us from the dominion of darkness and transferred us to the kingdom of his beloved Son, in whom we have redemption, the forgiveness of sins.
>
> He is the image of the invisible God, the first-born of all creation; for in him all things were created, in heaven and on earth, visible and invisible, whether thrones or dominions or principalities or authorities—all things were created through him and for him. He is before all things, and in him all things hold together. (vv. 12–17)

He is the Firstborn of all creation *because in Him* all things were created. This does not mean that He is the first of creatures. Jesus is not a creature. He is before all things; He is not one of the things. He is God's Son, but He becomes the one who makes all creatures firstborn. He is the one who has preeminence over all creation.

To whom does all creation belong? It belongs to Jesus Christ, the Firstborn.

St. Paul continues: "He is the head of the body, the church; he is the beginning, the first-born from the dead, that in everything he might be pre-eminent" (v. 18). He is not only preeminent over all creatures, but He holds the first place even among those who are dead.

There is a double teaching here: that Jesus is the Firstborn of all creation, and that He is the Firstborn from among the dead.

This is the plan of God: that the one by whom, through whom, and for whom all things were created would come to earth and live a creaturely life Himself, even taking upon Himself the sin of the world. He became a curse for those who are cursed. He became sin for those who are sinful. He even became dead, *in order that* He might be the Firstborn from among the dead, as the apostle says, because He has to be the Firstborn in everything. He not only has preeminence over all creatures, as the Lord God, but He has preeminence over all things because He takes upon Himself the sins of the world and dies on the Cross, and therefore, from among all the dead people, He is raised as the Firstborn, as the heir among them all.

In doing this, He redeems all the firstborn in creation. It is interesting that, in the first Pascha (Passover), it is the firstborn of Egypt who are killed, while Israel, God's firstborn, is saved. Then, in the second Pascha—the final Pascha, the Pascha of Christ—it is God's Firstborn who is slain, in order to save all those who were slain by sin and death.

He does all this for us so we can be what He is by grace. We have the status of firstborns, sons of God, anointed ones of God, beloved of God, chosen of God—in and through Him, because that is who *He is*.

The Psalms are fulfilled. That Son of David is the very Son of God. Jesus said to the leaders of the Jews:

> "What do you think of the Christ? Whose son is he?" They said to
> him, "The son of David." He said to them, "How is it then that David,
> inspired by the Spirit, calls him Lord, saying,
>> 'The Lord said to my Lord,
>> Sit at my right hand,
>> till I put thy enemies under thy feet'?
> If David thus calls him Lord, how is he his son?" (Matt. 22:42–45)

This is what got Jesus killed and allowed Him to become the Firstborn from among the dead.

This Firstborn of all creation and the Firstborn from among the dead is none other than the Lord Jesus Christ: God from God, who becomes Man of Mary, in order to be the Firstborn and the preeminent in all things. That is who Jesus is: the Firstborn of many brethren, the Firstborn of all creation, and the Firstborn from among the dead—all so that we could become firstborn sons of God in and through Him.

CHAPTER 38

Jesus the

CHOSEN AND BELOVED

Jesus, like Israel as a whole in the Old Testament, is called "God's Chosen One" and "God's Beloved." He is called the one who is elected and also the one in whom God is well pleased, or upon whom is God's *evdokia*, God's "good will," God's "good pleasure."

That word *evdokia* is in the glad tidings of the angels to the shepherds—"Glory to God in the highest, and on earth peace, *goodwill* [*evdokia*] toward men" (Luke 2:14 NKJV).

The chosen and the beloved of God *are* the people of Israel. God chose Abraham, Isaac, and Jacob. That choice of God sometimes appears to be rather arbitrary. God very often does not choose the firstborn. Isaac is chosen, but he is not the firstborn. He is the only-born of Sarah, but Ishmael was born before him. Then, of course, there is Jacob, whose name becomes Israel. We know the story about how the birthright is stolen and God decides not to choose the firstborn, Esau.

God chooses David to be king. He becomes the one to whom God promises there would be no end to his kingship, and from whose line would come the messianic King, the Son of God, Jesus, who would bring the final, ultimate Kingdom of God to the world. With David, God chose the seventh son, the lowliest of the sons of Jesse. Thus, God often does not operate "by the rules," or according to the pattern human beings might expect. He does whatever He wills, acting by grace, doing what He has to do in order for His plan to be accomplished—which, according to Scripture, was His plan from before the foundation of the world (see Eph. 1:4; 1 Pet. 1:20).

God wills to choose or elect certain people. If you look in a biblical concordance for *chosen*, *elect*, or *beloved*, you can see how often these terms are repeated about Israel: "Israel, My beloved," and even "My son," "My firstborn son," "Israel, My chosen," "Israel, the one with whom I am well pleased, upon whom I lavish My own goodwill."

God has sworn and cannot change His mind (see Ps. 110:4); He *has* chosen Israel. Israel is chosen to produce the Christ, the seed of Abraham, in whom all the families of the earth will be blessed and saved. All of Israel is reduced to that one Person who finally fulfills the will of God as His Chosen, as His Beloved, as the One in whom His good pleasure rests, and in whom and through whom His good pleasure comes to the whole world—Jesus Christ.

In the New Testament, Jesus is proclaimed *by God the Father* to be His Beloved and the One in whom His good pleasure abides. When Jesus is baptized by John in the Jordan River, the voice of the Father is heard, and the Spirit descends in the form of a dove and rests upon Him:

> In those days Jesus came from Nazareth of Galilee and was baptized by John in the Jordan. And when he came up out of the water, immediately he saw the heavens opened and the Spirit descending upon him like a dove; and a voice came from heaven, "Thou art my beloved Son; with thee I am well pleased." (Mark 1:9–11)

That could also be translated, "You are *My* Son, *the* Beloved, in whom I am well pleased" or "in whom I express My good pleasure." Those words are *exactly* the same in the Gospels of Matthew and Luke.

In Matthew and Mark, these are also exactly the same words spoken by God the Father at Christ's Transfiguration. Looking at how Matthew, Mark, and Luke are constructed in a literary sense, one can see the center of each *is* the Transfiguration. The beginning is the Baptism, the center is the Transfiguration, and the end is the Crucifixion and Resurrection. That is how the material is arranged, even though these three Evangelists tell the story differently to make different emphases and different theological points.

In the Baptism narrative of Luke, exactly the same words are used as in Matthew and Mark, but not at the Transfiguration. At the Transfiguration, the wording is slightly different. The New King James Version says, "This is My beloved Son. Hear Him!" But in Greek, it says, "This is My Son, the Chosen One [*ho eklelegmenos*]." This is very clever since, in the Old Testament, the *chosen* and the *beloved* are the same, and they are God's Son.

Matthew 12 includes a long quotation from the Prophet Isaiah that is very instructive. Jesus is doing all the messianic signs—healing the sick, casting out demons. Jesus is doing everything God alone can do, and now He is doing this as a Man. Great multitudes followed Him and He healed people, but He commanded them not to make Him known yet (vv. 15–16).

The reason Jesus does these signs is

> to fulfill what was spoken by the prophet Isaiah:
> "Behold, my servant whom I have chosen,
> my beloved with whom my soul is well pleased.
> I will put my Spirit upon him,
> and he shall proclaim justice to the Gentiles.
> He will not wrangle or cry aloud,
> nor will any one hear his voice in the streets;
> he will not break a bruised reed
> or quench a smoldering wick,
> till he brings justice to victory;
> and in his name will the Gentiles hope." (vv. 17–21)

This quotation from Isaiah 42:1–4 is important because it refers to this Servant of Yahweh, "my servant," who is also "my beloved" and "my chosen."

There is a very interesting connection between this text and the Magnificat of the Virgin Mary in Luke 1. When the Virgin Mary greets Elizabeth, Elizabeth says, "Blessed are you among women, and blessed is the fruit of your womb! . . . And blessed is she who believed that there would be a fulfillment of what was spoken to her from the Lord" (vv. 42, 45). Then Mary sings her song:

> "My soul magnifies the Lord,
> and my spirit rejoices in God my Savior,
> for he has regarded the low estate of his handmaiden.
> For behold, henceforth all generations will call me blessed;
> for he who is mighty has done great things for me,
> and holy is his name.

And his mercy is on those who fear him
from generation to generation.
He has shown strength with his arm,
he has scattered the proud in the imagination of their hearts,
he has put down the mighty from their thrones,
and exalted those of low degree;
he has filled the hungry with good things,
and the rich he has sent empty away.
He has helped his servant Israel,
in remembrance of his mercy,
as he spoke to our fathers,
to Abraham and to his posterity for ever." (Luke 1:46–55)

Interestingly, in the sentence "He has helped his servant Israel," the term used for *servant* in the Greek text is masculine and singular. The Magnificat begins by saying, "He has regarded the low estate of his female slave," then ends with, "He has upheld His male slave, Israel." The Christian tradition understands this as referring to Jesus Himself—it is Jesus who is upheld. This corresponds exactly to what was quoted above from Matthew and Isaiah.

The expression *chosen of God* is repeated often in the Scriptures. In the Passion narrative of Luke, those who are mocking Jesus on the Cross say, "Why is He being crucified? Why is God not helping Him? He saved others; let Him save Himself if He *is* the Christ of God, the Chosen One" (see Luke 23:35).

The First Epistle of St. Peter states:

That word is the good news which was preached to you. So put away all malice and all guile and insincerity and envy and all slander. Like newborn babes, long for the pure spiritual milk, that by it you may grow up to salvation; for you have tasted the kindness of the Lord.

Come to him, to that living stone, rejected by men but in God's sight chosen and precious; and like living stones be yourselves built into a spiritual house, to be a holy priesthood, to offer spiritual sacrifices acceptable to God through Jesus Christ. (1 Pet. 1:25—2:5)

Jesus is rejected by men but chosen by God. And that statement can also apply to the followers of Jesus, because all those who follow Him and keep His commandments are rejected by men but chosen by God. When we know that Jesus is the Chosen, the Beloved, in whom is God's good pleasure, we know that all this is done for us and for our salvation. He is revealed, for our sake, as the Chosen One of God.

Those who are chosen in Christ, who is the Chosen One—those who are beloved of God in Christ, who is the Beloved One—are called to keep the commandments of God. They are called to show forth the love of God, perfectly and totally. They are called to do the will of God, without qualification or condition. They are chosen to serve God in every possible way for the salvation of all the nations and the whole world. They are called to be holy as God is holy.

Those who are called and chosen in Him are called to be saints. Practically every letter of the Apostle Paul begins with the words *klētoi agiois,* "called to be saints." Jesus Christ said, *"Many* are called"—this means *the multitude, everyone.* Everyone is called. But He said, "Few are chosen" (Matt. 22:14).

Those who are chosen are chosen to suffer with Christ. In Romans 8:14–17, this is put very sharply:

> For all who are led by the Spirit of God are sons of God. For you did not receive the spirit of slavery to fall back into fear, but you have received the spirit of sonship. When we cry, "Abba! Father!" it is the Spirit himself bearing witness with our spirit that we are children of God, and if children, then heirs, heirs of God and fellow heirs with Christ, provided we suffer with him in order that we may also be glorified with him.

After this, Paul speaks about what Christians have to go through with patient endurance, but then he says:

> We know that in everything God works for good with those who love him, who are called according to his purpose. For those whom he foreknew he also predestined to be conformed to the image of his Son, in order that he might be the first-born among many brethren. And those whom he predestined he also called; and those whom he called he also justified; and those whom he justified he also glorified. (Rom. 8:28–30)

We know that we are called. Christians are called; the baptized are called. Those who are sealed with the Spirit, those who participate in the broken

Body and shed Blood of Christ, they are the ones who prove they are chosen. But those who are chosen by God are chosen to suffer with Him.

Those whom God chose are the ones He *knew* would keep His commandments; those He *knew* would love Him in return; those He *knew* would love everyone, including their worst enemies, the way Christ did and commanded. Colossians 1:13–14 says, "He has delivered us from the dominion of darkness and transferred us to the kingdom of his beloved Son, in whom we have redemption, the forgiveness of sins." So we become sons of God's love in Jesus. That is what it means to be a beloved son: to be the son of His love, to be made sons because He loved us.

Revelation 17:14 says, "they will make war on the Lamb, and the Lamb will conquer them, for he is Lord of lords and King of kings, and those with him are called and chosen and faithful."

But those who are called, chosen, and faithful are those who *suffer*. That is the point. Only the Suffering Servant is the Chosen and the Beloved. Only those who suffer together with Him are chosen, the ones upon whom the goodwill of God rests. The "goodwill toward men" is only for those who serve God, by which they become sons.

They are only those who co-suffer with Jesus, who die with Him, not just in the sacrament of baptism but in every moment of their lives; who are sealed with the gift of the Holy Spirit, not only at their chrismation, but are constantly sealed and acting by the Holy Spirit in every moment, with every breath; who eat and drink the broken Body and shed Blood of Christ at the table of the Kingdom, so their bodies can be broken and their blood can be shed, so they can demonstrate and prove they are indeed the chosen and the beloved of God, those who have answered the call.

When Jesus hung on the Cross in total silence, the leaders of the people scoffed at Him: If He *is* the Chosen, why cannot He save Himself and come down from the Cross? But there they made a tragic error: He hung on the Cross, crucified and silent, because He is the Chosen One, and as the Chosen, the Beloved, He gives His life to the Father.

So when He says in St. John's Gospel, translated literally, "It is fulfilled" (John 19:30), it means, "My being chosen, My being beloved, My being God's only Son is now being fulfilled, when I give up Myself for the life of the world." And all those who belong to Him, by faith and by grace, and by the Holy Spirit's power, are called to be chosen and faithful and beloved for doing exactly the same thing. He does it, not so that we do not have to, but so that *we* may do it together with Him—that we, with Him, may be chosen and beloved, and may be revealed as those upon whom rests God's goodwill.

CHAPTER 39

Jesus the

BRIDEGROOM

One of the earliest titles given to Jesus is *the Bridegroom*. In the Gospel of Mark, the Pharisees and the disciples of John the Baptist came to Jesus and asked Him,

> "Why do John's disciples and the disciples of the Pharisees fast, but your disciples do not fast?" And Jesus said to them, "Can the wedding guests fast while the bridegroom is with them? As long as they have the bridegroom with them, they cannot fast. The days will come, when the bridegroom is taken away from them, and then they will fast in that day." (Mark 2:18–20)

Of course, Christians do fast, because our Bridegroom has been taken away, but we are waiting for Him to return again.

In Matthew, the Lord relates the parable about the wise and foolish virgins:

> "Then the kingdom of heaven shall be compared to ten maidens who took their lamps and went to meet the bridegroom. Five of them were foolish, and five were wise. For when the foolish took their lamps, they took no oil with them; but the wise took flasks of oil with their lamps. As the bridegroom was delayed, they all slumbered and slept. But at midnight there was a cry, 'Behold, the bridegroom! Come out to meet him.' Then all those maidens rose and trimmed their lamps. And the foolish said to the wise, 'Give us some of your oil, for our lamps are going out.' But the wise replied, 'Perhaps there will not be enough for us and for you; go rather to the dealers and buy for yourselves.' And while they went to buy, the bridegroom came, and those who were ready went

in with him to the marriage feast; and the door was shut. Afterward the other maidens came also, saying, 'Lord, lord, open to us.' But he replied, 'Truly, I say to you, I do not know you.' Watch therefore, for you know neither the day nor the hour." (Matt. 25:1–13)

Another parable speaks of the marriage feast of a king's son, another bridegroom. It mentions the wedding garment one was supposed to wear in order to enter into the wedding as a guest. In those days, the garment was provided by the host, so if you did not have a wedding garment, it meant you did not belong there (see Matt. 22:11–14).

The very first miracle Jesus does, recounted in John 2, is at a wedding feast. Then John 3 says:

> And they came to John, and said to him, "Rabbi, he who was with you beyond the Jordan, to whom you bore witness, here he is, baptizing, and all are going to him." John answered, "No one can receive anything except what is given him from heaven. You yourselves bear me witness, that I said, I am not the Christ, but I have been sent before him. He who has the bride is the bridegroom; the friend of the bridegroom, who stands and hears him, rejoices greatly at the bridegroom's voice; therefore this joy of mine is now full. He must increase, but I must decrease." (vv. 26–30)

In John 4, Jesus meets with a woman at a well in Samaria, and says to her, "Give me a drink" (v. 7). In the Old Testament, some prominent people met their brides at wells. Abraham sends his servant to go find a wife from among his own people for his son Isaac, and the servant goes and sees Rebecca at a well. Jacob meets Rachel at a well. Moses meets the daughter of the Midianite, Zipporah, at a well.

One might wonder: Is Jesus meeting His bride, also, at a well? There is a sense in which the answer is yes, because Jesus' bride is sinful humanity. Jesus' bride is the whole of humanity that will belong to Him and go with Him to the house of His Father to live in God's Kingdom forever—that is, the Church.

This Samaritan woman is traditionally called Photini, which means "the illumined one." He tells her to go get her husband. She says, "I don't have a husband." He says, "You're speaking truly, because the man you're living with now is not your husband. You've had five husbands" (see John 4:16–18).

This Samaritan woman is about as bad as you can get for a Jew because, first of all, she's a Samaritan, whom the Jews call "dogs." Jews were not even supposed to talk with them. Then, in addition, she is a sinful woman; she is not living with her husband. She epitomizes the person for whom Christ comes into the world—the one who needs to be illumined and saved, the one who is living in sin, the one who is far from God, who is a heretic, worse than a Gentile.

In the Old Testament, the imagery of bride and bridegroom and husband and wife is pervasive. It is by far the most used analogy for the relationship of God and His people. Isaiah says,

> How the faithful city
> has become a harlot,
> she that was full of justice!
> Righteousness lodged in her,
> but now murderers. (Is. 1:21)

God calls Jerusalem a harlot, an adulterous bride. Isaiah 54 says:

> "Sing, O barren one, who did not bear;
> break forth into singing and cry aloud,
> you who have not been in travail!
> For the children of the desolate one will be more
> than the children of her that is married, says the Lord. . . .
> "For your Maker is your husband,
> the Lord of hosts is his name;
> and the Holy One of Israel is your Redeemer,
> the God of the whole earth he is called.
> For the Lord has called you
> like a wife forsaken and grieved in spirit,
> like a wife of youth when she is cast off,
> says your God." (vv. 1, 5–6)

In Jeremiah 2:1–3, this is written:

> The word of the Lord came to me, saying, "Go and proclaim in the
> hearing of Jerusalem, Thus says the Lord,
>   I remember the devotion of your youth,

your love as a bride,
how you followed me in the wilderness,
in a land not sown.
Israel was holy to the Lord,
the first fruits of his harvest.
All who ate of it became guilty;
evil came upon them,
says the Lord."

But then the people forsake their Bridegroom. They commit adultery with the Baalim, with the idols, with the Canaanite fertility gods. Jeremiah continues later on:

"For my people have committed two evils:
they have forsaken me,
the fountain of living waters,
and hewed out cisterns for themselves,
broken cisterns,
that can hold no water." (Jer. 2:13)

"For long ago you broke your yoke
and burst your bonds;
and you said, 'I will not serve.'
Yea, upon every high hill
and under every green tree
you bowed down as a harlot." (Jer. 2:20)

"How can you say, 'I am not defiled,
I have not gone after the Baals'?
Look at your way in the valley;
know what you have done." (Jer. 2:23)

And the Lord said to me, "Faithless Israel has shown herself less guilty than false Judah. Go, and proclaim these words toward the north, and say,
  'Return, faithless Israel,
  says the Lord.
  I will not look on you in anger,
  for I am merciful,
  says the Lord;
  I will not be angry for ever.'" (Jer. 3:11–12)

"Surely, as a faithless wife leaves her husband,
so have you been faithless to me, O house of Israel,
says the Lord." (Jer. 3:20)

This imagery continues in Hosea 1:2:

When the Lord first spoke through Hosea, the Lord said to Hosea, "Go,
take to yourself a wife of harlotry and have children of harlotry, for the
land commits great harlotry by forsaking the Lord."

In Hosea, God says He will stay faithful to His adulterous wife and harlot,
the people of Israel, even though they go after false lovers and forget the
Lord, who waits for their return. As God says through Hosea, "I will betroth
you to me in faithfulness; and you shall know the Lord" (Hos. 2:20). He says
the same thing to Israel in Hosea as He does in Isaiah and Jeremiah: "You
were unfaithful; I remain faithful. I will not reject you."

The covenant of love is broken by faithless Israel. In Ezekiel, the Lord says:

"And as for your birth, on the day you were born your navel string was
not cut, nor were you washed with water to cleanse you, nor rubbed
with salt, nor swathed with bands. No eye pitied you, to do any of these
things to you out of compassion for you; but you were cast out on the
open field, for you were abhorred, on the day that you were born.

"And when I passed by you, and saw you weltering in your blood, I
said to you in your blood, 'Live, and grow up like a plant of the field.' And
you grew up and became tall and arrived at full maidenhood; your breasts
were formed, and your hair had grown; yet you were naked and bare.

"When I passed by you again and looked upon you, behold, you were
at the age for love; and I spread my skirt over you, and covered your
nakedness: yea, I plighted my troth to you and entered into a covenant
with you, says the Lord God, and you became mine. Then I bathed
you with water and washed off your blood from you, and anointed you
with oil. I clothed you also with embroidered cloth and shod you with
leather, I swathed you in fine linen and covered you with silk. And I
decked you with ornaments, and put bracelets on your arms, and a
chain on your neck." (Ezek. 16:4–11)

"But you trusted in your beauty, and played the harlot because of your
renown, and lavished your harlotries on any passer-by. You took some

of your garments, and made for yourself gaily decked shrines, and on them played the harlot; the like has never been, nor ever shall be. You also took your fair jewels of my gold and of my silver, which I had given you, and made for yourself images of men, and with them played the harlot; and you took your embroidered garments to cover them, and set my oil and my incense before them." (Ezek. 16:15–18)

It continues like this for pages. Then, of course, God says He is going to remain faithful to her; He is never going to abandon her.

The Old Testament includes one book that contains the most erotic, conjugal love-writing in the entire Bible—the Song of Solomon. Some people call this the most mystical book of the whole Bible. One had to be thirty years old to read it in Israel. And this is how it begins:

O that you would kiss me with the kisses of your mouth!
For your love is better than wine,
your anointing oils are fragrant,
your name is oil poured out;
therefore the maidens love you.
Draw me after you, let us make haste. (Song 1:2–4)

The book probably was originally a marriage poem. But it is taken as an allegory for Israel and God, for Christ and the Church, for the soul and the Lord. The beginning of the third chapter says:

Upon my bed by night
I sought him whom my soul loves;
I sought him, but found him not;
I called him, but he gave no answer.
"I will rise now and go about the city,
in the streets and in the squares;
I will seek him whom my soul loves."
I sought him, but found him not.
The watchmen found me,
as they went about in the city.
"Have you seen him whom my soul loves?" (Song 3:1–3)

In this love poem, the lover says to the beloved:

> You have ravished my heart, my sister, my bride,
> you have ravished my heart with a glance of your eyes,
> with one jewel of your necklace.
> How sweet is your love, my sister, my bride!
> how much better is your love than wine,
> and the fragrance of your oils than any spice!
> Your lips distil nectar, my bride;
> honey and milk are under your tongue;
> the scent of your garments is like the scent of Lebanon.
> A garden locked is my sister, my bride,
> a garden locked, a fountain sealed. (Song 4:9–12)

> "Open to me, my sister, my love,
> my dove, my perfect one;
> for my head is wet with dew,
> my locks with the drops of the night." (Song 5:2)

These are all names the bridegroom bestows upon his beloved. This is considered to be a prefiguration of the love of Christ and the Church.

St. Paul writes to the Christians in Corinth: "I feel a divine jealousy for you, for I betrothed you to Christ to present you as a pure bride to her one husband" (2 Cor. 11:2).

Ephesians 5:22–28, which is read at Orthodox weddings, says:

> Wives, be subject to your husbands, as to the Lord. For the husband is the head of the wife as Christ is the head of the church, his body, and is himself its Savior. As the church is subject to Christ, so let wives also be subject in everything to their husbands. Husbands, love your wives, as Christ loved the church and gave himself up for her, that he might sanctify her, having cleansed her by the washing of water with the word, that he might present the church to himself in splendor, without spot or wrinkle or any such thing, that she might be holy and without blemish. Even so husbands should love their wives as their own bodies. He who loves his wife loves himself.

Revelation 19:6–7 says:

> Then I heard what seemed to be the voice of a great multitude, like the sound of many waters and like the sound of mighty thunderpeals, crying,

> "Hallelujah! For the Lord our God the Almighty reigns.
> Let us rejoice and exult and give him the glory,
> for the marriage of the Lamb has come,
> and his Bride has made herself ready." (Rev. 19:6–7)

Then, later, the angel says, "Blessed are those who are invited to the marriage supper of the Lamb" (Rev. 19:9), when Christ becomes one with His people.

In Revelation, St. John calls the New Jerusalem the Bride of Christ:

> And I saw the holy city, new Jerusalem, coming down out of heaven from God, prepared as a bride adorned for her husband. (Rev. 21:2)

> Then came one of the seven angels who had the seven bowls full of the seven last plagues, and spoke to me, saying, "Come, I will show you the Bride, the wife of the Lamb." And in the Spirit he carried me away to a great, high mountain, and showed me the holy city Jerusalem coming down out of heaven from God. (Rev. 21:9–10)

Revelation ends by saying, "The Spirit and the Bride say, 'Come.' And let him who hears say, 'Come.'" (Rev. 22:17). We are all invited to enter into the bridal chamber. The final prayer in Revelation is "Come, Lord Jesus" (Rev. 22:20). Come to take us to Yourself as Your beloved bride.

When Jesus is crucified, He cries with a loud voice, "'*Eli, Eli, lama sabachthani?*' that is, 'My God, my God, why hast thou forsaken me?'" (Matt. 27:46). He is quoting Psalm 22(21):1. That verb, *forsake* or *abandon*, is used in only one other place in the entire Old Testament—Genesis 2:24: "Therefore a man leaves his father and his mother and cleaves to his wife, and they become one flesh." To this Jesus adds, "What therefore God has joined together, let not man put asunder" (Matt. 19:6; Mark 10:9).

So when Jesus cries, "My God, My God, why have You forsaken Me?" we could dare to imagine that God the Father would answer Him, "My Son, You know why I must abandon You on the Cross. I must abandon You so that You can go and *cleave unto Your wife* and become one flesh with her."

Who is the wife? She is adulterous Israel. She is harlot humanity. She is all the human race who worship false gods and do not worship the one, true, and living God who has chosen them as a bride to love and ravish with beauty and glory and splendor and joy forever and ever. That bride is symbolized by the Samaritan woman, a heretic, a Gentile, and a sinful woman—that is the Bride of Christ. He came for the sinners, and we are those sinners.

He died for us, to prove to us that He loves us to the end. St. John Chrysostom said the Son of God loves us like a young man madly in love with a whore. As the hymn in 2 Timothy says, "If we are faithless, he remains faithful— / for he cannot deny himself" (2 Tim. 2:13).

He became one flesh with us in the Incarnation. He entered into Hades with us, into the realm of the dead, so that He could raise us up and take us home into that bridal chamber in the heavens.

During Holy Week, the hymn that begins the whole Passion celebration is:

> Behold, the Bridegroom comes at midnight, and blessed is the servant whom He shall find watching, and again unworthy is the servant whom He shall find heedless. Beware, therefore, O my soul, and do not be weighed down with sleep, lest you be given up to death, lest you should be shut out of the Kingdom, but rouse yourself, crying, "Holy, holy, holy are You, O God! Through the Theotokos, have mercy on us!"

At Matins during Holy Week, when the sun is beginning to shine, we sing the "hymn of light":

> I see Your bridal chamber all adorned, O my Savior, and I have no wedding garment that I may enter. O Giver of Life, enlighten the vesture of my soul and save me.

We have many hymns like these during Holy Week. We want to enter into that bridal chamber with Him and become one flesh with Him, become everything He is in this union of love. Thérèse of Lisieux, a famous Roman Catholic saint, said, "The Cross is the bed on which God consummates His love affair with His creaturely bride."

We not only enter into the marriage-feast as guests, but we enter into the bridal chamber as the bride, to become one flesh, one spirit, one life with Christ Himself. Therefore, being the wife of the Lamb, we have the one true God as our Father, and we live forever in the mansions of God, in the coming Kingdom, with the whole of redeemed humanity.

He is our Bridegroom, and we are His Bride. No matter how sinful, how apostate, how wretched, how insane we become; no matter how much we flee from Him, He chases after us and finds us—even in the pit of Hades, in the realm of death—and there He consummates His love affair with us, and He makes us—if we surrender to His love—His beloved Bride.

Christ is the Bridegroom, divinely beautiful; and He chooses us, the Church, as His Bride so that we can share that very same beauty, that very same glory, that very same splendor, and that very same life and reality with Him, forever.

CHAPTER 40

Jesus the

FIRSTFRUIT

We have already reflected about Jesus as the Firstborn. There is another biblical image applied to Christ that is very similar to *prōtotokos*, "firstborn," and that is the imagery of the *aparchē*, the "firstfruit."

For some reason in the English translations of the Scriptures, this word is translated in the plural, *firstfruits*, but technically, it is singular, the *firstfruit*. In the Law, this firstfruit, the first that was harvested, is to be offered to God. Each book of the Pentateuch (or Torah, the five Books of Moses—Genesis, Exodus, Leviticus, Numbers, and Deuteronomy) has a law about or makes reference to the offering of the firstfruit.

At each harvest or feast, according to the Torah, the firstfruit of each crop had to be offered to God. So we might even dare to say that all the feasts of the Lord in the Law began as agricultural and cosmic celebrations. Pascha, Pentecost, the Feasts of Tabernacles and Booths—these were times for offering the harvest to God.

Later, these feasts received historical meanings. Pascha was connected first with the Israelites' exodus from Egypt and later with Christ's Crucifixion and Resurrection, as He is the Firstfruit from among the dead. Pentecost itself—which was, in the Old Testament, also a feast of resurrection and victory—in the New Testament was connected with the risen and glorified Christ sending the Holy Spirit into the world. The Holy Spirit was the Firstfruit, bringing forth the firstfruit from among humanity—the firstfruit of those who belonged to Christ, who were filled with His Holy Spirit.

This term, *firstfruit*, is connected with another Greek word used by St.

Paul, *arrabon*, which is like a promise made for everyone. The Holy Spirit is the *Arrabon*, or the "Pledge" or "Token," the guarantee of everlasting life in the age to come.

From agriculture, fertility, and cosmos, we move into the historical acts of God's wonders among men: saving them from Egypt, giving the Law on Sinai, and then finally the ultimate Pascha, raising Christ from the dead, which is the fulfillment of Sinai. The wonders continued on Pentecost, when God gave the Holy Spirit to people's hearts instead of just commandments in letters on stone. All of this will be fulfilled in the age to come, the age dawning after the Second Coming of Christ, when everything will be filled with the Holy Spirit and enter into communion with God.

In the Law are commandments about offering the firstfruit generally, and then at very particular times and festivals, particularly at Passover or Pascha. In Exodus 23, God commands both the keeping of a feast after the harvest and the giving of the firstfruit to Him:

> "You shall keep the feast of harvest, of the first fruits of your labor, of what you sow in the field. You shall keep the feast of ingathering at the end of the year, when you gather in from the field the fruit of your labor." (v. 16)

> "The first of the first fruits of your ground you shall bring into the house of the Lord your God." (v. 19)

Leviticus 23 describes the appointed feasts:

> And the Lord said to Moses, "Say to the people of Israel, When you come into the land which I give you and reap its harvest, you shall bring the sheaf of the first fruits of your harvest to the priest; and he shall wave the sheaf before the Lord, that you may find acceptance; on the morrow after the sabbath the priest shall wave it. And on the day when you wave the sheaf, you shall offer a male lamb a year old without blemish as a burnt offering to the Lord." (vv. 9–12)

Then it goes on to describe Pentecost:

> "And you shall count from the morrow after the sabbath, from the day that you brought the sheaf of the wave offering; seven full weeks shall they be, counting fifty days to the morrow after the seventh sabbath;

then you shall present a cereal offering of new grain to the Lord. You shall bring from your dwellings two loaves of bread to be waved, made of two tenths of an ephah; they shall be of fine flour, they shall be baked with leaven, as first fruits to the Lord." (vv. 15–17)

Numbers 28:26–27 says:

"On the day of the first fruits, when you offer a cereal offering of new grain to the Lord at your feast of weeks, you shall have a holy convocation; you shall do no laborious work, but offer a burnt offering, a pleasing odor to the Lord: two young bulls, one ram, seven male lambs a year old."

This is a double offering: the offering of the fruit of the earth and the offering of the animals. Deuteronomy 16 gives the same statute:

"You shall count seven weeks; begin to count the seven weeks from the time you first put the sickle to the standing grain. Then you shall keep the feast of weeks to the Lord your God with the tribute of a freewill offering from your hand, which you shall give as the Lord your God blesses you." (Deut. 16:9–10)

Here again, what has to be offered is the first: "from the time you first put the sickle to the standing grain." This is repeated in other books. During the reign of King Hezekiah, one of the rare good kings of Judah, there was a renewal of all these wonderful festivals, and the people were told again that these festivals must be kept.

As soon as the command was spread abroad, the people of Israel gave in abundance the first fruits of grain, wine, oil, honey, and of all the produce of the field; and they brought in abundantly the tithe of everything. (2 Chr. 31:5)

The same thing took place in the time of Ezra and Nehemiah, when the temple was being rebuilt, after the tribes of Judah and Benjamin returned to the Holy Land after the deportation to Babylon.

Proverbs 3:9–10 says:

Honor the Lord with your substance
and with the first fruits of all your produce;

then your barns will be filled with plenty,
and your vats will be bursting with wine.

Besides the command to offer the firstfruit of the harvest, in the Old Covenant, the people of Israel were chosen by God as a firstfruit of all humanity, to offer themselves to God as the chosen portion of the human race. Their task was to prepare for the salvation of all the nations. So Israel is called God's son, His firstborn son, His heir, His portion, His *klēronomia* or "inheritance," but they are also called the firstfruit. That expression is used about the people themselves. Jeremiah 2:1–3 says this:

> The word of the Lord came to me, saying, "Go and proclaim in the
> hearing of Jerusalem, Thus says the Lord,
>> I remember the devotion of your youth,
>> your love as a bride,
>> how you followed me in the wilderness,
>> in a land not sown.
>> Israel was holy to the Lord,
>> the first fruits of his harvest.
>> All who ate of it became guilty;
>> evil came upon them,
>> says the Lord."

Jeremiah goes on to inveigh against the people God chose as His firstfruit because they were not faithful to God. And then the whole of Israel culminates in that Suffering Servant of Yahweh, who is literally the Firstfruit, and that is Jesus Christ Himself. Jesus is the Firstfruit offered to God from among humanity, who will then abide forever in the Kingdom of God to come.

St. Paul says in 1 Corinthians:

> Now if Christ is preached as raised from the dead, how can some of
> you say that there is no resurrection of the dead? But if there is no
> resurrection of the dead, then Christ has not been raised; if Christ has
> not been raised, then our preaching is in vain and your faith is in vain.
> We are even found to be misrepresenting God, because we testified of
> God that he raised Christ, whom he did not raise if it is true that the
> dead are not raised. For if the dead are not raised, then Christ has not
> been raised. If Christ has not been raised, your faith is futile and you are

still in your sins. Then those also who have fallen asleep in Christ have perished. If for this life only we have hoped in Christ, we are of all men most to be pitied.

But in fact Christ has been raised from the dead, the first fruits of those who have fallen asleep. (1 Cor. 15:19–23)

Since Christ is the Firstfruit, those who belong to Him also become the firstfruit. We who are baptized, who have put on Christ, in Him and through Him and with Him become the firstfruit unto God. In the same way Israel was the firstfruit of the Old Covenant, now the New Israel—the Church—is the firstfruit: those who believe in Jesus as the Christ and who accept Him at His coming. In Romans, St. Paul writes:

We know that the whole creation has been groaning in travail together until now; and not only the creation, but we ourselves, who have the first fruits of the Spirit, groan inwardly as we wait for adoption as sons, the redemption of our bodies. (Rom. 8:22–23)

The Spirit comes and gives this firstfruit to us in and with Christ, and then we become the firstfruit together with Him, being adopted by God.

Sometimes even individuals are referred to as firstfruit. For example, in Romans 16:5, when St. Paul is greeting everybody at the end of the letter, he says, literally, "Greet my beloved Epaenetus, who was the firstfruit in Asia for Christ." In the Revised Standard Version, it says, "the first convert," but in Greek it says, "the firstfruit."

In 1 Corinthians 16:15, when Paul is greeting people, he speaks this way: "Now, brethren, you know that the household of Stephanos were the firstfruit in Achaia." James 1:18 speaks about the people of God, as a whole, becoming the firstfruit together with Christ to God: "Of His own will He brought us forth by the word of truth that we should be a kind of firstfruit of His creatures."

Israel was created to be the firstfruit of all the peoples, and as God's people, they offered the firstfruit of the fruits of the earth and the firstborn of the animals, symbolizing the offering of themselves to God as the firstfruit. Christ fulfilled this at His coming, and He became *the* Firstfruit. We see this also in Revelation:

> It is these who have not defiled themselves with women, for they are
> chaste; it is these who follow the Lamb wherever he goes; these have
> been redeemed from mankind as first fruits for God and the Lamb, and
> in their mouth no lie was found, for they are spotless. (Rev. 14:4–5)

It is interesting that in the earliest years of the Church, the Feast of Pentecost—which we now think about almost exclusively in terms of the coming of the Holy Spirit—was actually the final day of the celebration of the Resurrection of Christ from the dead. And because it was originally connected with the harvest, it came to be understood as a kind of harvest of all those who are saved. Jesus Himself was considered to be the Firstfruit of the renewed humanity.

Philo, an Alexandrian Jewish philosopher who died around AD 50, interpreted the festival of Pentecost in the Mosaic Law as the expression of thanksgiving, forgiveness, deliverance, and jubilee. All this is fulfilled in Christ and with the coming of the Holy Spirit.

St. Cyril of Alexandria said of Pentecost:

> We say that it is the mystery of the Resurrection of the Lord which
> is signified by the feast of the firstfruit. For indeed it is in Christ
> that human nature first flowered anew, henceforth doing away with
> corruption and doing away with the old age of sin.

St. Cyril also said:

> The death of Emmanuel for us is the Paschal feast, but the feast
> immediately following it, which is in no way inferior to it, is the
> resurrection from among the dead which shook off corruption and
> caused us to pass over to a new life. Indeed we have stripped off the
> old man and put on the new man, who is Christ. Then, we contemplate
> Christ as the Firstfruit of renewed humanity, that is Christ Himself in
> the figure of the sheaf and in the firstfruit of the field and the first ears of
> grain offered in holy oblation to God the Father.

The way the priests entered into the holy place, offering the firstfruit of the earth, Christ enters into the sanctuary not made by hands in the heavens, offering Himself as the Firstfruit of our salvation. And He takes us with Himself when He ascends into heaven and enters the holy place,

304

and we become, together with Him, the firstfruit that is offered to God.

This is a jubilee festival. Everyone is liberated. All the sins are pardoned when that is done. On Pentecost, Christ offers Himself as the Firstfruit, and the Holy Spirit is poured out upon us as a kind of firstfruit within us, making us the firstfruit. In these actions, all the sins of the world are washed away and pardoned.

This is our faith: Christ is the Firstfruit. This is the teaching of the Apostle Paul, together with the entire New Testament, that we also, in Christ, have the status of firstfruit, the status of firstborn, and the status of sons of God.

CHAPTER 41

Jesus the

HEIR

God has given all things to His Son, Jesus Christ. He has made Him the Heir of all the promises to Israel.

The ones to whom God wills all things are the people of Israel themselves, as a whole. And Israel, in turn, is reduced to Jesus Christ, in whom everything is recapitulated. In some sense, everything is reduced. The only real human being is Jesus. The only real Jew, the only real seed of Abraham, is Jesus. Being the Firstborn and the only Son, He is God's Heir.

The Greek term for "heir" is *klēronomos*. It is made up of two words: *klēros*, which means "portion" or "part" or "lot," and *nomos*, which means "law." The words *heir, inherit, inheritance,* and *heritage* occur hundreds of times in Holy Scripture. The Old Testament shows Israel as the heir of all God's promises, but it also includes a saga of who inherits what.

God chose Abraham and promised that, in his seed, all the families of the earth would be blessed. Then He made the same promise to Isaac and Jacob. Through Moses, He promised many things. He promised that the Israelites would inherit the land—typifying the meek inheriting the earth and the inheriting of God's Kingdom. Israel would inherit all the nations, and then the Gentiles would also enter into the inheritance of God. The New Testament illustrates the inheritance of eternal life, the inheritance of everything that was promised—in fact, the inheritance of all things.

The term *inheritance*, in the Old Testament, is never in the plural. There is *the* inheritance that God gives to His people. As Psalm 61(60):5 says, "For thou, O God, hast heard my vows, / thou hast given me the heritage

306 ✠ THE NAMES OF JESUS

of those who fear thy name." This is applied to Christ. But there is another translation: "You have given Your inheritance to *all* who fear Your name." And then it immediately speaks about the king: "Prolong the life of the king; / may his years endure to all generations" (v. 6). That king, of course, is Jesus.

Another line that is used in Orthodox services is from Psalm 28(27):8–9:

> The Lord is the strength of his people,
> he is the saving refuge of his anointed.
> O save thy people, and bless thy heritage;
> be thou their shepherd, and carry them for ever.

The line "O Lord, save thy people and bless thine inheritance" appears also in the dismissal hymn for the Holy Cross, which served as a kind of imperial anthem for the Christian Roman (Byzantine) Empire. The Cross is the standard, the flag of Christians. Each year on September 14 at the Exaltation of the Holy Cross, it was lifted up for veneration. When the Cross was lifted up, this hymn was sung: "O Lord, save Your people and bless Your inheritance. Grant victory to Orthodox Christians [originally, the rulers, the king] over their adversaries, and by the power of Your Cross, preserve Your *klēronomia*," that is, "Your portion."

The Christian Roman (Byzantine) Empire thought of itself as God's heritage in the world, a kind of successor to the biblical Kingdom of Israel. But no earthly kingdom can, by itself, be the inheritance or the inheritor of God. The real inheritors are those who believe in God, who receive the inheritance by faith.

Many times in Holy Scripture, there is a sense in which God seems not to follow His own laws. He does not always give His inheritance to the firstborn, for example. He gives it to whomever He wills. He gives it according to His providential plan for the salvation of the world. Those whom God chooses for His inheritance are those who fear His name, but they are also the ones on whom He bestows grace. And sometimes, in the Old Testament, they are not very faithful, but He keeps His promise.

If Israel is God's inheritance, the one He has chosen by grace, it is chosen as an instrument for the salvation of all. The Old Testament says the nations will come into God's inheritance (see Psalm 82[81]:8). The nations will stand as children of Abraham. The inheritance is given to all, but not all receive it. It is given providentially, to those who fear His name, who keep His commandments, who do His will.

Not only was Israel the portion or the inheritance of God on behalf of all people, but *within* the people of God, there was a portion, a *klēros*—the priesthood, who had no portion of the land, but whose main portion was God alone. That is where we get the word *clergy*. In the words "O Lord, save Your *people* and bless Your *inheritance*," the *laos* or "people" [this is where we get the words *laity* and *laymen*] are *all* the people.

The same thing takes place in the final covenant, the New Covenant in Christ. All the Christians are God's portion. All the believers are God's inheritance, because Jesus is the Heir. All become children of the promise, because Jesus is the Promised One to whom all is given. There is a sense in which all Christians act as the *klēros,* the clergy, on behalf of humanity. As we say in the Divine Liturgy, they stand together with Christ before the face of God, filled with the Holy Spirit; they stand on behalf of all and for all.

So, in one sense, in the same way Israel was called apart as the chosen people for God's service, so in the New Testament, *all* the people are called apart to be the *klēros* of God, the *klēronomia* of God. They are all heirs together with Christ.

But within those who are the total portion, there are the particular people—the clergy—who have a second laying-on of hands after their baptism to be that portion *within* the portion, the *klēros* within the *laos*. This is spelled out in Timothy and Titus. The clergy are within the people, of the people, and for the people.

Metropolitan Kallistos Ware once said that, when it comes to the inheritance—the priesthood, the prophetic life, and the kingship—there is one and one alone for Christians: Jesus Christ Himself. He alone is the Priest; He alone is Adam; He alone is Israel; He alone is the Firstborn; He alone is the Son of God; He alone is the Son of Man. But in Him, it is everyone!

The Synoptic Gospels include a parable of a vineyard let to tenants.

> "Hear another parable. There was a householder who planted a
> vineyard, and set a hedge around it, and dug a wine press in it, and

built a tower, and let it out to tenants, and went into another country. When the season of fruit drew near, he sent his servants to the tenants, to get his fruit; and the tenants took his servants and beat one, killed another, and stoned another. Again he sent other servants, more than the first; and they did the same to them. Afterward he sent his son to them, saying, 'They will respect my son.' But when the tenants saw the son, they said to themselves, 'This is the heir; come, let us kill him and have his inheritance.' And they took him and cast him out of the vineyard, and killed him. When therefore the owner of the vineyard comes, what will he do to those tenants?" They said to him, "He will put those wretches to a miserable death, and let out the vineyard to other tenants who will give him the fruits in their seasons." (Matt. 21:33–41)

A Christian interpretation is that the servants who are sent to the tenants are the prophets. They are the holy ones of the Old Testament, the ones God raised up to teach His people; but they rejected them. Certainly the heir in the parable is Jesus. He will own the vineyard. He will own the whole of creation. When the people try to seize the inheritance, God is not going to give it to the wicked husbandmen. He is going to give it to those who bring the fruit of it.

This is repeated in other places in the New Testament. For example, in Hebrews 1, terms relating to inheritance are used three times:

In many and various ways God spoke of old to our fathers by the prophets; but in these last days he has spoken to us by a Son, whom he appointed the heir of all things, through whom also he created the world. He reflects the glory of God and bears the very stamp of his nature, upholding the universe by his word of power. When he had made purification for sins, he sat down at the right hand of the Majesty on high, having become as much superior to angels as the name he has obtained is more excellent than theirs. (vv. 1–4)

Are they not all ministering spirits sent forth to serve, for the sake of those who are to obtain salvation? (v. 14)

Jesus is the Heir, but through Him all become heirs. In Romans 8:16–17, St. Paul writes:

> It is the Spirit himself bearing witness with our spirit that we are
> children of God, and if children, then heirs, heirs of God and fellow
> heirs with Christ, provided we suffer with him in order that we may also
> be glorified with him.

That "joint" or "co-" is a wonderful thing. In Greek, it is the prefix *syn-*,
meaning "together with." If we co-live with Him, co-endure with Him,
co-suffer with Him, and co-die with Him, then we shall be co-glorified with
Him and co-reign with Him.

Galatians 3:27 gives exactly the same teaching: "For as many of you as
were baptized into Christ have put on Christ." That verse is sung at baptisms,
when the newly baptized walks around the baptismal font three times,
indicating that he now belongs to the unending Kingdom of God. It is also
sung at the Divine Liturgy in place of the Trisagion Hymn on great festival
days like Pascha, Epiphany, Christmas, Pentecost, and Lazarus Saturday.

> For as many of you as were baptized into Christ have put on Christ.
> There is neither Jew nor Greek, there is neither slave nor free, there
> is neither male nor female; for you are all one in Christ Jesus. And if
> you are Christ's, then you are Abraham's offspring, heirs according to
> promise. I mean that the heir, as long as he is a child, is no better than a
> slave, though he is the owner of all the estate. (Gal. 3:27—4:1)

> But when the time had fully come, God sent forth his Son, born of
> woman, born under the law, to redeem those who were under the
> law, so that we might receive adoption as sons. And because you are
> sons, God has sent the Spirit of his Son into our hearts, crying, "Abba!
> Father!" So through God you are no longer a slave but a son, and if a
> son then an heir. (Gal. 4:4–7)

God has made us heirs through His Son, Jesus Christ. In Ephesians, St. Paul
writes:

> [God] has made known to us in all wisdom and insight the mystery of
> his will, according to his purpose which he set forth in Christ as a plan
> for the fullness of time, to unite all things in him, things in heaven and
> things on earth.
> In him, according to the purpose of him who accomplishes all things
> according to the counsel of his will . . . (Eph. 1:9–11)

In Jesus, we are chosen as an inheritance. Those who were chosen as the inheritance have been sealed with the Holy Spirit and have received a promise that they would inherit all things. This promise was first made to Abraham, and now it is made to all of us through Jesus Christ.

The Holy Spirit is the *Arrabon* in Greek, the "Pledge," "Token," "Foreshadowing," and "Certitude." He is the guarantee of the inheritance. As St. Paul says in Ephesians 1:17–18:

> That the God of our Lord Jesus Christ, the Father of glory, may give you a spirit of wisdom and of revelation in the knowledge of him, having the eyes of your hearts enlightened, that you may know what is the hope to which he has called you, what are the riches of his glorious inheritance in the saints.

In Titus 3, this term is used again:

> But when the goodness and loving kindness of God our Savior appeared, he saved us, not because of deeds done by us in righteousness, but in virtue of his own mercy, by the washing of regeneration and renewal in the Holy Spirit, which he poured out upon us richly through Jesus Christ our Savior, so that we might be justified by his grace and become heirs in hope of eternal life. (vv. 4–7)

James echoes this, saying: "Listen, my beloved brethren. Has not God chosen those who are poor in the world to be rich in faith and heirs of the kingdom which he has promised to those who love him?" (James 2:5).

The Kingdom of God is given to those who love Him, who fear Him. There is no contradiction between fear of God and love of God. If we love God, we hold Him in awe and fear Him.

First Peter 3:7 speaks about those who are married being joint heirs of the grace of life. So men and women together are the joint heirs of Christ.

In Revelation 21:7, the same words are used: "He who conquers shall have this heritage, and I will be his God and he shall be my son."

In Colossians, St. Paul writes, "Whatever your task, work heartily, as serving the Lord and not men, knowing that from the Lord you will receive the inheritance as your reward; you are serving the Lord Christ." (3:23–24). In 1 Corinthians 6:9–10, he writes:

> Do you not know that the unrighteous will not inherit the kingdom
> of God? Do not be deceived; neither the immoral, nor idolaters,
> nor adulterers, nor sexual perverts, nor thieves, nor the greedy, nor
> drunkards, nor revilers, nor robbers will inherit the kingdom of God.

At the end of the same letter, St. Paul writes: "I tell you this, brethren: flesh and blood cannot inherit the kingdom of God, nor does the perishable inherit the imperishable" (1 Cor. 15:50).

We are sown perishable and raised imperishable, indestructible, undefiled (see 1 Cor. 15:42); and in that sense, we become by grace everything Christ is by His nature. This does not happen through the Law; it is by grace and faith. It has always been that way, even in the Old Testament. God does say that if you keep the Law you will inherit, but in fact nobody keeps the Law; everyone has gone astray, each to his own way. Only Christ, the Heir, has done all things rightly and to the fullest.

Christ alone is the Heir. As we read in Hebrews, once again, "In many and various ways God spoke of old to our fathers by the prophets; but in these last days he has spoken to us by a Son, whom he appointed the heir of all things, through whom also he created the world" (Heb. 1:1–2). We have received that inheritance in Christ along with Christ. Jesus Christ is the Heir, and we are the co-heirs together with Him.

CHAPTER 42

Jesus the

HOLY ONE OF GOD

In St. Mark's Gospel, no human being calls Jesus the Son of God until the centurion at the Cross says, "Truly this man was the Son of God!" (Mark 15:39). But the *demons* know who He is. After John the Baptist is arrested and Jesus comes into Galilee preaching, Mark 1:23–24 says:

> And immediately there was in their synagogue a man with an unclean spirit; and he cried out, "What have you to do with us, Jesus of Nazareth? Have you come to destroy us? I know who you are, the Holy One of God."

Mark 3:11 says, "And whenever the unclean spirits beheld him, they fell down before him and cried out, 'You are the Son of God.'"

In the Nicene Creed, Jesus is confessed as "Light from Light and true God from true God." Jesus is also the Holy One from the Holy One. In the Old Covenant, God is the only Holy One. This is confessed in the Psalms: "You alone are holy." That line is used in the Great Doxology: "You alone are holy. You alone are the Lord, Jesus Christ." Jesus is holy because He is *everything* that God is. He has the same divinity as God Himself.

Since God is the Holy One, His people have to be holy also, with the same holiness that God Himself is. In Exodus, God tells Moses to tell the people of Israel:

> "Now therefore, if you will obey my voice and keep my covenant, you shall be my own possession among all peoples; for all the earth is mine, and you shall be to me a kingdom of priests and a holy nation. These

are the words which you shall speak to the children of Israel." (Ex. 19:5–6)

In Leviticus 20:26, God gives this commandment: "You shall be holy to me; for I the Lord am holy, and have separated you from the peoples, that you should be mine."

A little later comes this commandment concerning the priests: "You shall consecrate him, for he offers the bread of your God; he shall be holy to you; for I the Lord, who sanctify you, am holy" (Lev. 21:8).

The Prophet Isaiah had a famous vision of God in the temple:

> In the year that King Uzziah died I saw the Lord sitting upon a throne, high and lifted up; and his train filled the temple. Above him stood the seraphim; each had six wings: with two he covered his face, and with two he covered his feet, and with two he flew. And one called to another and said:
> "Holy, holy, holy is the Lord of hosts;
> the whole earth is full of his glory!" (Is. 6:1–3)

"Holy, holy, holy," the thrice-holy hymn, is central to all Orthodox prayers. In the Liturgy, we pray, "Holy God, holy Mighty, holy Immortal, have mercy on us" and "Holy, holy, holy, Lord God Almighty." In the Trisagion Hymn, the "Holy, holy, holy" is applied to the three Persons of the Trinity: Holy God, Holy Mighty, and Holy Immortal.

In Revelation, this very same vision is shown to the seer of the Apocalypse, St. John:

> And the four living creatures, each of them with six wings, are full of eyes all round and within, and day and night they never cease to sing,
> "Holy, holy, holy, is the Lord God Almighty,
> who was and is and is to come!" (Rev. 4:8)

But then the seer sees the Lamb, and the same glory and honor and dominion are given to Him who is seated on the throne and to the Lamb. That evokes memories of the Book of Daniel, when the Son of Man approaches the Ancient of Days, is seated at His right hand, and receives all glory, honor, dominion, thanksgiving, and worship, as they are given to God Almighty Himself.

Isaiah says:

> "Fear not, you worm Jacob,
> you men of Israel!
> I will help you, says the Lord;
> your Redeemer is the Holy One of Israel." (Is. 41:14)

In the Old Testament, the Redeemer is God, but the redeeming action of God is done through Christ. We are redeemed by the broken Body and shed Blood of Christ.

This expression of Jesus as the Holy One is also confessed in the Acts of the Apostles. In the very first sermon in the Christian era, given on the streets of Jerusalem, the Apostle Peter says:

> "Men of Israel, hear these words: Jesus of Nazareth, a man attested to you by God with mighty works and wonders and signs which God did through him in your midst, as you yourselves know—this Jesus, delivered up according to the definite plan and foreknowledge of God, you crucified and killed by the hands of lawless men. But God raised him up, having loosed the pangs of death, because it was not possible for him to be held by it. For David says concerning him,
>
>> 'I saw the Lord always before me,
>> for he is at my right hand that I may not be shaken;
>> therefore my heart was glad, and my tongue rejoiced;
>> moreover my flesh will dwell in hope.
>> For thou wilt not abandon my soul to Hades,
>> nor let thy Holy One see corruption.
>> Thou hast made known to me the ways of life;
>> thou wilt make me full of gladness with thy presence.'
>> [Ps 16(15):8–11]
>
> "Brethren, I may say to you confidently of the patriarch David that he both died and was buried, and his tomb is with us to this day. Being therefore a prophet, and knowing that God had sworn with an oath to him that he would set one of his descendants upon his throne, he foresaw and spoke of the resurrection of the Christ, that he was not abandoned to Hades, nor did his flesh see corruption. This Jesus God raised up, and of that we all are witnesses. Being therefore exalted at the right hand of God, and having received from the Father the promise of the

Holy Spirit, he has poured out this which you see and hear. For David did not ascend into the heavens; but he himself says,

'The Lord said to my Lord, Sit at my right hand,
till I make thy enemies a stool for thy feet.'

"Let all the house of Israel therefore know assuredly that God has made him both Lord and Christ, this Jesus whom you crucified." (Acts 2:22–36)

In Acts 3, Peter and John are on the street, and again they do an act in the name of Jesus, and here again Peter preaches:

"Men of Israel, why do you wonder at this, or why do you stare at us, as though by our own power or piety we had made him walk? The God of Abraham and of Isaac and of Jacob, the God of our fathers, glorified his servant Jesus, whom you delivered up and denied in the presence of Pilate, when he had decided to release him. But you denied the Holy and Righteous One, and asked for a murderer to be granted to you, and killed the Author of life, whom God raised from the dead. To this we are witnesses." (vv. 12–15)

The Holy One came to make us holy. Probably the most-quoted text on that point is this:

As obedient children, do not be conformed to the passions of your former ignorance, but as he who called you is holy, be holy yourselves in all your conduct; since it is written, "You shall be holy, for I am holy." (1 Peter 1:14–16)

Everything that serves God can bear the adjective *holy*: Holy Scriptures, holy temple, holy tabernacle, holy Law, holy place, holy of holies. Everything is holy to the Lord when it is consecrated by God and sanctified to His purposes. And certainly the people of God are called to be holy as God Himself is holy.

What does it mean to be holy?

Two different words are used in English for one and the same word in Hebrew and Greek. In Hebrew, that word is *qadosh*; in Greek, it is *hagios*. But in English, we often do not realize that the term *holy* and the term *saint* have exactly the same meaning. A holy person is a saint. If you say "Saint

Nicholas" in English, it is the same as if you said "Holy Nicholas." So to say "Holy Saint Nicholas" is actually redundant.

But what does the term *holy* mean? It literally means "separate," "different," "uncommon." It means "not like anything else." It means "that which is pure and unstained." There is a sense in which it could also mean "originally" or "uncreated." Created things become holy because the holy God has consecrated and sanctified them to become holy. The verbs *consecrate* and *sanctify* have the same root as the term *saint*, in every single language. They mean "to make God-like."

God alone is different from all creation. Therefore, one cannot say that anything in creation by itself is holy. Only God is holy, and Jesus is the Holy One of God because He is divine. He is a divine Person who became human. No creature by itself could be called holy, except by the grace of God, but Jesus is the Son of God by nature, not by grace. He *is* the Holy One of God, begotten by the Father before all ages.

The expression "Holy is His name" is often used in Scripture, and sometimes it is hard to tell whether it means that God's name is to be kept holy, or that His actual name is "the Holy One." In fact it means both things. The name of God—the Tetragrammaton, the Hebrew consonants corresponding to "YHWH"—was such a holy name that it was not even uttered, except by the priest once a year. Instead, they would say "the Lord."

But when Jesus is going to be born, the angel says to Mary, "the child to be born will be called holy, the Son of God" (Luke 1:35). That holiness is given to the name of Jesus right from the very beginning, before He is even conceived in Mary's womb. And it happens by the *Holy* Spirit.

Sometimes, in Latin, it is said that God is *totaliter aliter*, or "totally other." Isaiah says several times that God, the Holy One, is not like anything else; there is nothing in heaven or on earth that can compare with God.

This leads to another important affirmation. Sometimes we say that we speak anthropomorphically about God. We speak about God as having eyes, ears, hands, a mouth. We speak about God walking in the garden. Even God speaks about His soul and His arm in Isaiah. But the truth of the matter is that we are made in God's image. As Karl Stern has said (see his book *Pillar of Fire*), "We must always keep in mind that we are theomorphic; God is not anthropomorphic." In other words, we do not imagine God as *we* are, but we are the way we are because we, in created forms, *image* what is beyond understanding in God, who is holy.

So when we say that God is holy and is completely other than anything else, we are saying that He is not like anything we can possibly imagine. But then we quickly add that this God, who is holy, has decided to create. And what He brings into being, He consecrates with His own holiness.

In this sense, the term *holy* does not carry a moral or ethical meaning. God is not ethical. God is God, and He is holy by His very nature. This has to do with the being of things, not with their behavior. I think we can say that the non-human creatures—animals, plants, rocks, stars, moons, galaxies— show forth the glory and the holiness of God in their very being, and we human beings must glorify God by our very being. But the problem with human beings is that we are not rocks or plants or animals. We are self-conscious creatures, made in the image and likeness of God, with freedom to exercise our holiness, to believe our holiness, to receive our holiness, to actualize and realize our holiness that is given to us as a gift from God.

The Old Covenant had holiness codes in the Torah. Whenever a creature is in touch with what is holy, the creature is said to be rendered unclean and has to do a purification rite because of, paradoxically, its contamination by the holiness of God. Those holy things were the things that had to do with the direct action of God in human life—with birth, death, and blood. This is why, if a man had an emission of semen or a woman was menstruating, it rendered them unclean. They had to purify themselves.

When the priests went and served in the temple, in the holy place, or touched the Holy Scriptures, they also had to purify themselves. When a woman had a baby, she had to be purified. When a person was in touch with diseases and suffering, leprosy, sores of any kind, sicknesses of any kind, he or she had to be purified because God was involved in that activity. When living human beings touched corpses or were in the presence of death, they also had to undergo a rite of purification.

Etymologically, the term *hagios* ("holy") is connected to another term, *agnoi*, for "pure" or "clean." When an impure person is in touch with the holiness of God, the holiness reveals his or her impurity. For a woman to have a baby is not sinful. To touch a corpse is not sinful. To have a disease with sores or leprosy is not sinful. To emit semen or to ovulate is not sinful. It has to do with sinful people being in touch with the holy, but the acts themselves are not sinful.

This holiness is a grace, a gift, an act that God does. The ultimate, final, everlasting sanctification and consecration of human beings and of the whole of creation is done by Christ, the Holy One of God. In Jesus, there is no unholiness at all. His human body is completely and totally holy. And the bodies of those who belong to Him *can* become holy only through Him. We receive His holy words, which make us holy, especially when we receive them and follow them. And then, of course, we partake of His holy Body and Blood, by the power of His Holy Spirit.

So we are sanctified, glorified, and even deified through Jesus, who is the Holy One of God. That is why, in the New Testament, the Christians are called "the saints." First John says, "But you have been anointed by the Holy One" (1 John 2:20). And in all the letters of the Apostle Paul, the Christians are greeted as saints and those who are called to be saints. They are the holy ones. In the Nicene Creed, the Church is the "one, holy, catholic, and apostolic Church."

If we actualize the gift of the holiness of God, we really do become saints, and that is proven by our behavior. We act in a holy manner. We keep the holy commandments. We do God's holy will. We keep His holy words. We eat Christ's holy Body and drink His holy Blood. We share the holiness of God, *provided that we suffer with Him.*

So this is our faith. We confess Jesus, who, alone among human beings, is *the* Saint, the Holy One of God. Then we confess that if our God is holy, through the Holy One of God, Jesus Christ, *we* are to become holy, too. The whole creation is sanctified by the power of God's own Holy Spirit.

Holy, holy, holy, Lord God Almighty! Heaven and earth are full of Your glory.

CHAPTER 43

Jesus

SIN AND CURSE

There are two texts in Holy Scripture that require us to make a very particular and daring reflection—that Jesus has received the title of *sin* and *curse*. He was made sin; He became a curse. He not only became an offering for sin, not only was He cursed, not only did He put Himself in the condition of all those who are cursed under the wrath of God, but He *became* a curse, He *became* sin. This reveals the great depth to which humanity descended through its Fall, that the Holy One of God would become sin; that the blessed of God, the Chosen and Beloved of God, would become a curse.

Jesus is totally without sin. That is the very clear scriptural teaching, that He has no sin. Hebrews says this clearly: "For we have not a high priest who is unable to sympathize with our weaknesses, but one who in every respect has been tempted as we are, yet without sin" (4:15), and "For it was fitting that we should have such a high priest, holy, blameless, unstained, separated from sinners" (7:26). Hebrews also says,

> But we see Jesus, who for a little while was made lower than the angels, crowned with glory and honor because of the suffering of death, so that by the grace of God he might taste death for every one. For it was fitting that he, for whom and by whom all things exist, in bringing many sons to glory, should make the pioneer of their salvation perfect through suffering. . . .
>
> Since therefore the children share in flesh and blood, he himself likewise partook of the same nature, that through death he might destroy him who has the power of death, that is, the devil, and deliver

319

all those who through fear of death were subject to lifelong bondage. For surely it is not with angels that he is concerned but with the descendants of Abraham. Therefore he had to be made like his brethren in every respect, so that he might become a merciful and faithful high priest in the service of God, to make expiation for the sins of the people. For because he himself has suffered and been tempted, he is able to help those who are tempted. (Heb. 2:9–10, 14–18)

He is really human. He became flesh and blood, suffering everything we suffer. He was tempted in every way we are tempted. He went through everything we go through, yet He does this as God's Son without sinning at all. This is what it says very specifically in the fourth chapter of Hebrews: "For we have not a high priest who is unable to sympathize with our weaknesses, but one who in every respect has been tempted as we are, yet without sin" (Heb. 4:15).

"Yet without sin," *chōris hamartias* in Greek, can also mean "apart from sin" and "having no sin." This is important because it is clearly a doctrine that the Lord Jesus Christ did not sin in any way. He is the righteousness of God, the Holy One of God. He is divine in every way in His humanity, and His humanity was completely and totally sanctified when it was united to His divinity. He is everything that we are, like his brethren in every respect, yet without sin, apart from sin.

The chapter continues, "Let us then with confidence draw near to the throne of grace, that we may receive mercy and find grace to help in time of need" (Heb. 4:16).

Jesus became one of us, human in every possible way, suffering everything we can suffer, offering Himself as the high priest according to the order of Melchizedek, with great prayers and supplications and tears (see Heb. 5:7), giving Himself totally and completely to God on our behalf. And, in doing this as the high priest and becoming the Victim, he becomes an offering for sin in that the sins are forgiven. He is also an offering for peace, reconciliation, purification, and cleansing. He becomes the offering for everything there were offerings for in the Old Testament according to the levitical Law and the levitical priesthood.

Even more astounding than this, however, Scripture says that not only did He became an offering for sin, but He *became* sin. This is, literally, what St. Paul says in 2 Corinthians 5:21: "For our sake he made him to be sin who knew no sin, so that in him we might become the righteousness of God."

Jesus is made sin that we might become righteousness. He became sin; it does not say He became a sinner, but that He became sin. Not knowing sin in any way, being without sin, He became sin. God made Him sin, so that in Him who has become sin, we might become the righteousness of God.

Here, it does not say "He became an offering for sin" or "He became a sin-offering." That is certainly a teaching of Holy Scripture, but here, it says He *became* sin, so that through Him, we might become righteousness.

St. Irenaeus of Lyons wrote a short treatise called *A Complete Exposition of the Apostolic Preaching*, never quoting one sentence from the New Testament. He quotes only the Scriptures of the Law, the Psalms, and the Prophets, to show what the apostolic teaching is concerning Jesus Christ. He said that Christ, in the Incarnation, became completely and totally like us so that we could be completely and totally like Him. Another way of putting it would be: He became what we are so that we could become what He is. Later, St. Athanasius the Great would say that God became human to make humans god. God became man to make man divine. St. Maximus the Confessor concurs, saying that God became everything we are so that, by grace and faith, we could become everything God is according to His divinity. A human being is a being with a commandment to be, by grace and by faith, everything that God is by nature. Those are classical teachings of ancient Christianity.

Jesus assumes and takes upon Himself *the condition of being a sinner*, without being a sinner. He not only becomes a human being, He also takes on the sin of the world and actually experiences what it means to be a sinner, again without being a sinner. God did not make Him *to sin*, but made Him *sin* itself because of His complete and total identification with human beings in their sinful, fallen, corrupted condition.

Vladimir Lossky, in his book *Mystical Theology*, said that when you contemplate the Incarnation, the Son of God becoming human, the first aspect of the Incarnation is simply becoming human. This he calls the "first moment." He becomes a human being. But the "second moment" is that He becomes sin. He voluntarily takes upon Himself the sin of the world to such an extent, to such a depth, that the Scripture can actually say that God made Him to be sin. He, the Sinless One, had the condition of being a sinner so that we could truly become righteous people.

The Scriptures teach that the wages of sin is death, and therefore He had to become sin in order to take on the sin of the world, to die, and to raise the dead. All this He did by His free will, by grace. He has the power to keep Himself alive. He has the power to forgive sins. He has the power to open the eyes of the blind. He has the power to raise the dead. He can say, "Your sins are forgiven you." And yet, He becomes sin and dies on the Cross. One could even say that He became death when He became a corpse.

This is the mystery of our salvation, that the Holy One of God not only became Man, but became a slave, obedient to death, and took upon Himself the sin of the world. Being the Lamb of God who was sacrificed, the Suffering Servant, the Man of Sorrows, He was made sin, while being totally righteous and holy.

He not only became sin, but He became a curse as well. St. Paul teaches this in Galatians 3:10: "For all who rely on works of the law are under a curse; for it is written, 'Cursed be every one who does not abide by all things written in the book of the law, and do them.'"

Here St. Paul quotes Deuteronomy 27:26. Anyone who is under the Law is, by definition, cursed, because there is no one who has kept the Law perfectly, beginning even with Adam. St. Paul continues, "Now it is evident that no man is justified before God by the law; for 'He who through faith is righteous shall live'" (v. 11).

No one can be considered righteous according to the Law; according to the Law we are all cursed, because we have all broken the Law. And, because we have all broken the Law of God, we are all subject to death, for "the just shall live by faith." This last part is a quotation from the Prophet Habakkuk (Hab. 2:4). This text from Habakkuk was quoted very much in the Dead Sea Scrolls, and it is also referenced in the canon sung at Matins on Pascha:

> He brings all of them up with a hook,
> he drags them out with his net,

he gathers them in his seine;
so he rejoices and exults.
Therefore he sacrifices to his net
and burns incense to his seine;
for by them he lives in luxury,
and his food is rich.
Is he then to keep on emptying his net,
and mercilessly slaying nations for ever?
I will take my stand to watch,
and station myself on the tower,
and look forth to see what he will say to me,
and what I will answer concerning my complaint.
And the Lord answered me:
"Write the vision;
make it plain upon tablets,
so he may run who reads it.
For still the vision awaits its time;
it hastens to the end—it will not lie.
If it seem slow, wait for it;
it will surely come, it will not delay.
Behold, he whose soul is not upright in him shall fail,
but the righteous shall live by his faith." (Hab. 2:1–4)

St. Paul makes a point of this connection between faith, righteousness, and life. Abraham was righteous before God because he *believed* in Him, not because of circumcision or by works of the Law. In the time of Abraham, there was no Mosaic Law. The righteous are made righteous by their *faith*— this is the teaching of the Law and the Prophets of the Old Testament, as well as the teaching of the Apostle Paul in the New Testament.

St. Paul says in Galatians 3:12, "but the law does not rest on faith, for 'He who does them shall live by them.'" Here he makes reference to Leviticus 18:5: "You shall therefore keep my statutes and my ordinances, by doing which a man shall live: I am the Lord."

But, St. Paul writes:

Christ redeemed us from the curse of the law, having become a curse for us—for it is written, "Cursed be every one who hangs on a tree" [Deut. 21:23]—that in Christ Jesus the blessing of Abraham might come upon

the Gentiles, that we might receive the promise of the Spirit through
faith. (Gal. 3:13–14)

We receive righteousness through faith. The faith is believing that God
has made the Suffering Servant, His Son Jesus Christ the Messiah, *sin* for us
so that, even though He has no sin, through Him we might become righteous
and righteousness. We become righteousness by faith and by grace, and we
receive the blessing of God by faith in Him who not only was made sin, but
who became a curse for us.

Galatians 3:13 says, "Christ redeemed us from the curse of the law."
In Greek, it says: "*Christos hēmas exēgorasen ek tēs kataras tou nomou.*"
Exēgorasen means "bought," bought as one would buy back a slave. So
Christ has bought us back, redeemed us, purchased us from out of the curse
of the Law.

Then it says in English, "having become a curse for us." Since Christ
became a curse for us, we have received from "the blessing of Abraham . . .
that we might receive the promise of the Spirit through faith." In the same
way that we become righteousness because He was made sin, so, according
to the Holy Scripture, we receive the blessing of God because He has become
a curse.

Deuteronomy 21:22–23 says:

> "And if a man has committed a crime punishable by death and he is put
> to death, and you hang him on a tree, his body shall not remain all night
> upon the tree, but you shall bury him the same day, . . . for a hanged
> man is accursed by God."

This is why Joseph of Arimathea went to take Jesus' body down from the tree
of the Cross—because, according to the Law of Moses, a dead man cannot
be hanging on a tree, and certainly not on a great Sabbath, overnight. He
must be taken down or the land will be defiled. So, to keep the land pure for
the celebration of the festival, all who were crucified had to be taken down
from the tree.

St. Paul says Jesus *had to* become a curse so that, through His being
cursed, we could be blessed. He became sin so we could become righteous.
He became a curse so that we could be blessed.

This is the lowest point of defilement, vileness, pollution: to become sin and curse. So much did Jesus identify with sinners that He not only died (because the wages of sin is death), but He died by execution. He died by being executed *as a sinner.* He became sin and was executed as a sinner, and thereby became curse because He was put to death by being hanged upon a tree.

God made Him to be sin, and by God's will He was given over to death by being crucified, hanged upon a tree, which, according to the law of God in Moses, is to become accursed. In this passage, St. Paul shows us to what extent—beyond which it is impossible to go—God has acted through His Son, Jesus Christ, for our forgiveness, redemption, expiation, propitiation, healing, cleansing, restoration, renewal, sanctification, glorification, and deification.

Who is the One who takes us up to heaven and seats us on the throne of God? The same One who has descended into the pit of death, becoming sin and curse. This is what we confess about our Lord Jesus Christ, and these are among His names and titles. He is not only the Righteous One; He is sin. He is not only the righteousness of God; He is human sin. He is not only the blessed of God, but He is the cursed. He is not only the blessing, He is the curse. This is who our Lord Jesus Christ is and what He has become for our salvation.

We have become righteousness and blessedness in God through Jesus, but we have become this way because God made Jesus to be sin and curse.

CHAPTER 44

Jesus

FRIEND AND BROTHER

Orthodox Christians are, perhaps, most well-known among all Christians for affirming the divinity of Christ, affirming that He is really God's divine Son with the same divinity as God the Father, that He is really God in human flesh. We relate to Jesus constantly as our Lord and God, our Master, our Savior, and our Redeemer. We glorify Him to the highest degree. Perhaps this is because of the historical and contemporary tendency to say that Jesus is "just a man like us, in no way different" and maybe "the best and the highest of creatures, but not divine like God," as Arius said in the fourth century and as some modern-day Arians do as well.

It is a *dogma* of the Eastern Orthodox Church that Jesus is divine with exactly the same divinity as the one God and Father, and also the Holy Spirit—but He is also truly human. The Council of Chalcedon, the fourth Ecumenical Council, said this quite specifically—that He is of one divine being with God the Father, and that He is of the very same nature with all human beings. Jesus Christ is, therefore, perfectly and completely divine and perfectly and completely human.

But sometimes, in stressing the divinity of Jesus, we lose a real sense of His humanity. He was a real Man. Jesus had all the qualities of being human. He had a human mind, a human body, a human soul, human passions (the blameless ones, such as hunger, thirst, tiredness), and human emotions. He had a human time, a human place, a human nationality. At the Incarnation, the invisible God became visible. The uncircumscribable became circumscribed. The immortal became mortal. The all-powerful became weak. He became a real human being in every way except for sin, without diminishing in any way His divinity—for He is the God-Man, the *Theanthropos*.

Besides the names and titles that refer to His divinity, Jesus also has names and titles referring to His humanity. One of them is "our Friend" and another is "our Brother"—because Jesus is not only our God and Master, He is also, in His humanity, our Friend and our Brother.

In the Old Testament, all those who were God-fearing were called the "friends of God." And that term, *friend*, in Greek is *philos*. Though this term is used only once in the New Testament, it is used often in the Orthodox Divine Liturgy, where Christ is called *Philanthropos*, or the "Friend of man." This is related to the word *philanthropy*, "love of humanity."

God is our Friend; He is not our enemy. He is not hostile to us. He is not our adversary. He is the one who is always there. A friend is trustworthy. Jesus is not a fair-weather friend. He is not just our friend when things are going well; He is also our friend when things are going badly. He is our friend not only when we do well, but He remains our friend even when we sin.

If you have a really good friend, that person will be your friend even when you sin against him, even when you offend him. This is often how friendship is tested. A true friend is there all the time, no matter what. A true friend is the one who is always at your side, never betraying, never fleeing, and never going away, no matter what.

A friend is also someone with whom you are intimate. You can tell anything to a friend, and it will not break the friendship. You could share the most horrid things, and that friend will still be your friend; he will not change his mind about you. The friend knows everything about you and can be trusted perfectly. He will not do or say anything to harm you. He will not retaliate or return evil for evil. He is not vindictive or vengeful, nor does he take offense and hold a grudge.

A friend may become angry about something, but that is a sign of friendship—it is a sign that he cares. As the Scripture says, "Be angry, but sin not" (Ps. 4:4). If you do not love someone and he is not your friend, you do not care what he does. If some person you do not like very much and do not consider a friend does bad, stupid, or destructive things, you could not care less. But when your *friend* does those things, you become disappointed and get angry. So anger is actually a sign of friendship.

Friends argue, hopefully civilly and not in any mean, embarrassing, or shaming way; but you can get angry and show your feelings to someone who is your friend because you know the friendship is not going to be broken. You can be who you are with a friend, your friend can be who he is with you, and you will remain friends. That is what friendship is about.

Jesus insists that He is our Friend. This is what He says in St. John's Gospel:

> "This is my commandment, that you love one another as I have loved you. Greater love has no man than this, that a man lay down his life for his friends. You are my friends if you do what I command you. No longer do I call you servants, for the servant does not know what his master is doing; but I have called you friends, for all that I have heard from my Father I have made known to you. You did not choose me, but I chose you and appointed you that you should go and bear fruit and that your fruit should abide; so that whatever you ask the Father in my name, he may give it to you. This I command you, to love one another." (John 15:12–17)

This text is important for us because we are servants of Christ. St. Paul uses that expression regularly. We are servants of God. Christ Himself was the Servant of God, and we become co-servants of God together with Christ. But we also, according to Scripture, become servants of Christ, slaves of Christ. St. Paul uses that expression many times. For example, in Romans, he speaks about becoming slaves of Christ, slaves of God, slaves of the Lord. And he even says that, as we were slaves of sin, we should become slaves of righteousness: "having been set free from sin, [you] have become slaves of righteousness" (Rom. 6:18). We are slaves of that which we obey, either God or sin.

Christians are to be slaves of God; we cannot give up that term. Jesus become a slave to transform us into sons, so that we would no longer have the status of slaves, but the status of children of God.

Thinking of the term *friend*, we see that, as servants of God and servants of Christ, we become friends of God. Our friendship is not slavish but is paradoxically a servitude based on friendship. A real friend is, in a sense, the slave of his friend. He serves his friend out of a spirit of love, devotion, and sacrifice. In friendship, there is mutual belonging. I belong to my friend, and my friend belongs to me; we are members, one of another. That is what constitutes our friendship.

Jesus says, effectively, "You are my friends: you know everything I'm doing; I've hidden nothing from you. Everything I have, I have given to you. Everything God has told Me, I've told to you. You are My friends. I no longer call you servants; I call you friends" (see John 15). But in the end of St. John's Gospel, Jesus encounters the Apostle Peter and asks him three times, "Do you love Me?" (see John 21:15–19).

After Jesus' arrest, Peter had denied Him three times; he had disowned Him. Peter cursed and swore and said, "I don't know the Man" (see John 18:15–27). Then, after His Resurrection, Jesus revealed Himself to the disciples and Peter. They had a miraculous catch of fish, and the risen Christ ate and drank with them. When they had eaten, Jesus said to Simon Peter, "Simon, son of John, do you love Me more than these others?" And Peter answered him, "Yes, Lord. You know that I love you." This is interesting because, when Jesus asks the question "Do you love Me?" He says, in the Greek text, "*Agapas Me*—Do you love Me with *agapē* love?" *Agapē* is the name for God in the Scriptures, when St. John says, "God is love" (1 John 4:16). *Agapē* means "charitable love." Do you do good to Me; do you share with Me; do you give your life to Me? That is *agapē*.

Peter answers, "Yes, Lord, You know that I love You." This could be translated: "You know that I'm Your friend," because Peter does not use the verb from *agapē*; he uses the verb from *philia*. Then, the second time Jesus speaks to Simon—He does it three times, to reinstate him, so to speak, after his threefold denial—He says again, "Simon, son of John, *agapas Me*—do you love Me?" Peter again answers, "*Philos se*—I am Your friend; I love You." He again does not use *agapō*. But the third time, Jesus asks him, "*Philis me*—Are you My friend really?" He switches the verb from the *agapē* word to the *philia* word: "Are you My friend? Are you really My friend?"

And here, Peter gets a little upset and he says, "Lord, You know all things. You know everything. You know that *philō se*, that I am Your friend, I love You."

It is interesting that the verb used there is the verb for friendship. Twice the verb is from *agapē*, but *four* times the verb is from friendship. Peter uses the friendship verb three times in his answers, and Jesus uses it one time out of the three. So to be a friend is very important.

Saying that Jesus is our Friend is completely scriptural. Yes, He is majestic, awesome, fearful, glorious, and holy, but He has made Himself our Friend.

The recently glorified elder St. Porphyrios said, "Christ is our Friend; He is our Brother. He shouts it out, 'You are My friends! I want you to see Me as one of your own, as your Friend. I want you to embrace Me. I want you to feel Me in your souls—Me, your Friend, who, in truth, is the Fountain of Life.'"

Not only is Jesus our Friend, He is our Brother. Jesus is God's Son, and He has said and accomplished all that He has done in order to make us also sons of God. We all have received the adoption of sonship. He has made us all into sons of God; every single human being can become a son of God now, through what Jesus has done for us—especially by being crucified, raised, and glorified.

So, if we are sons of God and children of God, then we are all brothers and sisters in Christ. But we could also say we are all brothers and sisters *of* Christ. We are Christ's brothers and sisters because by His grace we are what He is by nature, in relationship to God. We become, so to speak, God's household. We become the new people who are the family of God, the people of God. And the people of God are all brothers and sisters with each other and with Christ. He has become our Brother in every respect. He became like His *brethren* in every respect, except sin (see Heb. 2:17 and 2 Cor. 5:21).

In Hebrews, St. Paul writes:

> For it was fitting that he, for whom and by whom all things exist, in
> bringing many sons to glory, should make the pioneer of their salvation
> perfect through suffering. For he who sanctifies and those who are
> sanctified have all one origin. That is why he is not ashamed to call them
> brethren, saying,
> "I will proclaim thy name to my brethren,
> in the midst of the congregation I will praise thee."
> And again,
> "I will put my trust in him."

And again,
 "Here am I, and the children God has given me."
 Since therefore the children share in flesh and blood, he himself likewise
 partook of the same nature, that through death he might destroy him
 who has the power of death, that is, the devil. (Heb. 2:10–14)

Jesus is the Child of God; He is the Son of God. Through Him, we become children of God; we become His brothers and sisters. So we can relate to Jesus as our Brother, and that is fantastic to think about—that in the Person of Christ, God Almighty becomes our Brother and our Friend.

Nowhere in the Law and the Psalms and the Prophets would any human being be called a brother or sister of God. They might be called a *friend* of God, like Abraham, but not a sibling. God is our Friend, and we are His friends when we keep His commandments (see John 15:14); but in the New Testament, we are called not only friends, but brethren. We are brothers and sisters of Christ, and therefore He is our Brother.

So, if He calls us friends—"You are My friends"—then we can say He is our Friend. If He says, "You are My brothers and we bear the same humanity. I became what you are, and I'm not ashamed to call you brothers and sisters, because I've become exactly what you are, and even more than that, I've taken on your sins and become a curse and everything else," then we can say He is our Brother.

It is absolutely scriptural to say that Christ is not only our Friend, but also our Brother. It is marvelous to think that, in and through Jesus Christ, in all that He said and did and in everything He became, He becomes our Friend and our Brother. We become His brothers and sisters, and we have God His Father as our Father.

The love, friendship, affection, and even the *eros* of God are ours in Jesus Christ. This is how deep, true, and real the Incarnation is. The holy, ineffable, invisible, incomprehensible, unspeakable, inexpressible God became a Man not to be served, but to serve; not to be honored, but to suffer dishonor to the point of making Himself to be sin and a curse. The Righteous One came to love sinners, to be our Friend and Brother. All these things are *real*, and they are part of who and what Christ is for us. And also we, for Him, are His friends and His brothers and sisters.

CHAPTER 45

Jesus

ANGEL AND APOSTLE

There are two titles we do not normally think about as being applicable to Jesus. One is *Angelos,* "Angel," and the other word is *Apostolos,* "Apostle." Nevertheless, in the Holy Scriptures and in the Church Tradition, these words are used for Jesus and are two of His titles.

The term *angelos,* which we normally translate in English as "angel," literally means "messenger" or "the one who bears a message." This is important for Christians because we believe in the gospel of Christ, and the term *gospel* in Greek is *evangelos. Gospel* means "a good message" or "good news." The Greek term comes from the two words: *ev-,* meaning "good," and *angelos,* which means "a messenger," or "a good message."

The Christian faith appeared on earth as a gospel. St. Paul used this term *gospel* in all his letters *before* the actual four Gospels were written. In his greeting to the church of the Thessalonians, he writes, "for our gospel came to you not only in word, but also in power and in the Holy Spirit and with full conviction" (1 Thess. 1:5).

St. Paul refers to the gospel throughout his writings. The gospel, *to evangelion,* is the good message. The one who brings the good message is the messenger, the *angelos.*

The Scriptures call St. John the Baptist a messenger. The Prophet Malachi prophesies the coming of John the Baptist, saying, "Behold, I send my messenger to prepare the way before me, and the Lord whom you seek will suddenly come to his temple; the messenger of the covenant in whom you delight, behold, he is coming, says the Lord of hosts" (Mal. 3:1). St. John the

Baptist is called the Forerunner; he is the messenger sent to prepare the way for Jesus. In ancient Christian iconography, the figure of John the Baptist is sometimes shown with wings on his back like an angel. This is to show that he is the messenger, the angel who brings the Good News.

But what about Jesus? Can we really call Jesus an Angel? In the New Testament, He is never called *Angel*. He is, after all, not a ministering spirit but the Son of God, having the same divinity as the Father and the Holy Spirit. The Prophet Isaiah says, in the Septuagint, "Not an elder or an angel, but the Lord Himself saved them from all their tribulation, because He loved them and spared them. He redeemed and took them up, and lifted them up all the days of old" (Is. 63:9 OSB).

Yet, in the Old Testament, He is called *Angel* or *Messenger*. Immediately after prophesying the coming of St. John the Forerunner, Malachi prophesies the coming of Christ, calling Him the Messenger of the covenant:

> "and the Lord whom you seek
> will suddenly come to his temple;
> the messenger of the covenant
> in whom you delight,
> behold, he is coming,
> says the Lord of hosts." (Mal. 3:1)

Jesus is sent into the world by God with the message of salvation. He is the Messenger of salvation, the Messenger of the New Covenant. It says very clearly in the synoptic Gospels that Jesus was sent to preach the gospel, to announce the glad tidings of God. He is the very Word of God Himself, and He brings the words of God. In that sense, He is the *Angelos*.

But there are still more references to Jesus as the Messenger in the Old Testament. In the Septuagint version of Daniel 3 is the well-known story of the three young men in the fiery furnace. Their story is read in the Orthodox Church every Holy Saturday.

King Nebuchadnezzar of Babylon, called "the most evil king in any land," had built a big golden idol in the plain of Dura and commanded that, when the peoples of his kingdom should hear the sound of musical instruments, they must bow down and worship this idol. Then he discovered that three

Hebrew youths, Shadrach, Meshach, and Abednego (or Azariah, Ananiah, and Misael), refused to obey his command to worship the big golden idol. This defiance enraged Nebuchadnezzar, who had the three youths thrown into a burning fiery furnace. But, while the three holy youths were in the furnace, they danced around and sang a marvelous canticle that begins,

> "Blessed are You and praiseworthy, O Lord, the God of our fathers,
> And praised and glorified is Your name unto the ages.
> For You are righteous in all You did for us,
> And all Your works are true.
> Your ways are upright,
> And all Your judgments are true." (Dan. 3:26–27 OSB)

Nebuchadnezzar's servants kept stoking the furnace to the point where the fire escaped its bounds and killed many of the Chaldeans around it. "But the Angel of the Lord went down into the furnace to join Azariah and his companions, and shook off the fiery flame of the furnace. He made the inside of the furnace to be as though a dew-laden breeze were blowing through it, so the fire did not touch them at all, or cause them pain, or trouble them" (Dan. 3:49–50 OSB).

But when Nebuchadnezzar heard them singing praises, he marveled and said, "Did we not cast three men bound into the fire?" They replied to the king, "Truly, O king." Then the king said, "Behold, I see four men untied and walking in the midst of the fire, yet they are not destroyed; and the vision of the fourth is like the Son of God" (vv. 91–92 OSB). Then he said, "Blessed is the God of Shadrach, Meshach, and Abednego, who sent His Angel and saved His servants who trusted in Him" (v. 95 OSB).

The descent of the Son of God into the burning fiery furnace and the deliverance of the three holy youths prefigures the Resurrection of Christ and the general resurrection of all mankind.

So that term *Angel* is applied to the one like unto the Son of God. But there is also another place in the Old Testament where Jesus is called *Angel*, in a famous canticle in Isaiah 9:6–7. In the Hebrew version, it says:

> For to us a child is born,
> to us a son is given;

and the government will be upon his shoulder,
and his name will be called
"Wonderful Counselor, Mighty God,
Everlasting Father, Prince of Peace."
Of the increase of his government and of peace
there will be no end,
upon the throne of David, and over his kingdom,
to establish it, and to uphold it
with justice and with righteousness
from this time forth and for evermore.
The zeal of the Lord of hosts will do this.

But in the Septuagint, this text is a bit different:

> For unto us a Child is born, unto us a Son is given; and the government
> will be upon His shoulder. His name will be called the Angel of Great
> Counsel, for I shall bring peace upon the rulers, peace and health by
> Him. Great shall be His government, and of His peace there is no end.
> His peace shall be upon the throne of David and over His kingdom,
> to order and establish it with righteousness and judgment, from that
> time forward and unto ages of ages. The zeal of the Lord of hosts shall
> perform this. (Is. 9:5–6 OSB)

Thus the Scriptures attest to Jesus Christ, the prophesied Messiah, as the Son
of God and the Messenger or Angel.

What about the title *Apostle*? Is Jesus ever called *Apostle* in the Scriptures?
We know that those He sent, He called apostles. In addition to the Twelve
Apostles, Jesus also sent out seventy others, whom the Church names as
apostles. But also, St. Paul refers to some Christians as apostles—not just the
Twelve and the Seventy. In Ephesians, he says:

> And his gifts were that some should be apostles, some prophets, some
> evangelists, some pastors and teachers, to equip the saints for the work of
> ministry, for building up the body of Christ, until we all attain to the unity
> of the faith and of the knowledge of the Son of God, to mature manhood,
> to the measure of the stature of the fullness of Christ. (Eph. 4:11–13)

But what does the word *apostolos* or "apostle" mean? Why is it used? The
literal meaning of *apostolos* is "someone who has been sent." In the Gospels,

Jesus *sends* people to preach, teach, bear witness, and testify. These He *names* *apostles*. Luke 6:13 says, "And when it was day, he called his disciples, and chose from them twelve, whom he named apostles." Not all of Jesus' disciples were named apostles, although in some sense everyone is sent to testify to Him, to bear witness, to be a martyr. Apostles are, broadly speaking, people sent on a mission, those who have a commission to represent the one who sent them. The apostles Jesus sends have the mission to preach His gospel.

In the Orthodox Church, we not only have apostles of the Twelve and Seventy, but those called "Equals of the Apostles," *eisapostoloi* in Greek. These include St. Mary Magdalene, who was an apostle to the Apostles; St. Thekla, a friend of St. Paul and the first female Christian martyr; St. Nino, who evangelized Georgia; Ss. Constantine and Helen; Ss. Vladimir and Olga; and even closer to our own time, St. Nicholas of Japan.

We know from Scripture that Jesus sends the apostles and commissions them to preach. They have this very particular mission and ministry of being sent by Him to preach, but primarily they are not just preachers, but apostles. Their title comes from the verb *to send*, which in Greek is *apostelō*, "I send."

In all four Gospels, but particularly in John, Jesus insists that He Himself has been sent by God. Therefore, in that He has been sent by God, He can be called *Apostle*. In St. John's Gospel, Jesus speaks of the one God and Father as "Him who sent Me."

In John 4:34, Jesus says, "My food is to do the will of him who sent me, and to accomplish his work." In John 5:24, He says, "Truly, truly, I say to you, he who hears my word and believes him who sent me, has eternal life." And in John 6:38, He says, "For I have come down from heaven, not to do my own will, but the will of him who sent me."

Jesus is the Sent One; in that sense, He is the Apostle. But is He ever called *Apostle* in the Scriptures? Yes. There is one place where He actually has the title *Apostle*, in Hebrews 3:1–2:

> Therefore, holy brethren, who share in a heavenly call, consider Jesus,
> the apostle and high priest of our confession. He was faithful to him
> who appointed him, just as Moses also was faithful in God's house.

So, in the Scriptures, Jesus is called the Apostle. He is the quintessential Apostle. *He* is sent by God, and then He sends His own apostles. These apostles also carry the message of His gospel, so, in that sense, they are also angels, because they are messengers. This is interesting. In Revelation, the bishops of the seven churches are called the "angels" of those churches.

The Holy Spirit is also sent. God sends the Holy Spirit into the world through Christ. Christ sends the Holy Spirit to the world from the Father, and, in that sense, the Holy Spirit is an *Apostolos* also. He is sent to bear the message of the gospel, to bring the word of God, to do the work of God, to accomplish the will of God; He is sent as a Servant and also a Messenger of God. So, the Holy Spirit is also, in that sense, an Angel.

Apostles are sent not only to bring the Good News of salvation, but also for other things: to govern, administer, oversee, serve, bear witness, and testify as martyrs. Those two words—*angelos* and *apostolos*, messenger and the one who has been sent, angel and apostle—are terms the Scriptures apply not only to God's creatures, but also to the Second and Third Persons of the Holy Trinity, Jesus Christ and the Holy Spirit.

Jesus Christ is the Son of Man who came as the Messenger of God to pull the people out of the fiery furnace, to raise them up from the dead. He is God's *Angelos*, the *Angelos Megalēs Voulēs*, the Angel of Great Counsel (Is. 9:6, LXX), the Messenger of the gospel of salvation. He is *the* Angel, with the definite article, and He is also *the* Apostle of our confession. He is the One who is sent from God to bring this salvation.

CHAPTER 46

Jesus

PASTOR AND BISHOP

In 1 Peter, there is a sentence in which Jesus is given the titles *Pastor* and *Bishop*, according to the King James Version (KJV). The New King James Version (NKJV) translates the titles as *Shepherd* and *Overseer*:

> For to this you were called, because Christ also suffered for us, leaving us an example, that you should follow His steps:
>   "Who committed no sin,
>   Nor was deceit found in His mouth";
> who, when He was reviled, did not revile in return; when He suffered, He did not threaten, but committed *Himself* to Him who judges righteously; who Himself bore our sins in His own body on the tree, that we, having died to sins, might live for righteousness—by whose stripes you were healed. For you were like sheep going astray, but have now returned to the Shepherd [*Poimen*] and Overseer [*Episkopos*] of your souls. (1 Pet. 2:21–25 NKJV)

In Greek, the last line would sound like this: "For as sheep you were wandering—*ēte gar hōs provata planōmenoi.*" *Planē* (sometimes transliterated *plani*), in Slavonic *prelest*, is the word used for *straying* (it could also be translated "wandering") in the text. It is a technical term in classical Orthodox Christian spiritual literature that means "delusion." The sheep were delusional. They were wandering all over the place, lost, not even knowing what was happening to them.

Jesus is called the Shepherd or the Pastor, with all the connotations of tending, guarding, caring for, feeding, nourishing, and protecting His people, His flock. But in this particular text, we have not only the term *Poimen*, but *Episkopos*: "the Shepherd and Bishop of your souls."

The term *episkopos*, "bishop," is used primarily in the New Testament for the heads of Christian communities, for those whom the apostles put in charge over the churches. Technically, the term *episkopos* means an "overseer." *Epi-* is "over" or "on," and *skopos* means "to see," as in the words *telescope* or *microscope*. Another word for *overseer* would be *supervisor*.

In Acts 1:20, for example, when the apostles are choosing a successor to replace Judas, they say, quoting Psalm 109(108):8, "Let another take his *episkope*." Let another take the supervising or overseeing position he had as one of the Twelve. It is certainly the teaching of the New Testament that the apostles, especially the Twelve, exercised *episkope*; they oversaw the Church of Christ. Christ placed them in that position as overseers, superintendents, caretakers, and pastors.

This term *episkopos* is applied to Jesus, first and foremost. It is very interesting how this term is used in Scripture. It refers to the one who is set over others for the sake of their good. St. Augustine of Hippo said, in effect, "When it comes to me as a bishop, I am the superintendent. I am the overseer. I am the head, even. But when it comes to myself as a Christian, then I'm a Christian in exactly the same way as everybody else."

The bishop, the *episkopos*, first has to be a human being and a Christian; then he can be the one who oversees. He is chosen from among the flock to be the one who oversees the flock. The shepherds, priests, and pastors of the Old Covenant were chosen from among the people, and often, by the grace of God, in ways the people did not expect. God chose David, the seventh of the sons of Jesse. He chose Jacob and not Esau; He chose Isaac and not Ishmael. And He chose Jesus, who is the Chosen One. Jesus was the one who was chosen as the Virgin's Child and as the very Son of God who has become Man, but He was still taken from among His brethren, for as it says in Hebrews:

> For he who sanctifies and those who are sanctified have all one origin.
> That is why he is not ashamed to call them brethren, saying,
> "I will proclaim thy name to my brethren,
> in the midst of the congregation I will praise thee." (Heb. 2:11–12)

As a Man, Jesus is a member of Israel, God's chosen people, and as such He is chosen from among the people to be the Christ. He has all the qualities necessary for that particular service and ministry; He is capable of doing all these things because, as a Man, He has fulfilled everything it is necessary to have in order to be the *Episkopos*.

He has all the qualifications, humanly speaking, and He has them because the Spirit of God is in Him and upon Him from the time He is conceived in His mother's womb. All through His childhood, He increased and grew by the Holy Spirit (see Luke 2:52). Then, when He is baptized in the Jordan, the Spirit is seen to descend and rest upon Him, making Him to be, humanly speaking, what He is as a Man.

St. Athanasius and St. Basil, in their letters on the Holy Spirit, and St. Gregory the Theologian also, say that Jesus has to do all these things as a Man in order to fulfill His ministry to be both the Good Shepherd, the Pastor who lays down His life for the flock, and the Lamb of God who takes away the sins of the world. He is to be the High Priest who offers Himself in sacrifice, and He is to be the *Episkopos* who cares for and governs the members of the Church, the members of His Body, of which He is the Head.

The term *episkopos*, in the ancient world, actually referred to a slave who oversaw other slaves, who was a caretaker for a property, or who supervised the household as the chief servant. So it is interesting that the term for a chief slave is given to Jesus. He is the *Episkopos*, the Chief Servant. To be an overseer or a caretaker, one first has to be a servant.

He is the Servant of all the servants; He is the Servant set over the other servants, because all the members of the household of God are servants, slaves of God, and the slaves become sons by the grace of God through Jesus.

Jesus said to His disciples, "No longer do I call you servants, for the servant does not know what his master is doing; but I have called you friends, for all that I have heard from my Father I have made known to you" (John 15:15). In Galatians, St. Paul writes, "So through God you are no longer a slave but a son, and if a son then an heir" (Gal. 4:7). The slaves become friends and sons. That is very important, but the servant element still remains. We begin as servants, and we always recognize ourselves as servants.

Jesus is the Servant of all servants. He is the Suffering Servant. He is the *Ebed Yahweh*, the Servant of the Lord, the *Païs Kyriou*. That is what He is in the prophecy of Isaiah. That is what He is in the teaching of the New Testament. That is what He is when He is suspended on the Cross and killed for us. He is the Lord who becomes our slave. The Son of God became the Servant of God so that the servants of God could become the sons of God. God becomes Man to make humans divine; God became a Slave to make slaves sons. Even the daughters have the status of sons, of inheritors according to the Law.

The *episkopos* in the household of the master is not the master, and *nothing* belongs to him; it all belongs to the master. A synonym for *episkopos* in Scripture is *oikonomos*, meaning the chief steward.

The *episkopos*, the chief servant, is not the master, the *despotis*, nor is he king or *vasilevs*, nor is he lord or *kyrios*. He is a servant, a slave, a *doulos*, *but* he is in charge of everything that belongs to the master and the lord. He is in charge of all the master's servants, goods, and property. He has all the master's power and authority. He has everything that belongs to the master. He functions *in persona*, "in the place of" the master. When you see him, you see the master. When you hear him, you hear the master. When he commands, you hear the command of the master. When he orders you to do something, you obey him as you would the master. But he is not *really* the master; the *real* master is the master.

In the Christian Church, this is very important, because the real Master, the real Lord, the real *Episkopos* is Christ Himself. The human *episkopoi*, the human bishops, exercise the functions of their office by the grace of God in Christ. They are icons of Christ, presences of Christ. They are surrogates. They stand in His place, as representatives making Him present. But He is not absent. He is there, acting in and through them. That is the Christian view.

When a priest celebrates the Divine Liturgy, Christ is the one who offers and is offered. When a teacher teaches, it is Christ who is teaching. When a deacon serves, it is Christ who is serving. When a prophet prophesies, it is Christ who is prophesying. As members of the Body of Christ, we become the hands, the feet, the eyes, the nose, the ears, the presence of Christ—but we are not Christ. Only Christ is Christ. That is why, in traditional language, the head of a Christian community is called an *episkopos*, because he is a chief servant. But he is only a servant. He is not the lord; he's a servant.

The Word of God, in becoming Man, became a slave and a servant, but remains Lord and God. He is Lord and God and slave and servant all at one time in His own Person. Through Him, *we* become by grace everything He is by nature. We become christs by grace and faith, and are servants with Him, suffering with Him as co-sufferers and co-slaves. Then, in that we have suffered with Him, we become sons and lords with Him. We even become gods; we are deified through Him. So what Christ is in Himself—Master and Lord, as well as *Episkopos, Doulos, Oikonomos,* and *Poimen*—all these things we can become by faith and grace, through Him.

When we contemplate the names and the titles of Jesus, we know that all names and titles that are given to humans belong, first of all, to Jesus Himself. In this sense, Jesus is the only human being, even the only Adam. Jesus is the only Jew or Israelite. He is the only Israel, the only King, the only Servant. Everything is reduced to, or fulfilled in, this one Person. It is all fulfilled and completed in Him. It all becomes Him, but He alone *is it*. We are it by participation, by resemblance, by grace, by faith, but He *is it*. He is not only the only High Priest, the only Prophet, the only Teacher, but He is also the only Shepherd and the only Bishop.

CHAPTER 47

Jesus

TRUE & FAITHFUL WITNESS

The words *witness, bear witness, testify, testimony,* and *make a testimony* are all forms of the same word in Greek: *martyreō, martyria, martyrion,* and *martys.* In the Book of Revelation, there are two texts where Jesus is specifically called by the noun *Martys.* The first is in the first chapter, where John, the one who receives this revelation, writes: "Grace to you and peace . . . from Jesus Christ the faithful witness, the first-born of the dead, and the ruler of kings on earth" (Rev. 1:4–5). *Faithful* could also be translated here as *true,* in the sense that God is faithful and true.

In Revelation 3:14, this same expression is used for Jesus in the letter written by the Spirit to the angel, or bishop, of the church in Laodicea: "And to the angel of the church in Laodicea write: 'The words of the Amen, the faithful and true witness, the beginning of God's creation.'" *The Beginning* could also be translated as *the Start* or *the Origin* of God's creation. A more literal translation might be, "And the Amen says these things, the Amen who is the faithful and true Witness, the Chief (or the Head or the Source) of creation." He is the beginning of creation in the sense of being the source of creation.

In St. John's Gospel, the verb *martyreō,* meaning "to bear witness" or "to testify" or "to affirm, to confirm, to demonstrate, to prove, to bring evidence," is used forty-four times. In John 3:10–12, Jesus says to Nicodemus:

> Jesus answered him, "Are you a teacher of Israel, and yet you do not understand this? Truly, truly, I say to you, we speak of what we know, and bear witness to what we have seen; but you do not receive our

testimony. If I have told you earthly things and you do not believe, how
can you believe if I tell you heavenly things?"

Jesus is saying that He and John the Baptist are testifying to what they
know. They are bearing witness to what they themselves know, what they
themselves have seen. Jesus is questioning Nicodemus about why he does
not accept this argumentation, this testimony, which is based on eyewitness
experience. Later in the chapter, John the Baptist says:

> "He [Christ] bears witness to what he has seen and heard, yet no one
> receives his testimony [his *martyria,* his witness]; he who receives his
> testimony sets his seal to this, that God is true. For he whom God has
> sent utters the words of God, for it is not by measure that he gives the
> Spirit; the Father loves the Son, and has given all things into his hand.
> He who believes in the Son has eternal life; he who does not obey the
> Son shall not see life, but the wrath of God rests upon him." (John
> 3:32–36)

Jesus bears witness to the things He learned from God when He was with
God before the world was made. In John 5:30–37, Jesus says:

> "I can do nothing on my own authority; as I hear, I judge; and my
> judgment is just, because I seek not my own will but the will of him who
> sent me. If I bear witness to myself, my testimony is not true; there is
> another who bears witness to me, and I know that the testimony which
> he bears to me is true. You sent to John, and he has borne witness to the
> truth. Not that the testimony which I receive is from man; but I say this
> that you may be saved. He was a burning and shining lamp, and you
> were willing to rejoice for a while in his light. But the testimony which
> I have is greater than that of John; for the works which the Father has
> granted me to accomplish, these very works which I am doing, bear me
> witness that the Father has sent me. And the Father who sent me has
> himself borne witness to me. His voice you have never heard, his form
> you have never seen."

So what Jesus says is this: "John the Baptist bore witness. He made his
testimony. You didn't believe him. Why didn't you believe him? He was a
burning and shining lamp; you were willing to rejoice. Yet, the testimony
that I am bringing is far greater than his." Jesus tells those who do not

accept His testimony, "behold, something greater than Jonah is here. . . . behold, something greater than Solomon is here" (Matt. 12:41–42). "Your father Abraham rejoiced that he was to see my day; he saw it and was glad" (John 8:56).

The whole of the Old Testament bore witness to Him—Moses testified to Him, David testified to Him, "that everything written about me in the law of Moses and the prophets and the psalms must be fulfilled" (Luke 24:44). So this testimony, this witness Jesus makes about Himself is *greater* than the testimony of John and all the prophets before him.

The Prophet Isaiah, in the Old Testament, calls the Servant of God a Witness:

> "You are my witnesses," says the Lord,
> "and my servant whom I have chosen,
> that you may know and believe me
> and understand that I am He.
> Before me no god was formed,
> nor shall there be any after me." (Is. 43:10)

But how is the testimony of Jesus greater than that of the Prophets? Jesus answers, "Because of My acts, My *erga*. My works are the testimony. What I *do* is the testimony. I am the *Martys*, the Witness." He is the *Martys* because His words *and* His deeds are His testimony. These deeds, and not just His words, bear witness that God His Father is the one who sent Him. In saying, "And the Father who sent Me has Himself borne witness to Me," Jesus is saying, in effect, "*God* is My witness."

In John 8, it is very clear that Jesus is claiming divinity and bearing witness to Himself:

> Again Jesus spoke to them, saying, "I am the light of the world; he who follows me will not walk in darkness, but will have the light of life." The Pharisees then said to him, "You are bearing witness to yourself; your testimony is not true." (John 8:12–13)

Before this, Jesus said, "If I bear witness to myself, my testimony is not true" (John 5:31), and here the Pharisees say, "You bear witness of Yourself; Your witness is not true." They are claiming that He is not a Faithful Witness.

Why? Because, in rabbinic legal disputation, according to the Law of Moses in the Torah, witness had to be borne *by another*. A person could not testify about himself as such; he had to have other witnesses, and there had to be at least two or three. Otherwise, the testimony was thrown out of court. But Jesus answered:

> "Even if I do bear witness to myself, my testimony is true, for I know
> whence I have come and whither I am going, but you do not know
> whence I come or whither I am going. You judge according to the flesh,
> I judge no one. Yet even if I do judge, my judgment is true, for it is not I
> alone that judge, but I and he who sent me." (John 8:14–16)

He is saying, "I and my Father together are judging." And He will say later, "I and my Father are one. The Father is in Me and I am in Him. So, when you hear Me, you hear the Father. When you see Me, you see the Father. When the Father speaks, He speaks through Me, and We are joined together; you cannot separate the Father and the Son" (see John 10).

Language to this effect is also in the First Letter of John: "No one who denies the Son has the Father. He who confesses the Son has the Father also" (1 John 2:23). The doctrine of the Son is the doctrine of God. The doctrine of God is the teaching of Jesus.

Then, again, in John 8, Jesus quotes to the Pharisees their own Law: "In your law it is written that the testimony of two men is true; I bear witness to myself, and the Father who sent me bears witness to me" (John 8:17–18). And later on, Jesus says the Holy Spirit is going to come and *also* bear witness to Him. So, John the Baptist bears witness to Him, God the Father bears witness to Him; Jesus bears witness to Himself, and the Holy Spirit bears witness to Him.

In John 5, Jesus tells them, "You search the scriptures, because you think that in them you have eternal life; and it is they that bear witness to me" (v. 39). So, the Scriptures also bear witness to Him—the Law, the Psalms, and the Prophets. In John 10, the Jews are about to stone Jesus for blasphemy, and He speaks of His works bearing witness to Him: "If I am not doing the works of my Father, then do not believe me; but if I do them, even though you do not believe me, believe the works, that you may know and understand that the Father is in me and I am in the Father" (vv. 37–38). All of these witnesses are mentioned in St. John's Gospel. That is why the word is used so frequently.

In this Gospel, we see something of the relationship between the Persons of the Holy Trinity. The Father reveals Himself through the Son, bearing witness to the Son; the Son bears witness to the Father; and the Holy Spirit acts in the Son and bears witness to the Son, thereby bearing witness to the Father. So in John 8, Jesus is saying, in effect, "I bear witness to Myself. My words bear witness to Me. God the Father bears witness to Me. They all bear witness about who I am, where I am from, what I am about, and what the truth is." He explains this more fully in John 16:13–15:

> "When the Spirit of truth comes, he will guide you into all the truth; for
> he will not speak on his own authority, but whatever he hears he will
> speak, and he will declare to you the things that are to come. He will
> glorify me, for he will take what is mine and declare it to you. All that
> the Father has is mine; therefore I said that he will take what is mine
> and declare it to you."

St. John's Gospel contains a continuous teaching about Jesus bearing witness, testifying of Himself, claiming that He testifies of the true God, and claiming that God testifies and bears witness about Him. The whole Gospel is about testimony, about *martyria*, about who is the *Martys*, the Witness.

In the tradition of Christianity, from the beginning, the Christians were those who bore witness to Christ. The whole life of a Christian has to be a testimony to Christ. Every Christian is called to be a martyr and to make the good confession when put to trial. Throughout the New Testament, the apostles and the first Christians bore witness to Christ, and all the saints since have imitated them.

This term, *witness*, was at first a general term for all the saints: all the holy ones, all those who were Christians, all those who were baptized, all those who believed, and all those who had the Holy Spirit. They all bore witness to Christ, to God, to the Spirit, and to the gospel. *Martyr* was a term applied to all holy people.

The kontakion hymn for All Saints Sunday says, "The universe [the whole

creation] offers to You the God-bearing *martyrs* as the firstfruits of creation."
I think it might have been better, in that particular hymn, to translate it as
witnesses, lest people think it refers only to those who were killed. The hymn
is speaking about all the saints together, not just those who were put to death.
Not all of Christ's witnesses are put to death for their testimony, but they all
still suffer with Him. One cannot be with Christ and not die with Him—in a
spiritual sense, if not also in the literal shedding of blood.

Christ is the Martyr, the Witness. He is the one who is *pistos* and
alēthenos—faithful and true. He is the Witness of God, who witnessed to
Himself and who sent the Holy Spirit, who bears witness to *Him*. And, as
such a Witness, He was killed.

If we do not die with Him, we do not live with Him. We may not die
physically, but we still have to die spiritually; we have to die to ourselves and
die to this world. That is our testimony, that we are *dead* to this world and
alive to God in Christ Jesus. This is the measure of a holy person, of a saint.

Jesus Christ is the faithful and true Martyr. He is the one who testifies,
and He is the one who *dies* for His testimony, who gives His life for His
testimony. So it is fitting and proper, meet and right to confess Jesus Himself
as *the* Witness, faithful and true, the true and faithful *Martys*.

CHAPTER 48

Jesus the

PHYSICIAN

The Gospels present Jesus as a healer, as the Physician, from the very beginning of His public ministry. After He was baptized in the Jordan and tempted in the wilderness, He sojourned among the people, healing all their diseases. He cured epileptics, lunatics, paralytics, demoniacs, and all who were suffering. They came to Jesus knowing He had the power of healing, knowing that, with a word alone, He could cleanse lepers, open the eyes of the blind, make the deaf to hear, the dumb to talk, and the lame to walk. His healing and preaching were simultaneous.

He announced the forgiveness of sins together with the healing of soul and body. He even connected the two. When a paralyzed man was brought by his friends to Jesus, He told him, "My son, your sins are forgiven." But when the scribes, with questioning in their hearts, accused Him of blasphemy, Jesus said to them:

> "Why do you question thus in your hearts? Which is easier, to say to
> the paralytic, 'Your sins are forgiven,' or to say, 'Rise, take up your pallet
> and walk'? But that you may know that the Son of man has authority on
> earth to forgive sins"—he said to the paralytic—"I say to you, rise, take
> up your pallet and go home." And he rose, and immediately took up the
> pallet and went out before them all; so that they were all amazed and
> glorified God, saying, "We never saw anything like this!" (Mark 2:8–12)

Jesus refers to Himself as a Physician and connects the healing of souls through the forgiveness of sins to the healing of bodily maladies. When the Pharisees were indignant that Jesus ate with tax collectors and sinners, He told them, "Those who are well have no need of a physician, but those who are sick; I came not to call the righteous, but sinners" (Mark 2:17).

In the Gospel of Luke, Jesus begins His public ministry by referencing a prophecy of Isaiah. In Nazareth, where He grew up, He goes into the synagogue as was His custom on the Sabbath day, and there He reads the following:

> "The Spirit of the Lord is upon me,
> because he has anointed me to preach good news to the poor.
> He has sent me to proclaim release to the captives
> and recovering of sight to the blind,
> to set at liberty those who are oppressed,
> to proclaim the acceptable year of the Lord."
> And he closed the book, and gave it back to the attendant, and sat down;
> and the eyes of all in the synagogue were fixed on him. And he began
> to say to them, "Today this scripture has been fulfilled in your hearing."
> And all spoke well of him, and wondered at the gracious words which
> proceeded out of his mouth; and they said, "Is not this Joseph's son?"
> And he said to them, "Doubtless you will quote to me this proverb,
> 'Physician, heal yourself.'" (Luke 4:18–23)

So He is called a Physician; we can say that is a name and title given to Him in Scripture. It shows His activity as a healer, and not just a healer of bodies, but a healer of souls as the one who can forgive sins.

No one can read the Gospels without seeing how Jesus is healing on practically every page—forgiving sins, healing souls and bodies, making peoples' lives whole again. And, of course, the ultimate healing is the restoration to life of the four-days-dead Lazarus.

Jesus has the power to heal. For example, Luke 5:17 says, "On one of those days, as he was teaching, there were Pharisees and teachers of the law sitting by, who had come from every village of Galilee and Judea and from Jerusalem; and the power of the Lord was with him to heal."

This power is with Him to such a degree that people come up to Him to touch the fringe of His garment and are healed because power goes out from Him. *Power* is the word for the healing miracles in Matthew, Mark, and Luke. In John, the miracles are called *signs*. He heals by a word, He heals by touch; some even receive healing without asking Him, just by touching His clothing.

The physical healings are not, however, the main point of His work of healing. His healings are not primarily for the body, but for the soul, for the whole person. This is why He says, "Your sins are forgiven," "Go and sin no more," and even "Follow Me." That is the point He makes to the paralytic in St. John's Gospel: "You're paralyzed in body, but don't be paralyzed in soul. Follow Me. Do not sin anymore."

Again, when He heals the blind young man, Jesus says, "Do you believe in the Son of Man, the Son of God?" The healed man says, "Who is He?" And He says, "The one you *see*." By healing him, Jesus immediately takes the blind man from physical sight to spiritual sight. Meanwhile He says to the Pharisees, who objected to His healing of the blind man, "For judgment I came into this world, that those who do not see may see, and that those who see [that is, the Pharisees and those who said His signs were not from God] may be made blind" (John 9:39).

Jesus' healing power is holistic—extending to the spirit and mind as well as the body. He restores those who are not in their right mind—demoniacs and the insane. When Jesus casts out the legion of demons from the Gerasene demoniac, people see the man afterward "sitting there, clothed and in his right mind" (Mark 5:15). Jesus gives people sanity as well as bodily soundness and health. This cannot be denied; these are the signs the prophets said Messiah would do.

Scripture is clear that human beings have diseases of mind and body because of sin. There is an ontological, organic connection between evil and disease. This point is made in Genesis. When Adam and Eve are in Paradise, obeying God and enjoying life in the Garden, there is no disease, sickness, sorrow, or suffering. But when they break communion with God through disobedience and are cast out of Paradise, then they are plunged into a world of disease and even terror.

Human beings were made to be sons of God—Adam is called the son of God. Yet, because of sin, we die like any beast of the field. We perish because we broke communion with God through disobeying His commandments. The scriptural teaching is clear: If we would keep the commandments of

God, remain in communion with Him, and live by the Spirit of God, then we would have power over every evil spirit, every disease, and every sickness. Then we would be able to keep ourselves alive; but none of us can do this.

The whole tragedy of humanity, as set forth in the Old Testament, is that we broke communion with God and died, having been overcome by all the powers of corruption, disease, and darkness. However, the teaching is also that, if we could maintain the Law of God, if we could keep all the commandments, then we would have control over all the elemental powers of the universe, both spiritual and material, and every possible cosmic power. We would be able to keep ourselves alive.

Yet the final point of scriptural teaching in the Old Testament is that none of us can keep from dying, because none of us is righteous. We are all sold in bondage to death. Even the most righteous person on earth—Christ's mother, Mary—still died a natural death.

In the Old Testament, the worst kind of death you could die—especially for a man—was to be stricken with some kind of disease or struck down by an enemy in the height of your life, in the prime of your power. Then the only hope or consolation you could have would be in your children, so if you were childless, you were really the most to be pitied.

Jesus of Nazareth, the incarnate Son of God, shows that He identifies with us in our poorest, lowest, weakest, most diseased and sinful state by being struck down in mid-life by crucifixion, leaving no progeny except all those who believe in Him, who are His by adoption. Jesus came into the world to bear our infirmities and to heal our diseases by taking them upon Himself. He shows that He does this voluntarily and has the power to do so. He shows this before He is crucified. He shows His power through healing, and He shows the voluntary nature of His suffering through raising the dead.

Before Jesus raised Lazarus from the dead, some of the Jews mocked Him, saying, "Could not he who opened the eyes of the blind man have kept this man from dying?" (John 11:37). Likewise, when Jesus was crucified, they taunted Him, saying, "He saved others; let him save himself, if he is the Christ of God, his Chosen One" (Luke 23:35). And one of the criminals crucified with Him railed at Him, saying, "Are you not the Christ? Save yourself and us" (Luke 23:39).

The answer is: Of course He could have saved Himself, but the only way He could *ultimately* heal the world—heal all diseases and raise the dead from all ages—was by obliterating sin, corruption, and death in their very essence—at the root, so to speak—by dying Himself. He took it all upon Himself, and in so doing healed it all by His own blood and suffering. He destroyed death and suffering by Himself undergoing the same. The Blood of Christ makes possible our ultimate healing.

When we look at Jesus as the Physician, we see that His healings are always in connection to His own death and Resurrection. When He heals or raises the dead, it is not in the ultimate sense. Each dead person He raised during His earthly ministry died again, one way or the other—either by disease, martyrdom, or something else. The same is true for the healings and resurrections wrought by the apostles and all the saints. Ultimate healing, wholeness, and resurrection do not take place in this life, but in the next.

We all have to pass through death. We only enter the Kingdom of God by affliction and suffering. Only the life after death is a new reality where, as the Prophet Isaiah said, there is neither sickness, nor sorrow, nor suffering, but life everlasting without any death, because in that life, there is no longer any sin. There is only the total righteousness of Jesus, given by grace to those who believe in Him and who want the righteousness of God that comes through Him.

It is certainly a teaching of Holy Scripture that only God has the power of healing and resurrection. Human beings have this power only through the grace of God. As St. Peter told the man lame from birth who was begging at the gate of the temple in Acts 3:6, "I have no silver and gold, but I give you what I have; in the name of Jesus Christ of Nazareth, walk." He healed the man by power that was given to him, not by power he himself possessed outright.

The great difference between Jesus Christ our Lord and the prophets and apostles is that Jesus heals the sick and raises the dead in His own name, by His own power. Sometimes, when He heals, He even prays to the Father, saying He is doing the work for the sake of the people, so that they may believe in Him. He healed simply by saying, "I say to you," and forgave sins simply by saying, "I forgive your sins." This is what made His actions so blasphemous in the eyes of the Jewish religious authorities. Only *God* could do things like that! Jesus does them by His own power, the power He has as God's Son, as the Second Person of the Trinity.

God alone is the Physician of our souls and bodies, and so *Christ* is the Physician of our souls and bodies. He shows this in His humanity, by His human activity. The one Christ, the God-Man, *heals* us. Anyone else who miraculously shows the power of God does it by prayer, faith, and grace, not by his or her own power or person. Jesus is the very Power of God; that is another of His titles. He is the Power of God, the *dynamis* that comes from God.

There is a connection between forgiveness of sins and healing. It is interesting that, when Jesus does a healing on the pages of Scripture, it is often translated into English, "and the person was made whole" or "the person was healed"; but in Greek, the verb used is *sōson*, "saved." Before He does a miracle, Jesus sometimes asks the sick person, "Do you want to be *saved*?" That is the more literal translation of the Greek, but in most translations, it is worded, "Do you want to be healed?" When a person is healed, the text does not say, "Your faith has *healed* you" or "Your faith has *made you whole*"; it says, "Your faith has *saved* you."

Faith is necessary in order for healing to occur. Mark's Gospel says even Jesus Himself could not do certain healings and signs in certain places because the people there had no faith; they were not open to the healing power of God; they rejected it, not wanting to be saved. Healings are connected with salvation and faith, since the ultimate healing is eternal salvation in the coming Kingdom of God.

Therefore, any type of physical healing is always a function of spiritual healing. Physical healing is never an end in itself; it is for the greater purpose of salvation. In Greek, the word *soteria*, "salvation," can also mean "victory" or even "healing." It represents victory over diseases, demons, darkness, and death. The healing, victory, and salvation Christ brings are bound together; they are indivisible.

Jesus Christ is the Physician of our souls and bodies and has the healing power of God Himself. The Father has given everything to the Son, from all eternity. And so, when Jesus is on earth, He does acts of healing. But He never does them just to show off. He always does them to show the power of God. He always does them to show that He is the Messiah. He always does them to show that He has the power to forgive sins and to raise up paralytics and to cast out demons and to heal the mentally ill. He always does them for the sake of salvation.

And He does them to show that He voluntarily gives Himself over unto death. He bears our infirmities; He carries our diseases; He takes upon Himself the sins of the world; and He dies on the Cross, being wounded for our transgressions, so that He can raise up the dead from all ages and destroy the power of death, giving us a life free of sickness, disease, sin, sorrow, and suffering—a life that will come to us when He returns in glory.

Jesus Christ is the Healer, the one and only Physician of souls and bodies, who heals, who saves, who makes whole, and who brings victory. Ultimate healing, salvation, wholeness, and victory can only be found in Him, in the age to come. Until then, healing is not an end in itself. It is for the glory of God and the salvation of souls—our own and those of others. This is a great mystery, but it is the ancient, scriptural, and traditional teaching of Orthodox Christianity.

CHAPTER 49

Jesus the

CORNERSTONE, SHRINE, AND TEMPLE

To understand Jesus Christ as the Cornerstone, it is necessary to examine the temple of God in the Old Testament. God commanded the Israelites to build a tabernacle in the wilderness in which sacrifices could be offered and the people could worship Him. The tabernacle was a tent the people carried with them during their forty-year wandering in the desert. When the tabernacle was set up, it defined a holy place, called in the Septuagint a *naos*. *Naos* means a "shrine" or a "sanctuary," a "holy dwelling place." The term *naos* was used also by the idolaters, the pagans, to describe their shrines.

After the Israelites had conquered the Promised Land and David had taken Jerusalem as a capital for his kingdom, God commanded that this be a holy city, and that a temple—a permanent structure for the worship of Yahweh—should be built there. Solomon built the temple of God, the place where God Himself came to dwell. It was also the place where the Jews were to come to worship Him.

So there was the *hieron*, the temple, and in the center of the temple was the *naos*, and this was the *oikos tou Theou*, the "house of God." Each of these different words is used in Holy Scripture.

The temple had many parts: outer courts, inner courts, the inner shrine, the holy of holies, the temple precincts. When Scripture says, "They went into the temple," or "Mary and Joseph presented Jesus in the temple," it means the temple precincts, the temple courts. They were not going into the

holy place, where only the priests went, where the sacrifices were offered.
When Solomon completed the temple, he said:

> "But will God dwell indeed with man on the earth? Behold, heaven and
> the highest heaven cannot contain thee; how much less this house which
> I have built! Yet have regard to the prayer of thy servant and to his
> supplication, O Lord my God, hearkening to the cry and to the prayer
> which thy servant prays before thee; that thy eyes may be open day and
> night toward this house, the place where thou hast promised to set thy
> name, that thou mayest hearken to the prayer which thy servant offers
> toward this place. And hearken thou to the supplications of thy servant
> and of thy people Israel, when they pray toward this place; yea, hear
> thou from heaven thy dwelling place; and when thou hearest, forgive."
> (2 Chr. 6:18–21)

In the New Testament, Jesus preached in the temple. He also cleansed the
temple, chasing the moneychangers out. He calls that temple a house, an
oikos tou Theou, or "the house of My Father." The Gospel of John says:

> The Passover of the Jews was at hand, and Jesus went up to Jerusalem.
> In the temple [*hieron*] he found those who were selling oxen and sheep
> and pigeons, and the money-changers at their business. And making
> a whip of cords, he drove them all, with the sheep and oxen, out of the
> temple [*hieron*]; and he poured out the coins of the money-changers
> and overturned their tables. And he told those who sold the pigeons,
> "Take these things away; you shall not make my Father's house [*oikos*]
> a house of trade." His disciples remembered that it was written, "Zeal
> for thy house will consume me." The Jews then said to him, "What sign
> have you to show us for doing this?" Jesus answered them, "Destroy this
> temple [*naos*], and in three days I will raise it up." The Jews then said, "It
> has taken forty-six years to build this temple [*naos*], and will you raise it
> up in three days?" (John 2:13–20)

Three different Greek words are used in this passage to refer to the temple:
hieron, *oikos*, and *naos*. *Hieron* refers to the courts of the temple—simply
called *the temple*—where animals are being sold and people exchange
money. Jesus drives them out of the temple, out of the *hieron*.

When He says, "You shall not make My Father's house a house of trade,"
the word used is *oikos*. *Oikos* is also used later in the New Testament to refer

to the Church itself as the gathering of God's people, the household of God. We also use the term *oikos* in the Divine Liturgy when we pray "for those who enter into this house (*oikos*)."

But when Jesus says, "Destroy this temple, and in three days I will raise it up," the word used for temple is *naos*, the word for "shrine." *Naos* does not refer to the whole temple complex but specifically to the holy place. "But he spoke of the temple [*naos*] of his body," as it says in John 2:21. In this sense, another title or name for Jesus can be the Temple, the Shrine, or the Holy Place, in that He refers to His Body in these terms. In the heavenly New Jerusalem that will appear after Christ returns in glory, there will be no *naos*. As Revelation 21:22 says, "And I saw no temple in the city, for its temple is the Lord God the Almighty and the Lamb." The Lamb, of course, is Christ.

Though Revelation says there is no temple in the New Jerusalem, it does mention the city having foundation stones, the Twelve Apostles: "And the wall of the city had twelve foundations, and on them the twelve names of the twelve apostles of the Lamb" (Rev. 21:14).

Foundations have cornerstones, and Jesus Christ as the Cornerstone was prophesied in the Old Testament. Isaiah says, "Behold, I lay for the foundations of Zion a costly stone, a chosen and precious cornerstone for its foundations, and whoever believes in Him will not be put to shame" (Is. 28:16 OSB).

Psalm 118(117) gives another prophecy of Christ as the Cornerstone. Some people think it was even the psalm that was sung by Jesus and His disciples at the Last Supper:

> The stone which the builders rejected
> has become the head of the corner [*eis kephalēn gōnias*].
> This is the Lord's doing;
> it is marvelous in our eyes.
> This is the day which the Lord has made;
> let us rejoice and be glad in it.
> Save us, we beseech thee, O Lord!
> O Lord, we beseech thee, give us success!
> Blessed be he who enters in the name of the Lord!
> We bless you from the house [*oikos*] of the Lord.
> The Lord is God,

and he has given us light.
Bind the festal procession with branches,
up to the horns of the altar. (vv. 22–27)

Jesus quotes this psalm about Himself in the Synoptic Gospels. In Luke, Jesus is teaching in the temple and is telling the people the parable of the man who planted a vineyard and let it out to tenants and then went into another country. He sent servant after servant to get his harvest from the tenants, but the evil tenants treated them shamefully and sent them away empty-handed. Finally, he sent his son, thinking they would respect him. But him the tenants killed, thinking they could then have the son's inheritance for themselves. Then Jesus said to them:

> "And they cast him out of the vineyard and killed him. What then will the owner of the vineyard do to them? He will come and destroy those tenants, and give the vineyard to others." When they heard this, they said, "God forbid!" But he looked at them and said, "What then is this that is written:
> 'The very stone which the builders rejected
> has become the head of the corner'?
> Every one who falls on that stone will be broken to pieces; but when it falls on any one it will crush him." (Luke 20:15–18)

In the last sentence, Jesus alludes to another prophecy of Isaiah:

> "And he will become a sanctuary, and a stone of offense, and a rock of stumbling to both houses of Israel, a trap and a snare to the inhabitants of Jerusalem. And many shall stumble thereon; they shall fall and be broken; they shall be snared and taken." (Is. 8:14–15)

Christ as the Cornerstone was part of the earliest teaching of Christianity. In Acts 4, after healing a crippled man, the Apostle Peter mentions this prophecy of the Cornerstone in his answer to the high priest:

> "Rulers of the people and elders, if we are being examined today concerning a good deed done to a cripple, by what means this man has been healed, be it known to you all, and to all the people of Israel, that by the name of Jesus Christ of Nazareth, whom you crucified, whom God raised from the dead, by him this man is standing before you well.

> This is the stone which was rejected by you builders, but which has become the head of the corner. And there is salvation in no one else, for there is no other name under heaven given among men by which we must be saved." (Acts 4:8–12)

St. Peter expands upon this theme in his first epistle, saying, "Come to him, to that living stone, rejected by men but in God's sight chosen and precious; and like living stones be yourselves built into a spiritual house, to be a holy priesthood, to offer spiritual sacrifices acceptable to God through Jesus Christ" (1 Pet. 2:4–5). He goes on to quote the Cornerstone prophecies of both Isaiah and Psalm 118(117).

Thus, Jesus is the Cornerstone, the Head of the Corner, the Stone which the builders rejected. This is a theme that runs throughout the New Testament.

The Apostle Paul tells the Corinthians, "You are God's . . . building" (1 Cor. 3:9), and the word he uses is *oikodomē*. *Oikos* is "house," and *oikodomia* means "edification" or "building up." So, "You are the house, the building that God has built up." Then he says:

> According to the grace of God given to me, like a skilled master builder [*architektōn*] I laid a foundation, and another man is building upon it. Let each man take care how he builds upon it. For no other foundation can any one lay than that which is laid, which is Jesus Christ. (1 Cor. 3:10–11)

Later, he says, "Do you not know that you are God's temple [*naos*] and that God's Spirit dwells in you?" (1 Cor. 3:16). The word for "dwells" here is *oikei*. St. Paul is saying, "God has made you His house, His holy sanctuary." Then he says, "If anyone destroys God's temple [*naos*], God will destroy him. For God's temple is holy, and that temple you are" (v. 17). You are that *naos*.

In Ephesians, this same imagery is used:

> So then you are no longer strangers and sojourners, but you are fellow citizens with the saints and members of the household of God, built upon the foundation of the apostles and prophets, Christ Jesus himself being the cornerstone, in whom the whole structure is joined together and grows into a holy temple in the Lord. (Eph. 2:19–21)

St. Paul is telling the Ephesian Christians that they are all built together, fitted together, into a *naos*, a shrine, that is holy. They are, in Christ, made into one building—together with the apostles and prophets—to be the dwelling-place of God in the Spirit of God, with Christ as the Cornerstone.

The Church made up of different people is now fitted together into one holy temple or shrine and called the house, dwelling-place, and household of God. The people are now the dwelling-place of God, and together they form the living temple of God. That is the teaching of the Apostle Paul. There is no more physical temple. Jesus Christ has ascended into heaven, and so the temple of His Body becomes the Church, His people. The people become His members; they become living stones in His Body; and therefore the temple is now composed of those who are members of Christ, who is the living Temple, risen from the dead.

St. Paul calls the heavenly New Jerusalem mentioned in Revelation "our mother": "But the Jerusalem above is free, and she is our mother" (Gal. 4:26). The Old Testament temple was fulfilled in Christ, and the physical building was razed. Christ is, Himself, the living Temple, and we, through baptism and entry into the Church, become His members, members of His Body. He is the Cornerstone, and we have become stones in the building, having been built up to be a living shrine, a living sanctuary of Jesus Christ. When Revelation says there is no temple in the New Jerusalem, God and the Lamb, God the Father and the Lord Jesus Christ, *are* the temple—and members of the Church share in that as members of Christ's Body.

All these things, however, are symbols. They interact with one another, not always neatly. They are used different ways in different contexts.

Jesus is the living Temple. When He said, "Destroy this *naos* (shrine) and in three days I will raise it up," He was speaking of His own Body. And we are also the Body of Christ, having become members of it, living stones in that Temple. We have been built up into that Temple by becoming members of Christ. In the temple that we are is the Cornerstone, the one that holds the edifice together, and this is Christ.

Christ is the only foundation—no other can be laid but Him, as St. Paul says—yet we also speak of the prophets and apostles as foundations, with

Christ as the Cornerstone of the foundation. We are all members of this living temple in Him.

So we have the same situation we have with every other name and title of Jesus. Jesus Himself is *the* Cornerstone, and even *the* Temple in His own Body. But, through divine grace and our faith, we become what He is. We become living stones. We become temples, individually and all together as the Church. As the fellowship of Christians, we make up the *oikos*, the household of God. When we gather as a church, then we are constituting that household, becoming the *naos*, the shrine or sanctuary. That is what Jesus claimed for Himself in the Holy Scriptures.

When we, by grace, become members of His Body, both physically and spiritually, we become one flesh, one body, one mind, and one spirit with Christ. Then we constitute the living Temple. We become members of Christ, who is the Temple, the Shrine, and the Cornerstone that the builders rejected. The stone which the builders rejected has become the cornerstone, the head of the corner, the *kephalēn gōnias*, the One on whom it all hangs together. This is the Lord's doing. It is marvelous in our eyes. The one who was rejected by men and crucified, God has made the Cornerstone, the Foundation prophesied by the prophets and preached by the apostles. He becomes the living Temple of God, which we become, together with Him.

This is the Christian gospel. This is our faith. The Cornerstone, the Head of the Corner, the Foundation that no one else can lay is Christ, with His prophets and apostles. He is the Temple, through and in whom we also become co-temples, co-houses, co-shrines, so to speak. We are God's holy place because of the One who is the Holy Place, Christ.

By faith in Him, by His grace, by His Holy Spirit, by the will of God His Father, we worship and adore Him as the Temple not made by hands, the Cornerstone of the building in which God Himself dwells. This is a divine building of living stones and living people in the coming Kingdom of God, the New Jerusalem, in which there is no physical temple, for God and the Lamb are its Temple. And we become deified; we become sons of God and christs. We become members of Christ, precious stones in that very Temple, because of Christ, our Savior.

CHAPTER 50

Jesus the

HEAD

Usually, when Christians contemplate Jesus as Head, we think of Him as the Head of the Church. This follows the teaching of St. Paul, who insists on Jesus as the Head of the Body, which is the Church. In Romans, St. Paul writes, "I appeal to you therefore, brethren, by the mercies of God, to present your bodies as a living sacrifice, holy and acceptable to God, which is your spiritual worship" (Rom. 12:1). Then he continues: "For as in one body we have many members, and all the members do not have the same function, so we, though many, are one body in Christ, and individually members one of another" (Rom. 12:4–5).

In 1 Corinthians, St. Paul writes: "For just as the body is one and has many members, and all the members of the body, though many, are one body, so it is with Christ" (1 Cor. 12:12).

In both epistles, St. Paul emphasizes the integral unity of the Church by comparing it to Christ's Body. Jesus Christ is the Head of the Church, which is His Body. He is Himself a *member* of the Body. The head is a member of the body, not something separate from it. Christ is the member who is the Head, the Head of the Church. In Ephesians, St. Paul says:

> Rather, speaking the truth in love, we are to grow up in every way into
> him who is the head, into Christ, from whom the whole body, joined
> and knit together by every joint with which it is supplied, when each
> part is working properly, makes bodily growth and upbuilds itself in
> love. (Eph. 4:15–16)

In Colossians, he says:

> He is the head of the body, the church [hē ekklēsia]; he is the beginning
> [the source], the first-born from the dead, that in everything he might
> be pre-eminent. For in him all the fullness of God was pleased to dwell,
> and through him to reconcile to himself all things, whether on earth or
> in heaven, making peace by the blood of his cross. (Col. 1:18–20)
>
> For in him [Christ] the whole fullness of deity dwells bodily, and you
> [being His Body] have come to fullness of life in him, who is the head of
> all rule and authority. (Col. 2:9–10)

Here, St. Paul expands on the concept of Christ as Head, from Christ as the
Head of the Church to Christ as the Head over all rule and all authority in
creation.

We have to hold fast "to the Head, from whom the whole body, nourished
and knit together through its joints and ligaments, grows with a growth that
is from God" (Col. 2:19). This is a very clear teaching. The community of
faith, the final covenant community in the Messiah, is headed by the Messiah
Himself, the God-Man, Jesus Christ; and the members of that community
actually constitute Christ's own Body.

Jesus, who is the Head of the Church, is in fact the Head over everything.
In Ephesians 1:20–23, St. Paul says that God

> raised him from the dead and made him sit at his right hand in the
> heavenly places, far above all rule and authority and power and
> dominion, and above every name that is named, not only in this age but
> also in that which is to come; and he has put all things under his feet and
> has made him the head over all things for the church [or, for the sake of
> the church], which is his body, the fullness of him who fills all in all.

He says that, because Christ suffered, died, arose, and was enthroned and
glorified, He was made the Head over all rule and authority and power and
dominion.

If you remember, the passage of the Old Testament that is most quoted
in the New Testament is Psalm 110(109):1: "The LORD says to my lord: /
'Sit at my right hand, / till I make your enemies your footstool.'" If all your
enemies and even all things are under your feet, then you are the head over

all things. So He is the Head over everything. That is exactly what St. Paul says: the Head *over*—not the Head from which everything comes, but the Head which is *over* everything.

There are a few other texts to consider when we contemplate Jesus as the Head, not only of the Church, which is His Body, but the Head over everything—and these relate to patriarchy, that the man is the head of a woman in marriage and the head of a family.

In Ephesians, in a passage read at Orthodox weddings, St. Paul writes, "Be subject to one another out of reverence for Christ" (Eph. 5:21). There is to be a mutual subjection, a mutual submission in marriage, according to St. Paul. That is incredibly important. He continues, "Wives, be subject to your husbands, as to the Lord. For the husband is the head of the wife as Christ is the head of the church, his body, and is himself its Savior" (Eph. 5:22–23).

St. Paul is saying that we can understand the Church by understanding the married couple, and we can understand marriage by understanding Christ and the Church. The same way Christ is the Head of the Church, so the husband is supposed to be the head of the wife. St. Paul continues:

> As the church is subject to Christ, so let wives also be subject in
> everything to their husbands. Husbands, love your wives, as Christ
> loved the church and gave himself up for her, that he might sanctify
> her, having cleansed her by the washing of water with the word, that he
> might present the church to himself in splendor, without spot or wrinkle
> or any such thing, that she might be holy and without blemish. Even so
> husbands should love their wives as their own bodies. He who loves his
> wife loves himself. For no man ever hates his own flesh, but nourishes
> and cherishes it, as Christ does the church, because we are members of
> his body. "For this reason a man shall leave his father and mother and
> be joined to his wife, and the two shall become one flesh." This mystery
> is a profound one, and I am saying that it refers to Christ and the
> church; however, let each one of you love his wife as himself, and let the
> wife see that she respects [or holds in awe or holds in fear] her husband.
> (Eph. 5:24–33)

What St. Paul is saying is that, in the family—St. John Chrysostom calls the family "the small church"—there is the same kind of structure, order, and headship as in the Church, but the Head of the family is, ultimately, Christ

Himself. The Head of the man is Christ. The man exercises the headship within the family, but it is not a headship of tyranny or domination or subjugation or chauvinism. It is the headship of love, the same as Christ's headship of the Church.

Just as Christ as Head of the Church gives everything He has and invigorates the whole Body and cannot even be the Head without the Body, neither can the Body be the Body without the Head. Otherwise, it is a corpse. It is the same thing with man and woman—there has to be this total union, this communion, this unity, a one-flesh reality. This reality exists by a mutual subjugation, a mutual submission. Christ actually submitted Himself to the Church because He died for the Church. That is why St. Paul says that the husband has to be the head of the wife just as Christ is the Head of the Church, which is His Body—and He gave Himself for her; He was crucified for her.

Christ said, "The Son of man came not to be served but to serve, and to give his life as a ransom for many" (Matt. 20:28). He came to die for us so that we could become one flesh and one body with Him as our Head.

That is how we understand the headship of the man over the woman in marriage and that of the father in a family. In Ephesians 3:14–15, St. Paul writes, "I bow my knees before the Father, from whom every family in heaven and on earth is named." In the Orthodox Christian tradition, every human community has to have a father, thus patterning or imaging the very structure of the Godhead.

Probably one of the most amazing sentences in the Scriptures on the issue of headship is in 1 Corinthians 11, where the Apostle Paul says, "I want you to understand that the head of every man is Christ, the head of a woman is her husband, and the head of Christ is God" (1 Cor. 11:3).

According to Orthodox theology, following the Holy Scriptures, God the Father is not greater than the Son of God in divinity. He is greater only in the order of relationship, because the Son is begotten of the Father, but the teaching of the Holy Trinity from the Council of Nicaea is that the Son of God is of one essence with the Father.

So here is a paradox (Orthodoxy is "paradoxy"): The Father is the Head of the Son, but they are equal; they are identical, even. Not only identical, they have exactly the same divinity, being yet two distinct Persons. And God the Father does not lord it over His Son, but is the Head of Christ as the Father of His divine Son, not just of Christ as a human being.

When Jesus says in St. John's Gospel, "The Father is greater than I" (John 14:28), St. Basil the Great, commenting on this, says (paraphrased), "When people say this refers only to Christ's humanity, this is not true, because if Jesus were a mere man and said, 'The Father is greater than I,' you could say, 'Really? Is God really greater than you, a creature?'" But Christ is not a creature. Arius was condemned by all the Holy Fathers and Ecumenical Councils for teaching that Jesus Christ was a mere creature. He is not; He is the only begotten Son of the Father, begotten of the Father before all ages. God is literally His Father, so He is equal and identical and perfectly one with God the Father in His divinity.

Nevertheless, the Head is still the Father, not the Son. The *Archē*, the *Principium*, the "Source," "Beginning," or "Foundation" of the divinity is still the Father. The Father is *over* the Son. The Son is not only *from* the Father, but the Father is *over* the Son. The Son receives everything *from* the Father. The Son *obeys* the Father. The Son speaks the Father's words; He does the Father's works; He accomplishes the Father's will. This is the teaching of Holy Scripture.

There is an order of reality, and the order exists even between those who are of the very same nature and are absolutely one in value, worth, and being. So we can say the same thing about humanity that we say about divinity: As the Father, Son, and Holy Spirit are one God, so all human beings are one humanity, exactly the same in value, worth, and being. Men and women have the same humanity. They are of the same worth and value. But, as they relate to each other, the one who functions in the headship, imaging Christ Himself in the Church and God the Father in the Holy Trinity, is the man, not the woman. Later on in 1 Corinthians 11, St. Paul says, "Nevertheless, in the Lord woman is not independent of man nor man of woman; for as woman was made from man, so man is now born of woman. And all things are from God" (1 Cor. 11:11–12).

Thus, men and women have an identical nature, value, and worth. When it comes to sanctity and holiness, here too there is no difference at all between men and women: both partake of the grace of God; both can become saints. But when it comes to how they interrelate, man as man and woman as woman, and not simply as human beings, but precisely in their gender-specific reality, there is a God-ordained order. That order does not involve any degradation or humiliation. It is, instead, a union of love, of faith, of reality, and as the Father, Son, and Holy Spirit are one God and one Godhead and one divine nature, so all men and women and children on earth are one humanity, with one and the same human nature. The headship is one of love and service, of origin and governance. But there is no tyranny, subjugation, or enslavement inherent in this headship.

Christ is our Head; He is the Head over all things. He is the Head over all rule and authority, and He is certainly the Head of the Church, even in His humanity. He was made the Head over all things when He was crucified, raised, glorified, and enthroned—in His human flesh and blood, in His Body—on the right hand of the throne of God the Father, being forever the God-Man Jesus Christ, one of the Holy Trinity who shares our human nature and is our Head.

The Head of everything is Christ. The Head over all humanity is Christ. The Head over all rule and authority, even over the angelic realm, is Christ. Christ Jesus was *made* the Head over everything through what He suffered. He won the right to be the ruler and the governor of the living and the dead because of what He suffered. According to Christianity, humanity should image this, should pattern this, should actualize this in every relationship. Our churches, dioceses, parishes, monasteries, homes, families, institutions, and even nations should be this way, to the measure that we can incarnate it in human reality, because the headship of Christ is shared with us as well. It is given to us in the various activities of our life. Each human being on earth—each man, woman, and child—has a certain function in this headship, in the particular conditions of his or her life.

That headship must always actualize and exemplify the headship of Christ, who alone is the Head. We become heads over everything only in and with Him. And, by the Holy Spirit, we exercise *His* headship in all of our human affairs in one way or another.

It is an organic, ontological headship that is rooted in the very nature of things, and it comes from the Holy Trinity. For the Head of Christ is God. The head of human beings is Christ. He is the Head of all human beings, and especially the Head of the Church. He is the Head, as St. Paul said, *hyper panta*, over all things. Christ, for Christians, is always and forever, in every way, *the* Head.

CHAPTER 51

Jesus

MEDIATOR & INTERCESSOR

In several places in the New Testament, our Lord Jesus Christ is called the Mediator. In Greek, the word is *mesitēs*. Jesus, as Mediator, lives eternally to make intercession, to intercede, to plead, and to make appeal on our behalf as Intercessor.

Most people are probably familiar with one passage from Holy Scripture that refers to Jesus as Mediator, 1 Timothy 2:5: "For there is one God, and there is one mediator between God and men [human beings], the man Christ Jesus."

Jesus Christ, Jesus the Messiah, Jesus of Nazareth is definitely a Man. The Nicene Creed sums this up when it says, "who for us men [human beings] and for our salvation came down from heaven, was incarnate of the Holy Spirit and the Virgin Mary, *kai enanthropēsanta*—and became human." The Logos, the divine Son of God, became human, and not in an abstract sense, but specifically as a first-century Jew, Mary's child by birth, Joseph's child by the Law. This is a *dogma* of ancient Christianity.

And it was a dogma that was hard-won, because practically every heresy about Jesus in the first thousand years of Christian history was somehow a *compromising* of the humanity of Jesus Christ. The Council of Chalcedon in 451 said that He is *Theos* (divine, God), with the same divinity as God the Father, being of one essence with the Father, but He is also *Anthropos*, with exactly the same human nature as all *anthropoi*, all human beings. He is truly God and truly Man; the *Theanthropos*, the God-Man.

The Mediator has to be what we are. If Jesus were not really and truly human, He could not function as a Mediator for us with God, because in that case He would be God only, the one with whom we have to have the mediation. It is the *Man* Jesus who is the *Mesitēs* according to the Scriptures. To have mediation, one has to have *two* parties. God is one; therefore, the mediator has to be *another* one.

God made a promise to Abraham that in his Seed—a human Seed because Jesus is the Son of Abraham—all the human beings of the earth would be blessed. As St. Paul says in Galatians:

> Now the promises were made to Abraham and to his offspring [or seed].
> It does not say, "And to offsprings," referring to many; but, referring to
> one, "And to your offspring," which is Christ. (Gal. 3:16)

In Galatians, St. Paul says that when the Seed should come to whom the promise was made, it was ordained by angels in the hand of a Mediator, so that there would be a Mediator between God and man.

Hebrews 7:25 says of Jesus Christ, "Consequently he is able for all time to save those who draw near to God through him, since he always lives to make intercession for them."

St. Paul says that Christ as Mediator is more excellent than Moses: "But as it is, Christ has obtained a ministry which is as much more excellent than the old as the covenant he mediates is better, since it is enacted on better promises" (Heb. 8:6). Those old promises are the ones made to Abraham, that in him—in his Seed, Christ—all the nations, all the peoples of the earth, all human beings would be saved.

Hebrews says that Christians have not simply come to where Moses was—to a mountaintop, to fire, to the giving of the Law—but to the city of the living God, to the heavenly Jerusalem, to the assembly of innumerable angels, to the general assembly of the firstborn who are enrolled in heaven, to the *Ekklesia*, the Church, "to a judge who is God of all, and to the spirits of just men made perfect, and to Jesus, the mediator of a new covenant, and to the sprinkled blood [Christ's Blood] that speaks more graciously than the blood of Abel" (Heb. 12:23–24).

The Mediator is alive, and He makes intercession for us. In speaking about this mediation and this living to make intercession, which is what Jesus does for us, we must understand that, in every context where this teaching is made, it is connected with God's promise to Abraham about his Seed, and it is always connected to His death, His broken Body, His shed Blood. Christ's mediation and intercession is always in the context of *leitourgia*, of offering, of sacrifice, of worship, of entering into the presence of God on our behalf. He is the Mediator before the face of God the Father. He lives to make intercession on our behalf, through His blood.

In Scripture, the term *Mesitēs,* or "Mediator," is often connected with another of Jesus' titles, *Archierevs,* or "High Priest," because the *Archierevs,* and the priesthood (*hierosynē*) in general, is by definition a mediating ministry. The priest mediates before God on behalf of human beings and the whole cosmos. He intercedes, offers, pleads, appeals, prays, worships, and stands on behalf of the people. This was the Old Testament priesthood.

In the New Testament, this High Priest who is the Mediator, the Intermediary, is not according to the order of Aaron or Levi, but according to the order of Melchidezek. It is a new priesthood, an everlasting priesthood, an eternal priesthood. It is not a priesthood that takes place on earth; it is a priesthood that takes place in heaven, because the Mediator enters into the presence of God to intercede on our behalf. He is made alive, never to die again; and eternally He appeals, pleads, and intercedes as the Intermediary and Mediator between God and man, as the One who was killed and shed His Blood in order to reconcile us to God.

The scriptural texts on mediation are all connected to the concepts of ransom, redemption, offering of blood, sacrifice, and priestly offering. The Mediator is the great High Priest, and He is the *Paraklētos.* He is also the Advocate. That is how all these things come together.

To put the reading from Hebrews into broader context, it says this: There were many priests in the Old Testament, but then a new priesthood arose according to the order of Melchizedek. In Hebrews 7, the name *Melchizedek* is used at least five times, in reference to the new priesthood that Christ enacts. Of the Old Testament priesthood—that of Aaron and Levi—Hebrews says, "The former priests were many in number, because they were prevented by death from continuing in office" (Heb. 7:23).

The Old Covenant priesthood could not be eternal, because the priests kept dying, and new priests were always needed. Likewise, they kept having to offer more and more sacrifices. "But he [Christ] holds his priesthood permanently, because he continues for ever" (Heb. 7:24). The Greek term corresponding to "permanently" is *aparavaton,* and it does not mean "permanent," but "intransmittable." He cannot transmit it to anyone else. It is *hapax,* "once and for all." Why? Because He is not dead. The next sentence continues, in the King James Version (KJV), "Wherefore He is able also to save those to the uttermost" (Heb. 7:25). That is, He is able to save them forever, always, and entirely because He lives forever to make intercession for them: "*pantote zōn eis to entynchanein.*" Then it continues:

> For it was fitting that we should have such a high priest, holy, blameless, unstained, separated from sinners, exalted above the heavens. He has no need, like those high priests [of the Old Covenant], to offer sacrifices daily, first for his own sins and then for those of the people; he [this one High Priest according to the order of Melchizedek] did this once for all when he offered up himself. (Heb. 7:26–27)

Jesus the Mediator effects mediation by offering up Himself on the Cross in death and then, after His Resurrection and Ascension, living forever and entering into the sanctuary not made by hands in the heavens. He serves forever as our High Priest and Mediator before the face of God, living forever to make intercession on our behalf. He has a more excellent *leitourgia* ("liturgy") than either the angels or the priests of the Old Covenant because He is the *Mesitēs,* the Mediator, of a better covenant, which was established upon the promises, a covenant that would be everlasting, that would be forever and would *literally* never end.

This is always connected with Jesus' self-offering, ransoming, priestly sacrifice, Crucifixion, Resurrection, Ascension, entrance into the presence of God, and remaining alive forever. Hebrews 9:12 says:

> He entered once for all into the Holy Place, taking not the blood of goats and calves but his own blood, thus securing an eternal redemption [an *aionian lytrosin,* a redemption that is everlasting, eternal, forever].

The blood of bulls and goats—the sacrifices of the Old Testament priesthood—could not, ultimately, do this for us. Their function was only temporary and a foreshadowing of what was to come with Christ's sacrifice. St. Paul continues in Hebrews 9:14–15:

> How much more shall the blood of Christ, who through the eternal Spirit offered himself without blemish to God, purify your conscience from dead works to serve the living God.
>
> Therefore he is the mediator of a new covenant, so that those who are called may receive the promised eternal inheritance, since a death has occurred which redeems them from the transgressions under the first covenant.

He is the Mediator of the New Covenant, which He offers in His death to become an *apolytrosin*, to make a redemption, in order that we could have the inheritance of God by becoming the heirs of the promises that were made to Abraham.

Jesus' mediation is connected with His priesthood. It is connected with His sacrifice, with His death, and with the redemption He brought. It is everlasting because it is made by the everlasting Spirit. It enters into the heavens; it is not earthly, not a part of creation. This is the kind of mediation that Christ does in order to make intercession on our behalf.

This blood of Jesus' mediation speaks more eloquently than the blood of Abel and the blood of the bulls, calves, and goats (see Heb. 12:24). It is the Blood by which the mediation between God and man is effected in the Person of Jesus, the one *Sperma*, the one Seed, the one *Anthropos*, the one Man, the one High Priest, the one *Paraklētos*, the one Paraclete. This is who Jesus is.

He is the one Mediator, the one *Mesitēs*. He lives to make intercession. By faith, by grace, by being *en Christo*—"in Christ," by receiving the same Holy Spirit, by entering with Christ into the Holy of Holies not made by hands and existing above the heavens, by sacrificing ourselves and by being sacrificed together with Him, *we also* become mediators who live to make intercession. That is the theological foundation for the intercession of the saints, and the fact that the saints, the holy people, are mediators. In our Eastern Orthodox Christian tradition, the first and chief mediator after Christ is His mother, Mary.

Jesus is one Mediator between God and man. He is God's Son. He is the High Priest according to the order of Melchizedek who has no human generation. He is the incarnate Logos of God. He is the one who emptied Himself on the Cross in order to *be* the Mediator and to make the intercession. In Him, the real Man, the one Seed, the one Mediator, the one Man, the one Adam, the one High Priest, the one Teacher, the one Prophet, the one everything, we become by grace what He is by nature. That is an absolute, unchanging principle and a central conviction of Christianity. He became everything we are so that we could become everything He is.

If He is Mediator, we can be mediators, too. If He lives to make intercession, we can live to make intercession, too. Right now, all who are dead in Christ are alive in Christ already. On earth, it has not happened yet, but in eternity, in the everlasting Kingdom, it already has. What has not yet happened on earth has happened already in Christ in the heavens. As Hebrews says, Christians have come into "the assembly of the first-born who are enrolled in heaven, and to a judge who is God of all, and to the spirits of just men made perfect" (Heb. 12:23).

We believe that the dead in Christ are already in Christ. They are already in the presence of God. Christ has filled Sheol, the realm of death, with Himself. Death is no more. Sheol has become as Paradise. No one remains in the tomb any more as far as God is concerned. It is our teaching that we relate, not only to Christ God Himself, but to all who have died in Christ, as to those already risen and glorified, because they are all now with Christ. So, it is very important that human beings, mere human beings, sinful human beings, by faith and grace, can act as mediators and intercessors for other people.

Anybody who has ever read the New Testament will know that this teaching certainly applies to those of us still on earth. The Apostle James says, "The prayer of a righteous man has great power in its effects" (James 5:16).

When we pray on earth for each other, we do so in Christ. We even say, "In Christ's name we do this." We always offer our prayers to God in the name of Jesus. There is even a formula in Western Christianity: "We ask this in Jesus' name." We are never just standing by ourselves in our mediation and intercession. We always do this in Christ, invoking His name, asking for His mercy, praying for His will to be done.

There are some Christians who say, "The only Mediator between God and man is Jesus." But, actually, that is not the teaching of Scripture. The Scripture says, translated literally from the Greek, "The Mediator between God and man is one; the man, Christ Jesus" (1 Tim. 2:5).

However, that one Mediator includes us in His one mediation. That one Intercessor includes us in His intercession. He does it alone, so to speak, but He invites us to do it with Him. That is how kind He is. That is how merciful and generous and gracious God is. Jesus Christ does not simply say to us, "Don't pray. Don't mediate. Don't intercede. I'll do it all for you. You don't have to do anything." He does these things so that we also can do them. And we have to do them if we follow Him. We pray, mediate, and intercede with Him, since we cannot do these things effectively without Him.

Jesus Christ alone is the one Mediator and the one Intercessor before God the Father on behalf of all and for all, and He does this because He is filled with the Holy Spirit and He is filled with all the fullness of God, even *somatikos*, "bodily," as it says in Colossians. But we enter into that. He mediates for us. He intercedes for us. And He gives us the grace and power to mediate, to intercede, and to offer ourselves and our bodies as sacrifices for each other. We then enter into the mediating and interceding power of the one Mediator, the one Intercessor, the one Intermediary between God and man, the only Savior, the only Lord, the only great High Priest, the only Redeemer, the only Savior, our Lord Jesus Christ.

And then, in and through Him, we participate in that mediating, interceding, sacrificing, and saving activity of God Himself. How wonderful all this is! But it all happens *only* and *exclusively* because of the one Man, the last Adam, Jesus Christ, who alone is the Mediator, who lives to make intercession on our behalf.

CHAPTER 52

Jesus

PIONEER & PERFECTER

A major theme of Hebrews is that everything in the Old Covenant was but a shadow, a prefiguration of what would be perfected and fulfilled in Christ. In Hebrews 12, Jesus is called the Pioneer and Perfecter of our faith—in essence, the One who initiates and the One who completes.

> Therefore, since we are surrounded by so great a cloud of witnesses, let us also lay aside every weight, and sin which clings so closely, and let us run with perseverance the race that is set before us, looking to Jesus the pioneer and perfecter of our faith, who for the joy that was set before him endured the cross, despising the shame, and is seated at the right hand of the throne of God. (Heb. 12:1–2)

In the Revised Standard Version (RSV), Jesus is called the Pioneer and the Perfecter. In the New King James Version (NKJV), He is called Author and Finisher. In Greek, these words are *Archēgon* and *Teleiōtēs*. *Archēgon* is "Author" or "Pioneer," and this same word is used in Hebrews 2 as well, where Jesus is called the *Archēgon tēs sōtērias*, the author of salvation (Heb. 2:10).

The term *archēgon* also means "leader," the "first one," the "source," the one from whom everything comes. This word is also used for Jesus in Acts 5:31, where it is translated "Leader" in the RSV and "Prince" in the NKJV. In Acts 3:14–15, *Archēgon* is used again. St. Peter, delivering his first sermon at Pentecost, says, "But you denied the Holy and Righteous One, and asked for a murderer to be granted to you, and killed the Author of life, whom God raised from the dead. To this we are witnesses."

Teleiōtēs can be translated as "Finisher" or "Perfecter." It comes from the word that means *perfect*, as a noun, and *to perfect* as a verb. *Teleiōtēs* refers to the one who perfects, the one who accomplishes, the one who finishes, the one who fulfills. Probably the best-known use of that particular term occurs in the last words of Jesus from the Cross in John 19:30, when He says, "*Tetelestai*—it is fulfilled; it is accomplished; it is finished; it is perfected."

So, He is the Author and the Finisher, the Beginner and the Ender. In Hebrews 6:20, He is even called the *Prodromos*, the "Precursor" or the "Forerunner."

In Him, everything begins. In Him, everything ends. Everything starts from Him; everything is accomplished by Him; everything is finished in Him. All is completed in Him. There is nothing before Him. He is before all things—as it says in Colossians 1:17. There is nothing after Him that is going to be beyond Him. He is the final act; He is the final word; He is the final One.

In Revelation, this same teaching is put another way. Not only is He the Author, Prince, and Pioneer of life, of salvation, of the New Covenant; He is the Accomplisher of life, salvation, and the New Covenant in His broken Body and spilled Blood. Revelation also identifies Jesus three times as the Alpha and the Omega, the First and the Last, the Beginning and the End.

Revelation 1:8 says, "'I am the Alpha and the Omega,' says the Lord God, who is and who was and who is to come, the Almighty [the *Pantokrator*]." The term *Almighty* is used six or seven times in Revelation. It is almost like a formula, resembling other divine titles in Scripture: the Lord God Almighty, *Yahweh Elohim, El-Shaddai, Kyrios Theos Pantokrator.*

There is a kind of theological nuance here, because, in Revelation, everything that is said concerns God the Father, the One who sits on the throne. But every single time, it also adds, "and the Lamb": "Him who sits upon the throne . . . and the Lamb, the one who was dead and is alive again." So, the expression in Revelation 1:8 is referring to both God the Father and God the Son.

In Greek, it sounds very nice, and in many Greek Orthodox churches, this text is written around the dome of the church. But the image in the dome is of Christ. God the Father is invisible; He cannot be seen. God is able to be seen in the Person of His Incarnate Son, who is Light from Light, true God of true God, *Yahweh* from *Yahweh*, *Pantokrator* from *Pantokrator*, Almighty from Almighty, who receives the same honor, dominion, glory, and majesty that are given to the Father. The Son of God, the Lamb, sits on the throne with the Father. He is also the Son of Man, the Lord who sits at the right hand of the Father with all His enemies under His feet.

Translated literally from the Greek, Revelation 1:8 would say, "*Egō eimi to Alpha kai to Omega legei kyrios ho theos*—I am the Alpha and the Omega, says the Lord God—*ho ōn kai ho ēn kai ho erchomenos, ho pantokrator*—who is and who was and who is to come, the Almighty." That is interesting, because "*ho ōn*" is a present participle: "the being, the one who is." "*Ho ēn*" means "the one who was." But then, it does *not* say, "the one who *will be*." Instead, it says, "the one who is coming, the coming one, *ho erhomenos*." That is really lovely, because when we pray to God, we see Him as the one who is *coming* to us.

How does God Almighty come to us? He comes to us as He always comes to us: in the Person of His Son, the Lamb of God, Jesus Christ. So, who is the "coming one"? At the end of Revelation, to whom will it be said, "Come!"? To the Lord Jesus: "Come, Lord Jesus," because when You come, You bring God with You. God comes and Christ comes, and they come together, so to speak. You do not have one without the other, but God is always acting and doing everything through the Person of His Son.

Also in Revelation, when there is an expression about "I am," it does not simply say "Alpha and Omega," but it also says "First and Last." In Revelation 1:17, when John, the seer and visionary who is writing the book, sees Him who sits upon the throne and the Lamb, he falls down on his face in front of them. He worships. He is scared to death. And he sees, not only Him who sits upon the throne, but the Son of Man, Jesus Christ, clothed with a garment down to the foot and a golden girdle. He has hair like white wool; His face is like snow; His feet are like brass burned in a furnace; and His voice is like the sound of many waters. Anyone who knows Scripture knows that is simply a repetition of the words of Daniel the Prophet, from when he saw the Ancient of Days sitting upon the throne and the Son of Man came to him. But now this one is described as the Son of Man also.

Then the seer, the apocalyptic visionary John, says:

When I saw him, I fell at his feet as though dead. But he laid his right hand upon me, saying, "Fear not, I am the first and the last, and the living one; I died, and behold I am alive for evermore, and I have the keys of Death and Hades." (Rev. 1:17–18)

In Greek, He says, "*Eimi zōn*—I am living—*eis tous aiōnas tōn aiōnōn*—forever, unto ages of ages." That is a liturgical formula: "unto ages of ages."

The same thing that is said about God the Father is said about the Lamb: Alpha and Omega, First and Last. At the end of Revelation, it says not only "First and Last" and "Alpha and Omega," but also, "Beginning and End" (Rev. 22:13).

Then He says, "Behold, I am coming soon" (Rev. 22:12). What *soon* means for God may not mean what *soon* means for us, but the Apostle Peter explains the reason: "The Lord is not slow about his promise as some count slowness, but is forbearing toward you, not wishing that any should perish, but that all should reach repentance. But the day of the Lord will come like a thief" (2 Pet. 3:9–10).

It is not fulfilled until it is all fulfilled. The Fulfiller is Jesus. He fulfills it all on the Cross when He saves us at His Crucifixion, but the ultimate fulfillment comes only at the end of the world, when all things will be made new: a new heaven, a new earth, a new creation. We shall finally have the kingship of God when Christ returns in power, He who in His Person is also the Power of God.

In Revelation 22:12 He says, "*Idou*—behold—*erhomai tahy*—I am coming quickly, and My reward [recompense] is with Me, to give to every person according to his work." That is very important: He gives to each of us according to how our work is: "*hōs to ergon estin avtou*," or, as it says later on, "*kata ta erga*—according to the works." This same phrase is in Proverbs and the Psalms, and that is very important, especially when answering people who say we are saved by faith alone. We are saved by faith and by grace, but it is for works. The only way you can prove your faith is by what you do, and it is written in Revelation that He comes to give to every person according to his works.

Then, in Revelation 22:13, He says, "*Egō eimi to Alpha kai to Omega*—I

am Alpha and Omega, the First and the Last, the Beginning and the End."
In Greek it says, "*Ho prōtos kai ho eschatos hē archē kai to telos.*" From
archē, of course, we get the word *archēgōn* used in Hebrews. *Archē* means
"source," "principle," or "beginning." The Bible begins, "In the beginning—
En archē." St. John's Gospel begins, "In the beginning was the Word—*En
archē ēn ho Logos.*"

In Colossians, St. Paul says that Jesus is the *Archē*, the Beginning. He is
before all things. He is not a creature. Some, such as Jehovah's Witnesses
today and Arians in the fourth century, say, "Jesus is the first of God's
creatures." But we Orthodox Christians say, "No! He is the Beginning
of everything, the Cause of everything, the Principle and the Source of
everything." *Archē* is the word used in Greek. In Slavonic, it is *Nachalo*, and
in Latin, *Principium*. And He is also the Fountain—in Greek, the *Pēgē*; in
Latin, the *Fons*, and in Slavonic, the *Istochnik*.

He is a divine Source. He is the *Demiurgos*. He is the One by whom,
through whom, for whom, in whom, and toward whom all things were
created, according to St. Paul. He is the *Archē*, and He is the *Telos*, the
Beginning and the End.

But who is the one who is coming? Who says, "I am coming soon"? It
is Christ. It is the Lamb, but He also brings God, so we could say that God
is coming quickly, too. God is still coming. God was, God is, and God
is coming. But He was and He is and He is coming in the Person of His
Son, Jesus Christ, who was dead and who is alive again. He Himself puts
it so beautifully: "I am the Alpha and the Omega, the first and the last, the
beginning and the end" (Rev. 22:13).

And then He says what He is coming to do. He is coming to bring the
Kingdom of God to the world, to bring the Kingdom of God that will last to
the ages of ages.

Jesus Christ is the Beginning and the End; the First and the Last; the Alpha
and the Omega; the *Archēgōn* and the *Teleiōtēs*; the Prince and the Author;
the Perfecter and the Pioneer; the Captain, the Forerunner, the Fountain, and
the Finisher. All of these are titles for Jesus that we find in the Holy Scriptures.

All of this is for us and for our salvation. All of this tells us that Jesus
is not a mere man. He is *the* Man. He is the Mediator. He is the Final and

Last Adam, the Man from heaven, the real Man. But He is also God, and He brings God the Father, and God the Father is in Him, and He is in God the Father. He brings what He has heard and received from God the Father from before the foundation of the world, since He is the Beginning, the Source, the One through whom all things were made, the One through whom all things came to be. He is the One who sums it all up.

When we spoke of the term *Head*, we had virtually the same teaching, but there is a wonderful word in Hebrews, *Anakephalaiosis*, "the One who brings everything to a head." Christ begins everything, and He ends everything. He starts everything; He finishes everything. He is the source of everything; He is the summation of everything. In fact, He is everything. And we could even end our reflection on the names and titles of Jesus here, with St. Paul saying, "Christ is all, and in all" (Col. 3:11). When everything is put under His feet, and He submits everything to God the Father, God becomes all and in all, and Christ Himself is all and in all, as the Beginning and the End, and even as the Forerunner and the inn along the way.

CHAPTER 53

Jesus

NAME ABOVE EVERY NAME

We have now come to the end of our reflections on the names and titles of Jesus in Holy Scripture, referring also to how they are sometimes used in the Holy Liturgy of the Church. Now we want to reflect on the subject of the name itself, the importance of *name*, and the name of Jesus, which is bestowed upon Him by God. It is the name above every other name, the name at which every knee, ultimately, will bow.

If we were to take a biblical concordance and look up the term *name* or *name of the Lord*, we would see just how many times that word *name* is used in the Holy Scripture, and in so many different ways. This is important, because the name, in biblical and Christian tradition, is a sacred and holy thing—*every* name, not just the name of the Lord God and the name of Jesus Christ, but the name in general.

The name is a presence and a power of the reality of that which is named. The name somehow reveals the very being, substance, presence, and action of the reality. Genesis contains two creation narratives, both of which we believe are inspired by God, and both of which reveal to us theological truths about reality having its beginning with God Himself. In the second narration, in Genesis 2, God is called the Lord God, *Yahweh Elohim*, whereas in the first narration, in Genesis 1, He is called the Most High God, the *Elohim*.

There are several different versions of the name of God in Scripture. It is important to see that, in the second narrative, it is the Lord God. Each reference to Him in the second narrative is *Yahweh Elohim*, and in that particular revelation of God, it says that Adam, the "earth-creature" (which is what *Adam* means in Hebrew), is made first. In the first narrative, human beings are made last, male and female. There is no *name* given to the earth-creature in the first narrative. He is simply called "*anthrōpos, 'ish* and *'ishshah*—man, male and female."

But in Genesis 2, the Lord God puts man in the Garden of Eden, gives him the commandment not to eat the fruit from the Tree of the Knowledge of Good and Evil, and says, "It is not good for man to be alone" (Gen. 2:18). God creates the *'ezer kenegdo*, the "helper fit for him" (Gen. 2:18), the fulfillment of his very reality as a human being in the image of God, male and female:

> So out of the ground the Lord God formed every beast of the field and every bird of the air, and brought them to the man to see what he would call them; and whatever the man called every living creature, that was its name. The man gave names to all cattle, and to the birds of the air, and to every beast of the field; but for the man there was not found a helper fit for him. So the Lord God caused a deep sleep to fall upon the man, and while he slept took one of his ribs and closed up its place with flesh; and the rib which the Lord God had taken from the man he made into a woman [from the *'ish* came the *'ishshah*] and brought her to the man. Then the man said,
>
> "This at last is bone of my bones
> and flesh of my flesh;
> she shall be called Woman [*'ishshah*],
> because she was taken out of Man [*'ish*]."
>
> Therefore a man leaves his father and his mother and cleaves to his wife, and they become one flesh. And the man and his wife were both naked, and were not ashamed. (Gen. 2:19–25)

After this, in Genesis 3, is the narration of how Adam and Eve fall, through listening to the word of the serpent. Then, at the end of Genesis 3, it says, "The man called his wife's name Eve [Hebrew for *living*], because she was the mother of all living. And the Lord God made for Adam and for his wife garments of skins, and clothed them" (Gen. 3:20–21). Then they are driven out of Paradise and into this present world, into the world as it is outside Eden.

So the name is extremely important. Adam, man—until Eve appears he is not Adam, but the "earth-creature"—is commanded by God to give names to everything in order to show what they are. This a very interesting sentence: "and brought them to the man to see what he would call them; and whatever the man called every living creature, that was its name" (Gen. 2:19). The naming is done by man, which is a way of saying that man has control over all things. God intends for man to govern and even to know what everything is.

For example, in St. John's Gospel, Jesus says about the good shepherd that he knows and calls his sheep by name because he really knows them. He knows what they are. He knows who they are. He knows how they are. He knows why they are. He knows what form they are. He knows what to do with them. He can see into their very reality, and that is revealed in this symbolical way of speaking: "They know the name; they give the name; they name the name."

Here in Genesis also, it is very important that the man names his wife. God does not name the woman. *Man* names the woman, and he names her, as it says in the RSV, "Eve," because she was the mother of all living. In the Septuagint, the name of Adam's wife is *Zōē*, which simply means "Life." So in Hebrew, it is "the Mother of the Living," and in Greek it is simply "Life."

Names are very important throughout Genesis, and some key figures even get their names changed. Abram, for example, and his wife Sarai end up becoming Abraham and Sarah. Their names are changed. He will be not just the exalted father, Abram, but the father of many nations, of all nations: Abraham.

Jacob, the son of Isaac and father of the twelve patriarchs, has his name changed to Israel after wrestling with the Angel of the Lord. There are debates about what *Israel* means—"blessed by God" or "chosen by God"—but I think the most plausible meaning is "the one who fights with God," "the one who has striven with God, who has struggled with God." This in itself symbolizes the fact that each human being has to end up struggling with God. God is with us, and we are with God. We delight in Him; we rejoice in and with Him; we praise His holy name, but there is a struggle there, as well.

There are also name changes in the New Testament. Simon is renamed *Cephas* or Peter, the rock. Jesus even gives nicknames, calling James and John the "Sons of Thunder." Because names play such an important role throughout Holy Scripture, they are worthy of note and ought to be carefully contemplated.

When it comes to God Almighty and His name, perhaps one of the most important texts in the Bible is in Exodus, in the story of the burning bush.

> Now Moses was keeping the flock of his father-in-law, Jethro, the priest of Midian; and he led his flock to the west side of the wilderness, and came to Horeb, the mountain of God. And the angel of the Lord appeared to him in a flame of fire out of the midst of a bush; and he looked, and lo, the bush was burning, yet it was not consumed. And Moses said, "I will turn aside and see this great sight, why the bush is not burnt." When the Lord saw that he turned aside to see, God called to him out of the bush, "Moses, Moses!" And he said, "Here am I." Then he said, "Do not come near; put off your shoes from your feet, for the place on which you are standing is holy ground." And he said, "I am the God of your father, the God of Abraham, the God of Isaac, and the God of Jacob." And Moses hid his face, for he was afraid to look at God. (Ex. 3:1–6)

After this, God gives a rather long discourse to Moses, telling him to lead His people out of Egypt, out of slavery, out of the hands of Pharaoh. God says, "I will send you to Pharaoh that you may bring forth my people, the sons of Israel, out of Egypt." And then Moses says to God, "Who am I that I should go to Pharaoh, and bring the sons of Israel out of Egypt?" (vv. 10–11). It is interesting that here they are called the sons of Israel, but above, it says, "the God of Abraham, Isaac, and *Jacob*." Now He is called the God of Israel. The names switch there.

Moses says, "Who am I?" And then God says to him, "But I will be with you; and this shall be the sign for you, that I have sent you: when you have brought forth the people out of Egypt, you shall serve God upon this mountain." Then, Moses says to God: "If I come to the people of Israel and say to them, 'The God of your fathers has sent me to you,' and they ask me, '*What is his name?*' what shall I say to them?" And God says to Moses, "I AM WHO I AM" (vv. 12–14).

"I Am Who I Am." In Hebrew, that is the Tetragrammaton, the YHWH. There is debate about how exactly to say it because of the lack of vowels in ancient Hebrew, but *Yahweh* is commonly used. In English translation, it is not only "I am who I am," but it could also be "I am what I am," or "I will be what I will be," or "I will cause to be what I will cause to be," or "I will do what I will do." Then God says:

> "This is my name for ever, and thus I am to be remembered throughout all generations. Go and gather the elders of Israel together, and say to them, 'The Lord, the God of your fathers, the God of Abraham, of Isaac, and of Jacob, has appeared to me, saying, "I have observed you and what has been done to you in Egypt; and I promise that I will bring you up out of the affliction of Egypt."'" (Ex. 3:15–17)

Essentially, He is saying, "Until now, you did not know Me as the Lord, as *Yahweh*. You only knew me as God, the Almighty God. Now I have a new name. And this new name is the name by which I'm going to be known for forever."

Then the Holy Scripture continues, saying lots of things about this name. Later in the Law of Moses, in the Pentateuch, it says that this name is holy, that His name is the jealous God, that He is the fear of Israel, He is the Almighty. And there are commandments never to profane or blaspheme His name, namely the third of the Ten Commandments: "You shall not take the *name* of the Lord your God—*Yahweh Elohim, ho Kyrios Theos*—in vain" (Ex. 20:7). In other words, do not use the name of God in any empty way; *in vain* means "empty, without purpose." Keep it holy, because that name is "fearful and glorious," as it says in the Law of Moses (see Deut. 28:58).

Scripture also says, "Holy is His name" (Psalm 111[110]:9; Luke 1:49), as if "*ho hagios*" was the very name. It can be translated both ways: His name is holy, or *Holy* is a proper name for God. In the New Covenant, Jesus Christ has *commanded* us to call God "Father," which was an outrageous thing to do according to the Mosaic Law, the Psalms, and the Prophets. What human mortals would dare to call God *ho Pater* or *Abba? Abba* means "dear father," "intimate father," "papa-father," or "daddy-father." But Jesus gives the command, the privilege, and the daring possibility for human beings to actually *name* God as Father. As Christians become the children of God, so God becomes the Father of Christians.

In the New Testament, God is called *Father* because of the One who—in His composite *hypostasis*, in His divine-human Person as the God-Man—is the Son of God, the Word of God, the Wisdom of God, the Power of God, the Truth, the Life, the Glory of God, and the Man named Jesus. God *commanded* that Jesus would be His name. In the infancy narratives in the Gospels of Matthew and Luke, Joseph and Mary are told, "You will call His name Jesus" (see Matt. 1:21; Luke 1:31).

In St. John's Gospel, the term *name* is used fifteen times. John 1 mentions the name of Jesus and that we find salvation in His name: "But to all who received him, who believed in his name, he gave power to become children of God" (John 1:12). We call upon His name. We pray in His name. We act in His name. We baptize in His name. And we believe in His name.

This particular way of speaking runs throughout John, but in two places he uses what is called in literary terms an *inclusio poetica*, where something is stated in the beginning and then recapitulated at the end: in John 17, in Jesus' last prayer before His Passion; and in John 20, after the Apostle Thomas' declaration of faith in His Resurrection.

In Jesus' prayer in John 17, He says, "*I have manifested thy name* to the men whom thou gavest me out of the world; thine they were, and thou gavest them to me, and they have kept thy word" (v. 6). Then, a bit later, He says:

> "And now I am no more in the world, but they are in the world, and I am coming to thee. Holy Father, *keep them in thy name,* which thou hast given me, that they may be one, even as we are one. While I was with them, *I kept them in thy name,* which thou hast given me; I have guarded them, and none of them is lost but the son of perdition, that the scripture might be fulfilled." (vv. 11–12)

Jesus ends His prayer with these words:

> "O righteous Father, the world has not known thee, but I have known thee; and these know that thou hast sent me. *I made known to them thy name,* and I will make it known, that the love with which thou hast loved me may be in them, and I in them." (vv. 25–26)

Jesus has made known to His disciples His Father's name, and it is this name that we, as Christians, are called to believe in.

The second *inclusio poetica* relating to belief in Jesus' name is at the end of John 20:

> Now Jesus did many other signs in the presence of the disciples, which are not written in this book; but these are written that you may believe that Jesus is the Christ, the Son of God, and that *believing you may have life in his name.* (vv. 30–31)

This is a wonderful thing! Believe that Jesus is the Christ, the Son of God, and have life. How? In His name. Throughout John's Gospel, and especially in His last discourse before His Passion, Jesus says things like, "You have asked nothing in My name; now ask in My name," and "Keep things in My name," and "Whatever you ask in My name, I will do it." For a fuller example, we have in John 14 the following:

> "These things I have spoken to you, while I am still with you. But the Counselor, the Holy Spirit, whom the Father will send in my name, he will teach you all things, and bring to your remembrance all that I have said to you." (vv. 25–26)

The Holy Spirit is coming and being sent in Jesus' name. Then, in John 15, Jesus says:

> "You did not choose me, but I chose you and appointed you that you should go and bear fruit and that your fruit should abide; so that whatever you ask the Father *in my name*, he may give it to you. This I command you, to love one another." (vv. 16–17)

To pray *in the name of Jesus* does not simply mean tacking on the expression, "We ask in Jesus' name." *In the name of Jesus* means "according to Jesus, according to His presence, according to His power, according to His Person." With the name comes the presence and power of the person. To ask for something *in the name of Jesus* means to ask according to Christ Himself, according to who He is, what He has, and what He does.

To ask, then, for something *in Jesus' name* has certain implications, the foremost of which is that the name of Jesus, together with His presence and power, belong not to us who say the name, but to Him whose name it is. To pray in the name of Jesus means also that we keep the commandments of Jesus and do the will of Jesus. If we would attempt to pray in the name of Jesus, but not for that which is according to Jesus, we would not be praying in the name of Jesus at all, but would be using a kind of magic formula. There are certain things for which we cannot pray in Jesus' name because they are not according to Jesus' Person, His presence, His power, His teaching, His word.

The apostles went around doing many kinds of things in the name of Jesus. They baptized in His name. They preached in His name. They did miracles in His name. They claimed that everything they were doing was according to the name of Christ.

In Acts, when Peter is preaching, he speaks about belief in Jesus' name. The healed man he mentions is a man lame from birth whom Peter and John had healed earlier "in the name of Jesus Christ of Nazareth" (Acts 3:6).

> "The God of Abraham and of Isaac and of Jacob, the God of our fathers, glorified his servant Jesus, whom you delivered up and denied in the presence of Pilate, when he had decided to release him. But you denied the Holy and Righteous One, and asked for a murderer to be granted to you, and killed the Author of life, whom God raised from the dead. To this we are witnesses. And his name, by faith in his name, has made this man strong whom you see and know; and the faith which is through Jesus has given the man this perfect health in the presence of you all." (Acts 3:13–16)

His name is repeated twice: Jesus' name and faith in His name made the lame man strong. Acts 4:8–12 says this:

> "Rulers of the people and elders, if we are being examined today concerning a good deed done to a cripple, by what means this man has been healed, be it known to you all, and to all the people of Israel, that by the name of Jesus Christ of Nazareth, whom you crucified, whom God raised from the dead, by him this man is standing before you well. This is the stone which was rejected by you builders, but which has become the head of the corner. And there is salvation in no one else, for there is no other name under heaven given among men by which we must be saved."

The Apostle Paul repeats this teaching in his letters again and again, saying that Christ's name has to be proclaimed over all the earth. The Christians are even named Christians in Antioch because of the name of Christ.

Two texts from St. Paul are extremely important to this topic. The first is from what could be the longest sentence in the entire Bible. It is in Ephesians 1, where St. Paul is saying that God has raised Jesus up and put Him at His own right hand, "far above all rule and authority and power and dominion, *and above every name that is named,* not only in this age but also in that which is to come" (v. 21).

The second text is from Philippians 2:9–11, which comes from a beautiful early Christian hymn:

> Therefore God has highly exalted him and bestowed on him the name which is above every name, that at the name of Jesus every knee should bow, in heaven and on earth and under the earth, and every tongue confess that Jesus Christ is Lord [*Kyrios, Yahweh,* I AM], to the glory of God the Father.

That is the Christian faith.

We also sing about Jesus, "Blessed is He who comes in the name of the Lord." All those who are in Christ come in the name of the Lord.

The Psalms also speak of the name of God, for example, "Save me, O God, by thy name" (Ps. 54[53]:1) and "Our help is in the name of the Lord, / who made heaven and earth" (Ps. 124[123]:8). But now, in the Final Covenant, there are two very important names: God, who is now *Abba,* Father; and Jesus, the name above every name: *Yeshua,* "God saves."

For Orthodox Christians from the days of the holy apostles until the present, the very name *Jesus* is the presence and the power of the Person of Christ Himself. When we say that name, He is there. When we invoke that name, Jesus is present. His power is present. His might is present. His saving power is present. He is present! The invocation of the name of Jesus is a *parousia,* a "presence," "arrival," or "official visit" that happens before and, in a way, in anticipation of the Second Coming of the Lord at the end of the ages, when every knee in heaven and on earth and under the earth will bow down before Him, to the glory of God the Father.

Those who resist the lordship of Christ and do not sanctify, bless, and glorify His holy name—the very presence of that name destroys them. That is why many people cannot stand to hear the name of Jesus. That is why, when you say the name of Jesus, the devils flee. And that is why St. John Climacus said in the sixth century, "Whip the demons with the name of Jesus! There is no more powerful weapon in heaven and on earth." You just say that name, and the demons flee.

The Lord's Prayer, the prayer that Jesus taught His disciples to pray, teaches us to address God as "Our Father who is in the heavens" and to say, "may Your name be holy" and "let Your Kingdom come, let Your will be done." Those last phrases are equivalent because, if God's name is sanctified and kept holy and not blasphemed, then it means His Kingdom and His Kingship is there, and His will is being done. And when His will is being done, then His name is being sanctified and His Kingdom is there. Those three statements amount to the same thing: may Your name be holy, may Your Kingdom come, and may Your will be done—as in the heavens. "On earth as it is in heaven" is equivalent to "as in Christ Himself, so also in us, His members on earth, who bear His name." As we pray with and in His name, we sanctify His name and, as a result, we sanctify our own names.

In Orthodox Christian tradition, we also have the Jesus Prayer: "Lord Jesus Christ, Son of God, have mercy on me, a sinner," or a variant thereof. This is yet another example of the importance of the name to prayer.

The Holy Fathers defended the holiness of that name. In the same way St. Stephen the New refused to step on an icon because it was the image of the Lord, so those who were defending the holy name of Jesus refused to step on a piece of paper on which was written *Iēsous*, "Jesus," the name of Christ, because that would be desecrating the name. There is a definite correspondence between the name and the icon—they are both presences of the Person and the power of Christ Himself.

This name is very important; and we can say that all the names on which we have commented in this series were titles of the one name, *Jesus*. We believe there is no other name that is saving. Whether people know it or not, if they are saved, it is because of Jesus Christ: His Person, His presence, and His power. So we glorify that name; but we also have to know, as our Holy

Fathers teach us, even the name of Jesus has to be somehow qualified and transcended, because the God who is holy is not like anything else. If God's name is holy, and if Christ is the Holy One of God, then even the name of Jesus takes us beyond itself into the realm of perfect silence beyond every name that is named in heaven and on earth. It is beyond it all.

In some sense, the reality of Christ Himself is beyond even the name of Jesus. The name guarantees His presence, but the presence itself is above the name. It is the name that reveals the presence, but the presence is prior to it and beyond it; it is inexpressible, inconceivable, invisible, incomprehensible, and nameless.

He dwells in ineffable silence, but He breaks that silence by revealing His name—I Am, the Lord, Jesus, Father—and allowing Himself to be named, to be called upon.

He has revealed a multitude of names; and He is beyond all names. But when it comes to a name that we can speak, the only name by which we can be saved is Jesus. And that name of Jesus, given to Him by God the Father because of the suffering He endured, is the name above every name, the name that causes every creature in heaven and on earth and under the earth to bow, to the glory of God, His Father. Amen.

In Loving Memory of

PROTOPRESBYTER
THOMAS HOPKO

March 28, 1939 to March 18, 2015

MEMORY ETERNAL!

Listen to Fr. Hopko's podcasts on Ancient Faith Radio:

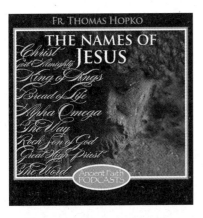

Explaining the significance of each of the names of Christ

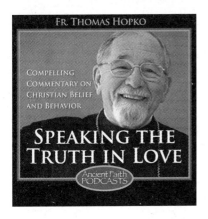

Compelling Commentary on Christian Belief and Behavior

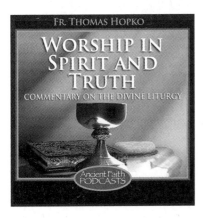

A series of reflections on the Divine Liturgy of the Orthodox Church

Also by Fr. Thomas Hopko

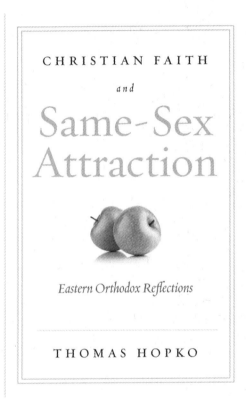

CHRISTIAN FAITH

and

Same-Sex
Attraction

Eastern Orthodox Reflections

THOMAS HOPKO

Combining theological and pastoral insights with a humble and loving
spirit, this small gem will aid pastors, those who experience same-sex
desires, and anyone seeking a deeper understanding of the nature
of our identity and our sexuality.